William D. Whitney

The Atharva Veda Prâtiçâkhya Or Çâunakîyâ Caturâdhyâyakâ

William D. Whitney

The Atharva Veda Prâtiçâkhya Or Çâunakîyâ Caturâdhyâyakâ

ISBN/EAN: 9783741184666

Manufactured in Europe, USA, Canada, Australia, Japa

Cover: Foto ©Andreas Hilbeck / pixelio.de

Manufactured and distributed by brebook publishing software (www.brebook.com)

William D. Whitney

The Atharva Veda Prâtiçâkhya Or Çâunakîyâ Caturâdhyâyakâ

THE

ATHARVA-VEDA PRÂTIÇÂKHYA,

OR

ÇÂUNAKÎYÂ CATURÂDHYÂYIKÂ:

TEXT, TRANSLATION, AND NOTES.

BY

WILLIAM D. WHITNEY,

PROFESSOR OF SANSKRIT IN YALE COLLEGE.

[FROM THE JOURNAL OF THE AMERICAN ORIENTAL SOCIETY, VOL. VII, 1862.]

NEW HAVEN:

FOR THE AMERICAN ORIENTAL SOCIETY,

PRINTED BY E. HAYES, PRINTER TO YALE COLLEGE.

MDCCCLXII.

SOLD BY THE SOCIETY'S AGENTS:

NEW YORK: B. WESTERMANN & CO., 440 BROADWAY:

LONDON: TRÜBNER & CO.; PARIS: BENJ. DUPRAT;

LEIPZIG: F. A. BROCKHAUS.

INTRODUCTORY NOTE.

THE distinctive title of the work here published is *Çâunakîyâ catur-âdhyâyikâ*, 'Çâunaka's Treatise in Four Chapters.' We have for it, however, only the authority of the signatures to the different portions of the manuscript containing the treatise; no reference to the latter by name has yet been discovered, so far as I am aware, in any other work of the Sanskrit literature. As regards the gender of the word, whether feminine or neuter, there is some question. In the signature to the first section (*pâda*) of the first chapter (*adhyâya*), it is styled *caturâdhyâyikâ*, as also at the close of the first chapter. With this accords, farther, the name, *caturâdhyâyî-bhâshya*, given to the commentary in the signature of chapter IV, section 1, and at the close of the whole work. The neuter form, and the ascription to Çâunaka, are found only in the final signature, which reads as follows (unamended): *iti çâunakîyacaturâdhyâyike caturthaḥ: caturâdhyâyibhâshya samâptaḥ.** The treatise was first brought to light, and its character determined, by Roth (see the Preface to his Nirukta, p. xlvii). It was recognized by him as being what is indicated by our title, a Prâtiçâkhya to a text of the Atharva-Veda. That it has any inherent right to be called *the* Prâtiçâkhya to *the* Atharva-Veda is not, of course, claimed for it; but, considering the extreme improbability that any other like phonetic treatise, belonging to any of the other schools of that Veda, will ever be brought to light, the title of Atharva-Veda Prâtiçâkhya finds a sufficient justification in its convenience, and in its analogy with the names given to the other kindred treatises by their respective editors, Regnier, Weber, and Müller.† Any special investigation of the questions of the authorship and date of our treatise, its relation to the other Prâtiçâkhyas and to the present received text of the Atharva-Veda, and the like, is reserved for the commentary and the additional notes: it will be sufficient to say here, in a general way, that it concerns itself with that part of the Atharvan text which is comprised in its first eighteen books, and with that

* Weber (Cat. Berl. MSS., p. 87; Ind. Literaturgeschichte, p. 146) calls the treatise *caturadhyâyikâ*; and Müller (Hist. Anc. Sansk. Lit., p. 139, etc.) styles it *câturâdhyâyikâ*—each by a different emendation of the name given in the manuscript: I do not see the necessity of departing from the authority of the latter.

† Prâtiçâkhya du Rig-Véda. Par M. Ad. Regnier, etc. Published in the Journal Asiatique, V^{e} série, Tomes vii-xii, Paris, 1858-58.—Das Vâjasaneyi-Prâtiçâkhyam. Published by Prof. Albrecht Weber, in his Indische Studien, Vol. iv, Berlin, 1858.—Müller's edition of the Rig-Veda Prâtiçâkhya includes only the first six chapters, one third of the whole, and forms part of his text-edition of the Rig-Veda itself, which also remains a fragment.

alone, and that it covers the whole ground which the comparison of the other treatises shows us to be necessary to the completeness of a Prâtiçâkhya, differing from any of them not more than they differ from one another.

The manuscript authority upon which the present edition is founded is a single codex (Chambers collection, No. 143; Weber, No. 361), belonging to the Royal Library of Berlin, a copy of which was made by me in the winter of 1852–3; it contains, besides the text of the Prâtiçâkhya, a commentary upon it, by an author not named, which styles itself simply *caturâdhyâyî-bhâshya*, 'Commentary to the Four-chaptered Treatise,' as already noticed above. It is briefly described in Weber's Catalogue of the Berlin Sanskrit Manuscripts (p. 87–8). The signature at the end is as follows (with one or two obvious emendations): *çrîr astu: lekhakapâṭhakayoḥ çubham bhavatu: çrîcaṇḍikâyâi namaḥ: çrîrâmaḥ: samvat* 1714 *varshe jyâishṭhaçuddha* 9 *dine samâptalikhitam pustakam.* The date corresponds to May, 1656; but it must, as in many other cases, be doubtful whether this is the date of the manuscript in our possession, or of the one from which this was copied; in the present instance, the latter supposition may be regarded as decidedly the more probable. Most unfortunately, considering the extreme rarity of the work, the manuscript is a very poor one. Not only is it everywhere excessively incorrect, often beyond the possibility of successful emendation; it is also defective, exhibiting *lacunae* at several points. Some may be of opinion, then, that the publication of the Prâtiçâkhya upon its authority alone is premature, and should not have been undertaken. This would certainly be the case, were any other copies of the work known to be in existence: to neglect to procure their collation before proceeding to publish would be altogether inexcusable. But, so far as is hitherto known, the Berlin codex is unique. No public or private library in Europe, nor any in India accessible to Europeans, has been shown to possess a duplicate of it. For assistance in procuring a second copy, I made application some years since to Prof. Fitz-Edward Hall, then of Benares, whose knowledge, experience, and public and private position made him the person of all others most likely to be of service in such a way; and he was kind enough to interest himself zealously in my behalf in searching for the work: but entirely without success; while he collected for me a mass of valuable materials respecting the other Prâtiçâkhyas, for that of the Atharva-Veda nothing could be found. Considering, then, the faintness of the hope that additional manuscripts would later be obtainable, and considering the peculiar interest of this class of works—well attested by the triple publications, within a few years past, of Regnier, Weber, and Müller—and the desirableness of placing as speedily as possible before the eyes of scholars the whole material furnished by them, in order to the greater force and conclusiveness of the results which some are already hastening to draw from them for the literary history of India, it has seemed best to publish the treatise without farther delay. Several circumstances deserve to be noted as supporting this decision, by diminishing the disadvantages arising from the scantiness and poorness of the manuscript material. In the first place, as regards the *lacunae*, they are, with two exceptions, of insignificant importance, and do not either cause the loss of a rule or render its interpretation doubtful; while, in the two instances (both occurring in chapter III) in which one or more rules are lost, the loss at least lies within the limits of a certain definite subject, and, though much to be regretted, is of no great extent or essential consequence. As concerns, again, the corruption of the readings, it is to be observed that the commentary is generally full enough to establish the true version of the rules, and yet, at the same time, too poor and scanty to render its own restoration important. The general method of the commentator is as follows: he first states the rule, then restates it in the baldest possible paraphrase, merely supplying the lacking copula, and adding the specifications, if any, of which the presence is inferrible from previous rules; next follow the illustrative citations; and finally, the rule is given once more, along with the one next following, which is euphonically combined with it, and of which the paraphrase and illustration then follow in their turn. As an example, I cite here in full rule i. 7, with its commentary, beginning from the final repetition of the next preceding rule:

स्पर्शाः प्रथमोत्तमा न वकारः। न वकारः पदो भवति। बहुलवकाः। न वकारः पद-
यान्तानि पूर्वो॰

Thus we have everywhere (unless, as is sometimes the case, a few words have dropped out from the copy) a threefold repetition of each rule, and its true form is almost always restorable from their comparison, notwithstanding the corruptions of the manuscript. If, now, the commentary were as full and elaborate as those of the other known Prâtiçâkhyas, it would have been alike trying and unsatisfactory either to endeavor to edit it, or to disregard it: while, as the case actually stands, it has itself attempted so little that we care comparatively little to know precisely what it says. Wherever its usual meagre method is followed, accordingly, little attention will be found paid to it in the notes. Nor has it seemed to me otherwise than a needless labor to notice, except in special cases, the corrupt readings of the manuscript—and this the more especially, as my distance from the original renders it impossible to test by a renewed collation the accuracy of my copy.* The citations from the Atharvan text are also given in their correct form, without farther remark; since, whatever the disguise under which the manuscript may present them, it has generally been not difficult for one familiar with the Atharvan, and in possession of a verbal index to its text, to trace them out and restore their true readings. There are a few notable instances in which the commentator abandons his customary reticence, and dispreads himself upon the subject with which he is dealing: and in such cases the attempt is made to follow him as closely as the manuscript will allow. Much more frequently than he ventures to speak in his own person, he cites the *dicta* of other authorities; occasionally referring to them by name; more often introducing his quotations by a simple *aparu âha*, 'another has said;' and very frequently making extracts without any introduction whatever, as if of

* Prof. Weber has had the kindness to verify for me, during the progress of publication, sundry passages, of special importance or of doubtful reading, which I took the liberty of submitting to him.

matter which might lawfully be woven in as an integral part of his own comment. The work, if it be a single work, from which these anonymous citations are made, is written in the common *çloka*, and is seemingly of the same general character with our treatise itself, or a kind of metrical Prâtiçâkhya to the Atharva-Veda; wearing, however, more the aspect of a commentary than does the metrical Prâtiçâkhya to the Rig-Veda.

What has here been said of the commentary applies only to that part of it which ends with the third section of the fourth chapter: the concluding section, on the *krama-pâṭha*, is of an entirely different character, as will be explained at the place.

While thus but imperfectly aided by the native commentator, I have enjoyed one compensating advantage over those who have undertaken hitherto the publication of works of this class, in that I have been able to avail myself of the results of their labors. Had it not been for their efficient help, much in the present treatise might have remained obscure, of which the explanation has now been satisfactorily made out; and I desire here to make a general acknowledgment of my indebtedness to them, which I shall have occasion to repeat hereafter in particular cases. I have thought it incumbent upon me to refer, under every rule, or in connection with every subject treated of, in the work here published, to the corresponding portions of the other Prâtiçâkhyas, giving a briefer or more detailed statement of the harmonies and discrepancies of doctrine which they contain. To the Rig-Veda Prâtiçâkhya reference is made primarily by chapter (*paṭala*) and verse (*çloka*),* the number of the rule cited being then also added, according to the enumeration of both Regnier and Müller; the latter (in the first six chapters only) in Roman figures, the former in Arabic. The Vâjasaneyi Prâtiçâkhya is cited from Weber's edition, already referred to, and according to his enumeration of its rules. For my ability to include in the conspectus of phonetic doctrines the Tâittirîya Prâtiçâkhya of Kârttikeya, I have to thank Prof. Hall, as above acknowledged; the excellent manuscripts of the text and of the text and commentary (*tribhâshyaratna*) which he procured for me will be made, I trust, to help the publication of that treatise in the course of the next year, either by myself or by some one else. The mode of reference to the Tâittirîya Prâtiçâkhya which has hitherto been usual I have abandoned. The work is divided into twenty-four chapters (*adhyâya*), which are classed together in two sections (*praçna*), each of twelve chapters: and Roth—as also Weber, following his example—has cited it by section and chapter, omitting any enumeration and specification of the rules into which each chapter is divided. But the *praçna* division is of as little account as the corresponding division of the Rik Prâtiçâkhya into three sections (*adhyâya*); and there appears to be no good reason why this treatise should not be cited, like those pertaining to the Rik, the White Yajus, and the Atharvan, by chapter and rule simply; as I have done. To Pâṇini's grammar

* In the first chapter, of which the verses are numbered differently by Müller and Regnier, the former counting in the ten prefixed introductory verses, the reference is according to Regnier: to find the corresponding verse in Müller, add ten to the number given.

(in Böhtlingk's edition) reference is also frequently made—in all cases, it is hoped, where the comparison would be of any particular interest. The special relation exhibited by our treatise in many points to the system of general grammar whereof Pâṇini is the authoritative exponent would perhaps have justified a more detailed comparison; but I have both feared to be led too far, and distrusted my ability to draw out the correspondences of the two in a perfectly satisfactory manner. To determine in full the relations of Pâṇini and the Prâtiçâkhyas, when the latter shall have been all made public, will be an important and a highly repaying task for some one more versed than I am in the intricacies of the Paninean system.

The peculiar method, so commonly adopted in our treatise (e. g. i. 64, 65, 85), of applying a rule to the series of passages or words to which it refers, by mentioning only one of them and including the rest in an "etc." (*âdi*) which is to be filled out elsewhere—or the familiarly known *gaṇa*-method of Pâṇini—and the remissness of the commentator, whose duty it was to fill out the *gaṇas*, but who has almost always failed to do so, have rendered necessary on the part of the editor a more careful examination of the Atharvan text, and comparison of it with the Prâtiçâkhya, than has been called for or attempted in connection with any other of the kindred treatises. It has been necessary to construct, as it were, an independent Prâtiçâkhya upon the text, and to compare it with that one which has been handed down to us by the Hindu tradition, in order to test the completeness of the latter, fill up its deficiencies, and note its redundancies. The results of the comparison, as scattered through the notes upon the rules, will be summed up in the additional notes, to which are also relegated other matters which would otherwise call for attention in this introduction. In examining and excerpting the text, full account has been taken of the nineteenth book, and of those parts of the twentieth which are not extracted bodily and without variation from the Rig-Veda. References are made, of course, to the published text of the Atharva-Veda;* if a phrase or word occurs more than once in the text, the first instance of its occurrence is given, with an "e. g." prefixed.

Readings of the manuscript which it is thought desirable to give are generally referred by numbers to the bottom of the page.

The occurrence, here and there in the notes, of emendations of the published text of the Atharvan calls for a few words of explanation here. The work of constructing the text was, by the compelling force of circumstances, so divided between the two editors that the collation of the manuscripts, the writing out of a text, and the preparation of a critical apparatus, fell to myself, while Prof. Roth undertook the final revision of the text, and the carrying of it through the press after my return to this country. Such being the case, and free communication being impossible, occasional misconceptions and errors could not well be avoided. Moreover, the condition of the Atharvan as handed down by the tradition was such as to impose upon the editors as a duty what in the case

---

* Atharva-Veda Sanhitâ, herausgegeben von R. Roth und W. D. Whitney. Erster Band. Text. Berlin, 1856. roy. 8vo.

of any of the other Vedas would have been an almost inexcusable liberty—namely, the emendation of the text-readings in many places. In so treating such a text, it is not easy to hit the precise mean between too much and too little; and while most of the alterations made were palpably and imperatively called for, and while many others would have to be made in translating, there are also a few cases in which a closer adherence to the manuscript authorities might have been preferable. Farther, in the matter of modes of orthography, where the usage of the manuscripts was varying and inconsistent, our choice was not always such as more mature study and reflection justify. Whenever cases of any of these kinds are brought up in connection with the rules and illustrations of the Prâtiçâkhya, I am free to suggest what appears to me a preferable reading or usage. In referring to the manuscripts of the Atharvan, I make use of the following abbreviations (which are also those employed in the margin of the edited text, in books xix and xx): 1st, *saṁhitâ* MSS.: "B." is the Berlin MS. (Ch. 115, Weber 338), containing books xi–xx; "P." is the Paris MS. (D. 204, 205), and contains the whole text, and books vii–x repeated; "M." and "W." are manuscripts of the Bodleian library at Oxford, M. in the Mill collection, and W. in the Wilson: M. is a copy of the same original, by the same hand, and in the same form, as P., and it lacks the part of the text which is found double in the other: W. lacks book xviii; "E." is the East India House manuscript, Nos. 682 and 760; "H." is in the same library, No. 1137, and contains only books i–vi; "I." is the Polier MS., in the British Museum: a copy made from it for Col. Martin is also to be found in the East India House library, Nos. (I believe) 901 and 2142. 2nd, *pada* MSS. These are all in the Berlin library. "Bp." is Ch. 8 (Weber 332) for books i–ix, and Ch. 108 (Weber 335) for books x–xviii: these are two independent manuscripts, but are included under one designation for convenience's sake, as complementing one another. "Bp.²" is Ch. 117 (Weber 331) for book i, and Ch. 100, 107 (Weber 333, 334) for book v, and books vi–ix: the two latter are accidentally separated parts of the same manuscript, and stand also in very close relationship, as respects their original, with Bp. (Ch. 8): the other is independent. Of book xix there is no *pada*-text to be found, and probably none was ever in existence: and the *pada* MSS. of book xx are only extracts from the Rik *pada*-text.

The mode of transcription of Sanskrit words is the same with that which has been hitherto followed in this Journal.

ATHARVA-VEDA PRÂTIÇÂKHYA.

CHAPTER I.

CONTENTS:—SECTION I. 1–2, introductory, scope of the treatise; 3–9, sounds which may occur as finals; 10–13, aspirates, nasals, surds, and sonants; 14–17, description of accents; 18–28, description and classification of sounds according to their place and organ of production; 29–36, do. according to the degree of approximation of the organs; 37–39, the ṛ and ḷ vowels; 40–41, diphthongs.

SECTION II. 42, *visarjanîya*; 43–48, *abhinidhâna*; 49–50, conjunction of consonants; 51–54, quantity of syllables; 55–58, division into syllables; 59–62, quantity of vowels.

SECTION III. 63–66, abnormal alterations and interchanges of sounds; 67–72, occurrence of nasalized vowels; 73–81, *pragṛhya* vowels; 82, treatment in *pada*-text of *pragṛhya* vowels followed by *iva*; 83–91, occurrence of long nasalized vowels in the interior of a word.

SECTION IV. 92, definition of *upadhâ*; 93, what makes a syllable; 94, only an unaspirated consonant allowed before an aspirated; 95, mode of application of rules respecting conversion of sounds; 96, special case of accent; 97, special cases of omission of *pluti* before *iti*; 98, conjunction of consonants; 99, *yama*; 100, *nâsikya*; 101–104, *svarabhakti* and *sphoṭana* and their effect; 105, cases of *pluti*.

चतुर्णां पदजातानां नामाख्यातोपसर्गनिपातानां सन्ध्यपद्यौ गुणौ प्रातिज्ञम् ॥१॥

1. Of the four kinds of words—viz. noun, verb, preposition, and particle—the qualities exhibited in euphonic combination and in the state of disconnected vocables are here made the subject of treatment.

Here is clearly set forth the main object of such a treatise as we are accustomed to call a *prâtiçâkhya*: it is to establish the relations of the combined and the disjoined forms of the text to which it belongs, or of the *saṁhitâ*-text and the *pada*-text: *sandhyapadyâu* might have been directly translated 'in the *saṁhitâ* and *pada* texts respectively.' The ultimate end to be attained is the utterance of the sacred text (*çâkhâ*, 'branch' of the Veda), held and taught by the school, in precisely the form in which the school receives and teaches it. The general material of the text must, of course, be assumed to be known, before it can be made the subject of rules: it is accordingly assumed in its simplest and most material-like form, in the state of *padas* or separate words, each having the form it would wear if uttered alone, compounds being also divided into their constituent parts, and many affixes and inflectional endings separated from their themes; and the Prâtiçâkhya teaches how to put together correctly this analyzed text. An essential part of such a treatise is also its analysis, description, and classification of the sounds of the spoken alphabet, as leading to correctness of utterance, and as underlying and explaining the complicated system of phonetic changes which the treatise has to inculcate. These two subjects—a theoretical system of phonetics, and the rules, general and particular, by which *pada*-text is converted into *sanhitâ*—are the only ones which are found to be fully treated in all the Prâtiçâkhyas; although none of the treatises confines itself to them alone. Thus, our own work gives in its fourth chapter the rules for the construction of the *pada*-text itself, as does also the Vâjasaneyi Prâtiçâkhya; and likewise, in the final section of that chapter (which is, however, evidently a later appendix to the work), a brief statement of the method of forming the *krama*-text, of which it has also taken account in more than one of the rules of its earlier portions: and the Prâtiçâkhyas of the Rik and the Vâjasaneyi have corresponding sections. Nor are the instances infrequent in which it more or less arbitrarily oversteps the limits it has marked out for itself, and deals with matters which lie properly beyond its scope, as will be pointed out in the notes. A summary exhibition of these irregularities, and a comparative analysis of the other Prâtiçâkhyas, will be presented in an additional note.

As the Prâtiçâkhya deals with words chiefly as phonetic combinations, and not as significant parts of speech (as *Wörter*, 'vocables,' not *Worte*, 'words'), their grammatical character is unessential, and the distinction of the four classes made in the rule is rather gratuitous: the names of the classes do not often occur in the sequel, although our treatise is notably more free than any other of its class in availing itself of grammatical distinctions in the statement of its rules. For a fuller exhibition of the fourfold classification of words as parts of speech, see Rik Pr. xii. 5–9, and Vâj. Pr. viii. 52–57.

In illustration of the term *sandhya*, the commentator says: "words that end thus and thus take such and such forms before words that begin so and so." To illustrate *padya*, he cites rule 8, below—a by no means well-chosen example. To show how it is that the treatise has to do only with the qualities of words as exhibited in *sanhitâ* and *pada*, he cites an instance of what must be done by a general grammarian in explanation of a derivative form, as follows: *sandhyapadyâv iti kim artham: lîḍham ity atra ho-ḍha-tvam: paracaturthatvam:* (MS. *padaca°*) *shṭunâ-shṭu-tvam: ḍho-ḍhe-lopo dîrghatvam iti vâiyâkaraṇena vaktavyam:* 'why is it said "the qualities in *sanhitâ* and *pada*"? Because the general grammarian must say, in explanation of *lîḍha*, "here applies the rule *ho ḍhaḥ* (Pâṇ. viii. 2. 31), that for the change of the following letter into its aspirated sonant, the rule *shṭunâ shṭuḥ* (Pâṇ. viii. 4. 41), the rule *ḍho ḍhe lopaḥ* (Pâṇ. viii. 3. 13), and that for the lengthening of the vowel."' These rules teach the formation of the participle *lîḍha* from the root *lih*, through the following series of changes: *lih-ta, liḍh-ta, liḍh-dha, liḍh-ḍha, li-ḍha, lîḍha;* and they are for the most part taken directly from Pâṇini, or at least correspond precisely with his rules; only, in the second case, *paracaturthatvam* takes the place of Pâṇ. viii. 2. 40, *jhashas tathor dho 'dhaḥ;* and, in the last case, *dîrghatvam* stands for *ḍhralope pûrvasya dîrgho 'ṇaḥ* (Pâṇ. vi. 3. 111). Whether the commentator thus deviates arbitrarily or through carelessness from the letter of the great grammarian's rules, or whether he cites from some other authority, anterior to or independent of Pâṇini, and with whom the latter agrees only in part, is a question of which the solution need not be attempted here: while the former supposition may appear the more probable, the other, in the present state of our knowledge respecting the relations between Pâṇini and the Prâtiçâkhyas and their commentators, is not to be summarily rejected as impossible.

एवमिहेति च विभाषाप्राप्तं सामान्ये ॥२॥

2. Farther, that respecting which general grammar allows diversity of usage is made subject of treatment, to the effect of determining the usage in this *çâkhâ*.

This is a broadly periphrastic translation of the rule, which reads more literally: '"thus and thus it is here"—to this effect, also, that which is allowed to be diversely treated in the general language (is made the subject of the rules of the treatise).' The commentator's exposition is as follows: *evam iha iti ca: asyâṁ çâkhâyâṁ tat prâtijñam manyante: yaro 'nunâsike 'nunâsiko vâ 'ti vibhâshâprâptaṁ sâmânye: kiṁ sâmânyam: vyâkaraṇam: vakshyati: uttamâ uttameshv iti:* '"thus it is here:" in these words also: i. e., in this *çâkhâ* they regard this as matter of precept: by the rule (Pâṇ. viii. 4. 45) "the letters from *y* to *s* may or may not be made nasal before a nasal," a choice of usage is allowed in general grammar—*sâmânya* means *vyâkaraṇa*, 'grammar'—but the Prâtiçâkhya is going to say (ii. 5) "mutes other than nasals become nasals before nasals."' The rule is somewhat obscure and difficult of construction, and the commentary not unequivocal, substituting, as before, an illustration in place of a real exposition of its meaning, but I am persuaded that it is fairly rendered by the translation above given. Müller, having occasion to refer to it, gives it somewhat differently, as follows (p. xii): "what by the grammatical text books is left free, that is here thus and thus: so says the Prâtiçâkhya." But this leaves the *ca* unexplained, and supposes the *iti* to be in another place, making the rule to read rather *evam iha vibhâshâprâptaṁ sâmânya iti;* nor does it accord with the commentator's exposition. It seems necessary, in order to account for the *ca*, to bring down *prâtijñam* as general predicate from the preceding rule; and the *iti* must be understood as pointing out that the Prâtiçâkhya says *evam iha*, 'so and so is proper here,' respecting any matter which the rules of grammar leave doubtful.

The rule is properly neither an addition to, nor a limitation of, the one which precedes it, but rather a specification of a particularly important matter among those included in the other; for the Prâtiçâkhya does not overstep the limits of its subject as already laid down, in order to determine points of derivation, form, etc., which general grammar may have left unsettled; nor does it restrict itself within those limits to matters respecting which general usage is allowed to vary: it does not at all imply or base itself upon the general science of grammar and its text book, but is an independent and a complete treatise as regards its own subject.

Of which *çâkhâ* of the Atharva-Veda this work is the Prâtiçâkhya, it gives us itself no information whatever, nor does it even let us know that it belongs to the Atharvan. The name by which it is called, however, leads us to suppose that it was produced in the school of the *Çâunakas*, which is mentioned in the Caraṇavyûha among those of the Atharvan (see Weber's Indische Studien, iii. 277–8). Its relation to the only text of the Atharvan known to be now in existence will be made the subject of an additional note.

पदान्त्यः पद्यः ॥३॥

3. A letter capable of occurring at the end of a word is called *padya*.

This is simply a definition of the term *padya*, which, in this sense, is peculiar to the present treatise; it is not found at all in either of the Yajur-Veda Prâtiçâkhyas, or in Pâṇini, and in the Rik Prâtiçâkhya it means 'member of a compound word.' The term signifies, by its etymology, 'belonging to a *pada*, or disjoined word' (in the technical sense), and it is evidently applied specifically to the last letter of such a word as being the one which is most especially affected by the resolution of *samhitâ* into *pada*.

As instances, the commentary cites a series of four words, ending respectively in guttural, lingual, dental, and labial mutes, which he gives also repeatedly under other rules; viz. *godhuk* (p. *go-dhuk:* e. g. vii. 73. 6), *virâṭ* (p. *vi-râṭ:* e. g. viii. 9. 8), *dṛshat* (ii. 31. 1), *trishṭup* (p. *tri-stup:* e. g. viii. 9. 20).

अनॢकारः स्वरः पद्यः ॥४॥

4. Any vowel, excepting *ḷ*, may occur as final.

The Rik Prâtiçâkhya treats of possible final letters in xii. 1, and excepts the long *ṝ*-vowel, as well as *ḷ*, from their number. The latter is also excluded by the introductory verse 9 to the first chapter, as given by Müller (p. x). The Vâjasaneyi Prâtiçâkhya also pays attention to the same subject, in i. 85–89, and its rule respecting the vowels (i. 87) precisely agrees with ours. It farther specifies, however (i. 88), that *ṛ* is found only at the end of the first member of a compound, which is equally true as regards the Atharvan text.

The illustrations brought forward by the commentator are *brahma* (e. g. i. 19. 4), *çâlâ* (ix. 3. 17), *mâlâ* (not found in AV.), *dadhi* (in *dadhi-vân*, xviii. 4. 17), *kumârî* (x. 8. 27), *madhu* (e. g. i. 34. 2), *vâyû* (only in *indravâyû*, iii. 20. 6), *kartṛ* (no such case in AV., nor any case of this word as member of a compound: take instead *pitṛ-bhiḥ*, e. g. vi. 63. 3; *pitṛ-lokam*, xviii. 4. 64), *cakshate* (e. g. ix. 10. 26), *asyâi* (e. g. ii. 36. 1), *vâyo* (e. g. ii. 20. 1), *tâu* (e. g. iii. 24. 7).

लकारविसर्जनीयौ च ॥५॥

5. Also *l* and *visarjanîya.*

The instances given by the commentator are *bâl* (e. g. i. 3. 1), and *vṛkshaḥ* (e. g. iv. 7. 5). The word *bâl*, an onomatopoetic exclamation, is the only one in the Atharvan ending in *l*—excepting the similar words *çal* and *phal*, in xx. 135. 2, 3, a part of the text of which our treatise takes no account. Both the other Prâtiçâkhyas (R. Pr. xii. 1; V. Pr. i. 86) omit *l* from the number of possible finals, no word in their texts, apparently, ending with it.

स्पर्शाः प्रथमोत्तमाः ॥६॥

6. Of the mutes, the first and last of each series.

That is to say, the unaspirated surds and the nasals, or *k*, *ṭ*, *t*, *p*, and *ṅ*, *ṇ*, *n*, *m*; *c* and *ñ* being excepted by the next following rule. In speaking of the mutes, our treatise follows the same method with that of the other Prâtiçâkhyas, calling the surd, the surd aspirate, the sonant, the sonant aspirate, and the nasal, of each series or *varga*, the "first," "second," "third," "fourth," and "last" of that series respectively. The Vâj. Pr. alone also calls the nasal by the name "fifth."

The commentator gives no instances under this rule: they may be added, as follows: *pratyak* (e. g. iv. 18. 2), *vashaṭ* (e. g. i. 11. 1), *yat* (e. g. i. 2. 3), *tri-shṭup* (e. g. viii. 9. 20); *arvâṅ* (e. g. iii. 2. 3), *brahmaṇ-vatîm* (vi. 108. 2), *asmân* (e. g. i. 1. 4), *teshâm* (e. g. i. 1. 1). The guttural nasal, *ṅ*, appears only as final of masculine nominatives singular of derivatives of the root *añc*; the lingual, *ṇ*, only in a few instances, at the end of the first member of a compound, where, by a specific rule (iv. 99), it is left in the *pada* in its *saṁhitâ* form (the Vâj. Pr. [i. 88] expressly notices this as true of its text): *ṭ* is found almost only as euphonic substitute of a final *c*, *j*, *sh*, or *ç* (*viṭ-bhyaḥ*, iii. 3. 3: in the onomato poetic *phaṭ* [iv. 18. 3], it doubtless stands for either *sh* or *c*; *baṭ* [xiii. 2. 29], the only other like case, is doubtful): *k* and *p* are also comparatively rare, and especially the latter.

The Vâj. Pr. (i. 85) gives the same rule, comprising with it also the one here next following. The Rik Pr. (xii. 1) forbids only to the aspirates a place as finals; but the phonetic rules of its fourth chapter imply the occurrence only of surds at the end of a word: see the note to rule 8, below.

न चवर्गः ॥७॥

7. Excepting the palatal series.

The commentator mentions all the palatal mutes, *c*, *ch*, *j*, *jh*, *ñ*, as excluded from the final position by this rule; but it properly applies only to *c* and *ñ*, the others being disposed of already by rule 6. The Vâj. Pr. (i. 85) specifies *c* and *ñ*: the Rik Pr. (xii. 1) speaks, like our rule, of the whole class.

It does not belong to the Prâtiçâkhya, of course, to explain into what an original palatal is converted when it would occur as a final.

प्रथमान्तानि तृतीयान्तानीति शौनकस्य प्रतिज्ञानं न वृत्तिः ॥ ८ ॥

8. That the words thus declared to end in first mutes end rather in thirds is Çâunaka's precept, but not authorized usage.

That is to say, Çâunaka prescribes that those words which, as noted in rule 6 above, and as implied throughout the rest of the treatise, have for their final letters the unaspirated surd, must be pronounced with the unaspirated sonant instead: but, although the sage to whom the treatise is ascribed, or from whom the school to which it belongs derives its name, is thus honored by the citation of his opinion, the binding authority of the latter is denied. With regard to the question whether a final mute is surd or sonant, opinions seem to have been somewhat divided among the Hindu grammarians. Pâṇini (viii. 4. 56) does not decide the point, but permits either pronunciation. The Rik Pr. (i. 3, r. 15, 16, xvi, xvii) cites Gârgya as holding the sonant utterance, and Çâkaṭâyana the surd: it itself declares itself for neither, and at another place (xii. 1), as already noted, treats both surd and sonant as allowable: its phonetic rules, however (iv. 1), being constructed to apply only to the surd final. If the Rik Pr. were actually, as it claims to be, the work of Çâunaka, the rule of our treatise now under consideration would lead us to expect it to favor unequivocally the sonant pronunciation. The Vâj. Pr., as we have seen above (under r. 6), teaches the surd pronunciation. The Tâitt. Pr., liberal as it usually is in citing the varying opinions of the grammarians on controverted topics, takes no notice whatever of this point; but its rules (viii. 1 etc.), like those of all the other treatises, imply that the final mute, if not nasal, is surd.

It would seem from this that the sound which a sonant mute assumed when final in Sanskrit (for that an original surd, when final, should have tended to take on a sonant character is very hard to believe) wavered somewhat upon the limit between a surd and a sonant pronunciation: but that it verged decidedly upon the surd is indicated by the great preponderance of authority upon that side, and by the unanimous employment of the surd in the written literature.

In his exposition of this rule, the commentator first gives a bald paraphrase of it: *prathamântâni padâni tṛitîyântânî 'ti çâunakasyâ 'câryasya pratijñânam bhavati: na tu vṛittiḥ;* adding as instances the words already given (see under r. 3), *godhuk, virâṭ, dṛshat, trishṭup;* he then, without any preface, cites two or three lines from his metrical authority, which need a good deal of amendation to be brought into a translatable shape, but of which the meaning appears to be nearly as follows: "mutes other than nasals, standing *in pausa*, are to be regarded as firsts: a word ending in a first may be considered as ending in a third, but must in no case be actually so read (compare Uvaṭa to

R. Pr. iii. 8, r. 13, cc), owing to the non-exhibition of authoritative usage in its favor" (MS. *nâvasânânikân sparçân padyân* [*âdyân?*] *anunâsikân: prathamân tṛtîyân* [*prathamântâṅs tṛtîyântâṅç?*] *vidyât na tu paṭhet kva cit: vṛtter anudarçanât*).

अधिस्पर्शं च ॥ ९ ॥

9. Also *adhisparçam.*

The meaning and scope of this rule are exceedingly obscure, and the commentator so signally fails to throw any light upon it, that we can hardly help concluding that he did not understand it himself. His exposition, without any amendment, is as follows: *adhisparça ca pratijñâ* [*jâdin mâ 'vasitân sparçân padyân anunâsikân: tṛtîyân çaunakamatât*] *nam bhavati: na tu vṛttiḥ: kim adhisparçâ nama: vakshyati: yakâravakârayor leçavṛttir adhisparçam çâkaṭâyanasya* . . .* I have to thank Prof. Weber for the highly probable suggestion, made in a private communication, that the words *jâdin* to *matât*, or those enclosed in brackets, have strayed into the commentary, out of place; so that the true reading is *adhisparçaṁ ca pratijñânam bhavati: na tu vṛttiḥ:* '*adhisparçam* also is a *dictum* of Çâunaka, but not authoritative usage.' The interpolated words form part of a verse, and are apparently identical or akin in signification with the verses cited under the preceding rule: a restatement of the same thing, in slightly different terms, and so, we may conclude, by a different authority. To explain what *adhisparça* means here, the commentator simply cites rule ii. 24, in which the same word occurs again: a rule which informs us of the opinion of Çâkaṭâyana, that final *y* and *v*, the result of euphonic processes, are not omitted altogether, but imperfectly uttered *as regards the contact* (*adhisparçam*), the tongue and lips, in their pronunciation, not making the partial contact (i. 30) which is characteristic of the semivowels. But how can the use of *adhisparçam* in that rule, as an adverb, give a hint of its meaning here, where it seems to be treated as a noun? Are we to understand that it is taken as the name of that peculiar utterance of *y* and *v*, and that our rule means to say that the mode of utterance in question is also a teaching of Çâunaka, but not authoritative? This is scarcely credible: it does not appear hereafter that Çâunaka had anything to do with that utterance, which is sufficiently put down by the positive rules of the treatise against it, nor would its mention here, in a passage treating of *padyas*, be otherwise than impertinent. Or is *adhisparça* to be interpreted as the name of a slighted or imperfect utterance, and did Çâunaka teach such an utterance as belonging to a final mute, which wavered, as it were, between sonant and surd? This appears somewhat more plausible, but not sufficiently so to be accepted as at all satisfactory: there is no question of a difference of contact of the

* Here, as also in the citation of the rule ii. 6, under rule 2 above, the whole series of illustrative citations from the Atharvan text, as given by the commentary under the rules themselves, are rehearsed: I have omitted them as superfluous.

organs (*sparça*) in such a case, and it is one to which the prescription of *abhinidhāna* (i. 43) applies.*

द्वितीयचतुर्थाः सोष्माणः ॥१०॥

10. The second and fourth of each series are aspirates.

The term *ūshman*, literally 'heat, hot vapor, steam,' is in the grammatical language applied to designate all those sounds which are produced by a rush of unintonated breath through an open position of the mouth organs, or whose utterance has a certain similarity to the escape of steam through a pipe: they are the sibilants and aspirations or breathings (see below, i. 31). In the term *soshman*, 'aspirated mute,' and in its correlative *anūshman*, 'unaspirated mute' (i. 94), *ūshman* is to be understood not in this specific sense, but in that of 'rush of air, expulsion of unintonated breath.' To this rule correspond Rik Pr. i. 3 (r. 13, xiv) and Vāj. Pr. i. 54, the latter being also verbally coincident with it. The Tāitt. Pr. has nothing analogous, and does not employ the terms *soshman* and *anūshman*.

The commentator merely adds the list of surd and sonant aspirates to his paraphrase of the rule, citing no examples. For the sonant palatal aspirate, *jh*, the Atharvan text affords no example. He next cites a verse from his metrical authority: *sasthānāir ūshmabhiḥ pṛktās tṛtīyāḥ prathamāç ca ye: caturthāç ca dvitīyāç ca sampadyanta iti sthitiḥ*; 'thirds and firsts, when closely combined with *flatus* of position corresponding to their own, become fourths and seconds: that is the way.' The most natural rendering of *sasthānāir ūshmabhiḥ* would be 'with their corresponding *ūshmans* or spirants;' but this is hardly to be tolerated, since it would give us, for example, *ts* and *ds*, instead of *th* and *dh*, as the dental aspirates. This view is distinctly put forth, however, as regards the surd aspirates, by another authority which the commentator proceeds to cite at considerable length: the first portion, which alone bears upon the subject of our rule, is as follows: "another has said, 'the fourths are formed with *h*:'" (now begin the *çlokas*) "some knowing ones have said that there are five 'first' mutes; of these, by the successive accretion of secondary qualities (*guṇa*), there takes place a conversion into others. They are known as 'seconds' when combined with the qualities of *jihvāmūlīya*, *ç*, *sh*, *s*, and *upadhmānīya*. The same, when uttered with intonation, are known as 'thirds;' and these, with the second spirant, are known as 'fourths.' When the 'firsts' are pronounced with intonation, and through the nose, they are called 'fifth' mutes. Thus are noted the qualities of the letters." The remaining verses of the quoted passage treat of the combination and doubling of consonants, and I am unable in all points to restore and translate them.

---

* I add Weber's conjecture: "possibly—'as regards contact also' the view of Çāunaka is only a *pratijñānam*, and not *vṛtti*; that is, when the *padyas* enter into *sandhi*, they are to be converted into *tṛtīyas* before nasals (e.g. *tad me*, not *ten me*); but this is only *pratijñānam*, not *vṛtti*." I cannot regard this as the true explanation, since we have no doctrine of Çāunaka's, to the effect implied, anywhere stated, and since *sparça* is not, so far as I am aware, ever used of the contact or concurrence of one sound with another.

उत्तमा अनुनासिकाः ॥ ११ ॥

11. The last in each series is nasal.

The term *anunâsika* in this treatise means simply 'uttered through the nose,' and is applied to any sound in the production of which the nose bears a part: see rule 27, below. In ii. 35, it is used of the *l* into which a nasal is converted before an *l*: in all other cases of its occurrence, it designates a nasalized vowel, or what is ordinarily known as the independent and necessary *anusvâra*. Our treatise stands alone among the Prâtiçâkhyas in ignoring any such constituent of the alphabet as the *anusvâra*, acknowledging only nasal consonants and nasal vowels. For a comprehensive statement of the teachings of the other treatises respecting nasal sounds, see Roth, Zur Litteratur und Geschichte des Weda, pp. 68-82.

The Rik Pr. (i. 3, r. 14, xv) and Vâj. Pr. (i. 89) describe the nasal mutes as *anunâsika*; as does also the Tâitt. Pr. (ii. 30), including with them the *anusvâra*.

श्वासो ऽघोषेष्वनुप्रदानः । नादो घोषवत्स्वरेषु ॥ १२।१३ ॥

12. In the surd consonants, the emission is breath;
13. In the sonant consonants and the vowels, it is sound.

In this case and the one next following, two or three rules are stated and explained together by the commentator; that the division and enumeration is to be made as here given, is attested by the statement at the close of the section respecting the number of rules contained in it.

The Prâtiçâkhya here lays down with entire correctness the distinction between surd and sonant sounds, which consists in the different nature of the material furnished in the two classes to the mouth organs by the lungs and throat: in the one class it is mere breath, simple unintonated air; in the other class, it is breath made sonant by the vocal chords on its passage through the throat, and thus converted into sound. The same thing is taught by two of the other treatises: see Rik Pr. xiii. 2 (r. 4, 5), and Tâitt. Pr. ii. 8, 10: the Vâj. Pr. gives no corresponding definition, nor does it use the terms *aghosha* and *ghoshavant*, but adopts instead of them the arbitrary and meaningless designations *jit* and *mud* for the surds, *dhi* for the sonants (i. 50-53). No one of the treatises confuses itself with that false distinction of "hard" or "strong," and "soft" or "weak," which has been the bane of so much of our modern phonology.

The word *anupradâna* means 'a giving along forth, a continuous emission,' and hence, 'that which is given forth, emitted material:' compare Tâitt. Pr. xxiii. 2, where *anupradâna*, 'emitted material,' is mentioned first among the circumstances which determine the distinctive character of a sound. The Rik Pr. (xiii. 2) uses instead *prakṛti*, 'material.'

Our commentator gives the full list of the sonant letters: the vowels in their three forms, short, long, and protracted (*pluta*), the sonant mutes, the semivowels, *h*, and, by way of examples of the sonant *yamas* (see below, i. 99), those of *g* and *gh*.[1] He then cites again a verse from his metrical authority, as follows: *vyañjanaṁ ghoshavatsaṁjñam antasthā haḥ parāu yamāu: trayas trayaç ca vargāntyā aghoshāḥ çesha ucyate*; 'the consonants termed sonant are the semivowels, *h*, the two latter *yamas*, and the three last of each class of mutes: the rest are called surd.' There is one striking anomaly in this classification; namely, the inclusion among the sonants of *h*, which in our pronunciation is a surd of surds. The Sanskrit *h* is, as is well known, the etymological descendant, in almost all cases, of a guttural sonant aspirate, *gh*: are we then to assume that it retained, down to the time of establishment of the phonetic system of the language, something of its sonant guttural pronunciation, and was rather an Arabic *ghain* than our simple aspiration? or would it be allowable to suppose that, while in actual utterance a pure *h*, it was yet able, by a reminiscence of its former value, to exercise the phonetic influence of a sonant letter? The question is not an easy one to decide; for, while the latter supposition is of doubtful admissibility, it is equally hard to see how the *h* should have retained any sonancy without retaining at the same time more of a guttural character than it manifests in its euphonic combinations. The Prātiçākhya which treats most fully of the *h* is that belonging to the Tāittirīya Sanhitā: we read there (ii. 4–6) that, while sound is produced in a closed throat, and simple breath in an open one, the *h*-tone is uttered in an intermediate condition; and (ii. 9) that this *h*-tone is the emitted material in the consonant *h*, and in "fourth" mutes, or sonant aspirates. I confess myself unable to derive any distinct idea from this description, knowing no intermediate utterance between breath and sound, excepting the stridulous tone of the loud whisper, which I cannot bring into any connection with an *h*. The Rik Pr. (xiii. 2, r. 6) declares both breath and sound to be present in the sonant aspirates and in *h*, which could not possibly be true of the latter, unless it were composed, like the former, of two separate parts, a sonant and a surd: and this is impossible. The Tāitt. Pr., in another place (ii. 46, 47), after defining *h* as a throat sound, adds that, in the opinion of some, it is uttered in the same position of the organs with the following vowel; which so accurately describes the mode of pronunciation of our own *h* that we cannot but regard it as an important indication that the Sanskrit *h* also was a pure surd aspiration.

समानयमे ऽक्षरमुच्चैरुदात्तम् । नीचैरनुदात्तम् । आक्षिप्तं स्वरितम् ॥ १४ । १५ । १६ ॥

14. In a given key, a syllable uttered in a high tone is called acute;

15. One uttered in a low tone is called grave;

---

[1] MS. गं, so that, but for the following verse, it would be very doubtful what was meant.

16. One carried from the high to the low tone is called circumflex.

The word *samânayamam* signifies literally 'on the same pitch:' *yama* has this sense once in the Rik Pr. (xiii. 17), and several times in the Tâitt. Pr. (xv. 9, xix. 3, etc.). The specification which it conveys is omitted in all the other treatises, probably as being too obvious to require statement. The meaning evidently is that the acute and grave pronunciations are bound to no absolute or fixed tones, but that, wherever one's voice is pitched, a higher tone of utterance gives the acute, a lower the grave. Our treatise, the Vâj. Pr. (i. 108, 109), the Tâitt. Pr. (i. 38, 39), and Pâṇini (i. 2. 29, 30) precisely accord in their description of the *udâtta* and *anudâtta* accents: the Rik Pr. (iii. 1) tries to be more profound, describing the cause rather than the nature of their difference, and succeeds in being obscure: its definition of them, as spoken "with tension and relaxation respectively," would teach us little about them but for the help of the other authorities. As regards the *svarita*, the definitions virtually correspond, though different in form: the Tâitt. Pr. (i. 40) and Pâṇini call it a *samâhâra*, or 'combination,' of the other two; the Vâj. Pr. (i. 110) says that a syllable possessing both the other tones is *svarita;* the Rik Pr. (iii. 2), that a syllable is *svarita* into which the two other tones enter together. The term *âkshipta*, used in the definition of our treatise, is difficult of explanation. It corresponds with the term *âkshepa*, by which in the Rik Pr. (iii. 1) the accent in question is characterized, and which Regnier translates "addition," Müller "a clinging to, continuance, persistence (*anhalten*)," and Roth (Preface to Nirukta, p. lvii) nearly the same (*aushalten*, 'persistence, perseverance'); while Weber (p. 133) renders our *âkshiptam* "slurred, drawled (*geschleift*)." Regnier's translation is supported by the analogy of the corresponding expressions in the other treatises, nor would it imply too great an ellipsis in the connection in which it stands in his text; but to understand the participle here in a corresponding sense, as meaning 'exhibiting the addition of the other two to each other,' could hardly be tolerated. Uvaṭa's commentary explains *âkshepa* by *tiryaggamana*, which would admit of being rendered 'a passing through, or across, from one to the other;' and I have accordingly translated *âkshipta* as having the sense of 'thrown, transferred, or carried from one to the other of the two already mentioned.'

The words *udâtta* and *anudâtta* mean literally 'elevated' and 'not elevated'—that is to say, above the average pitch of the voice. *Svarita* is more difficult to understand, and has received many different explanations, none of which has been satisfactorily established. I have myself formerly (Journ. Am. Or. Soc., v. 204) ventured the suggestion that it might come from *svara*, 'vowel,' and mean 'vocalized, exhibiting a conversion of semivowel into vowel,' as would be necessary, in order to the full enunciation of the double tone, in the great majority of the syllables which exhibit it: but I am far from confident that this is the true explanation. The accent is once called in the Tâitt. Pr. (xix. 3) *dviyama*, 'of double tone or pitch.' The three Sanskrit accents, *udâtta*, *anudâtta*, and *svarita*, so precisely correspond in phonetic character with what we are accustomed to call acute, grave, and circumflex, that it has not seemed to me worth while to avoid the use of these terms in treating of them.

The commentator gives only a paraphrase, and no explanation, of these rules, which he states and treats together, as I have done. As illustrations of the accents, he cites *amâvâsyâ'* (e. g. vii. 79. 2) and *kanyâ'* (e. g. i. 14. 2), both circumflex on the final syllable, and the words *prâ' 'mú' ca roha*, which are not found in the Atharvan: but the reading is probably corrupt, and the phrase meant may be *prajā'm ca róha* (xiii. 1. 34); this would furnish instances of the *udâtta* and *anudâtta*—although, indeed, not better than a thousand other phrases which might have been selected.

स्वरितस्यादितो मात्रार्धमुदात्तम् ॥ १७ ॥

17. Half the measure of a circumflex, at its commencement, is acute.

Our treatise, with which the Vâj. Pr. (i. 126) precisely agrees, contents itself with this description of the *svarita* or circumflex, and we must commend their moderation. The other two treatises give way more or less to the characteristic Hindu predilection for hair-splitting in matters unessential, and try to define more particularly the degree of elevation of the higher portion, and the degree of depression of the lower. Thus the Rik Pr. (iii. 2, 3) describes the higher portion—which it allows to be either a half-mora or half the whole quantity of the syllable—as higher than *udâtta* or acute, while the after portion is indeed *anudâtta* or grave, yet has the *udâtta* pitch. The Tâitt. Pr. (i. 46) notices the doctrine held by our treatise as that of some teachers, and also remarks (i. 47) that some regard the whole syllable as a slide or continuous descent from the higher to the lower pitch. Its own doctrine (i. 41–45) is that, when the *svarita* follows an *udâtta*, its first half-mora only is higher than *udâtta*, its remaining portion being either the same as *udâtta*, or lower, or the same as *anudâtta*.

We have in this part of the work only the general description of the accents: a more detailed treatment of them, as they arise and as they affect one another in the combinations of the continuous text, is given in the third section of the third chapter (iii. 55 etc.).

The commentator merely cites, as offering instances of the circumflex accent, the following words: *amâvâsyâ'* (e. g. vii. 79. 2), *kanyâ'* (e. g. i. 14. 2), *dhânyàm* (e. g. iii. 24. 2), *âcâryàḥ* (e. g. xi. 5. 3), *râjanyàḥ* (e. g. v. 17. 9), *nyàk* (vi. 91. 2), *kvà* (e. g. ix. 9. 4), *svàḥ* (e. g. ii. 5. 2): they all appear again, as instances of the *jâtya* or original *svarita*, under iii. 57.

मुखे विशेषाः करणस्य ॥ १८ ॥

18. In the mouth there are differences of producing organ.

This rule is simply introductory to those that follow, respecting the place and mode of production of the different sounds of the spoken alphabet. As regards each of these, two circumstances are to be considered: the *sthâna*, or 'position,' and the *karaṇa*, or 'producer.' The distinction between the two is laid down by the commentator twice over, in identical phrase, under rules 19 and 25: *kim punaḥ sthânam: kim karaṇam: . . . yad upakramyate tat sthânam: yeno 'pakramyate tat karaṇam*; 'what, again, is "position," and what "organ"? that is position to which approach is made; that is organ by which approach is made.' The Tâitt. Pr. has a similar definition in its text (ii. 31–34): "in case of the vowels, that is position to which there is approximation; that is organ which makes the approximation: in the case of the other letters, that is position upon which contact is made; that is organ by which one makes the contact." That is to say; two organs are always concerned in the production of a sound, and by their contact or approximation the sound receives its character: of these, the more immovable one is called the *sthâna*, or place of production, and it is from this that the sound derives its class designation; the more movable or active one is called the *karaṇa*, or instrument of production. The *sthâna* does not require to be stated, since it is implied in the very name of the sound; but, lest it should chance to be erroneously imagined that all the sounds are produced by one and the same organ at the places indicated, we are expressly taught the contrary in this rule, and the treatise goes on to specify the different organs.*

कण्ठ्यानामधरकण्ठः ॥ १९ ॥

19. Of the throat-sounds, the lower part of the throat is the producing organ.

That is to say, as the commentator goes on to explain, the upper part of the throat, as place of production, is approached by the lower part of the throat, as instrument of production. As the sounds constituting the class, he mentions *a*, in its short, long, and protracted values, *h*, and the *visarjanîya*. The same sounds are defined as *kaṇṭhya* by the Rik Pr. (i. 8, r. 38–40, xxxix–xli), which also notices that some call *h* and *visarjanîya* "chest-sounds" (*urasya*). The Vâj. Pr. (i. 71) declares them formed in the throat, but (i. 84) by the middle of the jaw as organ—a strange description, and not very creditable to the accuracy of observation of its author. The Tâitt. Pr. (ii. 46) reckons only *h* and *visarjanîya* as throat-sounds, and then adds (ii. 47, 48) that some regard *h* as having the same position with the following vowel, and *visarjanîya* as having the same position with the preceding vowel. This latter is the most significant hint which any of the Prâtiçâkhyas afford us respecting the phonetic value of the rather problematical *visarjanîya*, indicating it as a mere uncharacterized breathing, a final *h*. There is an obvious propriety in detaching these two aspirations and *a* from the following class of "gutturals," *k* etc., in which the Paninean scheme (under Pâṇ.

* The meaning *i* under the title *karaṇa* in the Böhtlingk-Roth lexicon—viz. "Aussprache, Articulation"—is accordingly to be struck out: Weber's translation of the word, also—"*Hervorbringungsweise*, 'method of production'"—is both inaccurate and peculiarly cumbersome and unwieldy.

i. 1. 9) ranks them, as they receive no modifying action from any of the mouth organs: and the authority who called the aspirations chest-sounds may also be commended for his acuteness, since in their production it may even be said that the throat has no part: it is only, like the mouth, the avenue by which the breath expelled from the chest finds exit.

The commentator quotes a verse again, of which the general drift is clear, although I have not succeeded in restoring its readings so as to translate it with closeness. It speaks of the diphthongs as also containing an element of throat-sound, and says that they, as well as the nasal mutes, are declared to have a twofold position.

जिह्वामूलीयानां हनुमूलम् ॥ २० ॥

20. Of the gutturals, the base of the jaw is the producing organ.

The name *jihvâmûlîya*, by which the class of sounds here spoken of is called, means 'formed at the base of the tongue:' I retain for them, however, the brief and familiar appellation of "gutturals." They are stated by the commentary to be the ṛ vowels, short, long, and protracted, the guttural mutes *k*, *kh*, *g*, *gh*, *ṅ*, the *jihvâmûlîya* spirant, or that modification of *visarjanîya* which is exhibited before the surd gutturals *k* and *kh* (intimated by him by means of an illustrative instance, *purushaḥ khanati*: the phrase is a fabricated one, not occurring in the Atharvan text), and the vowel ḷ (also intimated by an example, *kḷptaḥ* [x. 10. 23]). Precisely the same series of sounds is stated by the Rik Pr. (i. 8, r. 41, xlii) to constitute the class of *jihvâmûlîyas*. The Vâj. Pr. declares the same, with the exception of the ḷ-vowel, to be formed at the base of the tongue (i. 65) by the base of the jaw (i. 83). The Tâitt. Pr. (ii. 35, 44) includes in the class only the guttural mutes and spirant, and reverses the relation of position and organ, making the jaw the former, and the tongue the latter. This is evidently the more natural way of defining the mode of production of the class, and the more analogous with the method of our own treatise elsewhere, as in the cases of the throat-letters, palatals, and labials, the lower and more mobile of the two organs concerned being taken as the producer. But the usage of naming the class from the *sthâna* seems to have required that the *jihvâmûla* be declared the *sthâna*, and not the *karaṇa*, of the sounds of which the well established name was *jihvâmûlîya*. By *hanumûla*, 'root or base of the jaw,' must be here understood, it should seem, the posterior edge of the hard palate, which might well enough be regarded as the base of the upper jaw, or of the bony structure in which the upper teeth are set. It is, in fact, by a contact produced at this point between the roof of the mouth and the nearest part of the upper surface of the tongue that our own gutturals, *k* and *g*, are uttered. That the ṛ-vowel should be included by the Prâtiçâkhyas among the guttural sounds, instead of among the linguals, where its euphonic value so distinctly places it, and where it is arranged in the Paninean scheme, is very strange, and would point to a guttural pronunciation of the *r* in certain localities or among certain classes; a guttural *r* is a well recognized constituent of many modern alphabets. The definition of the *ḷ*-vowel as a guttural by part of the authorities is probably explainable by its occurrence only in the root *kḷp*, after a guttural, where it might naturally enough be so far assimilated as to take on something of a guttural character, being removed to a point considerably posterior to that in which the common *l* is uttered. The Vâj. Pr. (i. 69) and the Paninean scheme make it dental. The *jihvâmûlîya* spirant and its compeer, the *upadhmânîya* or labial spirant, are nowhere expressly mentioned in our treatise, but are apparently necessarily implied in ii. 40, and are regarded by the commentator as forming part of the alphabet which the work contemplates. It does not seem probable that they were important modifications of the neutral breathing, the *visarjanîya*.

The commentator again closes his exposition with a verse, which, with some doubtful emendations, reads as follows: *jihvâmûlam ṛvarṇasya kavargasya ca bhâshyate; yaç*[1] *cai 'va jihvâmûlîya ḷvarṇaç ca 'ti te smṛtâḥ*[2]*:* 'the root of the tongue is declared the organ of the *ṛ*-vowels and the *k*-series; also the spirant which is *jihvâmûlîya*, and the *ḷ*-vowels are so explained.'

तालव्यानां मध्यजिह्वम् ॥ २१ ॥

21. Of the palatals, the middle of the tongue is the producing organ.

The sounds composing this class are stated by the commentator to be *e*, *âi*, *y*, *ç*, *c*, *ch*, *j*, *jh*, *ñ*, and the vowel *i*, in its short, long, and protracted values. In this enumeration, he follows the order of the half verse which he goes on to quote, as follows: *tâlv âiyaçacavargâṇâm ivarṇasya ca bhâshyate:* 'the palate is explained to be the place of production of *âi*, *y*, *ç*, the *c*-series, and the *i*-vowels.' The same sounds are specified by the Rik Pr. (i. 9, r. 42, xliii) as palatals, and are described by the Vâj. Pr. (i. 66, 79) as formed upon the palate, by the middle of the tongue, precisely as by our treatise. The Tâitt. Pr. (ii. 36) furnishes the same definition of the *c*-series and (ii. 44) of *ç*, but holds (ii. 40) that *y* is formed upon the palate by the middle and end of the tongue; and, as in other cases, it does not include any vowels in the class.

The ancient Sanskrit *c* and *j* can hardly have been so distinctly compound sounds as our *ch* and *j* (in *church*, *judge*), or they would have been analyzed and described as such by the phonetists. At the same time, their inability to stand as finals, the euphonic conversion of *t* and following *ç* into *ch*, the Prakritic origin of *c* and *j* from *ty* and *dy*, etc., are too powerful indications to be overlooked of their close kindred with our sounds, and deviation from strict simplicity of nature. That the *ç* was our *sh*, or something only infinitesimally differing from it, we see no good reason to doubt: and certainly, those who hold to the English *ch* and *j* pronunciation for the mutes cannot possibly avoid accepting the *sh* pronunciation for the sibilant.

It has already been noticed above (under r. 10) that one of the palatal mutes, *jh*, does not once occur in the Atharvan text.

---

[1] *yaç.*

[2] *ḷvarṇasye 'ti sa smṛtaḥ.*

मूर्धन्यानां जिह्वाग्रं प्रतिवेष्टितम् ॥ २२ ॥

22. Of the linguals, the tip of the tongue, rolled back, is the producing organ.

The sounds composing this class are *sh*, and the *ṭ* series, or *ṭ*, *ṭh*, *ḍ*, *ḍh*, *ṇ*; so says the commentator, and fortifies his assertion by adding the half verse *mūrdhasthānaḥ shakārasya ṭavargasya tathā matam*. They are known in all the Prātiçākhyas by the same name (R. Pr. i. 9, r. 43, xliv; V. Pr. i. 67, 78; T. Pr. ii. 37, 44), and the Vāj. Pr. and Tāitt. Pr. describe them in the same manner with our treatise, even to using the same verb to express the action of reverting or rolling back the tip of the tongue into the highest part of the mouth cavity. The semivowel and vowel *r* are in the Pāninean scheme, and in our customary classification of the Sanskrit alphabet, also reckoned as linguals; and, as the euphonic laws of the language show, with entire propriety, since it is in no inconsiderable measure under the assimilating influence of the *r* that the others have come into the alphabet, or won their present degree of extension in the spoken system of sounds. The only letter of nearly corresponding position in our modern European alphabets is the *r*, which in English, at least, is ordinarily pronounced smoothly over the tip of the tongue within the dome of the palate, although not at a point so far back as would seem to be indicated by the term *mūrdhan*. This word means literally 'head, *caput*,' and hence an exact translation of its derivative *mūrdhanya* would be 'capital,' and this would be the proper name by which to call the class, if the term had not in English another well recognized meaning as applied to letters. Müller (p. xviii) holds *mūrdhan* to be used directly in the sense of 'dome of the palate' (*Gaumendach*), and Weber (p. 108) accepts the same meaning for *çiras*, but it seems to me exceedingly doubtful whether words which mean so distinctly 'head,' as usually employed, can, without limiting addition, be taken as signifying a certain region in the mouth: especially when we see the Vāj. Pr. (i. 30) once use *bhrūmadhya*, 'the middle of the brows,' in a corresponding sense, and the Tāitt. Pr. (ii. 3) mention the mouth (*mukha*) along with the "head" (*çiras*) among the organs which give form to sound. *Mūrdhan* must be taken to mean 'dome of the palate' indirectly, if at all, in so far as that is the highest point in "the head" which the tongue is capable of reaching. Müller proposes "cacuminal" as a name for the class; a far from unsuitable term, but one which has not found acceptance, perhaps as being rather cacophonous. The name employed by Bopp and many other later grammarians, "lingual," seems as free from objection as any other. "Cerebral" does injustice to the Hindu grammarians, and obtrudes offensively a false and absurd theory.

षकारस्य द्रोणिका ॥ २३ ॥

23. Of *sh*, the trough-shaped tongue is the producing organ.

Our treatise is the only one which singles out *sh* from among the other lingual letters to make it the subject of a special description.

Both the commentator and his metrical authority regard the *sh* as included in the class which the last rule describes: we are to regard this, then, only as a specification which so far modifies the description already given. It is very possibly a later interpolation in the text of our treatise. The commentary, as usual, offers no explanation of the word *dronikâ*, which does not occur elsewhere in the grammatical language. It is a derivative from *droṇa*, 'wooden tub or trough,' and is explained in the Böhtlingk-Roth lexicon as "the tongue bent together in the form of a trough," which is undoubtedly the true rendering. It can hardly be claimed that this rule adds to the distinctness of our apprehension of the character of this sibilant, which is clearly enough exhibited by its relation to the other lingual sounds: it is not our *sh*—which is rather, as above noticed, the palatal *ç*—but such a sibilant as is formed by reverting the tip of the tongue into the dome of the palate; much more nearly resembling our *sh* than our *s*, because uttered at nearly the same point with the former, only with the tip, instead of the broad upper surface, of the tongue: an *s* can only be produced pretty close behind the upper teeth.

As an instance of this sibilant, the commentator cites the phrase *shaḍ bhûḥ çîtân shaḍ u mâsâḥ* (viii. 9. 17).

दन्त्यानां जिह्वाग्रं प्रस्तीर्णम् ॥ २४ ॥

24. Of the dentals, the tip of the tongue thrust forward is the producing organ.

The commentator makes this class include *l*, *s*, *t*, *th*, *d*, *dh*, and *n*, citing again a quarter verse to the same effect: *dantâ*[1] *lasatavargâṇâm*. The Vâj. Pr. adds the *ḷ*-vowel to the class, which it defines (i. 69, 76) as formed at the teeth by the tip of the tongue. The Rik Pr. (i. 9, 10, r. 44, 45, xlv, xlvi) composes the class of *l*, *s*, and *r*, besides the *t*-series, and calls them *dantamûlîyâs*, 'letters of the roots of the teeth.' The Tâitt. Pr. (ii. 38, 42, 44) defines the same letters, except *r*, as formed *dantamûleshu*, 'at the roots of the teeth,' the *t*-series and *s* by the tip of the tongue, and *l* by its middle part. The description of the two latter authorities is undoubtedly the more accurate, since the contact by which our "dentals" are produced is not upon the teeth themselves, but just at their base or behind them: between the tip of the tongue and the teeth, where no close contact is possible, are brought forth the English *th* sounds. What makes in all cases the peculiar character of an *l* is that in its production the tongue is in contact with the roof of the mouth in front, but open at the sides. The Tâitt. Pr., then, in defining the *l* as produced by the middle of the tongue, doubtless refers to the part where the escape of the breath takes place, while the others are thinking only of the part by which the contact is made.

ओष्ठ्यानामधरौष्ठम्[2] ॥ २५ ॥

25. Of the labials, the lower lip is producing organ.

---

[1] *dantyâ.*

[2] *-oshṭhyam*; as also in more than one instance in what follows.

That is to say, as in the case of the throat sounds (r. 19, above) the upper surface of the throat was regarded as the passive organ, or position, and the under surface as the active organ, or producer, so here the upper lip is passive organ, and the lower lip active: or, as the commentary phrases it, "the upper lip, the position (*sthâna*), is approached by the lower lip, the producer (*karaṇa*)." The labials are, according to the commentator, the diphthongs *o* and *âu*, in the normal and the protracted form, the *p*-series, or *p*, *ph*, *b*, *bh*, *m*, the *upadhmânîya* spirant (which is not named, but indicated by an example, *purushaḥ pibati*: the phrase is not found in the Atharvan), and the vowel *u*, short, long, and protracted. That the semivowel *v* is omitted here is doubtless the fault of the copyist only, since the sound is not provided with a place elsewhere. The verses cited from the metrical treatise are as follows: *sandhyaksharesku varṇeshu varṇântam oshṭhyam ucyate: upadhmânîyam ukâro vaḥ pavargas tathâ mataḥ*:[1] 'in the diphthongal sounds, the final sound is called labial; the *upadhmânîya*, *u*, *v*, and the *p*-series are also so considered.' The Rik. Pr. (i. 10, r. 47, xlviii) agrees with our treatise; the Vâj. Pr. (i. 70, 80, 81) also defines the same sounds as produced upon the lip, and by the lip,[2] but then adds farther that in the utterance of *v* the tips of the teeth are employed: the same specification as to the *v* is made by the Taitt. Pr. (ii. 43: its commentator explaining that in the utterance of that letter the points of the upper teeth are placed on the edge of the lower lip); and the latter treatise also, as in other cases, omits the vowels and diphthongs from the class. The descriptions of *v* given by the two Prâtiçâkhyas of the Yajur Veda, as well as that offered in the Paninean scheme (which declares its organs of utterance to be the teeth and lips), leave no room to doubt that at their period the *v* had already generally lost its original and proper value as English *w*—as which alone it has any right to be called a semivowel, and to rank with *y*—and, doubtless passing through the intermediate stage of the German *w*, had acquired the precise pronunciation of the English *v*. Whether the silence of the Rik and Atharvan Prâtiçâkhyas on this point is due to their prior date, or to a local or scholastic difference in their utterance of the *v*, or to the fact that, in view of the exclusively labial euphonic character of the sound they were willing to overlook the peculiarity of utterance distinguishing it from the other labials, I would not undertake to decide: but should consider the first supposition the least possible, and the second the most probable, of the three.

नासिक्यानां नासिका ॥२६॥

26. Of the nose-sounds, the nose is producing organ.

The commentary paraphrases *nâsikyâḥ* by *nâsikâsthânâ varṇâḥ*,

---

[1] *pavargaç ca tathâ mataḥ*.

[2] Weber misunderstands rule 80, *samânasthânakaraṇâ nâsikyaushṭhyâḥ*, to signify that the nasals and labials have the same *sthâna* and *karaṇa* with one another: the meaning evidently is that, in each of these two classes of sounds, *sthâna* and *karaṇa* are the same organ: in the one case, they are both the nose; in the other, both are the lips.

'sounds which have the nose as their place of production,' and cites, without farther explanation, as instances, *brahma* (e.g. i. 19. 4), *payânsi* (e. g. i. 9. 3), ह्नं ह्णं ग्नं ह्मं, and ṅ, ñ, ṇ, n, m: that is to say, the *nâsikya* (see below, i. 100), *anusvâra*, the *yamas* (see below, i. 99), and the nasal mutes. A verse from the metrical authority follows, containing this exposition: *nâsikye nâsikâ sthânaṁ tathâ 'nusvâra ucyate: yamâ vargottamâç câ 'pi yatho 'ktaṁ câi 'va te matâḥ;* 'in the case of *nâsikya*, as likewise of *anusvâra*, the nose is called the place of production; the *yamas*, and the finals of the several mute series are also understood to be as explained.' But there are grave objections to be made to this exposition. In the first place, the nasal mutes have been expressly declared above (i. 11) to be *anunâsika*, and the *anunâsikâs* are the subject, not of this rule, but of the next. Again, this treatise, as already noticed, acknowledges no *anusvâra*, and regards such syllables as the second of *payâṅsi* to contain nasalized or *anunâsika* vowels, which also fall under the next rule. We can hardly doubt that the commentator has here allowed himself to be misled by the authority on which he relies, and which may have treated the nasals in a manner essentially different from that of our treatise. The sounds to which the rule is meant to apply must be merely the *nâsikya* and the *yamas*. This conclusion is supported by the authority of the Rik Pr., which (i. 10, r. 48, xlix) gives the name of nose-sounds (*nâsikya*) to the *nâsikya*, *yamas*, and *anusvâra*;* and also by that of the Vâj. Pr., which (i. 74) declares the same sounds to be formed in the nose, and pronounces (i. 80) their place and organ of production to be the same, only specifying farther (i. 82) that the *yamas* are uttered "with the root of the nose." The doctrine of the Tâitt. Pr. (ii. 49–51) is less definite and distinct: it states that the nose-sounds are uttered with the nose, or else with the nose and mouth both, when their organ varies according to the *varga* or mute series to which they belong.

अनुनासिकानां मुखनासिकम् ॥ २७ ॥

27. Of the nasalized sounds, the mouth and nose together are the producing organs.

The commentator explains *anunâsikâḥ* by *anunâsikasthânâ varṇâḥ*, 'sounds which have for their place of production the *anunâsika*.' I know of no other case in which *anunâsika* is treated as the name of any part or organ in the mouth, and cannot but regard this paraphrase as an unintelligent and mechanical continuance of the same mode of explication which has been correctly applied to the class appellations in the preceding rules. Without any statement of what sounds are to be considered as referred to in this rule, the commentary cites the following illustrative instances: *dve ca me viṅçatiç ca* (v. 15. 2); *tisraç ca me triṅçac ca* (v. 15. 3); *catasraç ca me catvâriṅçac ca* (v. 15. 4); *puṁsâ*

* The commentary of one of Müller's manuscripts (see p. xix), by a noteworthy agreement in misinterpretation with our own, tries to bring in the nasal mutes also as belonging to the class.

puṅsaḥ (e. g. iii. 6. 1); *tatra puṅsuvanam* (vi. 11. 1): they are cases, wanting both in brevity and variety, of the nasalized vowels only. But, besides the nasal vowels, the rule must be intended to describe the character of the nasal semivowel *l* (ii. 35), and of the nasal mutes (i. 11). In the production of all these sounds, the mouth bears a part not less essential than the nose: each of them requires a given position of the mouth organs, to which the expulsion of the breath, in part or in whole, through the nose, then communicates a nasal quality.

The corresponding definition of the Rik Pr., "a nasal sound is produced by the mouth and nose together," does not occur until the latter portion of that treatise (xiii. 6, r. 20). The Vâj. Pr. (i. 75) gives an equivalent explanation; the Tâitt. Pr. (ii. 52) says, with equal justice, "nasal quality is communicated by the unclosing of the nose"—of course, in any given position of the mouth organs.

A verse is again cited by the commentator, as follows: *mukhanâsike ye varṇâ ucyante te 'nunâsikâḥ: samânâsyaprayatnâ ye te savarṇâ iti smṛtâḥ;* 'the sounds uttered in the mouth and nose together are called nasalized. Those produced by a like effort of the mouth are styled similar.' The term *savarṇa*, 'similar,' applied to sounds differing in quantity only, and not in quality, is used but once in our treatise (iii. 42), and is not defined by it: the cited definition is almost the same with that of Pâṇini (i. 1. 9): that of the Vâj. Pr. (i. 43) is more explicit: the other treatises, like our own, employ the word without taking the trouble to explain it.

रेफस्य दन्तमूलानि ॥ २८ ॥

28. Of *r*, the roots of the teeth are the producing organs.

By the 'roots of the teeth' must be understood, doubtless, the bases of the upper front teeth, at which, according to the Rik Pr. (i. 9–10) and the Tâitt. Pr. (ii. 38, 42), the whole class called in our treatise simply "dentals" (see rule 24, above) is produced. It seems strange to find them here called the *karaṇa*, instead of the *sthâna*, of *r*, and we are almost ready to assume a break in the *anuvṛtti* of the term *karaṇa*, and supply *sthâna* in place of it; and the more especially, as the cited verse favors the substitution: *rephasya dantamûlâni pratyag vâ tebhya ishyate: iti sthânâni varṇânâṁ kîrtitâni yathâkramam;* 'of *r*, the place is taught to be the roots of the teeth, or a point close to them: thus have the places of the sounds been set forth in order.' The commentator farther adds: *apara âha: hanumûleshu rephasya dantamûleshu vâ punaḥ: pratyag vâ dantamûlebhyo mûrdhanya iti câ 'pare;* 'another has said: "the place of *r* is at the roots of the jaw, or, again, at the roots of the teeth, or close behind the roots of the teeth: others say that it is a lingual."' A considerable difference of opinion among the Hindu phonetists respecting the position of the *r* is indicated by these citations and by the teachings of the different phonetic treatises. The Rik Pr., as we have seen (under rule 24), includes it with the other dentals, as *dantamûlîya*, but adds (i. 10, r. 48, xlvii) that some regard it as gingival. The Vâj. Pr. defines it as produced at the roots of the teeth (i. 68), by the tip of the tongue (i. 77); the Tâitt. Pr. (ii. 41), by the tip and middle of the tongue, at a point close behind the roots of the teeth: the Paninean scheme alone reckons it as *mûrdhanya*, 'lingual.' The separation of *ṛ* and *r* from one another, and of both from the lingual class, is the strangest and least defensible feature in the alphabetic classification of the Prâtiçâkhyas. By its effect in the euphonic system of the language, *r* is clearly a lingual, and can hardly be supposed to have been uttered otherwise than as our smooth English *r* is uttered, with the tip of the tongue reverted into the dome of the palate, to the lingual position. In this position, however, it cannot be vibrated or trilled; and it is possible that in the laborious and somewhat artificial pronunciation of the Vedic schools it was, for greater distinctness, thrown farther forward in the mouth, to the teeth or near them.

As instances of the *r*, the commentator cites *çaradaḥ purûcîḥ* (ii. 13. 3), *punâ rakshaḥ vâsaḥ* (not in AV.), *punâ rûpâṇi* (i. 24. 4), *jaghnû rakshâṅsi* (iv. 37. 1), *agnî rakshâṅsi* (viii. 3. 26), *agnî rakshaḥ* (xii. 3. 43).

स्पृष्टं स्पर्शानां करणम् ॥ २९ ॥

29. In the case of the mutes, the organ forms a contact.

From this contact (*sparça*) of the organ with the place of production, the mutes (*sparça*) derive their name.

The Rik Pr. (xiii. 3, r. 9) gives the same definition, with the addition that the organ is also *asthitam*, 'not stationary.' The Tâitt. Pr. (in ii. 33, 34, cited above, under i. 18) implies a contact in the case of all sounds excepting vowels and spirants (ii. 45), not laying down any distinction between the complete contact of the mutes, and the imperfect one of the semivowels.

The commentator cites a verse which establishes a noteworthy exception to this rule: *svaramadhye ḍaḍhâu yatra pîḍanaṁ tatra varjayet: mṛduprayatnâu uccâryâu îḍâ mîḍhaṁ nidarçanam;* 'where *ḍ* and *ḍh* occur between two vowels, there one must avoid a close contact; they are to be uttered with a gentle effort: instances are *îḍâ* (v. 12. 6) and *mîḍham* (*puru-mîḍham*, iv. 29. 4).' This corresponds, if it does not coincide, with the conversion of these letters in a like case into a lingual *ḷ*, unaspirated and aspirated, usual in the Rik and in some schools of the White Yajus, and taught by the Rik Pr. in i. 11, 12 (r. 51, 52, lii, liii), as resting upon the authority of Vedamitra, and by the Vâj. Pr. in iv. 143 as the doctrine of some teachers. Our verse does not indeed point out that the relaxation of the contact takes place at the sides of the tongue, and that the resulting sound is hence of the nature of an *l*; but this is altogether probable.

ईषत्स्पृष्टमन्तःस्थानाम् ॥ ३० ॥

30. In the case of the semivowels, it is partially in contact.

That is to say, the organs are so nearly approximated that their position may be called an imperfect contact. The Rik Pr. (xiii. 3, r. 10) calls it *duḥspṛṣhṭam*, 'imperfectly or hardly in contact.' The Tâitt. Pr., as just remarked, does not distinguish the degree of contact of the semivowels from that of the mutes.

The name by which the semivowels *y, r, l, v* are called—namely *antaḥsthâ*, 'intermediate, standing between'—is generally explained as indicating that the sounds in question, in the arrangement of the alphabet, stand between the mutes and the spirants. The Böhtlingk-Roth lexicon, however (*sub verbo*), defines it to mean 'occurring only in the interior of a sentence, never at its end.' This latter interpretation is exceedingly unsatisfactory: in the first place, the definition would be as true of the spirants and aspirates as of the semivowels; in the second place, it would not be true of the *l*; in the third place, no letter could be called *antaḥsthâ* in this sense which could occur at the beginning of a sentence, as all the semivowels do. But the other explanation also seems too indefinite and indistinctive. Is it not more likely that these sounds were named "intermediate" in reference to the mode of their formation, as being neither by a complete contact, like the full mutes, nor by an open position, like the vowels? The name *antaḥsthâ* would then be virtually accordant with our own "semivowel."

ऊष्मणां विवृतं च ॥३१॥

31. In the case of the spirants, it is also open.

The final *ca* of the rule indicates, according to the commentator, that *îshatspṛṣhṭam* is also to be inferred from the preceding rule: in the formation of the spirants (*ç, sh, s,* and *h* are specified by the commentary as constituting the class), the organ is both in partial contact and open—a rather awkward way of saying, apparently, that its position is neither very close nor very open. The Tâitt. Pr. (ii. 44, 45) declares that the spirants, in their order, are uttered in the positions of the mutes, but with the middle part of the producing organ opened. The Rik Pr. (xiii. 3, r. 11) includes the vowels, *anusvâra*, and the spirants together, as produced without contact, and with the organ stationary.

In the absence of a *varṇasamâmnâya*, 'list of spoken sounds,' or 'alphabet,' such as the other Prâtiçâkhyas give (Rik Pr., introductory verse, and i. 1, 2; Vâj. Pr. viii. 1–31; Tâitt. Pr. i. 1–10), it is not easy to assure ourselves how many spirants the treatise acknowledges, and in what order it would assume them to stand. As we have already seen, the commentary accepts the *jihvâmûlîya* and *upadhmânîya*, which are nowhere expressly mentioned in the text, but of which the existence seems necessarily implied in ii. 40. The class of spirants is then probably composed of *ḥ* (*visarjanîya*), *h*, *ḥk* (*jihvâmûlîya*), *ç, sh, s,* and *ḥp* (*upadhmânîya*). The Rik Pr. (i. 2, r. 10, xl) includes in the class these seven, along with *anusvâra*; the Vâj. Pr. (viii. 22), only *ç, sh, s, h*; the Tâitt. Pr. (i. 9), the seven of our treatise, with the exception of *visarjanîya*.

स्वराणां च ॥३२॥

32. In the case of the vowels also, it is open.

The commentator understands, and doubtless correctly, that *vivṛtam* only, and not *îshatspṛshṭam* also, is implied in this rule by inference from the preceding. He adds the whole list of vowels, both simple vowels and diphthongs, in their short, long, and protracted (*pluta*) form.

The Rik Prâtiçâkhya's doctrine respecting the vowels was cited under the last rule. The Tâitt. Pr., in its rules ii. 31, 32 (cited above, under i. 18), implies that in the utterance of the vowels the organs only approximate, and do not touch one another.

एके स्पृष्टम् ॥ ३३ ॥

33. Some consider it as forming a contact.

That is, the commentator says, some maintain that in the utterance of the vowels the organs are in contact; others, that they remain open. The former opinion is too obviously and grossly incorrect, one would think, to be worth quoting. No one of the other treatises favors it in any degree.

एकारौकारयोर्विवृततमम् ॥ ३४ ॥

34. In the case of *e* and *o*, it is very widely open.

The word *eke*, 'some,' is no longer in force, but this and the two following rules are more detailed explanations of our treatise itself under its own rule 32. For the pronunciation of the Sanskrit *e* and *o*, see below, under rule 40.

The commentator cites, as instances of these diphthongs, *eke taranti* (vi. 122. 2), *oko asya* (v. 22. 5).

ततो ऽप्याकारस्य ॥ ३५ ॥

35. And even more so, in the case of *â*.

The *a*-sound ("Italian *a*," as in *father*) is unquestionably the most open of all the sounds of the alphabet, the only one in the utterance of which all the mouth organs are removed, so far as is possible, from the path of the intonated breath, which is thus suffered to stream forth wholly unimpeded and unmodified.

संवृतो ऽकारः ॥ ३६ ॥

36. The *a* is obscured.

The modes of utterance of the short *a*, of the ṛ-vowel, and of the diphthongs *e* and *o*, taught by the Prâtiçâkhyas, are matters of special interest in their phonetical systems, as helping to characterize the period in the history of the language represented by these treatises. Neither of the sounds in question has fully retained, down to their time, that value which general considerations, and the euphonic system of the Sanskrit language, show to have been the original and proper one. As regards the short *a*, it was no longer generally spoken with the full openness of *á*, or as its correspondent short sound. See what Weber says upon the subject, under Vāj. Pr. i. 72—which rule, like the final one of Pāṇini's grammar (viii. 4. 68), prescribes that the short *a* is to be treated throughout as if coincident in quality with long *á*—a prescription which implies, of course, that in actual pronunciation it was different. Whatever degradation from its pure open quality the *a* had suffered must have been, it seems to me, in the direction of the neutral vowel (English "short *u*," in *but*, *son*, *blood*), which has so generally taken its place in the modern pronunciation of India, rather than toward an *e* or *o*, as suggested by Weber. The term *saṁvṛta*, 'covered up, enveloped, obscured' (antithesis of *vivṛta*, 'opened'), very well expresses the quality of this neutral sound, which differs from *a* only in not having the mouth freely opened for its utterance, and which does not, like *e* and *o*, call for a placing in position of any of the mouth organs. The Tāitt. Pr. does not separate *a* from *á*, but says of both (ii. 12) that they are to be spoken "with the lips and jaws not too much approximated, and not too widely parted"—a description too indefinite to derive any distinct idea from. The Rik Pr. also fails to note any difference of quality between the long and short values of this vowel. But it is very doubtful whether we are to regard the silence of these two treatises upon the point in question as any evidence that they are of notably earlier date than the others, as Weber seems inclined to do: their peculiarity is much more likely to be due to a local or a scholastic difference of pronunciation, or they may have simply disregarded, as of little account, the discordance of quality between *a* and *á*.

The commentary gives, as furnishing instances of short *a*, the words *açvaḥ* (e. g. ii. 30. 5), *ajaḥ* (e. g. iv. 14. 1), and *agniḥ* (e. g. i. 7. 4).

संस्पृष्टरेफमृवर्णम् ॥ ३७॥

37. The ṛ-vowels are combined with an *r*.

In the grammatical language of our treatise and of the Tāitt. Pr., *varṇa* appended to the name of a short vowel causes it to include also the long and protracted (*pluta*) vowels of the same quality: it is a designation of the quality, without distinction of quantity. The Tāitt. Pr. (i. 20) gives a special rule establishing the usage. Thus *ṛvarṇa* means *ṛkāra*, *ṝkāra*, and *ṛ3kāra*.

The commentator gives no explanation of this rule: he simply repeats it with an added *bhavati*, and then cites a couple of phrases containing the *ṛ*, viz.: *idam pitṛbhyaḥ pra bharāmi barhiḥ* (xviii. 4. 51), and *putrāir bhrātṛbhir aditiḥ* (vi. 4. 1). But he next proceeds to quote from his metrical authority a few verses which are more to the point; they read as follows, with the exception of the first and last lines, which are corrupt: . . . .[1] *ṛvarṇe svaramātrā yā tasyā madhye 'rdhamātrayā : repho bhavati saṁspṛshṭo yathā 'ṅgulyā nakhaṁ tathā : sūtre maṇir ive 'ty eke tṛṇe krimir ive 'ti ca :* . . . .[2] 'an *r* is combined with a half-mora

[1] *ṛvarṇasya madhye yugapac ca samarah.*
[2] *anena mātrayārdhayā praçlesha ā ubhayor api.*

in the middle of the vowel mora in the ṛ-vowel, just as a nail is with the finger; like a pearl on a string, some say; like a worm in grass, say others.' With this accords quite nearly the doctrine of the Rik Pr., which says (xiii. 14) that *r* forms part of the ṛ-vowel, and is found in the middle of it. Neither treatise attempts to define what constitutes the remainder of the vowel. In the analogous rule (iv. 146) of the Vâj. Pr., that remainder is (if the rule is in this point correctly interpreted by Weber, which is doubtful; my own manuscript of the commentary is too corrupt just here to be made anything of) declared to be of the character of *a;* so that, according to Weber, $ṛ = \frac{a}{4} + \frac{r}{2} + \frac{a}{4}$. The Tâitt. Pr. does not, any more than the Rik Pr. in the earlier and more genuine part of its text, take any notice of the presence of heterogeneous elements in the ṛ and ḷ vowels; it only says (ii. 18) that in their utterance the jaws are somewhat closely approximated, and the tip of the tongue brought near to the parts immediately above and behind the row of teeth. The etymological and euphonic character of the sound in question is simply that of a vocal *r*, an *r* which is employed with the value of a vowel, as *r* has been and is employed in other languages in different parts of the earth; and there seems no good reason for regarding it as having originally deviated in mode of pronunciation from the semivowel *r*. But it is clear that, at the time of the Prâtiçâkhyas, the Hindus had begun to find that difficulty in its utterance and use as a vowel which caused its entire disappearance in the later forms of the language, and has made of it in the mouth of the modern Brahmans the syllables *ri* and *rî*. If I may judge from experiments made in my own mouth, the bringing of the ṛ far enough forward in the mouth to be trilled would render very natural, and almost unavoidable, the slipping in, before and after it, of a fragment of the neutral vowel, our *u* in *but*, the "obscure (*saṁvṛta*) *a*" of our treatise: of this character, it can hardly be doubted, would be what elements the sound contained which were not *r*.

दीर्घप्लुतयोः पूर्वा मात्रा ॥३८॥

38. Of the long and protracted forms of the vowel, the first mora is so combined.

The commentary paraphrases thus: *dîrghaplutayos tu pûrvâ mâtrâ saṁspṛshṭarepham ṛvarṇam bhavati;* which is a palpable blunder for *saṁspṛshṭarephâ bhavati:* i. e. if the vowel is extended so as to occupy two or three moras, the *r*-element which it contains is not prolonged, but is found only in the first mora: the whole remainder of the sound is composed of the other element. The Rik Pr. says in like manner (xiii. 14) that the *r* is found only in the former half of long ṝ, and is either shorter or of the same length with that which enters into ṛ.

Two instances of the long ṝ are given by the commentator as illustrations: they are *kartṝn akshava* (x. 1. 14), and *pitṝ̃r upe 'mam* (xviii. 4. 40).

सल्कारम्ऌवर्णम् ॥ ३९ ॥

39. The *ḷ*-vowels are combined with *l*.

This doubtless means what is more clearly and unequivocally stated by the Rik Pr. (xiii. 14, r. 35): that when, in such combinations as those which have just been described, *l* takes the place of *r*, the result is the *ḷ*-vowel. The other two treatises, as we have seen above, treat the two vowels together, in the same rules. The use of the term *ḷvarṇa* in the rule would seem to imply the possible occurrence of the long and protracted forms of the vowel, which are, on the other hand, impliedly denied in rule 4 above; they are also ignored by the Tâitt. Pr., as they are by the Rik Pr. in its proper text (i. 1, r. 1); while the prefixed introductory verses to the latter treatise, and the Vâj. Pr. (viii. 7), acknowledge them.

The commentator cites, as instances of this vowel, *pañcadaçena kḷptâḥ* (viii. 9. 15), and *sinîvâly acîkḷpat* (vi. 11. 3): the Rik. Pr. (xiii. 14, r. 35) notices the fact that the *ḷ* occurs nowhere excepting in the root *kḷp*. He then adds a verse from his metrical authority: *ṛvarṇe ca ḷvarṇe*[1] *loḥ praçlishṭaç ca yadâ tayoḥ : ḷ iti tad ichanti prayogaṁ tadvido janâḥ*; the general meaning is clear enough, but the verse needs amending to be made translatable.

संध्यक्षराणि संस्पृष्टवर्णान्येकवर्णवद्वृत्तिः ॥ ४० ॥

40. The diphthongs are composed of combined vowels; their treatment is that of a simple vowel.

The term *sandhyakshara* means literally 'syllable of combination;' it is the usual name for a diphthong in all the treatises excepting the Tâitt. Pr. The correlative *samânâkshara*, 'homogeneous syllable,' is but rarely used, as indicating the simple vowels, when it is necessary to distinguish them from the diphthongs (in our treatise, only in iii. 42). The diphthongs are vowel sounds which, though not simple and homogeneous, yet form but a single syllable, and are treated as *if* they were simple sounds. They are *e, o, âi, âu*. The two former would be more properly written *ai, au*, since the euphonic processes of the language clearly show these to have been their original values, each containing a short *a* as its first element, followed by an *i* or an *u* respectively. That they should be so readily composable of *a* and *i*, *a* and *u*, in the accidental and momentary combinations of the phrase, and especially, that they should be so regularly resolvable into the same sounds, if they did not actually contain those sounds, is not to be credited. The same evidence proves the other two to be made up of long *â*, with *i* or *u* following. The mutual relation of *e* (*ai*) and *âi* must have been nearly that of our *I* and *aye*. In the Prakrit languages, however, *e* and *o* have gained the pronunciation of the *e* in *they* and *o* in *note*; they have become sounds intermediate between, instead of made up of, *a* and *i* and *a* and *u*; and they have acquired short values as well as long. As *e* and *o* they are likewise pronounced in the usage of the modern Brahmans. But even at the

---

[1] *ḷvarṇa*.

period of the Prâtiçâkhyas, and in the phonetic systems of the Vedic schools, they no longer had uniformly their original value. From the present rule, indeed, no such inference could be drawn; but the one which next follows establishes a distinction in value between them and *âi*, *âu*. The Rik Pr. (xiii. 16, r. 38) predicates doubleness of position of all the four, and goes on (r. 39) to cite Çâkaṭâyana to the effect that *a* forms half of each, and *i* and *u* the remaining half; but it adds (r. 40) that *e* and *o*, by reason of the fusion of their parts, have not a sound in which the separate components are distinct. This might, however, be fairly enough said of our own *ai* and *au* (in *pine*, *house*). The Vâj. Pr. (i. 73) defines only *âi* and *âu* as composed of two different elements (the commentary explains them to be ½*a*+1½*e* and ½*a*+1½*o* respectively), and directs them (iv. 142) to be treated as simple sounds, without seeing any reason for giving the same precept as to *e* and *o*. The Tâitt. Pr. is not less explicit: it says of *o* (ii. 13, 14) that in its enunciation the jaws are to be neither too nearly approached nor too widely sundered, while the lips are to be closer than in *a*; of *e* (ii. 15–17), that the lips are to be somewhat protracted, the jaws pretty closely approached, and the middle part and end of the tongue in contact with the upper rows of teeth (*jambhân*); and finally (ii. 23), that in *e*, as in *i*, the middle of the tongue is brought near the palate. More distinctive descriptions of our *e* and *o* could hardly be given: there is evidently no thought at all of the combination of two phonetic elements into one in them. On the other hand, *âi* and *âu* are defined with equal clearness (ii. 26–29) as containing each the half of an *a* (which some held to be of closer position than the ordinary *a*), followed by one and a half times *i* and *u* in the two cases respectively.

नैकारौकारयोः स्थानविधौ ॥४१॥

41. Not so, however, with *âi* and *âu*, in a rule of position.

The commentator's paraphrase is *âikârâukârayoḥ sthânavidhâne ekavarṇavad vṛttir na bhavati*. What the meaning and value of the rule is, is not altogether clear: I can see no other application of it than to forbid the inclusion of *âi* among the palatals only, and of *âu* among the labials only, since they are both throat-sounds as well. By implication, then, *e* and *o* would admit of being ranked as merely palatal and labial; but the commentary to rule 19, above, treated these, as well as the others, as of double position, and as containing an element of throat-sound.

A verse is added in the commentary, as follows: *âikârâukârayoç câ 'pi pûrvâ mâtrâ parâ ca yâ: ardhamâtrâ tayor madhye saṁspṛṣṭa iti smṛtâḥ*. The last *pâda* is corrupt, and I am too uncertain of the scope of the verse to venture to amend it: perhaps the meaning is that, while the beginning and end of *âi*, for instance, are clearly *a* and *i*, a mora in the middle of the sound is of a mixed character.

This rule ends the first section of the first chapter: the signature is *caturâdhyâyikâyâṁ prathamasyâ 'dhyâyasya prathamaḥ pâdaḥ: sûtra* 41: *ekacatvâriṅçat*. This is the only case in which the number of rules reckoned is assured by being expressed in words as well as in figures.

विसर्जनीयो ऽभिनिष्टानः ॥४२॥

42. *Visarjanīya* is *abhinishṭāna*.

The commentator vouchsafes no explanation of the rule, but merely paraphrases it, as follows: *visarjanīyo varṇaḥ: abhinishṭāno bhavati;* and adds, as instances of *visarjanīya*, *agniḥ* (e. g. i. 7. 4) and *vṛkshaḥ* (e. g. iv. 7. 5). The term *abhinishṭāna* does not form part of the grammatical language of the Prātiçākhyas or of Pāṇini: among the former, it occurs only in this place: a rule of the latter (viii. 3. 86) determines its derivation and orthography, and the instances given in the commentary show its equivalence with *visarjanīya;* the Böhtlingk-Roth lexicon also refers (*sub verbo*) to several vocabularies which contain the word, giving it the same meaning. More significant is its occurrence several times in the *gṛhya-sūtras* (as cited in the lexica of Böhtlingk-Roth and Goldstücker), also with the signification *visarga*.* It looks as if it had belonged to an earlier grammatical terminology than that of our treatises, and had been retained merely as a reminiscence of something formerly current: its introduction into our text is otherwise quite unexplained, and, so far as can be seen, without significance. Probably it is an ancient name of *visarjanīya* or *visarga*, crowded out of use by the latter terms. The Böhtlingk-Roth lexicon gives it, with reference to this passage, the meaning "an expiring or vanishing sound (*ein verklingender Laut*)," but this is merely a conjecture, and by no means so well supported by the etymology of the word (which would suggest rather 'a sounding forth, a resonance') as to be placed beyond the reach of question. Pāṇini's rule must be taken as conclusive respecting the derivation and form favored in his time, or by his school; but the analogy of the words *abhinidhāna*, *abhinihita*, *abhinihata*, *abhinipāta* cannot but suggest *abhinishṭhāna* as the true form, coming from the root *sthā* with the prefixes *abhi* and *ni*. This would not, however, relieve the obscurity investing the primitive meaning and application of the term; an obscurity which also attaches, in some measure, to the word *visarjanīya* and its more modern representative *visarga*.

व्यञ्जनविधारणमभिनिधानः पीडितः सन्नतरो हीनश्वासनादः ॥४३॥

43. The holding apart of a consonant is *abhinidhāna;* it is pinched, quite weakened, lacking breath and sound.

* That the word ever means 'a sound of the alphabet in general,' as stated in both the lexicons, seems to me very doubtful: I have not access to all the authorities referred to by Böhtlingk-Roth, but the commentary to Pāṇini, *abhinishṭāno varṇaḥ*, does not necessarily imply any thing of the kind, but may rather mean 'an *abhinishṭāna* letter;' while, in the citation given by Goldstücker as an instance of the general meaning, it evidently signifies *visarga*: *dīrghābhinishṭānāntam*, '(a name) ending in a long vowel or in *visarga*.' If the other cases relied on are not less equivocal than these, the general definition 'sound' must be rejected.

We have here one of those subtleties of phonetic analysis which are such marked characteristics of the Hindu science. In order to any satisfactory understanding of it, we must call in to our aid theoretical considerations, as the dark and scanty expositions of the grammatical treatises and their commentators are insufficient. The phenomenon forming the subject of the rule evidently is or includes a defective pronunciation or indistinctness of utterance, and the two next rules teach us that it affects a mute which is followed by another mute, and one which stands as final. In what does the peculiarity of utterance of such a letter in such a position consist? A mute is a sound produced by a complete closure of the organs of articulation in some defined position, entirely cutting off the escape of breath through the mouth; and it is by the breaking of the closure with the utterance of a following open sound that the mute is itself made audible. In speaking a *p*, for instance, so long as the lips are kept compressed, there is no audible sound; but as soon as the contact is severed with the expulsion of either unintonated or intonated breath, in the passing of the voice to the utterance of some other sound, the *p* is clearly heard. A sonant mute, as a *b*, is less absolutely a dumb letter before the breach of the contact, because it includes an expulsion of resonant breath from the throat into the cavity of the mouth during the closure of the organs, and this resonance is sufficient to indicate imperfectly the character of the contact. A nasal mute, as *m*, is yet less dependent upon the explosion for its distinctness of utterance, since it implies a free flow of sonant breath through the nose, and so is continuous and even quasi-vocalic in its nature; yet even the nasals, and still more the sonants, are explosive letters, and do not have a perfect utterance unless the contact is broken. A following vowel, of course, discovers them most completely; yet any open and continuable letter, as a semivowel or a sibilant, answers the same purpose, and in the syllables *pya*, *psa*, for instance, we feel that *p* is fairly enunciated. If, however, one mute letter follows another, the explosion of the former cannot properly occur; the organs are supposed to pass from one position of complete contact to another, without any intervening open sound: the former mute is imperfectly uttered. A like thing takes place when a mute is final, or when there is no following open sound to break the contact with: we then have only that very imperfect hint of its pronunciation which is given by the formation of the contact upon the preceding open sound. We are accustomed, indeed, in order to give distinctness to a final mute, to unclose the organs again after making the contact, thus whispering after it, as it were, a bit of a vowel; and the absence of this unclosure is remarked by phoneticists as a peculiarity of the pronunciation of some dialects of spoken Chinese, rendering their final mutes almost inaudible: it is hardly possible, too, to make one mute follow another so closely that there shall not slip out, in the transfer of the organs from one contact to the other, a bit of breath or sound, which greatly helps to make the former of the two audible: and of both these inorganic or involuntary additions or insertions we shall see hereafter that the Hindu theory takes note: but they do not wholly remedy the theoretic imperfection of the utterance. That the indistinct pronunciation thus described is the *abhinidhâna* of the Hindu theory, or at least the central and most important fact of those comprehended under that name, seems to me tolerably certain, although it must be confessed that there are difficulties attending such an explanation: none, I think, that may not be done away by supposing that the Hindus had not made a complete physical analysis of the phenomenon, and hence that their descriptions of it partake of vagueness and inconsistency; and also, that they have brought together under the name *abhinidhâna* things not entirely accordant, although analogous, in character. The difficulty of the subject is sufficiently attested by the doubtful and discordant views taken of it by those who have had occasion hitherto to examine it, as Müller, Regnier, Weber, Goldstücker (s. v. *abhinidhâna*). An alternate view to which I have myself been somewhat attracted is that by the *abhinidhâna* is meant the instant of silence which intervenes between the closure of the organs for the first mute, and their opening for the second: that the Hindu theory regards, in the word *âpta*, for example, the utterance of the *p* as complete by the closure of the lips upon the preceding *â*, and that of the *t* as complete by the unclosure of the tongue before the following *a*, while the brief interval of suspended utterance separating the two acts is *abhinidhâna*. This, better than anything else, would give meaning to the first word of our rule, "a holding apart of the consonants," and would accord well enough with the rest of the description, translating the last term 'deprived of both breath and sound.' Fatal objections, however, to this explanation are: the treatment of the phenomenon as something affecting the former consonant, not interposed after it; the difficulty of assuming any such interval of silence in the case of a concurrence with sonant and nasal mutes; and the non-applicability of the theory to the case of a final consonant. The term *vyañjanavidhâraṇam* must therefore be understood as used simply in antithesis to the *saṁyuktam* of rule 49: whereas, in other cases of concurrence of consonants, there is actual combination, with partial assimilation of the latter to the former (rule 50), here each is held apart from the other as distinct. This, it is true, applies only to the concurrence of consonants, and not to a final; but it is allowable to regard as contemplated in a general description or designation of a phonetic phenomenon its principal case only, although not to adopt an explanation of the phenomenon itself which should shut out any of the cases included by it. If I am not mistaken, the term *abhinidhâna* has also a similar meaning. Etymologically, and by its use in other than grammatical senses, it should signify, as a neuter noun, simply 'a setting down against' the following letter, as distinguished from an actual combination with it. That it is used in our treatise as a masculine is somewhat surprising, but cannot be regarded as an error of the manuscript. The word seems to be taken almost in the sense of *abhinihita*, as denoting the sound affected by the process rather than the process itself, and so to be attracted to the gender of *varṇaḥ* or *sparçaḥ*: the explanations which follow it in the rule, it will be noticed, apply rather to the altered letter than to the alteration. The Rik Pr. (vi. 5, r. 17, cccxciii) treats the word as neuter, and defines it clearly as a process: *saṁdhâraṇaṁ saṁvaraṇaṁ ca vâcaḥ*, 'a repressing and obscuring (holding together and covering up) of the voice.'

Our own commentary, as is its wont in difficult cases, leaves us here altogether without valuable aid. It simply paraphrases the rule, adds the *dicta* of a couple of other authorities, and closes with a verse; as follows: *vyañjanavidhâraṇam abhinidhâno bhavati: pîḍitaç ca çvâsanâdâbhyâm: apara âha: vyañjanavidhâraṇam abhinipâto mâtrâ jupano bhavati pîḍitaç ca çvâsanâdâbhyâm: apara âha: vyañjanavidhâraṇam abhinipâto mâtro jupane gurutâ bhavati: antaḥpade padânte vâ pîḍitaḥ sanna eva tu: avakṛshṭatara sthânâd avasannataraç ca saḥ: klaç ca çvâsanâdâbhyâṁ yo yatrârtho 'bhidhîyate.* I will not attempt to translate the passage, as I could do so but in part, and as it seems incapable of throwing any valuable light upon the subject in hand. The most noteworthy circumstance about it is its presentation of *abhinipâta*, 'a falling down against,' as a synonym of *abhinidhâna*.

स्पर्शस्य स्पर्शे ऽभिनिधानः ॥४४॥

44. A mute suffers *abhinidhâna* before a mute.

The phraseology of the rule would be the same, if *abhinidhâna* were here intended to be taken adjectively, as conjectured above, and if it were meant to say that 'a mute before another mute becomes *abhinidhâna*.' The commentary merely cites as instances the three words *bṛhadbhiḥ, samidbhiḥ, marudbhiḥ*, of which only the last is found in the Atharvan (p. *marut-bhiḥ*, e. g. ii. 29. 4).

The cases in which *abhinidhâna* alone ensues (only accompanied in part by duplication, according to iii. 28 etc.) are those in which a mute is followed by another mute (and, if itself non-nasal, then by another non-nasal) of the same or a succeeding series. Followed by a mute of a preceding series, it suffers also the intervention of *sphoṭana*, by ii. 38; if followed by a nasal, a *yama* is interposed, by i. 99. In an additional note at the end of the work will be presented a conspectus of all the consonantal combinations occurring in the Atharva-Veda, with an exhibition of the forms assumed by them according to the phonetic rules of our treatise.

The Rik Pr. (vi. 5, r. 17, cccxciii) pronounces not only the mutes, but also the semivowels, except *r*, to suffer *abhinidhâna* when followed by mutes. This would, however, in the Atharvan text, add only the groups *lk, lg, lp, lph, lb, lm*, and *v* to those which by our own treatise admit the modification, so that the extension of the rule is meant virtually to include merely the *l*, a letter which our rule 46 shows to be regarded as especially liable to *abhinidhâna*. The *l* requires so marked a contact of the tongue at its tip that the omission of the breach of that contact by a following open letter may well enough have been felt by the Hindu phonetists as needing to be looked upon as *abhinidhâna*.

पदान्तावग्रहयोश्च ॥४५॥

45. Also at the end of a word, or of the first member of a compound.

The commentator paraphrases as follows: *padânte avagrahe ca spar-*

padya sparçe parataḥ: abhinidhâno bhavati: but it is clear that the specification *sparçe parataḥ*, 'before a following mute,' has no business here: that case is included in the preceding rule, and the present precept applies to the pronunciation of a final as a final, without any reference to what may follow it. This appears partly from the nature of the case, partly from the analogy of the corresponding rule in the Rik Pr. (vi. 5, r. 18, ccccxiv), and partly from the cited illustrations of the commentator himself: the words given by him under the preceding rule would be cases of *avagraha* in the *pada*-text, and, of those which he presents under this, the last two are instances of *avagraha* before vowels. His citations are *tân: vaḥ: yaḥ: devânâm* (xi. 1. 5), *ap su* (e. g. i. 6. 2), *sâlârçkân-iva* (ii. 27. 5), and *khalvân-iva* (ii. 31. 1).

The rule of the Rik Pr., already referred to, *api câ 'vasâne*, 'also in pausa,' is coincident in meaning with our own. The Tâitt. Pr. takes no notice whatever of the doctrine of *abhinidhâna*, nor does the Vâj. Pr. directly. The latter, however, presents a couple of rules which are worthy of remark, as having to do with the same general subject. In i. 90, 91, it teaches that when a final mute stands either *in pausa* or before a following word, there takes place a release or separation of the organs of production, the passive and the active organ, or *sthâna* and *karaṇa*; that is to say, the contact is dissolved (Weber, and Goldstücker following him, have failed to apprehend the true meaning of the phenomenon described). This dissolution of the contact, in the case of the mute *in pausa*, is what was referred to above as taking place in our ordinary pronunciation after a final contact-letter, in order to make the mute more distinctly audible: as occurring before another word, it is analogous with the *sphoṭana* of our treatise (ii. 38), and the *dhruva* of the Rik Pr. (vi. 11), although having a different sphere of occurrence from both of them, as they from one another; it is a formal release of the organs of articulation from the position belonging to the close of one word, before they take up that belonging to the beginning of another, in order to the more distinct separation of the two independent members of the sentence.

लकारस्योष्मसु ॥ ४६ ॥

46. *L* suffers *abhinidhâna* before spirants.

The only spirants before which *l* is found actually to occur in the Atharva-Veda are *ç* and *h*: the commentary cites instances of both, as follows: *çatabalçâ vi roha* (vi. 30. 2); *sa gamishyati balhikân* (v. 22. 9); *vihalho nâma* (vi. 16. 2); nor are the combinations to be met with in the text in any other words than those here quoted. The rule and its comment are of particular interest as settling authoritatively the reading of the word *balhika*, 'of Balkh,' which, owing to the customary carelessness of the scribes, in not distinguishing *lh* from *hl* (our own manuscripts vary between the two), has often been read and explained as *bahlika*.

L is also noted by the Rik Pr. (vi. 6, r. 20, ccccxvi) as suffering *abhinidhâna* before spirants, according to the Çâkala doctrine, which is not that of the treatise itself. By the Vâj. Pr. (iv. 16) it is regarded as to be treated in the same manner as *r* in a like position. *R* before a spirant suffers *svarabhakti*, or the insertion of a vowel-fragment, according to all the other Prâtiçâkhyas (see below, rule 101); and the treatment of the Vâj. Pr. is virtually, though not formally, the same. The doctrine, then, of the Vâj. Pr., in admitting a *svarabhakti* between *l* and a spirant, would differ little from that presented in the Rik Pr.—which (by vi. 11) would admit a *dhruva*, or (by vi. 13, r. 47, ccccxxii) even a *svarabhakti*, after the *abhinidhâna* of the *l*—except by omission of the *abhinidhâna*, of which, as already remarked, it nowhere takes any notice; but our own treatise, by prescribing *abhinidhâna*, and not allowing even *sphoṭana* after it, differs quite notably from the others. I must confess myself unable to explain why either *l* before a spirant, or the nasals before *h*, as taught in the next rule, should suffer or be regarded as suffering the obscuring process of *abhinidhâna*.

ङणनानां हकारे ॥ ४७ ॥

47. Also the guttural, palatal, and dental nasals before *h*.

The instances cited by the commentary, in illustration of this rule, are as follows: *pratyaṅ hi* (iv. 19. 7); *gaṇ hi* (a fabricated case: the lingual nasal never occurs before *h* in the Atharvan text); *krimin hantu* (ii. 32. 1); *amûn hetiḥ* (vi. 29. 1).

The only consonants ever found to precede *h* in the Atharva-Veda are *r*, *l*, *ṅ*, and *n*. The first case, *rh*, is one of *svarabhakti* (i. 101); the second, *lh*, falls under the preceding rule; the other two are provided for by this rule, which is moreover, like many others in the treatise, cast in a theoretical form, or made more general than the requirements of the text justify. Since, according to the theory of this Prâtiçâkhya (see ii. 9), no nasal ever occurs immediately before a sibilant, rules 46 and 47 might have been cast together into the form: "the nasals and *l* suffer *abhinidhâna* before the spirants."

The cases which this rule contemplates are in the Rik Pr. (vi. 7, r. 28, ccccxix) included in a much more general precept of the Çâkalas, viz., that all the mutes except *m*, when final and followed by initial spirants or *y*, *r*, and *v*, suffer *abhinidhâna*.

आस्थापितं च ॥ ४८ ॥

48. *Abhinidhâna* is also called *âsthâpita*.

I translate in obedience to the commentator, who says: *âsthâpitasaṁjñaç ca bhavati: abhinidhânaç ca: etâny evo 'dâharaṇâni;* 'it both receives the name *âsthâpita* and *abhinidhâna*: the instances are those already given.' Unfortunately, this alternative title for the phenomenon which we have found so obscure does not notably help our comprehension of it: the word admits of being translated, in accordance with the explanation of *abhinidhâna* offered above, 'made to stand up to, or against;' but it may also be rendered 'stopped,' that is, 'silenced,' and so may favor another theory of the phenomenon.

अतो ऽन्यत्संयुक्तम् ॥ ४९ ॥

49. Any other combination of consonants is conjunct.

That is to say, all other combinations of consonants than those specified in rules 44–47 as accompanied with *abhinidhāna* are simply *saṁyukta*, 'yoked together, conjoined;' the precise nature of such conjunction being defined by the next rule. The commentator says: *ataḥ anye vyañjanasaṁdhayaḥ saṁyuktā bhavanti: anye abhinidhānāt padāntasparçāḥ:*[1] *antaḥsthoshmasu padādishu*[2] *ca saṁyujyante:* 'other combinations of consonants than these are conjunct; other final mutes than *abhinidhāna*, before semivowels and sibilants commencing a word, are conjoined with them;' and then, instead of citing from the text any actual cases, he goes on to put the series of words with which we are already acquainted, *godhuk, virāṭ, dṛshat, trishṭup* (see rules 5, 6), in lengthy and tedious succession, before *yāti, vayati, rathe, çete, shaṇḍe*, and *sāye*. This by no means exhausts all the possible cases to which the name *saṁyukta* applies; nor has there been any restriction of *abhinidhāna* to cases of contact between a final and an initial, as the commentator's language would seem to imply.

This rule has the appearance of restricting the term *saṁyoga* to such combinations of consonants as are not accompanied with *abhinidhāna*. But such is not its meaning, at least as regards the general usage of the treatise: *saṁyoga* is employed everywhere in the more general sense expressly attributed to it by a later rule of this chapter (i. 98).

Nothing is to be found in the other Prātiçākhyas corresponding to this rule and the one next following.

पूर्वरूपस्य मात्रार्धं समानकरणं परम् ॥ ५० ॥

50. The latter half-measure of the first constituent has the same organ of production with the second constituent.

The term *pūrvarūpa* is not elsewhere found in our treatise with this meaning, although it occurs twice in a like sense in the Rik Pr. (ii. 12, iii. 7). The construction of the rule is also irregular, and its ellipsis of *pararūpeṇa* or *pareṇa* at the end (*pareṇa* is added by the commentator in his paraphrase) is bolder and more obscure than is usual elsewhere. These anomalies may be owing to the fact that the rule is taken in its present form and extent from some other treatise, and a metrical one. Weber (p. 127) has noted that it forms a half-*çloka*, and it is actually cited as such by the commentator, along with the other half-verse, as follows: *pūrvarūpasya mātrārdhaṁ samānakaraṇam param: pratyayena bhavet kāryam etat saṁyuktam ishyate;* 'the latter half-measure of the first element must be made to have the same organ of production with the succeeding element; such a combination is regarded as conjunct.' We can hardly help, however, both here and in the rule, assuming a different meaning for *karaṇa* from that which it

[1] *padāntāt sparçaḥ.* [2] *padābhidhishu.*

has elsewhere in our treatise, and usually also in the other kindred works, and translating it rather 'mode of production' than 'organ;' and this is an additional indication of the foreign origin of the rule itself. The only instances given by the commentator are such as do not show any difference of organ between the two constituents of the conjunction: they are *vatsâu virâjaḥ* (viii. 9. 1), *stomâ âsan* (xiv. 1. 8), and *ayaṁ vaste* (xiii. 1. 16). Of the accuracy of the physical observations which could discover any actual assimilation of the first element of these and other similar combinations, in its final portion, to the latter, I find it hard to say much in praise: I am unable to discover that any part of the *t* in *vatsâu* becomes an *s*, or any part of the *s* in *vaste* a *t*, any more than the *s* and *t* respectively become converted in part into the following vowels *âu* and *e*.

ह्रस्वं लघ्वसंयोगे ॥५१॥

51. A syllable containing a short vowel, excepting before a conjunction of consonants, is light.

The distinction of syllables, as regards their metrical value, is properly into light (*laghu*) and heavy (*guru*); long (*dîrgha*) and short (*hrasva*) are terms to be used of vowels only. The neuter gender of the terms in the rule is to be explained by their agreement with *aksharam*, 'syllable,' understood.

The Rik Pr. (xviii. 19, r. 37) and the Tâitt. Pr. (xxii. 15) have rules closely agreeing with this. The former also adds (xviii. 20, r. 42, 43) that a short vowel with a consonant makes a light syllable, but without a consonant one still lighter—an unpractical and useless distinction. The Vâj. Pr. has no passage corresponding to our rules 51–54, but remarks, rather out of place, in iv. 105, that vowels which precede a conjunction of consonants or a final consonant, or which stand *in pausa*, are of double quantity; a loose and inaccurate statement, as compared with those of the other treatises, since it is the value of the syllable, and not the quantity of the vowels, that is increased in the cases mentioned.

The commentator gives as illustrations the indifferent words *dadhi* and *madhu*, which we have had already (under i. 4), and shall meet with many times more.

गुर्वन्यत् ॥५२॥

52. Any other is heavy.

That is, as the commentator goes on to explain, those syllables are heavy which contain a short vowel before a group of consonants, or a long vowel, or a protracted (*pluta*) vowel. As instances of the first case, he gives *takshati* (*takshati*, ix. 10. 21) and *rakshati* (e. g. viii. 9. 13); of the second, *çâlâḥ* (viii. 6. 10); of the third, *bhûyâs idâm* (ix. 6. 18).

The corresponding rules of the other treatises are Rik Pr. i. 4 (r. 20, 21, xxi, xxii) and xviii. 19 (r. 36, 37), Tâitt. Pr. xxii. 14, Vâj. Pr.

iv. 105. The Rik Pr. farther adds (xviii. 20, r. 40, 41) that, while a long vowel is heavy, it is yet heavier if accompanied by a consonant.

अनुनासिकं च ॥ ५३ ॥

53. Also a syllable containing a nasalized vowel.

The commentator's illustrative citations are the same which he has already once given us, under rule 27; it is unnecessary to repeat them here.

The other treatises have the same rule (R. Pr. i. 4, r. 21, xxii, and xviii. 19, r. 38; T. Pr. xxii. 14), but with the difference that the former, admitting the *anusvâra* as a separate constituent of the alphabet, declares a vowel followed by *anusvâra* to be heavy.

पदान्ते च ॥ ५४ ॥

54. And at the end of a word.

The commentator simply paraphrases the rule, and adds one of his staple lists of illustrations, viz. *godhuk* etc. (see under i. 3). The Vâj. Pr. (iv. 105, cited under r. 51, above) holds a like doctrine. The Taitt. Pr. (xxii. 14, 15) restricts the heaviness to such final syllables as end with a consonant, as our own commentator would seem to do by the instances he cites. It is not meant, of course, that in the combinations of the phrase the final syllables of words are heavy, but in the disjoined or *pada*-text, where each final is followed by a pause, or at the end of a verse or phrase. The Rik Pr. makes no mention of this case.

परस्य स्वरस्य व्यञ्जनानि ॥ ५५ ॥

55. Consonants belong to the following vowel.

This and the three succeeding rules concern the division of words into syllables, and the assignment of the consonants they contain to the proper vowels. It is a matter of pretty pure theory; the only practical bearing it can have must be in determining whether such and such a consonant shall receive one or another accent, as being that of the preceding or of the following vowel: and this itself must be almost unmixed theory, since it can hardly be claimed that even sonant consonants share at all in accentuation: certainly they do not do so consciously. The teachings of the different Prâtiçâkhyas are very nearly accordant upon the subject, and this general introductory rule is equivalently stated by all (R. Pr. i. 5, r. 23, xxiv, and xviii. 17, r. 32; V. Pr. i. 100; T. Pr. xxi. 2).

The commentator gives as instances again *dadhi* and *madhu*, which are to be divided *da-dhi* and *ma-dhu*.

संयोगादि पूर्वस्य ॥ ५६ ॥

56. The first consonant of a group belongs to the preceding vowel.

The commentator here does his work very unsatisfactorily: he fabricates his illustrations, instead of drawing them from the Atharvan text, giving *atra sati, âdravati, pradravati,* and he does not note for us the fact that, in the combinations which he presents, the former consonant is to be doubled, by iii. 28, and then inform us to which of the two products of duplication the precept of the rule applies. In the Rik Pr. (i. 5, r. 25, xxvi; also xviii. 16, r. 34), the name *saṁyogâdi* belongs to the second letter, as being the first of the original combination or *saṁyoga*, while the one preceding it is specifically the product of the duplication (*kramaja*): and the treatise allows it to be counted either with the preceding or following syllable: thus, either *at·tra* or *att·ra*. The Vâj. Pr. (i. 102) calls the first consonant of the group as it stands after duplication *saṁyogâdi*, and unites it with the former syllable: and in the same sense, probably, the term is to be understood in our own treatise and in the Tâitt. Pr. (xxi. 4): we are to write and divide *at·tra sati, âd·dravati, prad·dravati.*

The commentary adds: *apara âha: hasayamaṁ pûrvasye 'ti*, of which the meaning is obscure and the pertinence questionable. If it has to do with the disposition of the *yama*, it ought to come in under rule 58 or 104.

पदान्तं च ॥५७॥

57. As does also a final consonant.

The commentary offers once more *godhuk* etc. (as under i. 3).

The equivalent rules of the other treatises are Rik Pr. xviii. 17 (r. 32), Vâj. Pr. i. 101, and Tâitt. Pr. xxi. 3.

रेफहकारक्रमजं च ॥५८॥

58. And one generated by *krama* after *r* and *h*.

The commentator offers no explanation of the rule, merely adding to it, in his paraphrase, the words *pûrvasvarasya bhavati*, and proceeding at once to give his illustrations. These are the same which appear again under iii. 31, and also, in part, under i. 100: they are for the most part words which do not occur in the Atharvan text, and, being much corrupted, are in more than one case of doubtful reading. A comparison of the illustrations under some of Pâṇini's rules (viii. 3. 26, 27; 4. 46) is of important use in restoring their true form. They are *arkaḥ, arcâ* (so under Pâṇ. viii. 4. 46; MS. *artha, arcco*), *vartaḥ* (MS. *gartte, vartto*), *bhargaḥ* (MS. *bhagnaḥ, bhagaḥ*: found in AV. only at xix. 37. 1), *prâhṇaḥ, pûrvâhṇaḥ, aparâhṇaḥ* (ix. 6. 46), *apa hmalayati* (MS. *apa brahma layati, apa hyalati*), *vi hmalayati* (MS. under iii. 31 *vi hyalati*), *apa hnute* (omitted here), and *brahma* (e. g. i. 19. 4). In all these words, the consonant following the *r* or the *h* is doubled, by iii. 31, and the former of the two, which is regarded as the one that owes its existence to the *krama*, or duplication, is to be reckoned as belonging to the preceding syllable. Thus we are to read and divide *ark·kaḥ, arc·cā, vart·taḥ, bharg·gaḥ, prāhṇ·ṇaḥ, pūrv·vāhṇ·ṇaḥ, aparāhṇ·ṇaḥ, apahm·malayati, apahn·nute, brahm·ma.*

The rule i. 104 of the Vāj. Pr. corresponds in meaning with this, although more general in its form; the Tāitt. Pr. (xxi. 5) teaches that a consonant not combined immediately with a vowel belongs to the preceding syllable, which would leave only the final member of any group to be attached to the following vowel: there are some exceptions made, which need not be noticed here. In the Rik Pr., the simple and frequent case of a consonant doubled after an *r* does not seem to be provided for at all: its rule (i. 5, r. 26, xxvii) is constructed only for a case in which the consonant following the *r* is itself succeeded by another; one is tempted there to reject the commentator's interpretation, and understand the rule to mean "two consonants are reckoned as belonging to the preceding vowel, when there is duplication of the second of a group:" this would make it accord with our own.

एकमात्रो ह्रस्वः ॥५९॥

59. A short vowel is of a single mora.

The commentator gives us again, as instances, *dadhi* and *madhu*.

The word translated 'mora' is *mātrā*, 'measure,' a term common in this sense to all the Prātiçākhyas. It is the fundamental measure, which cannot itself be defined by anything else. Only the Rik Pr. (xiii. 20) attempts to fix the length of the short, long, and protracted vowels, by comparing them with the cries of certain birds.

The corresponding definitions of the other treatises are Rik Pr. i. 6 (r. 27, xxviii); Vāj. Pr. i. 55, 56; Tāitt. Pr. i. 33.

व्यञ्जनानि च ॥६०॥

60. The consonants are of the same length.

The commentator's illustrative instances are again *dadhi* and *madhu*.

All the other treatises (R. Pr. i. 7, r. 34, xxxv; V. Pr. i. 59; T. Pr. i. 37) agree in assigning but half a mora as the length of a consonant.

द्विमात्रो दीर्घः ॥६१॥

61. A long vowel has two moras.

The commentator's instance is *çālā* (ix. 3. 17).

There is no discordance among the Prātiçākhyas upon this point: compare Rik Pr. i. 6 (r. 29, xxx); Vāj. Pr. i. 57; Tāitt. Pr. i. 35.

त्रिमात्रः प्लुतः ॥६२॥

62. A protracted vowel has three moras.

The instance cited is *idā3m* (ix. 6. 18). All the cases of protracted vowels which the Atharvan text contains are rehearsed below, in rule 105.

Compare the accordant rules of the other treatises in Rik Pr. i. 6 (r. 30, xxxi); Vâj. Pr. i. 68; Tâitt. Pr. i. 36.

With this rule ends the second section of the first chapter. The signature in the manuscript is *prathamasya dvitîyaḥ pâdaḥ*: 62.

षट्पुरसोरुकारो ऽन्त्यस्य दशदाशयोरादेशश्च मूर्धन्यः ॥ ६३ ॥

63. The final of *shash* and *puras* becomes *u* before *daça* and *dâça* respectively, with substitution of a lingual for the following initial.

That is to say, *shash* before *daça* becomes *sho*, and the *daça* becomes *ḍaça*, making the compound *shoḍaça*; and *puras* with *dâça*, in like manner, forms *puroḍâça*. The commentator cites from the text the words themselves merely, viz.: *shoḍaçam* (iii. 29. 1), *puroḍâçâu* (e. g. ix. 6. 12). Neither of the words is analyzed, or restored to its theoretically regular form, by the *pada*-text; and our treatise, accordingly, according to its own programme, has nothing to do with them: and the same is true of the words referred to in the three following rules.

These two words, with others of somewhat analogous character, are treated in the Vâj. Pr., iii. 39–46.

कृपे रेफस्य लकारः ॥ ६४ ॥

64. In the root *kṛp*, *l* is substituted for *r*.

The whole commentary upon this rule is lost, and only its repetition before the next rule remains. Apparently, the copyist has carelessly skipped from the repetition of the rule in the commentator's paraphrase to that with which, as usual, the whole exposition closes. The loss is of very insignificant consequence: the missing passage would probably have afforded us some instances from the Atharvan text of verbal forms or derivatives of the root *kḷp* or *kalp*, which are frequent there. The rule may be taken as the assertion of an opinion that the original form of this root is *karp*; an opinion rendered plausible by the derivative noun *kṛp* (see the next rule), and by the analogy of the root *kar*, of which the other seems to be a secondary form. With it corresponds Pâṇini's rule viii. 2. 18; none of the other Prâtiçâkhyas offers anything equivalent. If our treatise has set itself to note the words in which a *l* appears in the place of a more original *r*, it should not pass over the words in which the root *car* becomes *cal*, as *avicâcala*, *pariçcali*, etc., *glaha* and *glahana*, which are hardly to be separated from the root *grah*, *udumbala* (viii. 6. 17), etc.

न कृपादीनाम् ॥ ६५ ॥

65. Not, however, in the words *kṛpâ* etc.

This is the first instance in our treatise of a rule stated in this form, the words or phrases to which the precept contained in the rule refers being conceived to form a series, or *gaṇa*, of which the first only is given in the rule, and the others comprehended in an *et cetera*. The form of statement is characteristic of the Atharva Prātiçākhya and of Pāṇini, and of them only: the Vāj. Pr. employs it but once (v. 38), the others not at all (R. Pr. iv. 39, where, for convenience's sake, a list is thus referred to in one verse which is given in full in the next, furnishes but an accidental and insignificant analogy). It would seem to be the business of a commentator to give the list in full, but the author of our commentary evidently does not think so, for he very seldom, if the *gaṇa* have any extent, presents us more than specimens from it. Here, he gives *kṛpā pāvaka* (xviii. 4. 59), and *kṛpāt svaḥ*[1] (vii. 14. 2: the reading doubtless is a corrupt one, and should be *kṛpā svaḥ*, as is read by both the Sāma and Yajur-Vedas, in their corresponding verses); also *kṛpaṇaḥ* (*kṛpaṇāḥ*, xi. 8. 28), and its derivative *kārpaṇyam* (not found in AV.). If these two words, which come from altogether another root, actually belong to the *gaṇa*, it should contain also *kṛpamāṇasya* (v. 19. 13) and *akṛpran* (xviii. 3. 23).

With this and the preceding and following rules are to be compared Pāṇ. viii. 2. 18, and the *vārttikas* upon it.

लकारस्य रेफः पादमङ्गुलिमित्येवमादीनाम् ॥ ६६ ॥

66. In *pādam aṅgulim* etc., *r* is substituted for *l*.

The instances given by the commentary as coming under this rule are *çaçre pādam aṅgurim* (iv. 18. 6 and v. 31. 11), *sahamūrān anu daha* (v. 29. 11), *yāhi mayūraromabhiḥ* (vii. 117. 1), and *açvasya vāraḥ purushasya vāraḥ* (x. 4. 2). The *gaṇa* should also include *pañcāṅguriḥ* (iv. 6. 4), *svaṅguriḥ* (vii. 46. 2), *anaṅgureḥ* (viii. 6. 22), and perhaps *tirya* (for *tilya*, from *tila*: iv. 7. 3): *aṅgurim* also occurs again in xx. 136. 13. As counter-instances, to show the necessity of constructing a *gaṇa*, of a limited number of instances, the commentator cites *aṅgulibhyo nakhebhyaḥ* (ii. 33. 6), and *bālās te prokshaṇīḥ santu* (x. 9. 3).

It is not in accordance with the usage of our treatise elsewhere to give, in citing a word or phrase in a rule, another form than that which it actually has in the text: we should have expected here पादमङ्गुरिमि°. The form *ity evam ādi*, instead of simply *ādi*, is found once more, in ii. 29.

नकारमकारयोर्लोपे पूर्वस्यानुनासिकः ॥ ६७ ॥

67. In case of the loss of a *n* or *m*, the preceding sound becomes nasalized.

The cases of elision of *n* and *m* are taught below, in ii. 32–34, which see for illustrations. The commentator offers here only the words

---

[1] *kṛpaṇiḥ*.

viñçatiḥ (e. g. v. 15. 2) and *payāñsi* (e. g. i. 9. 3)—which are very ill chosen, since, though each offers an example of a nasalized vowel, neither exhibits an elision of an original nasal mute, according to any rules contained in this treatise.

Corresponding rules to this and the following one of our treatise are offered by the other Prātiçākhyas: see Rik Pr. iv. 35 (r. 79, cccxix); Vāj. Pr. iii. 129, iv. 3; Tāitt. Pr. xv. 1: there are some differences of application, but chiefly dependent upon the different modes of treatment of the nasal mutes adopted by the different authorities, which will be explained in their place.

यरोष्मापत्तौ च ॥ ६८ ॥

68. Also in case of their conversion into *y*, *r*, or a spirant.

The instances given by the commentary are as follows: *rathāñ iva* (v. 13. 6), *sālāvṛkāñ iva* (ii. 27. 5), *khalvāñ iva* (e. g. ii. 31. 1)—in all these cases, the final *n* is first, by ii. 27, converted into the spirant *visarjanīya*, the latter then changed, by ii. 41, into *y*, and this finally, by ii. 21, dropped altogether; so that we have the successive steps *rathān iva*, *rathāñḥ iva*, *rathāñy iva*, *rathāñ iva*—farther, *ṛtūñr ṛtubhiḥ* (not found in AV.), *ṛtūñr ut sṛjate vaçī* (vi. 36. 2), *mo shu paṇīñr abhi* (v. 11. 7: the commentator repeats the first word in its *pada* form, *mo iti*, at the end of the citation), and *dasyūñr uta bodhi* (iv. 32. 6)—in these instances, the final *n*, by rule ii. 29, becomes *r*, and, the preceding vowel being nasalized, *ṛtūn ut* is converted into *ṛtūñr ut*.

As the *n* must always be converted into the spirant *visarjanīya* before it becomes *y*, it seems superfluous to make separate mention of the latter in the rule. The commentator apparently feels this objection, and ventures for once a defence, as follows: *ūshmaṇo grahaṇāt siddhe punar-grahaṇena kim: nityatvaṁ na syāt: ṛtūñr ut sṛjate vaçī*; 'when the matter is made certain by the use of the term *ūshman*, why any farther mention? it is because this does not apply to all cases, as is shown by the instance *ṛtūñr ut sṛjate vaçī*.' I do not see the point of this defence: it does, indeed, explain the mention of *r* in the rule, but it has nothing to do with that of *y*.

अनुनासिकस्य च पूर्वेणैकादेशे ॥ ६९ ॥

69. And in case of the combination of a nasalized vowel with a preceding vowel.

The only cases cited by the commentary are those of the combination of the initial vowel of *añça* with a preceding final vowel, by simple fusion or by the elision of the initial *a*; they are: *ubhāv upāñçu* (pada *upa-añçu*) *prathamā pibāva* (iv. 32. 7), *somasyā 'ñço* (vii. 81. 3), and *ye vrīhayo yavā nirupyante 'ñçavaḥ* (ix. 6. 14).

Compare Rik Pr. xiii. 10 (r. 20), Vāj. Pr. iv. 51, Tāitt. Pr. x. 11.

पुरुष आ बभूवाँ इत्यवसाने ॥ ७० ॥

70. In the passage *purusha ā babhūvāñ*, the vowel is nasal before the pause.

The passage referred to is x. 2. 28: *sarvâ diçaḥ purusha â babhûvâñ3*, where, in a case of doubt and questioning, the final *a* of *babhûva* is both protracted and nasalized. The *pada*-text reads simply *purushaḥ : â : babhûvâñ3*: and there would be no call for such a rule as that given here, but for the requirements of the *krama*-text, in which *babhûva*, as the last word in a verse, must suffer *parihâra* (iv. 117), or repetition with *iti* interposed, and in which it might be made a question whether the nasality of the vowel should or should not be preserved before the *iti*. This rule teaches us that the nasal quality is lost before the *iti*, as rule 97, below, teaches also with respect to the protraction; and the same things are taught once more by iv. 120, 121. The three last *kramapadas* of the verse will be, then: *purusha â babhûvâñ3 : â babhûvâñ3 ; babhûve 'ti babhûvâñ3*.

ऋवर्णस्य रेफात्परं यत् ॥७१॥

71. Of the *ṛ*-vowels, the part following the *r* receives the nasal quality.

We have seen above, in rules 37 and 38, that the *ṛ*-vowel is regarded as composed of a piece of an *r*, with a fragment of vowel sound preceding and following it, and that, when it is long or protracted, the *r*-quality is found only in the first mora. Here we learn that, when such a vowel is nasalized, the nasal quality does not affect the *r*, but only the part of a vowel which follows it. Any one may perceive, however, upon trying the experiment, that there is no physical difficulty in the way of nasalizing the *r* itself, supposing the *ṛ*-vowel to be properly accordant in pronunciation with that letter throughout.

The commentator cites *bhûmidṛñham acyutam pârayishṇu* (v. 28. 14), *dṛñha pratnân* (vi. 136. 2), and *janân dṛñhantam* (xii. 2. 9). The instances, as in many other cases, are wanting in variety and in completeness: as an example of the long vowel nasalized, we may take *pitṝ̃r upe 'mam*, already cited under rule 38: no case of the protracted vowel nasalized occurs in the text.

The other treatises offer nothing corresponding to this rule.

उकारस्येतावपृक्तस्य ॥७२॥

72. *U* is nasalized when standing alone, before *iti*.

In the *pada*-text of the Atharvan, as in those of the other Vedas, the particle *u* is always written *ûñ iti*. In this rule, its nasality in such a situation is noticed: in the rule next succeeding are taught its long quantity and its exemption from conversion into a semivowel before the following vowel.

The term *apṛkta* means 'uncombined with any other letter:' it is said also of the particles *â* and *o* (= *â* + *u*) in rules i. 79, iv. 118, below.

दीर्घः प्रगृह्यश्च ॥७३॥

73. In the same situation it is also long, and *pragṛhya*.

The term *pragṛhya* means, by implication, that the vowel to which it applies is not liable to the ordinary changes of *saṁdhi*, viz. fusion with, or conversion into a semivowel before, a following vowel. I say, by implication: for only in the Tâitt. Pr. (which uses, however, not *pragṛhya*, but the related term *pragraha*) does the pronouncing a vowel *pragṛhya* exempt it from change; all the other treatises find it necessary to teach by a specific rule (see iii. 33, below, and the quotations there given) that the vowels declared to be *pragṛhya* are not subject to euphonic alteration. The whole proceeding is somewhat analogous with that by which the Rik Pr. teaches the conversion of *visarjanīya* into *r*; first rehearsing all the cases in which the conversion takes place, and pronouncing their *visarjanīya* to be *rephin* or *riphita*, and then finally declaring the *riphita visarjanīya* convertible into *r*. The word *pragṛhya* is explained by Böhtlingk-Roth to mean literally "to be held apart, or isolated," i. e., from the combinations of *saṁdhi*.

Any satisfactory reason why the particle *u* should be treated in this peculiar manner by the framers of the *pada*-text is not readily apparent. There are but few cases in our text in which it assumes a long form in *saṁhitā* (viz. eight instances: they are given under iii. 4), so that it can hardly be said to exhibit any special tendency to protraction; it nowhere assumes a nasal quality in the combined text; and it has hardly a trace of a proper *pragṛhya* character: if, indeed, it be preceded by an uncombined vowel and followed by another vowel, it remains uncombined with the latter (by iii. 36, which see: only three such cases occur in our text); but, on the other hand, if preceded by a consonant, it combines regularly with a following vowel (of this also there are only four cases in AV.: see ii. 37). It seems as if the protraction must have been made in order to give the word more substance as an independent *pada* in the disjoined text, it being the only instance of a single short vowel possessing such a value; and as if the nasalization and addition of *iti* were intended to mark it more distinctly as an exceptional case, requiring a different treatment in the *saṁhitā*-text. Pāṇini (i. 1. 17, 18) allows it to be read either *u* or *ū̃*.

The treatise now goes on to detail the other cases of *pragṛhya* final vowels.

ईकारोकारौ च सप्तम्यर्थे ॥ ७४ ॥

74. Final ī and ū are also *pragṛhya*, in a form having a locative sense.

The instances cited by the commentator are *āṣṭrī padaṁ kṛṇute agnidhāne* (vi. 27. 3: the Rig-Veda, in the corresponding passage, has the proper locative form, *āṣṭryām*), *ato jātāso dhārayanta urvī* (xviii. 1. 32), *mahī no vātāḥ* (xviii. 1. 39), and *tanū dakṣam ā suvatām* (iv. 25. 5). This last, however, is a doubtful case, since the word *tanū́* may quite as plausibly, or more so, be taken as nominative dual, 'their very selves.' A more unequivocal case of ū is *madyū́* in xviii. 4. 4, and it is the only one which I have noted in the text. There is also a single case of a locative in ī not given by the commentary: it is *abhihrutī*, in

vi. 3. 3. As counter examples, of final *î* and *û* in other than a locative sense, and therefore not *pragṛhya*, the commentator offers *dhîtî vâ ye* (vii. 1. 1), *tasyâ 'mû sarvâ* (xiii. 4. 28). Of cases analogous with the former of these, where the *î* represents an instrumental case, there are several others in the text, as vii. 48. 1, 77. 1; ix. 9. 8.

The *pada*-text carefully notes these locatives in *î* and *û* as *pragṛhya*, in the usual manner, by writing an *iti* after them: thus, *dakshî iti*, *urvî iti*, *tanû iti*, etc. The commentator, in citing the several passages, under this and the following rules, always repeats at the end of each citation the *pragṛhya* word, in its *pada* form, or with *iti* appended: I have omitted such repetitions, as unnecessary here.

A corresponding rule in the Rik Pr. is found in i. 18 (r. 72, lxxiii): also in Pâṇini, i. 1. 19. The Vâj. Pr. notes no such cases as those to which this rule applies: and the Tâitt. Pr., instead of classifying and defining the *pragṛhya* terminations according to their grammatical values, describes them all in an entirely empirical way (in iv. 1–54), by their position and surroundings, whence its rules do not generally admit of detailed comparison with those of the other treatises.

द्विवचनान्तौ ॥ ७५ ॥

75. The same vowels, *î* and *û*, are *pragṛhya* as dual terminations.

The commentator's illustrations are *imau pârshṇî âbhṛte* (x. 2. 1), *indravâyû ubhâu* (iii. 20. 6), *ubhâv indrâgnî â bharatâm* (v. 7. 6).

Corresponding rules are Rik Pr. i. 18 (r. 71, lxxii) and Vâj. Pr. i. 93; both of them include also the cases noted by our treatise in the next following rule.

एकारश्च ॥ ७६ ॥

76. As is also *e*.

The commentator cites *atrâ dadhete* (v. 1. 3), *rathacakre vâvṛdhâte* (v. 1. 5), *saṁ pitarâv ṛtviye* (xiv. 2. 37).

अस्मे युष्मे त्वे मे इति चोदात्ताः ॥ ७७ ॥

77. Also the words *asme*, *yushme*, *tve*, and *me*, when accented.

The specification "when accented" is, of course, meant only for the two latter of the words named, as the others would never occur otherwise than accented. Of the four, *yushmé* and *mé* never occur in the Atharvan text: *tvé* is found once, in a Rik passage (AV. v. 2. 3 = RV. x. 120. 3), and also, according to the manuscripts, in viii. 9. 9, twice repeated, and each time written in the *pada*-text *tvé iti*, as a *pragṛhya*: but the accent and the addition of *iti* are hardly to be regarded otherwise than as a blunder of the tradition, since the word is evidently the enclitic or accentless *tve* of the Vedic language: no forms of this enclitic pronoun are found elsewhere in the Atharvan. The fourth, *asmé*, is also hardly an Atharvan word. It is found in three Rik passages, viz. iv. 21. 1 (RV. vi. 28. 1), xviii. 1. 3 (RV. x. 10. 3), 42 (RV. x. 17. 8): in another passage (iv. 31. 3), where the Rik (x. 84. 3) reads *asmé*, all the Atharvan manuscripts have *asmā'i*, which has been altered to *asmé* in the edition, in obedience to the requirement of the sense, and the authority of the Rik reading. Another precisely similar case is xix. 40. 4 (RV. i. 46. 6). The only passage where the Atharvan gives *asmé* independently is v. 1. 3, where all the manuscripts except P. and M. (copies of the same original, by the same scribe) agree in reading it (pada *asmé iti*): here also, however, the edition reads *asmā'i*.

The commentator cites no instances, but says *nigame yushmadbhyā vibhakter itvam ishyati: yushmâkam: asmâkam: tvam aham iti prâpte: asme yushme tve me iti ca vibhaktyâdeçaḥ kriyate.*

The Rik Pr. (i. 19, r. 73, 74, lxxiv, lxxv) notes *asme, yushme, tve*, and *amî* as *pragṛhya*: the third, *tve*, when accented, and not a member of a compound word. The Vâj. Pr. (i. 96, 97) notes *asme, tve*, and *me*, the latter when accented. *Asme* and *tve* are dealt with in Tâitt. Pr. iv. 9, 10.

अमी बहुवचनम् ॥ ७८ ॥

78. Also *amî*, as plural.

The examples cited by the commentator are *amî ye yudham* (vi. 103. 3), *amî ye vivratâḥ* (iii. 8. 5), and *amî açaṇe* (not found in AV.). To explain the addition of the specification "as plural," he gives a counter-example, *çamy atra*, which is plainly one of his own fabrication; nor can I find that the text contains anything which should render that addition necessary. The Vâj. Pr. says (i. 98) "*amî*, when a word by itself;" the other treatises (R. Pr. i. 19, r. 73, lxxiv; Tâitt. Pr. iv. 12) see no reason for appending any such limitations.

निपातो ऽपृक्तो ऽनाकारः ॥ ७९ ॥

79. Also a particle consisting of an uncombined vowel, unless it be *â*.

This rule is meant to apply solely to the particle *o*, composed of *â* and *u*, which is found in two passages of the text, viz. *o cit sakhâyam* (xviii. 1. 1) and *prâtaṁ havir o shu* (vii. 72. 2), both of which are cited by the commentator: the *pada*-text writes the *o* in the usual manner of a *pragṛhya*, viz. *ó íti*. To explain the addition of "unless it be *â*" to the rule, the commentator cites *punar â 'hi vâcaspate* (i. 1. 2), where the *pada*-text reads, of course, *â': ihi*.

The form of this rule is not a little strange: why *o* should thus be made an exception from the next rule, and why, when there is no other particle, except *â*, composed of a single vowel, it should be treated as if one of a class, it is very difficult to see: we cannot help suspecting here the influence of the general grammar: compare Pâṇ. i. 1. 14, the virtual correspondence of which with our rule is as close as possible. The Rik Pr. (i. 18, r. 69, lxx) has a similar precept.

ओकारान्तश्च ॥ ८० ॥

80. Also one ending with *o*.

That is to say, as we must infer from the preceding rule, and as the commentator fills out the ellipsis, a *nipâta* or 'particle,' having *o* for its final. This is a strangely inaccurate description: it was bad enough to have the *upasarga* or preposition *â* treated as a *nipâta* by the last rule, when combined with *u*: but here we have nouns, verbs, prepositions, and particles all confounded together under the same name. The particles, it is true, greatly preponderate in number and in frequency: thus we have *atho* (about 130 times in the whole Atharvan text), *mo* (15 times), *no* (12 times), *uto* (7 times), and *iho, yado, aṅgo, evo, dosho* (once each); but of prepositions we have *o* and *upo* (twice each), and *pro* (once); of verbs, *vidmo, datto, atto* (once each); and of nouns (pronouns), *teno* (twice), *yo*, and *so* (once each). In the form of the rule is perhaps to be seen again the influence of the general grammar: compare Pâṇ. i. 1. 15. The other treatises are not open to the same criticism: the Rik Pr. (i. 18, r. 70, lxxi) declares *pragṛhya* a final *o*, except of the first member of a compound; and the Vâj. Pr. (i. 94, iv. 89) constructs its rule in very nearly the same manner.

As regards the actual *pragṛhya* character of these words, there are, among the nearly 200 instances of their occurrence, but 11 cases in which they stand otherwise than before a consonant or an initial *a*, and so have an opportunity to exhibit that character distinctly. These cases are: before *â*, xx. 127. 13; before *i*, vi. 14. 3, xiv. 2. 4, xx. 130. 17, 13; before *u*, xi. 6. 7, xii. 1. 7, 9; before *e*, ii. 9. 1, vii. 56. 5, ix. 8. 7. In xx. 130. 19, and only there, an initial *a* is absorbed by such a final *o*; on the other hand, in iv. 9. 3, the metre shows that such an absorption of an initial *a* must be made in reading, though it be not so written. In *teno* (ix. 1. 20) and *yo* (xi. 4. 9), the metre shows that the combined particle *u* must be separated from the final of the original word, and that the two must be read *téna u* and *yá' u*.

The examples given by the commentary are *dosho gâya* (vi. 1. 1), *aṅgo nv aryaman* (vi. 60. 2), *atto havînshi* (xviii. 3. 44), and *datto asmabhyam* (xviii. 3. 14).

आमन्त्रितं चेतावनार्षे ॥ ८१ ॥

81. Also a vocative ending in the same letter, before an *iti* not belonging to the text.

Literally, 'before an *iti* not coming from the *ṛshis*,' or authors of the hymns: that is to say, before the *iti* by which, as already remarked, a *pragṛhya* word is followed in the *pada*-text. The vocatives in *o*, from themes in *u*, are not in a single instance treated as *pragṛhyas* in the *sanhitâ* of the Atharvan, but are always euphonically combined with the following vowel.* In the *pada*-text, however, they are invariably

* The cases are not numerous in which such a vocative occurs elsewhere than in pausa, before a consonant, or before an *a*; they are as follows: before *â*, v. 13. 6;

written as if they were *pragṛhyas*, with the usual *iti* annexed. The object of this rule, then, is to teach that they are exempt from euphonic combination only in the *pada*-text, while in other situations they are to be treated according to the general euphonic rules (iii. 40, ii. 21). The Vâj. Pr. (iv. 89) has a rule corresponding with that of our treatise; it, however, seems to be inconsistent with a previous rule (i. 94), which teaches that a final *o* is *pragṛhya* in general, and not before the *iti* of the *pada*-text alone. The usage of the *sanhitâ*-text is in accordance with the later rule, and not with the earlier, so far as I can judge from the passages which correspond with those of the Atharvan referred to in the marginal note: I am surprised that Weber has not taken any notice of this discordance between the text and the Prâtiçâkhya. The Tâitt. Pr. (iv. 6) says that *o* is *pragraha* when it is not the product of *sandhi*, and is followed by *a* or a consonant—which is a rather absurd way of saying that it is not *pragraha* at all in *sanhitâ;* since before a consonant its *pragṛhya* character could not, and before *a* need not, appear. The Rik Pr., after declaring the *o* of the vocative *pragṛhya* (i. 18, r. 68, lxix), is obliged later (ii. 27, r. 52, clvii) to except it from the rule that *pragṛhyas* are exempt from euphonic change, and to place it under the control of rules previously given for its combination with succeeding vowels. Finally, Pâṇini (i. 1. 16) gives a rule precisely corresponding to ours, but gives it upon the authority of Çâkalya. This whole state of things is something very peculiar. Why, when the *o* of *vâyo* is really no more exempt from change than the *e* of *agne*, should it be regarded by all the *pada*-texts as a *pragṛhya*, causing so much trouble to the different treatises to explain its treatment!

The commentator cites, as examples of the rule, *tvayy udite pre 'rate citrabhâno: citrabhâno iti* (iv. 25. 3), *yuvaṁ vâyo savitâ: vâyo iti* (iv. 25. 3), and *manyo vajrin: manyo iti* (iv. 32. 6). As counter-examples, to show that the vowel is unchangeable only before the *iti* of the *pada*-text, he gives *vâya ûtaye* (iv. 25. 6), *manya îḍitâ* (iv. 31. 4), and *babhra â me çṛṇuta* (v. 13. 5).

आर्त्नी इवादिष्विवादितिः[1] परः ॥ ८२ ॥

82. In *ârtnî iva* etc., the *iti* follows the *iva*.

This is a rule which concerns only the writing of the *pada*-text itself, and so, as dealing with a matter lying outside of the proper sphere of a Prâtiçâkhya, is extra-judicial, and has no correspondent in either of the other treatises. It grows out of the difficulty, in a few special cases, of combining two methods of writing usual in the *pada*-text. This text, in all the Vedas, always combines the enclitic particle *iva*, 'as if, like,' with the word to which it is attached, as if forming a compound with it, giving up often, in favor of this combination, the division which

---

before *i*, vii. 4. 1; before *î*, iv. 31. 4; before *u*, vi. 68. 1, vii. 26. 8 (*bis*); before *û*, iv. 25. 6. In iv. 32. 1, the final *o* absorbs a following initial *a;* everywhere else, it and the following *a* both remain unchanged.

[1] °वादिति परः

would otherwise be made of a preceding compound: thus, *uda-dhim* (iv. 15. 6), but *udadheḥ-iva* (i. 3. 8). When, now, the *iva* happens to follow a *pragṛhya* word, like *ártnī*, which ought to be followed in the *pada*-text by *iti*, in order to bring to light its *pragṛhya* quality, what is to be done? shall we separate the two parts of the compound word—a thing unheard of elsewhere—and introduce the *iti* between them, writing *ártnī iti 'vá "rtnī-iva?* or shall we allow the *iti* to lose its proper function, but still be retained at the end of the compound, in order to call attention to the *pragṛhya* quality of the first member of the latter, and write *ártnī ive 'ty ártnī-iva?* The second of these two alternatives is the one adopted by all the *pada*-texts, and the one which our rule here teaches us to choose. The Atharvan text offers but four such cases, which, for once, are all cited by the commentator; they are as follows: *ártnī ive 'ty ártnī-iva* (i. 1. 3); *gharmadughe ive 'ti gharmadughe-iva* (iv. 22. 4); *nṛpatī ive 'ti nṛpatī-iva* (viii. 4. 6); *yame ive 'ti yame-iva* (xviii. 3. 38).*

अनुनासिको ऽन्तःपदे ह्रस्वः ॥ ८३ ॥

83. A nasalized vowel occurring in the interior of a word is short.

Here we have the general fact laid down, and in the following rules, to the end of the section, are stated the exceptions to it. The Rik Pr., in one of its later books (xiii. 7–10), treats the same subject, and the commentator is at much pains (see Regnier's note to r. 22) to explain its introduction into the Prâtiçâkhya, into whose proper province such a matter does not enter. Our own commentator seldom troubles himself about little inconsistencies and redundancies of this kind, which are exhibited by all the treatises; they aid in the general purpose of a Prâtiçâkhya, which is to preserve the traditional text of the school from corruption. Thus, the Tâitt. Pr. presents (xvi. 1–31) a complete conspectus of all the nasalized vowels, short and long, found in its text in the interior of a word, and again (xiii. 6–14), a detailed exhibition of all cases of occurrence of the lingual nasal, ṇ.

The commentator cites a third time the whole series of instances given above, under rule 27, and repeated by him under rule 53.

दीर्घो नपुंसकबहुवचने ॥ ८४ ॥

84. In neuters plural it is long.

The commentator gives, as examples, *parûṅṣhi yasya sambhârâḥ* (ix. 6. 1), *yajûṅṣhi hotrâ brûmaḥ* (xi. 6. 14), *atto havîṅṣhi* (xviii. 3. 44).

An equivalent rule is found in the Rik Pr. (xiii. 7, r. 22), which farther specifies that the theme ends in a spirant, and that the long vowel precedes the terminations *si* and *shi*. The Tâitt. Pr., ignoring all help

* I have given the words here in the full form in which the *pada*-text presents them: our commentator, in his citations, leaves off the repetition of the compound, writing simply *ártnī ive 'ti*, etc.

from grammatical categories in the construction of its rule, as is its custom, says (xvi. 14) that â, î, and û are nasal before *si* and *shi* at the end of a word.

पांसुमांसादीनाम् ॥ ८५ ॥

85. Also in *pâṅsu*, *mâṅsa*, etc.

The commentator cites *pâṅsûn akshebhyaḥ* (vii. 109. 2), *mâṅsam mâṅsena* (iv. 12. 4), *çâṅçapena* (vi. 129. 1 [should be *çâṅçapena?* the manuscripts blunder somewhat over the word, but W. E. and H. read distinctly *çâṅçapena*]), and *çilâ bhûmir açmâ pâṅsuḥ* (xii. 1. 26). To the words thus instanced I have only to add *pâṅsure* (vii. 26. 4), which may perhaps be regarded as virtually included in *pâṅsu*.

The form of this rule is quite peculiar, in that it cites two words, instead of one, as heading of the *gaṇa*.

हनिगम्योः सनि ॥ ८६ ॥

86. Also in a desiderative form from the roots *han* and *gam*.

Of desiderative forms from the root *han* the text furnishes us *jighâṅsati* (e. g. iv. 18. 3) and *jighâṅsan* (vi. 99. 2). From *gam* we have no such forms, unless, in xii. 4. 29, 30, we are to amend *yadâ sthâma jighâṅsati* into *jigâṅsati*, which would very much improve the sense, if I am not mistaken. Could we trust implicitly to the Prâtiçâkhya to include in its rules no forms not actually to be found in the Atharvan text, this passage would be a sufficient warrant for making the alteration suggested: but that is not the case, as the very next rule, for instance, notably shows. The reason why these two roots are thus put together as the subject of such a grammatical precept may be to be sought in the general grammar; compare the equivalent rule in Pâṇini (vi. 4. 16), which offers also the same technical term, *san*, for a desiderative form.

The commentary offers as examples the word *jighâṅsati* (e. g. iv. 18. 3), and the passage spoken of above, *yadâ sthâma jighâṅsati;* and, although our manuscript here reads, like those of the text, *jighâṅsati*, the absence of any other citation or fabricated illustration of desiderative forms from *gam* gives a degree of color to the conjecture that our commentator may have meant to give *jigâṅsati*.

शान्मान्दानाम् ॥ ८७ ॥

87. As also from the roots *çân*, *mân*, and *dân*.

Of these three roots, only *mân* offers in the Atharvan text any forms falling under this rule. The commentator cites one of them, *mîmâṅsamânâḥ* (ix. 1. 3): the others are *mîmâṅsamânasya* (ix. 6. 24), *mîmâṅsitasya* (ix. 6. 24), and *amîmâṅsanta* (xii. 4. 42). The form *mâṅsta* (xi. 2. 8), as not being of desiderative origin, does not properly belong here, but, if genuine, should be included under rule 85: it may be a corrupted reading for *maṅsta;* we have the corresponding second person,' *maṅsthás*, in ix. 5. 4, and there also a part of the manuscripts (P. W. I.) read *mâṅsthâḥ*. For *çân* and *dân* the commentator evidently had no genuine instances at command, and he fabricates *çiçâṅsati*, *didâṅsanti*. Here also it is a auspicious circumstance that a rule of the general grammar (Pâṇ. iii. 1. 6) groups these three roots together: although, it is true, for a different purpose from that which calls forth our rule.

वस्वन्तस्य पञ्चपद्याम् ॥ ८८ ॥

88. Also in a strong case from a theme in *vaṅs*.

The strong cases (*pañcapadî*, 'five words or forms') are the masculine nominatives singular, dual, and plural, and the accusatives singular and dual. The suffix *vaṅs* is that which forms the perfect active participle: it is called in Pâṇini by the same name as here, *vasu*. The commentary cites as instances *paryivâṅsam* (xviii. 1. 49), *praviçivâṅsam* (iv. 23. 1), *utasthivâṅsaḥ* (vi. 93. 1), and *papivâṅsaḥ* (vii. 97. 3).

ईयसश्च ॥ ८९ ॥

89. As also from a theme in *îyaṅs*.

That is to say, in a strong case of a comparative of the ancient formation, or that produced by adding the primary suffix *îyaṅs* to the, generally gunated, root. The commentator gives as examples *çreyân*, *çreyâṅsau*, *çreyâṅsaḥ*; but the only strong case of this word occurring in the Atharvan text is *çreyâṅsam* (xv. 10. 2).

विदेश्च ॥ ९० ॥

90. As also from the root *vid*.

There are two damaging objections to be made to this rule: in the first place, it ought to be brought in, if at all, after rule 88, in order that *vasvantasya* as well as *pañcapadyâm* may be implied in it by inference from its predecessor; and in the second place, there is no need of any such precept at all, since there is no good reason why *vidvân*, the word to which it alone applies, should not be considered a *vasvanta*, and therefore regarded as disposed of by rule 88. The Hindu theory, indeed, does not regard *vidvân* as a perfect participle, and Pâṇini (vii. 1. 36) is obliged to teach that in it the perfect participial suffix is substituted for that of the present participle; and probably it is out of this circumstance that the introduction of the rule here in question has proceeded: yet, the substitution having been made, *vidvân* would have to be deemed and taken for a *vasvanta*, one would think, even by the Hindu theory itself.

The commentator gives all the strong forms of *vidvân*, of which only a part, however, are to be found in the Atharvan, and then winds up with an actual citation; as follows: *vidvân* (e. g. ii. 1. 2), *vidvâṅsau*, *vidvâṅsaḥ*, *vidvâṅsam* (e. g. ix. 9. 4), *vidvâṅsau*; *vidvâṅsam vrâtyam* (e. g. xv. 2. 1).

पुंसश्च ॥ ९१ ॥

91. As also from *puṅs*.

The commentary instances the five cases of *puṅs* to which the name *pañcapadî* belongs; only one of those to which the rule actually applies occurs in our text: *pumân* (e. g. i. 8. 1), *pumâṅsâu*, *pumâṅsaḥ*, *pumâṅsam* (e. g. iii. 23. 3), *pumâṅsâu*. Then he adds a counter-example, to show that the rule is meant for the strong cases alone: *puṅsi vâi reto bhavati* (vi. 11. 2).

Here ends the third section of the first chapter: the signature in the manuscript is *prathamasya tṛtîyaḥ pâdaḥ*: 91.

वर्णादन्त्यात्पूर्व उपधा ॥ ९२ ॥

92. A sound preceding a final sound is called its *upadhâ*.

This is simply a definition of the term *upadhâ*, and, to illustrate the rule, the commentator cites the two later rules, *nâmyupadhasya rephaḥ* (ii. 42) and *âkâropadhasya lopaḥ* (ii. 55), in which the term is employed. The Vâj. Pr. (i. 35) has precisely the same definition. In the Rik Pr. the word has a more general use, as 'preceding letter or word' (*upa-dhâ*, 'a setting against or next to'): it is probably on account of this less restricted signification current in some schools that the two treatises first spoken of deem it necessary to limit the term by a specific definition. The Tâitt. Pr. does not employ it at all.

स्वरो ऽक्षरम् ॥ ९३ ॥

93. A vowel is a syllable.

The precise scope of this rule it is not easy to determine; it seems to be rather a general and theoretic doctrine than a precept which enters in any active and practical manner into the system of rules of our treatise. The Vâj. Pr. and Rik Pr. have similar rules, and that of the former (i. 99) is expressed in identical terms with our own; it receives an easier interpretation than ours by being placed at the head of the rules for syllabication, which correspond to our rules 55–58, above. The Rik Pr. (xviii. 17, r. 31) states more fully that a vowel, whether pure, or combined with *anusvâra*, or combined with consonants, is a syllable; as also (i. 4, r. 10, xx) that both the short and the long vowels are syllables; making the former declaration an introduction to the rules for syllabication and quantity, and the latter, to the briefer treatment of the same subjects in the first chapter. We may perhaps regard our rule as a virtual precept that the accentuation, which in later rules (iii. 55 etc.) is taught especially of the vowels, extends its sway over the whole syllable: or, on the other hand, that the accents, which in rules 14–18 above were declared to belong to syllables, affect especially the vowels. With the subject of accent the commentator seems, at any rate, to bring it into special connection. Omitting his usual explanatory paraphrase (a small loss: it would doubtless have been *svaro 'ksharam bhavati*), he proceeds at once to give an exposition, of which a part occurs again at the close of the third section of the third chapter; it reads, unamended, as follows: *kim aksharasya svaryamāṇasya svaryate: ardham hrasvasya pādo dīrghasye 'ty eke: sarvam iti çāñkhamitraḥ* (under ii. 6 and iii. 74, *çāñkhamitriḥ*): *aksharasyāi 'shā vidhānaṁ* (*vidhāna*) *vidyate yad yad virasvarībhāvaḥ* (*yad yad visvarībhava:* the passage goes no farther under iii. 74): *svaram aksharam ity āhuḥ: svarād anyat vyañjanaṁ sarvaṁ pṛthak varṇasāmānyaṁ dvyaktāṁ rajyate budhāiḥ*. I translate, in part, as follows, not without some misgivings: 'what part of a circumflexed syllable is circumflexed? some say, half a short one, quarter of a long one: Çāñkhamitri says, the whole: here is found no rule for a syllable [*hrasva* and *dīrgha* are said of vowels only: see note to r. 51, above]; since, in each case, the vowel alone is contemplated [??]: now the vowel is declared to be the syllable ....,' and hence, perhaps, what is taught of the vowel must be understood to be said of the whole syllable. Yet all this would appear to be rendered unnecessary by the rules for syllabication, which, as we have seen, hardly have a meaning if they do not imply that each consonant shares in the accentuation of the vowel to which it is declared to belong.

सोष्मणि पूर्वस्यानूष्मा ॥ ९४ ॥

94. The sound preceding an aspirate becomes a non-aspirate.

The proper application of this rule, within the sphere of the Prātiçākhya, is only to cases of the doubling of the first or second consonant of a group, by the *varṇakrama*, as taught in rules iii. 28 etc., yet its form of statement is general, and there can be no doubt that it should apply to all cases arising in the course of derivation and inflection, and that forms such as *vṛḍhḍhi*, containing a double lingual sonant aspirate, are strictly excluded by it. Such forms, as is well known, occur in almost all the Vedic manuscripts, and those of our own text offer several instances of them;* which, however, we have not hesitated to amend in the printed text (except in ii. 5. 4, where the correction has been accidentally omitted) to *ḍḍh*.

Corresponding rules in the other Prātiçākhyas are: Rik Pr. vi. 1 (r. 2, ccclxxix), and xii. 3 (r. 9); Vāj. Pr. iv. 106; Tāitt. Pr. xiv. 5: that of the Vāj. Pr. and the former one of the Rik Pr. are restricted in terms to the cases of duplication arising under the rules of the *varṇakrama;* the others are general precepts, like our own.

The examples given by the commentary are such as illustrate the application of the rule to forms of derivation and inflection, as well as of *krama;* they are *iddham* (*sam-iddham*, vii. 74. 4), *dugdham* (e. g. x. 6.

* The details are as follows: ii. 5. 4, all the MSS. *ḍhḍh;* vii. 46. 1, all do.; vii. 97. 7, E. I. do., the rest *ḍh;* xi. 1. 29, Bp. *ḍh* only, all the rest *ḍhḍh;* xi. 1. 31, first time, all *ḍhḍh;* second time, Bp. *ḍh*, the rest *ḍhḍh;* xii. 2. 19, B. *ḍhḍh*, all the rest *ḍh;* xviii. 3. 42, all *ḍhḍh;* xviii. 4. 1 do.; xviii. 4. 86 do. The true reading, *ḍḍh*, is not given in a single instance by any of the MSS.

31), *nasv â ruruddhre* (iv. 31. 3: ordinary reading *rurudhre*; but in this instance, as occasionally elsewhere, the *pada* manuscript obeys the rules of the *krama*, and gives *ruruddhre*), *yo daddhre* (xviii. 3. 63, *dadhre*), *valagaṁ vâ nicakkhnuḥ* (x. 1. 18, *nicakhnuḥ*). The commentator then once more commences his citations from his metrical authority, and gives the verse *prathamâç ca dvitîyânâṁ saṁyoge pratyanantarâm: tṛtîyâç ca caturthânâm etat sarvatra lakshaṇam*; 'first mutes are substituted for seconds, when directly preceding the latter in a group; and thirds in like manner for fourths: this is a rule of universal application.'

आसन्नैषा वृत्तिः ॥ ९५ ॥

95. Conversion is according to propinquity.

That is to say, when any sound is ordered to be changed into another, of any class or description, we are to convert it into that one which is nearest to it, in situation or in character. The commentator, after his customary repetition of the rule, by way of paraphrase, with the bare addition of *bhavati*, proceeds, without any farther explanation, to cite three rules in the interpretation of which it needs to be applied. The first of these is ii. 31, to the effect that *m* before a mute is converted into a letter of the same position with it: which, by this rule, must be understood, *m* being a nasal, to mean the nasal letter of the series, and not either of the non-aspirate or aspirate surds or sonants. The second is ii. 40, by which the *visarjanîya* is to be made of like position with a following surd mute, and, by our rule, still a spirant of like position with the latter. The third example is iii. 39, which prescribes the conversion of a vowel into a semivowel; and this semivowel, by our rule, must be that of the same class with the vowel: we are not to change *i* into *v*, or *u* into *r*, etc. There are other rules to which the present precept applies; so, in explaining the one next preceding, it may be looked upon as determining the non-aspirate into which the duplication of an aspirate is converted to be surd or sonant according as the aspirate is surd or sonant (a matter which, in the other treatises, is expressly prescribed in the rules themselves, and not left for inference): and possibly its bearing upon that rule is the reason why it is introduced here, rather than elsewhere in the treatise. Similar prescriptions are found in the Rik Pr. (i. 14, r. 56, lvii) and the Vâj. Pr. (i. 142).

खण्वखाइ३ खैमखाइ३ इत्याकारादिकारो ऽनुदात्तः ॥ ९६ ॥

96. In *khaṇvakhâi* and *khâimakhâi*, the *i* following the *â* is unaccented.

This is a special rule, evidently intended to guard against an apprehended mispronunciation. The two words in question (iv. 15. 15) are meant for imitations of the croaking of frogs, and are probably for *khaṇvakhâi*, *khâimakhâi*, with protraction (*pluti*) of the final syllable: and it is feared that, without particular caution, the final *i* will be made to share in the irregular accent which falls upon the protracted vowel, both words being doubly accented, on the first and third syllables.*

अवशा आबभूवाँ इतीतावेकारो प्लुतः ॥ ९७ ॥

97. In *avaçâ* and *â babhuvẫ3*, with *iti*, the *e* is not protracted.

The commentator, after paraphrasing the rule, adds simply *avaçe 'ti, babhûve 'ti*. The two passages referred to are found at iii. 4. 42 and x. 2. 26, and they read, in the *pada* and *sanhitâ* texts, as follows:

p. वशा। इयाम्।३॥ अवंशा।३॥ इति॥—*s.* वशेयाऽमवशेति।

p. पुरुषः। आ। बभूवाँ॥ ४।३॥—*s.* पुरुष आ बभूवाँ३।

They are not analogous cases, as regards the action of the present rule, since one of them actually contains an *iti*, while, in the other, no *iti* follows the protracted vowel in either the *sanhitâ* or the *pada* texts, but only in the *krama*-text (see the note to rule 70). All the *sanhitâ* manuscripts, however, observe the precept of our treatise in making the combination of *avaçâ3* with the succeeding word, and accordingly its protraction, which is assured by this rule and by i. 105, and which is exhibited by the *pada*-text, entirely disappears in *sanhitâ*—a strange imperfection of the latter text, and one which, if it did not exhibit itself in all the manuscripts, we should be very loth to introduce, upon the sole authority of this rule of the Prâtiçâkhya.

By Vâj. Pr. iv. 86, a final *pluta* vowel retains its *pluti* before *iti*, and the closing *krama-pada* of our second verse would be *babhûvẫ3 iti babhûvẫ3*, instead of *babhûve 'ti babhûvẫ3*. Neither of the other Vedic texts appears to present any case analogous with the other one which forms the subject of our rule.

व्यञ्जनान्यव्यवेतानि स्वरैः संयोगः ॥ ९८ ॥

98. Consonants not separated by vowels form a conjunction.

With this definition of a *sanyoga*, a conjunction or group of consonants—which, as already noticed, is much more comprehensive than that which would seem to be implied in the definition of *sanyukta* given above, in rule 49—agree those of the other treatises (R. Pr. i. 7, r. 37, xxxviii; V. Pr. i. 48; T. Pr. offers nothing corresponding).

The commentator's paraphrase of the rule, with the accompanying examples, forms a verse, as follows: *vyañjanâny avyavetâni svarâiḥ*

* E. I. and H. read the first word *khaparkhá'si*, with a single accent only, and the printed text has—wrongly, as it seems to me—followed their authority instead of that of the other manuscripts: and also, by some inexplicable oversight, signs of accent have become attached to the *pluti* figures, as if the preceding *â*'s were circumflex, and the following *i*'s acute. The line ought to read as follows:

खपर्वखा३इ खिमखा३इ मध्ये तदुरि।

saṁyogo bhavati: agnir indraç ca tushṭaç ca vṛkshaḥ plaksho nidarçanam. The word *tushṭe* is not found in the Atharvan, nor *plaksha*, excepting in the form *plakshât* (v. 5. 5).

समानपदे ऽनुत्तमात्स्पर्शादुत्तमे यमैर्यथासंख्यम् ॥ ९९ ॥

99. After a non-nasal and before a nasal mute, in the same word, is made the insertion of *yamas*, suited to each case.

The commentator treats this intricate subject with the utmost possible brevity, merely paraphrasing the rule, as follows: *samânapade 'nuttamât sparçât: uttame parataḥ sparçe yamâir vyavadhânam bhavati: yathâsaṁkhyam*:—and adding as instances *sapatnam* (vii. 109. 3), *çrathnâti* (not found in AV.; the word most nearly resembling it is *çrathnânaḥ* [xiv. 1. 57], for which it may not impossibly be a false reading of the manuscript), *yajñaḥ* (e. g. iv. 11. 4), and *gṛbhṇâti* (MS. *gṛhṇâti*, which is no example of a *yama*: the only form in the AV. admitting *yama* is *gṛbhṇâmi* [iii. 8. 6]). Unfortunately, we cannot be permitted to dismiss the subject in such an off-hand manner, but must endeavor to ascertain, by the aid of the other treatises and of phonetical theory, what these *yamas* are.

We have already seen (under rule 43) that the euphonic system of the Prâtiçâkhya does not allow one mute to follow another by a simple consonantal conjunction, but regards the former of the two as suffering a modification which robs it of part of its distinct quality. Now we have the farther direction, which must be taken as to that extent limiting the former, that, within the limits of a simple word, if the latter consonant is nasal and the former not so, there is interposed between the two a *yama*, or 'twin' to one of the other letters. This is all that our treatise says of the *yamas*: none of its other rules mention them, although one or two may be regarded as referring to them, and are so interpreted by the commentator—from whose explication of rule 26, above, we have learned that they are of nasal character. The Tâitt. Pr. is not more explicit: it merely says (xxi. 12, 13): "after a mute not nasal, when followed by a nasal, are inserted, in each several case, nose-sounds (*nâsikya*): these some call *yamas*." The Vâj. Pr., where it teaches the occurrence of the *yamas* (iv. 160), calls them *vicheda*, 'separation,' a word which it does not elsewhere employ; its doctrine is: "within a word, a non-nasal before a nasal suffers separation"—that is, it is to be inferred, a separation or division of itself into two parts, which are as twins to one another—and the *yamas* have elsewhere been stated to be nose-sounds (i. 74), and formed by the root of the nose (i. 82). The Rik Pr. is decidedly more elaborate in its description. After stating (i. 10) that the *yamas* are nose-sounds, it goes on to say (vi. 8–10) that the non-nasal mutes, before following nasals, become their own "twins"—that is to say, if we rightly understand it, each becomes a pair of twins of its own nature; what is left of the original mute being one of the pair, and its nasal counterpart the other; the latter being especially the *yama*, or the twin which is added to make up the pair. The *yama* is then declared to be similar to its original (*prakṛti*); or, it is said, there is an audible utterance in the mouth, of the same quantity with the *yama;* but the office of the suffixed sound is not diverse from that of its original. All this seems intended to be very explicit, but it is so far from being perspicuous that it has led both the editors of the Rik Pr., or allowed them to fall, into the very serious error of supposing the *yama* to be something prefixed to the non-nasal mute, instead of interposed between it and the following nasal. Phonetic analysis does not, as it seems to me, help us to recognize the *yama* of the Hindu grammarians as any necessary accompaniment of the utterance of a mute and nasal, but will lead us to a plausible explanation of what they must have called by the name.* A nasal is a sound in the production of which there is an expulsion of intonated breath through the passages of the nose, at the same time that the mouth organs are closed in the position in which an ordinary mute is uttered; in any language, then, there will naturally be as many nasals as there are classes of mutes, and the unusually complete alphabet of the Sanskrit language recognizes and distinguishes them all. If, now, we pronounce a *t* before a following *m*, as in *ātma*, the *t*, in the first place, suffers *abhinidhāna*, losing the explosion which is essential to its full utterance: the organs pass, without intervening unclosure, from the dental contact to the labial contact, by which latter the *m* is produced, with expulsion of sound through the nose. By taking sufficient pains, we can make the nasal utterance so closely simultaneous with the labial explosion that nothing shall be audible except the *t* and the *m*. But we may also commence the nasal sound a perceptible interval before the explosion, and we shall even be most likely to do so in a labored utterance: if it be made to begin after the labial position is taken up, the nasal resonance is merely a preface to the *m*, and a dwelling upon it before the explosion: but if we utter sound through the nose before transferring the organs from the dental to the labial contact, we give origin to a kind of nasal counterpart to the *t*, as a transition sound from it to the *m*. If this is not the *yama* of the Hindu grammarians, I am utterly at a loss to conjecture what the latter should be. The theory which recognizes it might be compared with that which, in rule 50, above, taught a general assimilation of the former consonant of a group, in its final portion, to the latter; it is still more nearly analogous with the surd which, by ii. 9, is inserted between a final nasal and a following sibilant: this arises, like the *yama*, by an exchange of the emission (the *anupradāna*) belonging to the former letter for that belonging to the latter before the transfer of the organs from the one position to the other; and the *t* thus introduced, for example, between a *n* and a *s* has just as good a right to be called the *yama* or counterpart of the former letter, as has the *n* inserted after *t* before *m*. That the utterance of the intermediate sound thus described is not necessary, and can readily be avoided, is no objection to our interpretation of the Hindu theory: in the studied explicitness of the scholastic utterance, and with a phonetical science which delighted itself with subtleties, and of which the strong tendency was to grow from descriptive into prescriptive, such

* That Müller pronounces the theory (p. cxlii) "perfectly clear and physiologically comprehensible" must go for nothing, considering his entire misapprehension of the situation and character of the *yama*.

transition sounds would naturally enough rise to a distinctness and a generality of occurrence much beyond what they were originally entitled to. A much more serious difficulty is, that the theory of the *yama* allows its occurrence between an aspirate mute and a nasal: and we should suppose that the unclosure and brief emission of unintonated breath constituting the aspiration would form an impassible barrier between the two letters, the nasal utterance being unable to precede it, and the position of contact of the former letter to follow it, so that no nasal counterpart to the former letter could be uttered. I see no way of getting over this difficulty, excepting by supposing an inaccuracy in the analysis of the Hindu phonetists: a serious charge, it may seem, but one of which I should be glad to see them relieved by any other intelligible explanation of the *yama*. If the whole theory of the phenomenon were more solidly founded and more accurately worked out by them, I should not think they need have explained it in a manner to cause their interpreters so much perplexity. The perplexity, indeed, is not confined to the modern expositors: the ancient commentators themselves (see Müller, p. cxxiii) seem to have been somewhat in doubt as to how many different *yamas* there are, whether twenty, one for each of the non-nasal mutes, or a smaller number. The orthodox doctrine of the Rik Pr. seems to be that of twenty: but its commentator says that there are only four; one for all the first mutes, one for all the seconds, and so on; and the commentary to Tâitt. Pr. xxi. 12 supports the same view.* This latter view, however, appears to me peculiarly indefensible: I cannot at all see how the nasal counterparts of the *tenues* of the five mute series should be identical with one another; nor, on the other hand, how they should be physically different from the *yamas* of the following mutes of each series respectively; although it might well enough be loosely said, considering their title of "twins," that there are as many of them as of the sounds to which they sustain that relation. Physically, it would seem necessary that a nasal transition-sound between two mutes should be of the nature either of the first or of the second: if of the second, and that second a nasal, it would be indistinguishable from it; if of the first, it would be identical with the nasal of that series (except as being *abhinihita*, or wanting the explosion), and so the same for all the mutes of the series. The doctrine of our own treatise upon this point is not entirely clear, since its expression, *yathâsaṁkhyam*, 'according to their number,' might possibly be taken as referring either to the non-nasal or to the nasal mutes: yet it is, without much doubt, to be understood of the former; and we are to allow theoretically the existence of twenty *yamas*, although only thirteen of them—viz. those of *k*, *kh*, *g*, *gh*, *c*, *j*, *ṭ*, *t*, *th*, *d*, *dh*, *p*, *bh*†—occur in the Atharvan text.

---

* Weber (p. 128) suggests that the discordance among the authorities upon this point may have grown out of the circumstance that, in speaking of the *yamas*, those of a single series of mutes are sometimes taken as representatives of the whole class, and treated as standing for them all. This seems very plausible; but we can hardly acquit the later expositors of having been misled by this usage into the belief that there are only four *yamas*, and not twenty.

† For the details, see the additional note on the consonantal combinations in general.

In the examples which he gives under this rule, the commentator does not attempt to write the *yamas.* Above, under rules 13 and 26, where the *yamas* were instanced, they were—taking those of the guttural mutes as representatives of the class—written by the mutes with an *anusvâra* sign above: viz. कं । खं । गं । घं ; the *anusvâra* being evidently intended here exceptionally to indicate the nasal quality of the consonant itself, and not of the following vowel. The method of the commentary to the Rik Pr. (see Müller, p. xix) is the same, or, in other manuscripts, क्ङ । ख्ङ । ग्ङ । घ्ङ, and this last mode Weber (under I. 60) conjectures, with much plausibility, to have arisen from writing the guttural nasal ङ under the other letters, since this would be the most accurate method which the alphabet renders possible of writing the non-nasal and its nasal *yama.*

हकारान्नासिक्येन ॥ १०० ॥

100. After *h* is inserted in like manner a *nâsikya* before a nasal mute.

The commentator paraphrases with *hakârât nâsikyena samânapade vyavadhânam bhavati;* and adds as illustrations a part of the words already once given, under rule 58: viz. *prâhṇaḥ, pûrvâhṇaḥ, aparâhṇaḥ, apa hmalayati, vi hmalayati, vi hnute, brahma.*

The Tâitt. Pr. (xxi. 14) teaches the insertion of a *nâsikya* after *h* and before a following nasal in terms nearly equivalent to those of our own rule. The Rik Pr. (i. 10, r. 48, xlix) and the Vâj. Pr. (I. 74, 80) describe its mode of pronunciation, as a nose-sound; and the latter, in its latest portion (viii. 28), speaks of it again among the constituents of the spoken alphabet; but, strangely enough, neither of them gives any rule respecting its occurrence.

What the sound may be which is thus taught to form the step of transition from the aspiration to a following nasal, it is hard to say with confidence. I can only conjecture it to be a brief expulsion of surd breath through the nose, as continuation of the *h*, before the expulsion of the sonant breath which constitutes the nasal. The pure aspiration *h* is a corresponding surd to all the sonant vowels, semivowels, and nasals of the alphabet: that is to say, it is produced by an expulsion of breath through the mouth organs in any of the positions in which those letters are uttered; it has no distinctive position of its own, but is determined in its mode of pronunciation by the letter with which it is most nearly connected. Thus the *h*'s of *ha*, of *hi*, of *hu*, and those heard before the semivowels *w* and *y* in the English words *when* and *hue*, for instance, are all different in position, corresponding in each case with the following vowel or semivowel. *H* is usually initial in a word or syllable, and is governed by the letter which succeeds, and not by that which precedes it: but where it occurs before another consonant in the middle of a word—which is always its position in the Vedas before a nasal—the question may arise whether it shall adopt the mode of utterance of the letter before or after it: whether in *brahma,* for example, we divide *brah-ma,* and pronounce the *h* in the position of the a, or *brah·ma*, and in the position of the *m*, through the nose. According to the Hindu method of syllabication (see rule 56, above), the former is the proper division, and the Hindu phonetists doubtless regarded the *h* as belonging with and uttered like the *a*; and noticing at the same time the utterance, scarcely to be avoided, of at least a part of the *h* in the position of the *m*, they took account of it as a separate element, and called it *nāsikya*.

रेफादूष्मणि स्वरपरे स्वरभक्तिरकारस्यार्धं चतुर्थमित्येके
अन्यस्मिन्व्यञ्जने चतुर्थमष्टमं वा ॥ १०२ ॥ [॥ १०१ ॥

101. After a *r*, and before a spirant which is followed by a vowel, is inserted a *svarabhakti*, half a short *a*: some say, a quarter.

102. Before any other consonant, the *svarabhakti* after *r* is a quarter or an eighth of *a*.

The two rules are stated and explained separately in the manuscript, but I have put them thus together for the convenience of treating the whole subject of the *svarabhakti* at once.

The term *svarabhakti* signifies a 'fraction or fragment of a vowel,' and the theory evidently is, that a *r* cannot be pronounced in immediate combination with any following consonant: there must always be slipped in between them a little bit of a transition-vowel, varying in length, according to different authorities, from a half to an eighth of a mora, and longer before a sibilant or *h*, if these be followed in turn by a vowel, than before other consonants; while in quality it coincides with the *a*—that is to say, undoubtedly, with the *a saṁvṛta* (rule 36, above), or the neutral vowel. The theory is this time, at least, perfectly intelligible, and any one may readily convince himself by trial how very easy it is to introduce such a vowel-fragment after a *r*, if he pronounce the latter far enough forward in the mouth for it to require to be trilled—and perhaps especially, if he be one to whom the smoother utterance of the *r*, farther back, is more natural. The reason for distinguishing the case of a following spirant—and that, too, only when followed by a vowel—as requiring a longer insertion, is not so clear, and I confess myself unable to discover the pertinence of the distinction: it is, however, a marked and important one to the apprehension of the Hindu phonetists, as will appear by a comparison of the teachings of the other treatises.

The Vāj. Pr. (iv. 16) restricts the occurrence of anything like *svarabhakti* to cases in which a spirant is the second member of a group, and is itself followed by a vowel; but it allows it both after a *r* and a *l* (see above, under rule 46), and moreover defines it as being the *ṛ* and the *ḷ*-vowels respectively. Considering, however, that the same authority defines these vowels as ending each with quarter of an *a* (see above, under rule 37), its description of the character of the insertion cannot be regarded as differing essentially from that of our own treatise. The doctrine of the Tāitt. Pr. is very nearly the same: it teaches (xxi.

15, 16) that when *r* and a spirant form a group, a *r* vowel-fragment (*rephasvarabhaktiḥ*) is inserted, except when the spirant is subject to duplication (i. e., is not followed by a vowel) or is followed by a "first" mute: while the commentary explains that a fragment of that vowel which is akin with the *r*, or the ṛ-vowel, is meant. According to the Rik Pr. (vi. 13, 14), the *svarabhakti*, which is described as being like the ṛ-vowel (*ṛkāravarṇā*), is inserted between a *r* and a following consonant when the former is preceded by a vowel: if the following consonant is a spirant, and itself followed by a vowel, the *svarabhakti* is the longer one, which had before been defined (i. 7, r. 33, xxxiv) as being a half-mora in length; in other cases, the shorter one, of half this length (i. 7, r. 35, xxxvi), is interposed. The accordance of this with the doctrine of our treatise is as close as possible. But the Rik Pr. also allows a *svarabhakti* between a sonant letter and a following mute or spirant; and it then farther cites the views of different authorities, of whom some deny the existence of the *svarabhakti* altogether, others permit it only after a *r*, and others only before a spirant not duplicated (this is very nearly the doctrine of the Vāj. Pr. and Tāitt. Pr.), pronouncing it to agree in character with either the preceding or the following vowel.

As we shall see hereafter (under iii. 46), the manuscripts of the Atharvan acknowledge the virtual correspondence of the *r* followed by the longer *svarabhakti* with the ṛ-vowel, by writing the ṛ instead of *r*, where the former comes before a spirant, and should be, by iii. 46, converted into *r* after *a* or *ā*.

Our commentator gives us, under rule 102, the instances *aryamṇā* (e. g. i. 11. 1), *parva* (i. 12. 2), and *dharmaṇā* (e. g. vi. 132. 1)—the manuscript not attempting to write the interposed vowel-fragment. Under rule 101 he cites no examples, but, after the baldest possible paraphrase of the rule, proceeds to quote from other authorities, as follows: *apara āha: ṛkārasvarabhaktiḥ: ūshmasu svarapareshv ardhākāravarṇo vyañjanaṁ çesha iti*: 'another has said, "a vowel-fragment of the ṛ-vowel;" "before spirants followed by vowels is heard half an *a*-vowel; the rest is consonant."' These appear to be the *dicta* of two different teachers. Next follow several verses, a part of which are of a character which would render their introduction under rule 37, above, more appropriate, while one line, the second, belongs rather under rule 98; they read: *rephād anyad ṛkāre yat tasyā 'rdham pūrvasasvaram: vacanena vyavetānāṁ saṁyogatvaṁ vihanyate: ṛvarṇe 'pi tu rephasya cā 'rdhamātrā pratijñayā: ardhamātrāṁ svaraṁ vidyāt sa cāi 'vaṁ kriyate punaḥ: tān hrasvobhayataḥ kuryād yathā mātrā bhaved iti: darço varshaṁ tatha rtavaḥ:*[1] *barhiç cā 'tra nidarçanam: etāṁ ṛtiṁ vijānīyāt svarabhaktir yadā bhavet;* 'half of what there is in the ṛ-vowel different from *r* is of the same character with the preceding vowel. Of consonants separated by audible sound, the conjunction is destroyed. In the ṛ-vowels there is, by express rule, half a mora of *r*; half a mora is to be recognized as vowel, and that, again, is thus managed: put the parts upon both sides of the short vowel, so as to make out a mora: exam-

---

[1] ǀ —MS. *tathātamḥ*.

ples are *darça, varsha, tatha rtavah, barhih:* know this to be the way when a *svarabhakti* is to be produced.' I trust that either the commentator or the manuscript, and not the translator, is responsible for the inconcinnity of this passage.

तद्देव स्फोटनः ॥ १०३ ॥

103. Of the latter value is *sphoṭana.*

That is to say, if I do not misapprehend the meaning of the rule, *sphoṭana*, like the shorter *svarabhakti*, has a quarter or an eighth the quantity of a short *a:* or it may be that the emphatic *eva* would restrict the reference to the latter value, the eighth, alone. The commentator, as so often, gives not a particle of assistance in comprehending the rule. He simply paraphrases, as follows: *tad eva sphoṭano vyañjako bhavati*—explaining *sphoṭana* by its synonym *vyañjaka*, 'manifester'—and then cites the same instances of *sphoṭana* which are given later, under ii. 38. For the doctrine of *sphoṭana*, see the rule last mentioned, and the note upon it. The subject is not disposed of here, because the *sphoṭana*, unlike the other insertions treated of in this part of the work, arises only in the combinations of the phrase, when a final mute comes in contact with a following initial mute of an earlier series or *varga.*

पूर्वस्वरं संयोगाविघातश्च ॥ १०४ ॥

104. These belong to the preceding vowel, and do not effect the dissolution of a conjunction of consonants.

There is something wrong with the commentary to this rule; apparently we have a repetition of a part of the commentary to rule 102, with the loss of what should properly be given here: it reads as follows: *pûrvapûrvasvaraṁ ca tad bhavati: saṁyogasya ca vighâtaḥ yat tat rephât akârasya caturthaṁ vâ bhavaty ashṭamaṁ vâ: aryamâ purva dharmaṇâ.* It furnishes us, it will be seen, no hint as to how far back the teachings of the rule apply. I presume, however, that they may be properly considered as extending themselves to all the phonetic insertions taught in rules 99–103: all these, in the division of the word into syllables, are to be reckoned as belonging to the preceding vowel, and sharing in its accent; and whereas it might seem that the insertion of the vowel-fragment, and of its kindred *sphoṭana*, dissolved the conjunction of the consonants between which they were inserted—since, by rule 98, a conjunction of consonants can only subsist where there is no interposition of vowels—the contrary is expressly declared to be true. This would regard *pûrvasvaram* as belonging to some such word as *aṅgam* understood, and used in an indistinctive or collective manner of all that precedes. It may be, however, that the specification applies only to *svarabhakti* and *sphoṭana*, and that the neuter singular form of *pûrvasvaram* is owing to its agreement with one of the words denoting the quantity of those insertions, *caturtham, ashṭamam,* etc. The Rik Pr. specifies only of the *svarabhakti* (i. 7, r. 32, xxxiii) that it belongs to the previous syllable; the Vâj. Pr. (i. 103) says the same thing of the *yama* alone; while the Tâitt. Pr. (xxi. 6) teaches that the *svarabhakti* belongs to the preceding syllable, but (xxi. 8) that the *yamas* and *nâsikya* go with the following one. The Rik Pr. alone, besides our treatise, thinks it necessary to say (vi. 10, r. 35, ccccxi) that the *svarabhakti* does not dissolve the conjunction: in the Vâj. Pr. it is left to be pointed out by the commentator (see Weber, p. 217).

खण्वखा३इ खैमखा३इ मध्ये तदुरि [iv. 15. 15] । इदं भूया३ इदा३मिति [ix. 6. 18] । ऊर्ध्वो नु सृष्टा३स्तिर्यङ् नु सृष्टा३ः सर्वा दिशः पुरुष आ बभूवाँ३ [x. 2. 28] । पराञ्चमोदनं प्राशी३ः प्रत्यञ्चा३मिति [xi. 3. 26] । त्वमोदनं प्राशी३स्त्वामोदना३ इति [xi. 3. 27] । वशेया३मवशे३ति [xii. 4. 42] । यत्तदासी३दिदं नु ता३दिति [xii. 5. 50] । इति प्लुतानि ॥ १०५ ॥

105. . . . . : these are the cases of protracted vowels.

I have taken the liberty of separating by a stroke the different passages rehearsed in this rule; the manuscript puts them all in *sandhi* together. One or two of the signs of protraction have also been restored which the manuscript has accidentally omitted. On the other hand, I have retained the sign of protraction given by the manuscript to the second case in the last passage but one, *avaçe3'ti* (the MS. writes *avaçeti3*), although it is not written by the *sanhitâ* codices of the Atharvan text, and is forbidden by rule 97, above. Finally, I have added the accent marks which belong to each passage.

The commentator does not give any paraphrase of the rule, nor does he repeat it at the end of his exposition, yet I cannot question that it is actually the closing rule of the chapter, and not a gratuitous appendix of the commentator's own addition. He discourses respecting it more liberally than usual, in this wise: *kimarthaḥ paripâṭhaḥ: ita uttaram adhikam: etâvat svârtho 'pi: bahuvidhâs trividhâḥ plutayo bhavanti: svaraparâ abhinishṭânaparâ vyañjanaparâḥ: tâsâṁ yâḥ samânâksharaparâs tâ itâv aplutavad bhavanti itâv aplutavad bhavanti;* 'for what reason is this enumeration made? because any other instance than these is in excess: within these limits the protracted vowel is pointed out by its own meaning (?). Protractions are various; namely, of three kinds: those which affect a syllable ending in a vowel, in *visarjanîya*,* and in

* For the use of the term *abhinishṭâna* for *visarjanîya*—of which this is, I believe, the only case which our commentary affords—see rule 42, above, and the note upon it.

a consonant, respectively;* among these, those which affect syllables ending in simple vowels assume their unprotracted form before *iti*.'† No other reason, it would seem, is to be sought for the rule than that here given: it is intended to insure the absence of protraction in any other instances in the text than those here given; in all of which, the protraction is due to the requirements of the sense, and is not merely euphonic or accentual. A somewhat similar enumeration is made by the Vâj. Pr. in ii. 50–53, and, at the same time, directions are given as to the somewhat anomalous accentuation of the several cases. In Rik Pr. i. 6 (r. 31, xxxii), also, are mentioned the only three instances of protraction to be found in the Rig-Veda, all occurring in the latter part of its tenth book.

Our text and commentary say nothing respecting the accentuation of these words, except as regards the final *i* in the two instances contained in the first passage, for which see rule 70, above. From this we may perhaps conclude that the other protracted words offer no anomalies of accent. There is, however, some discordance among the manuscripts as to their treatment, which it may be well enough to notice here. Of the first passage (iv. 15. 15) we have already spoken, in the note to rule 96. In ix. 6. 18, all the manuscripts excepting I. read *bhûyâ3ḥ*, without accent, and our printed text has followed their authority: but I cannot consider this reading as anything but an error, possibly arising from a blundering confusion of the word with the verbal form *bhûyâs*, from the root *bhû*: we ought to read, with I., *bhû́yâ3ḥ*. In x. 2. 28, Bp. and E. accent the protracted syllable, *babhû-vấ'3n*: and this accent is somewhat supported by the analogy of the first *âsî́'3t* in Rig-V. x. 129. 5: but the case is still more nearly analogous with Vâj.-S. xxiii. 49, *ấ' viveçâ3n*, and Rig-V. x. 146. 1, *vindatî́3n*, and hence the reading of the published text is much the more likely to be correct. In xi. 3. 26, all the manuscripts except P. and M. accent *pratyáñcấ'3m*, which is accordingly the best supported reading. In xii. 5. 50 is only to be noted that the *pada* manuscript in the second instance omits the sign of *pluti*, but doubtless by a clerical error merely. The *pada*-text everywhere writes the vowel in its protracted form, and adds the sign of protraction, not immediately after the vowel, but after the final consonant of the syllable, and sometimes with a stroke, or even a double stroke, interposed.

Except in the first passage, which contains an imitation of animal sounds, we have in all these protractions only cases of doubtful questioning as between two alternatives, of hesitating indecision, of *mîmânsâ*, as it is called once in the text (xii. 4. 42).

The signature of the chapter is *caturâdhyâyikâyâm* ca *prathamo 'dhyâyaḥ samâptaḥ*: 13. The figures expressing the number of rules contained in it are obviously corrupt, but how they are to be amended, unless by simply altering them to 105, I do not know. That they mean 113, and that any part of the last section is lost, is not at all probable: I discover nowhere in the section any signs of a *lacuna*.

---

* These terms I translate rather according to the evident requirement of the sense than as they would seem naturally to mean.

† This is virtually a restatement of rule 97, above.

CHAPTER II.

CONTENTS:—SECTION I. 1, introductory; 2, final mutes before sonants; 3, do. as finals; 4, do. before surds; 5, do. before nasals; 6, do. before sibilants; 7, do. before *h*; 8, *ṭ* before *s*; 9, nasals before sibilants; 10, *n* before *ç*; 11, do. before sonant palatals; 12, do. before linguals; 13, *t* before *ç* and *l*; 14, do. before palatals and linguals; 15, dentals after palatals and linguals; 16, do. after *sh*; 17, *ç* after dentals; 18, loss of an initial *s*; 19, do. of *r* before *r*; 20, do. of a mute after a nasal and before another mute; 21, do. of final *y* and *v* after a vowel; 22–23, exceptions; 24, Çākaṭāyana's view of this combination; 25, insertion of a sibilant after *pum*; 26, do. after *n* before a surd palatal, lingual, and dental; 27, final *ān* before a vowel; 28, do. before *v*, in a special case; 29, insertion of *r* after final *in*, *ūn*, *ṛn*; 30, exceptions; 31, *m* before mutes; 32–33, do. before semivowels and spirants; 34, *n* in like position; 35, *m* and *n* before *l*; 36–37, *m* retained before semivowels; 38, *sphūrjana*; 39, *karshapa*.

SECTION II. 40, *visarjanīya* before a surd; 41–42, do. before a vowel; 43, do. before a sonant; 44–50, do. converted into *r* after *i* and *u*; 51–52, exceptions; 53–54, *as* converted to *o*; 55–59, loss of final *visarjanīya*.

SECTION III. 60–61, special cases of irregular *sandhi* of final *visarjanīya*; 62, conversion of *visarjanīya* into a sibilant before initial *k* and *p* of the second member of a compound word; 63–80, do. of an independent word.

SECTION IV. 81–101, conversion of final or initial *s* into *sh*; 102–107, exceptions.

संहितायाम् ॥ १ ॥

1. The following rules are to be understood as of force in the combined text.

The first chapter of the treatise has disposed of all matters of general phonetic theory, and laid down such rules as apply to words in their disjoined and independent form, and we now enter upon the consideration of those changes which may and must occur when the *padas* of the disjoined text are put together into the form of *sanhitā*. This rule is a general heading (*adhikāra*) belonging to the second and third chapters. The other treatises have equivalent or corresponding headings; the Rik Pr. at the head of its second chapter, the Vāj. Pr. of its third, the Tāitt. Pr. of its fifth. We shall see, however, that our treatise does not everywhere strictly limit itself to what concerns the conversion of *pada*-text into *sanhitā*.

पदान्तानामनुत्तमानां तृतीया घोषवत्स्वरेषु ॥ २ ॥

2. Finals not nasals become, before sonant consonants and vowels, unaspirated sonants.

Considering that, by i. 6, only the first and last of each series of mutes can occur as finals, this rule might have said *prathamānām*, 'first mutes,' instead of *anuttamānām*, 'mutes not nasal;' both this and the following rules, however, seem constructed in view of the disputed character of the final non-nasal mute, and of the doctrine of Çâunaka himself that it is a *media*, and not a *tenuis* (see i. 8). The corresponding rule of the Vâj. Pr. (iv. 117) is expressed in a precisely equivalent manner: those of the Rik Pr. (ii. 4, r. 10, cxiv, and iv. 1, r. 2, ccxxi) and Tâitt. Pr. (viii. 1, 3) use the term *prathama*, even although, as already noticed (under i. 6), the former work in theory recognizes the *media* as possible finals.

The commentator's examples are as follows: *yad yatra viçvam* (ii. 1. 1); *yad yâmaṅ cakruḥ* (vi. 116. 1); *tasmâd vâr nâma* (iii. 13. 3); *vrishad vishaḥ* (v. 17. 5); *yad râjânaḥ* (iii. 29. 1); *suhasto godhug uta* (vii. 73. 7); *sâ virâḍ ṛshayaḥ* (viii. 9. 8); and two which are not to be found in the Atharvan, and of which the latter, at least, is evidently fabricated: viz., *tad abhûtam* and *trishṭub atra.*

पदान्ते चाघोषाः ॥ ३ ॥

3. And at the end of a word they are surds.

This, in view of i. 6, is a superfluous precept, and its introduction is only to be accounted for by the considerations adverted to under the last rule.

The commentator cites once more his standard assortment of final mutes, viz. *godhuk* etc. (see under i. 3).

अघोषेषु च ॥ ४ ॥

4. As also before surd consonants.

Also an unnecessary specification; since final surds do not require to become surds before succeeding initial surds, but simply remain unchanged. Only the Vâj. Pr. (iv. 118), among the other treatises, gives an equivalent precept.

The commentator instances in illustration *vâk ca 'ndriyam ca* (xii. 5. 7), *virâṭ prajâpatiḥ* (ix. 10. 24), and *trishṭup pañcadaçena* (viii. 9. 20).

उत्तमा उत्तमेषु ॥ ५ ॥

5. Before nasals they become nasals.

The Prâtiçâkhyas are unanimous in this requirement: compare Rik Pr. iv. 1 (r. 3, ccxxii), Vâj. Pr. iv. 120, Tâitt. Pr. viii. 2. Pâṇini, as has already been noticed (under i. 2) allows either the unaspirated sonant or the nasal before a nasal, while manuscript usage is almost, if not quite, invariably in favor of the nasal.

The commentator cites in illustration the following passages from the Atharvan text: *ṛdhaṅmantro* (p. *ṛdhak-mantraḥ*) *yonim* (v. 1. 1); *ya addnaṃ nyâyanam* (vi. 77. 2); *arṇavân mahatas pari* (i. 10. 4); *madughân madhumattaraḥ* (i. 34. 4); *madhyân nicâiḥ* (iv. 1. 3); and *ya stâyan manyate* (iv. 16. 1); and finally, as the text affords him no instance of a final *p* before a nasal, he fabricates a case, out of words more than once employed by him elsewhere in a similar way, viz. *trishṭum nayati.*

द्वितीयाः शषसेषु ॥ ६ ॥

6. Before *ç*, *sh*, and *s*, they become aspirated surds.

On this point there is by no means an agreement of opinion among the different Prâtiçâkhyas. The doctrine of the Tâitt. Pr. (xiv. 12) accords most nearly with that of our treatise, only omitting its restriction to the case of a final before an initial; and the same view is by our commentator mentioned as held by Çâṅkhamitri, Çâkaṭâyana, and Vâtsya: his words are: *apadântânâm api çushasheshu dvitîyâ bhavanti: iti çânkhamitri-çâkaṭâyana-vâtsyâḥ:*[1] *tasyâ agnir vatsaḥ;*[2] 'Çâṅkhamitri, Çâkaṭâyana, and Vâtsya say that mutes even when not final become "seconds" before *ç*, *sh*, and *s*; as in the instance *tasyâ agnir vatsaḥ* (iv. 39. 2).' The Tâitt. Pr. (xiv. 13) adds that Vâḍabhîkâra* teaches the conversion of the mute into an aspirate only before a sibilant not of the same class;† and the doctrine of the Tâitt. Pr. in this form, as modified by Vâḍabhîkâra, is by the Vâj. Pr. (iv. 119) ascribed to Çâunaka, the putative author of our treatise and of the Rik Pr. The Rik Pr., ignoring all these views, and itself holding, like the Vâj. Pr., that the mute remains unchanged before the sibilant, remarks only (vi. 15, r. 54, ccccxxx) that some regard a *tenuis* before a sibilant as to be aspirated, unless it be a final. Finally, a *vârttika* to Pâṇ. viii. 4. 48, as noticed by Weber (p. 249), ascribes to Pâushkarasâdi the doctrine which our commentator attributes to the three other grammarians mentioned, and which is also taught by the Tâitt. Pr.—viz., that a mute in any situation becomes aspirated before a sibilant. This comparison of conflicting views is exceedingly curious, and it cannot but inspire us with some distrust of the accuracy, as well as completeness, with which the Hindu grammarians report one another's views.

The commentator, instead of citing from the text any genuine cases, proceeds to repeat a part of the cases which he has already once manufactured (under i. 49), in illustration of a *saṁyukta* combination of consonants, by putting his four words, *godhuk* etc. (see under i. 3), one after another, before *çete*, *shaṇḍe*, and *sâye*; and the manuscript uniformly fails to write the aspirate, except in the case of *dṛshat*. The cases which actually occur in the Atharvan text are *ks* (e. g. iii. 1. 4), *tç* (ix. 5. 21), *ts* (e. g. viii. 9. 9; but, by rule ii. 8, it is to be read *ṭts*), *ts* (passim), and *ps* (in *avagraha*; e. g. *ap-su*, i. 6. 2); *ksh* and *pç* are found only in the interior of words. The manuscripts of the Atharvan read always the simple surd before the sibilant, and in the printed text we have of course followed their authority rather than that of the Prâtiçâkhya. Weber (p. 250) notices that a single Berlin MS. of the Vâjasaneyi-Sanhitâ writes the surd aspirate before a *s* not followed by a consonant.

---

[1] *çâṅkhamitiçâkaṭâyanasyavâtsyâḥ.* [2] *vatsaḥ.*

* My manuscripts vary, as to the reading of this name, between *vâḍabhikâra*, *bâḍabhikâra*, and *bâḍavikâra*; Weber (p. 78) calls it once *vâḍabhîkâra*.

† Weber says (pp. 245, 250) "only before a sibilant of the same class;" apparently misled by an error of his manuscript.

तेभ्यः पूर्वचतुर्थो हकारस्य ॥ ७ ॥

7. After final non-nasal mutes, *h* becomes the aspirated sonant of the preceding letter.

The Rik Pr. (iv. 2, r. 5, ccxxiv) and Vāj. Pr. (iv. 121) agree precisely with our treatise upon this point; and the same doctrine is attributed by the Tāitt. Pr. (v. 38) to Plākshi, Kāuṇḍinya, Gāutama, and Pāushkarasādi. The Tāitt. Pr. (v. 39–41) goes on to state that in the view of some the *h* remains unchanged; while the Mīmānsakas, and Çāityāyana etc. (the "etc." means, according to the commentator, Kāuhalīputra, Bharadvāja, sthavira-Kāuṇḍinya, and Pāushkarasādi [sthavira-Pāushkarasādi?]) hold that an aspirated sonant* is inserted between the final surd and the *h*. Pāṇini's rule (viii. 4. 62), as is well known, allows the *h* either to remain unchanged, or to become the sonant aspirate; and there is but a very trifling phonetical difference between the two modes of treatment.

The illustrative citations of the commentator are *ud dharshantām maghavan* (iii. 19. 6), *ud dharshaya satvanām* (v. 20. 8), *uddharshiṇam munikeçam* (viii. 6. 17), *kad dha nūnam* (xviii. 1. 4), *pṛthivyām astu yad dharaḥ* (xviii. 2. 36), *tejasvad dharaḥ* (xviii. 3. 71).

टकारात्सकारे तकारेण ॥ ८ ॥

8. After *ṭ* is inserted *t* before *s*.

The same phonetic precept is found in the Tāitt. Pr. (v. 33), combined with a part of that contained in our next following rule: *t*, it is said, is to be inserted after *ṭ* and *n*, when they are followed by *s* and *sh*. The Rik Pr. (iv. 6, r. 17, ccxxxvi) also gives it as the view of certain teachers that *ṭ* and *n*, when followed by *s*, receive the appendix of a *t*.

The commentary quotes from the text *virāṭ svarājam* (viii. 9. 9), *pṛtanāshāṭ suvīraḥ* (xi. 1. 2), and *triṅçatāḥ shaṭ sahasrāḥ* (xi. 5. 2), which are the only examples of this combination presented by the Atharvan. In the first of the three, P. reads *ṭts*, in its second copy of the book, and by the emendation of a second hand: the other manuscripts give here, as do all of them in the other two cases, simply *ṭs*; and the printed text follows their authority.

ङणनेभ्यः कटतैः शषसेषु ॥ ९ ॥

9. After *ṅ*, *ṇ*, and *n* are inserted *k*, *ṭ*, and *t* before *ç*, *sh*, and *s*.

The form of this rule is a little ambiguous, since we might be left by it to query whether, for instance, after *ṅ*, was to be inserted *k* before *ç*, *ṭ* before *sh*, and *t* before *s*, or only *k* before all the three sibilants—in other words, whether the transition-sound should adapt itself to the character of the following or of the preceding letter. The commentator

* Weber (p. 251), by a *lapsus calami*, says "the unaspirated sonant."

either does not notice, or does not deign to relieve, this difficulty; he offers no explanation of the rule, and, in the instances which he cites, the manuscript persistently omits to write the transition-sound. For phonetic reasons, however, it cannot be doubted that the latter is determined by the preceding letter, and that after *ṅ* is to be uttered a *k*, after *ṇ* a *ṭ*, and after *n* a *t*, before all the sibilants. By no means all the cases, however, which the rule theoretically contemplates, are found actually to occur in practice. The guttural nasal, *ṅ*, precedes *s* six times in the Atharvan (iv. 11. 6. vi. 51. 1. xiii. 1. 56; 2. 3; 3. 16. xviii. 1. 26), but is never found before *ç* or *sh*: the manuscripts do not in a single instance write the transitional *k*, nor have we introduced it in the published text. The lingual nasal, *ṇ*, never occurs as a final, except before *v*, in the cases treated of in rule iv. 99. The case of *n* before *ç* is provided for by rules 10 and 17, below; *n* before *sh* is found three times in our text (viii. 9. 17. xiii. 1. 4; 3. 6), and nowhere do the manuscripts write a *t* between them (it is done by the edition, however, in the last two cases); *n* before *s* occurs times innumerable, and the usage of the manuscripts with respect to the *sandhi* is exceedingly irregular; there is hardly an instance in which they all agree together either to reject the *t* or to insert it, nor is any one of them consistent with itself in its practice. In the edition, therefore, we have followed the authority of the Prâtiçâkhya, and the *sandhi* is always made *nts* (except in one instance, viii. 5. 16, where the *t* has been omitted by an oversight).

The insertion of these *tenues* after the nasals is a purely physical phenomenon, and one which is very natural, and liable to occur in any one's pronunciation. There is to be made, in each case, a double transition in utterance: from the sonant nasal to the surd oral emission, and from the close to the partially open position of the organs. If, then, the former is made an instant earlier than the latter, if the nasal resonance is stopped just before, instead of exactly at the same time with, the transfer of the organs to the position of the sibilant, a *tenuis* of the same position with the nasal becomes audible. It is, as already remarked under i. 99, the counterpart of the nasal *yama*, asserted by the Hindu phonetists to be heard between a mute and following nasal. It is also closely analogous with the conversion of *nç* into *ñch*, as will be pointed out below (under rule 17).

The commentator, by way of examples of the combinations taught in the rule, puts *pratyaṅ* and *gaṇ* before *çete*, *shaṇḍe*, and *sâye* respectively (the MS., as already noted, always failing to write the transition-sound), and then quotes from the text two actual cases: viz. *shaḍ âhuḥ çîtân shaḍ u mâsaḥ* (viii. 9. 17), and *tânt satyâujâḥ* (iv. 36. 1).

The Rik Pr. does not itself teach these euphonic insertions, but merely records it as the opinion of some authorities (iv. 6, r. 16, 17, cccxxv, cccxxvi) that *k* is inserted after *ṅ* before a sibilant, and *t* after *n* before *s*. The Vâj. Pr. so far agrees with our treatise as to prescribe (iv. 14) the insertion of *k* after *ṅ* and *t* after *n*, before *s*, adding (iv. 15) that Dâlbhya is of the contrary opinion. The Taitt. Pr. (v. 32, 33) inserts *k* after *ṅ*, and *t* after *n*, before both *s* and *sh*, and so precisely accords with our own rule, only omitting such cases as are unnecessarily and vainly provided for in the latter.

नकारस्य शकारे ञकारः ॥ १० ॥

10. Before *ç*, *n* becomes *ñ*.

This rule is incomplete, except as taken in connection with rule 17, below, along with which, accordingly, it will be here treated. The commentator's illustrations are two of those which are given under rule 17, viz. *asmâñ chatrûyatîm abhi* (iii. 1. 3), and *divi shañ chukraḥ* (xviii. 4. 59).

चवर्गीये घोषवति ॥ ११ ॥

11. As also before a sonant palatal.

That is to say, before *j*; since *jh*, as already noticed, never occurs, and *ñ* is never found as initial.

This is another rule as to the observance of which the usage of the Atharvan manuscripts is quite various; and it may almost be said here, as of the insertion of *t* between *n* and *s*, that there is not a passage in which all the codices agree either to make or to neglect the assimilation. We find written in such cases either *anusvâra*, or *ñ*, or *n*; yet the first is notably the most frequent, and in the printed text has been made, in obedience to the authority of the Prâtiçâkhya, the universal usage. It might perhaps have been better, in order to avoid ambiguity, to write the palatal nasal expressly, instead of intimating it by the employment of the nasal sign over the preceding vowel: yet the cases are few in which a final *ñ* so written could be mistaken for one which arises from the assimilation of a final *m*.

The other treatises (R. Pr. iv. 4, r. 9, ccxxviii; V. Pr. iv. 92; T. Pr. v. 24) prescribe the conversion of *n* into *ñ* before any following palatal; and the Rik Pr. and Tâitt. Pr. include the palatal sibilant in the same prescription, their rules thus corresponding to our 10th and 11th together. In the Atharvan, *n* does not occur anywhere before an original *ch*, and *n* before *c* is treated in a later rule (ii. 26). The manuscripts of the Rig-Veda (see Müller, p. lxxxvii) show the same irregularity in their treatment of final *n* before a palatal which has been noted just now as characterizing those of the Atharva-Veda: but the editor does not appear to have attempted to carry out any principle in the readings which he has adopted.

The commentator cites *avapaçyañ janânâm* (i. 33. 2), *tṛṇahâñ janam* (v. 8. 7), *prâthyañ janam iva* (v. 22. 14), and *vidvâñ jâdîn* (xii. 5. 44).

टवर्गीये णकारः ॥ १२ ॥

12. Before a lingual mute, *n* becomes *ṇ*.

As no lingual mute is found at the beginning of any word in the Atharvan, any more than in the other Vedas, this rule is as unnecessary as is the inclusion of *ṇ* along with the other nasals in rule 9 of this chapter, and as is more than one rule or part of a rule in that which is to follow: such specifications are made merely for the sake of a theoretical completeness. None of the other kindred treatises has a corresponding precept.

The commentator fabricates, as illustrations of the rule, *bhavāṇ ḍīyate, mahāṇ ḍīyate.*[1]

तकारस्य शकारलकारयोः परसस्थानः ॥ १३ ॥

13. Before ç and *l*, *t* becomes of like position with those letters respectively.

There is no discordance among the different treatises with regard to the combination of *t* with either *ç* or *l*, although there are differences in the precise mode of statement of the rules. The corresponding precepts are Rik Pr. iv. 4 (r. 10, 11, ccxxix, ccxxx); Vāj. Pr. iv. 12, 93; Tāitt. Pr. v. 22, 25. The *sandhi* of *t* with *ç* is not complete without the addition of rule 17, below, which see.

The commentator cites one instance for each part of the rule, viz.: *ucchishṭe* (p. *ut-çishṭe*) *nāma* (xi. 7. 1), and *ghṛtād ulluptam* (v. 28. 14).

There follows a slight *lacuna* in the manuscript, the copyist heedlessly passing, as we may plausibly conclude, from the *takārasya* of the final repetition of this rule to that of the paraphrase of the next, thus overleaping the latter altogether, so that it has to be restored from its final repetition before rule 15. We may restore as follows, indicating by brackets the portion omitted: *ghṛtād ulluptam: takārasya [çakāralakārayoḥ parasasthānaç caṭavargayoç ca: caṭavargayoç ca takārasya] parasasthāno bhavati.* We have had occasion once before (under i. 64) to note such an omission, and more than one additional instance will appear hereafter. Here, nothing of any consequence is lost.

चटवर्गयोश्च ॥ १४ ॥

14. As also, before palatal and lingual mutes.

One part of this rule, again—viz. that relating to the lingual mutes—is altogether superfluous; and it has no correspondent in any of the other treatises. The assimilation of *t* to a following palatal is taught by them all (see R. Pr. iv. 4, r. 10, 11, ccxxix, ccxxx; V. Pr. iv. 92; T. Pr. v. 22, 23).

For the palatal combination, the commentator instances *uc ca tishṭha* (ii. 6. 2), and *yuñ jāmayaḥ* (xiv. 2. 61); and we may add *bṛhacchandāḥ* (iii. 12. 3). For the lingual combination, he fabricates the examples *agnicit ṭīkate, somasuḍ ḍīyate*: compare those given under the corresponding rule of Pāṇini (viii. 4. 41).

ताभ्यां समानपदे तवर्गीयस्य पूर्वसस्थानः ॥ १५ ॥

15. A dental mute following these in the same word is assimilated to them.

---

[1] *bhavār ḍīyate, mahār ḍīyate.*

This rule, in its extent as given, is an infringement of the limits laid down in i. 1 as those of a Prâtiçâkhya, and also of those laid down in ii. 1 as those of the chapter: and a more notable one, as it concerns in part the very case which is cited in the commentary to i. 1 as an illustration of what it does not belong to a Prâtiçâkhya to treat; the instances here quoted in the commentary for the assimilation of a dental to a preceding lingual—they are *mûḍhâ amitrâḥ* (vi. 67. 2), and *teshâm vo agnimûḍhânâm* (vi. 67. 2)—are precisely analogous with the one there given, and our rule teaches only one out of the series of changes which such a word must undergo, as drawn out in full by the commentator in his exposition. The only practical application of the precept is one which is not recognized, or at least not illustrated, by the commentator; namely, to those cases in which an initial *s* followed by a *t* or *th* is, by later rules (ii. 90 etc.), converted into *sh*: the following dental then becomes by this rule a lingual.

In illustrating the other part of the rule, that which prescribes the assimilation of the dental to a preceding palatal, the commentator first states, *vârttika*-like, the restricted form in which alone it applies—*cavargîyân nakârasya ca*, 'following a palatal mute, a *n* is assimilated'—and cites *yajñena yajñam* (vii. 5. 1), *somâya râjñe* (ii. 13. 2), and *somasya râjñaḥ* (vi. 68. 1). He might have added *yâcñyâya kṛṇute** (xii. 4. 30), the only instance in the Atharvan of a like assimilation after *c*.

The other treatises, combining the practical part of this rule with the one next following, teach that *t* and *th* are everywhere converted into *ṭ* and *ṭh* after *sh* (see R. Pr. v. 3, r. 11, cccxxviii; V. Pr. iii. 78; T. Pr. vii. 13, 14).

षकारान्नानापदे ऽपि ॥ १६ ॥

16. And even in a different word, after *sh*.

That is to say, a dental following *sh* is assimilated to it, and becomes lingual, not only when both letters occur within the same word, but also when the *sh* is final, and the dental the initial of an independent word. The commentary cites cases of the assimilation in the same and in separate words—viz. *shashṭiḥ* (e. g. v. 15. 6) and *shaṇṇavatiḥ*—but the former belongs under the preceding rule, and the other is such a case as never occurs in the Atharvan. The precept was evidently only intended for such combinations as *bahish ṭe* (i. 3. 1), in which, by the rules contained in the fourth section of this chapter, an original final *s* becomes lingualized, and the following *t* is assimilated to it.

The corresponding rules of the other Prâtiçâkhyas have been already referred to.

तवर्गीयाच्छकारः शकारस्य ॥ १७ ॥

17. After a dental mute, *ç* becomes *ch*.

This rule, taken in connection with rules 10 and 13, above, deter-

* The reading of the printed text, *yâñyâya*, is an error of the press.

mines the form to be assumed by the combinations *t + ç* and *n + ç*. Exception may fairly be taken, however, to the method in which the change is taught. By the other rules referred to, *t* and *n* are to become *c* and *ñ* before *ç*: and if those rules are first applied, there will be no dental mutes for *ç* to follow; while, if the present rule be first applied, the others are rendered wholly or in part superfluous, by the non-occurrence of *ç* after *t* and *n*. In the case of *t* there comes in the still farther difficulty that rule 6 of this chapter has converted it into *th*, so that a part of rule 13 is thereby also rendered incapable of application. These are incongruencies such as the authors of the Prātiçākhyas are very seldom guilty of. What is the intention of our treatise is, indeed, sufficiently clear: the combination of *t* and *ç* is to produce *cch*, by the conversion of the former into *c* and the latter into *ch*; and the combination of *n* and *ç*, in like manner, is to produce *ñch*. The Rik Pr. (iv. 4, 5, r. 9, 11, 12, ccxxviii, ccxxx, ccxxxi) teaches the same changes, only adding (r. 13, ccxxxii), that Çākalya would read instead *cç* and *ñç*. The Vāj. Pr. (iv. 93, 94) also agrees, only exempting the *ç* from conversion into *ch* when it is followed by a mute. The Tāitt. Pr. prescribes (v. 22, 24) the change of *t* and *n* into *c* and *ñ* before *ç*, and (v. 34, 35) the conversion of *ç* into *ch* when preceded by any mute excepting *m*, Vālmīki (v. 36) also excepting *p*, and Pāushkarasādi (v. 37) denying the conversion when *ç* is followed by a consonant, and denying in this case also the conversion of the preceding *n* into *ñ*.*

The commentator cites examples only of the combination of *n* and *ç*; they are *devāñ chlokaḥ* (xviii. 1. 33), *asmāñ chatrūyatām abhi* (iii. 1. 3), and *divi ṣhañ chukraḥ* (xviii. 4. 59): as an example illustrative of the other part of the rule, we may take *ārāc charavyāḥ* (i. 19. 1). In the orthography of this class of combinations, we have followed in the printed text the authority of the manuscripts, which, with hardly an exception, write simply *ch*, instead of *cch*. This orthography is also, to my apprehension, a truer representation of the actual phonetic result of combining *t* with *ç*. That these sounds fuse together into a *ch* is very strong evidence that the utterance of the Sanskrit surd palatals did not differ materially from that of our *ch* (in *church* etc.); and I conceive that the constant duplication of the *ch* and *jh* (wherever the latter occurs) between two vowels is to be looked upon simply as an indication of the heaviness of those consonants, and of their effect to make the preceding vowel long by position. The *c* and *j*, though strictly compound sounds, are too easy combinations to occasion position: in this respect they resemble the aspirate mutes, which are likewise really double in their nature: but they are too heavy to bear the farther addition of even so light an element as the aspiration without acquiring the quantity and phonetic value of double letters.

The conversion of *nç* into *ñch*, on the supposition of the compound nature of the palatal, as made up of a mute and a sibilant element, would be almost precisely analogous with that of *ns* into *nts*, as taught in rule 9, above, and would be readily and simply explainable as a phonetic process.

---

* Pāushkarasādi would read neither *pāpīyāñ chreyase* nor even *pāpīyāñ çreyase*, but *pāpīyān çreyase*; this is misunderstood by Weber (p. 238).

लोप उदः स्थास्तम्भोः सकारस्य ॥ १८ ॥

18. After the preposition *ud*, the *s* of the roots *sthâ* and *stambh* is dropped.

The commentary cites the only cases from the root *sthâ*, occurring in the Atharvan text, to which the rule properly applies; viz. *sá ghoshấ ut thuḥ* (vii. 52. 2), *tatas tvo 't thâpayâmasi* (x. 1. 29), and *ut thâpaya sîdataḥ* (xii. 3. 30); in each instance, the *pada*-text reads the *s*, leaving the irregular and mutilated *sandhi* for the *sanhitâ* to make. Wherever, however, the preposition receives the accent, and enters into a more intimate combination with the root, as in the participle *útthita*, the *pada*-text (by iv. 62) does not separate the compound, or restore the original *s*, but reads the same form which appears in *sanhitâ*. Of this kind is also the only example of the root *stambh* combined with the preposition *ud* which our text presents, viz. *satyeno 'ttabhitâ* (xiv. 1. 1), where the *pada* reads *úttabhitâ*, and not *út-stabhitâ*: the passage is cited by the commentator.

The Vâj. Pr. (iv. 95) notices the loss of *s* from the root *stambh*, but, as Weber remarks with surprise, omits all mention of *sthâ*. The Tâitt. Pr. (v. 14) includes these cases in a more general rule, that *s* is dropped when preceded by *ud* and followed by a consonant.

रेफस्य रेफे ॥ १९ ॥

19. *R* is dropped before *r*.

The corresponding rules in the other treatises are Rik Pr. iv. 8 (r. 26, cclvii), Vâj. Pr. iv. 34, Tâitt. Pr. viii. 16.

The *r* which is thus dropped must itself, of course, be the product of euphonic processes taught elsewhere (ii. 42, 43). The protraction of a preceding short vowel when a *r* is thus dropped is prescribed in a later rule (iii. 20).

स्पर्शादुत्तमादनुत्तमस्यानुत्तमे ॥ २० ॥

20. After a nasal, a non-nasal mute is dropped before a non-nasal.

This rule, also, is hardly in place as a part of the Prâtiçâkhya, unless it be meant that in the words to which it applies the non-nasal mute is not to be omitted in the *pada*-text. The most frequent cases occurring under the rule are those of forms of conjugation coming from roots exhibiting a nasal before their final mute, and formed by affixes commencing with a consonant: as, from *indh*, *indhe* instead of *inddhe*, for *indh-te*; from *chind*, *chintam* instead of *chinttam*, for *chind-tam*; from *añj*, *ântam* instead of *ânktam*, for *âñj-tam*; from *yuñj*, *yundhi* instead of *yungdhi*, for *yuñj-dhi*, etc. In all such cases, however, the *pada* manuscripts, as well as the others, omit the intermediate mute, nor is it at all likely that they ought to do otherwise: the rule is one properly of supererogation, yet finding a sufficient excuse in the peculiarity of the mode of utterance which it inculcates, and in the desirability that this should be noticed in the grammatical text-book of the school. Neither of the other known Prâtiçâkhyas teaches the same omission, or even notices it as prescribed by any authority.

The citations of the commentator are *paṅtir atra* (fabricated: no such case in AV.), *pāṅtaṁ chandaḥ* (xii. 3. 10), and *sapatnān me bhañdhi* (x. 3. 13). As counter-examples, to show that the omission takes place only after a nasal and before a non-nasal mute, he instances *tasyā vāyur vatsaḥ* (i. e. *vattsaḥ*: iv. 39. 4), *utso vā tatra* (i. e. *uttso* and *tattra*: vi. 106. 1), *apsarasaḥ sadhamādam madanti* (i. e. *appsarasaḥ*: xiv. 2. 34), and *sudāmā enam apa rudhmaḥ* (i. e. *ruddhmaḥ*: xii. 3. 43).

The Atharvan manuscripts are quite consistent in observing this rule, although there are cases in which one or another of them preserves the mute of which the omission is here directed. In the published text, it is uniformly followed—with, I believe, but one accidental exception, viz. *anuprayuṅktām* (xii. 1. 40): and here, for once, all the manuscripts happen to agree in retaining the *k*.

स्वराद्यवयोः पदान्तयोः ॥२१॥

21. Final *y* and *v*, following a vowel, are dropped.

This rule applies, on the one hand, to the *y* and *v* of the syllables *ay*, *av*, *āy*, *āv* (the latter, however, being excepted by the following rule), into which, by iii. 40, *e*, *o*, *āi*, and *āu* are converted before a vowel; and, on the other hand, to the *y* into which, by ii. 41, *visarjanīya* theoretically passes before an initial vowel. An equivalent rule is found in the Vâj. Pr., at iv. 124. The teachings of the Tâitt. Pr. upon the subject are found at x. 19–23: that treatise is here, as on so many other points, especially liberal in the citation of the opinions of discordant authorities. According to it, *y* and *v* are dropped when preceded by *a* and *ā*; Ukhya, however, maintaining the contrary; Sâṅkṛtya denying the loss of *v*; Mâcâkîya allowing the elision of both when followed by *u* or *o*; Vâtsapra holding that they are not lost altogether, but only imperfectly pronounced. The treatment of final diphthongs and *visarjanīya* by the Rik Pr. does not include the exhibition of a final semivowel which requires to be got rid of, and hence it has no precept corresponding with the one now in question.

The commentator instances *ka āsañ janyāḥ ke varāḥ* (xi. 8. 1), *ushṇena vāya udakene* '*hi* (vi. 68. 1), *asyā ichann agruvāi patim* (vi. 60. 1), *sa u eva mahāyamaḥ* (xiii. 4. 5), and *tā imā āpaḥ* (xv. 15. 7). In these passages, *ke*, *vāyo*, and *agruvāi* are converted into *kay*, *vāyav*, and *agruvāy*, by iii. 40, prior to the elision of the semivowels: while *saḥ*, *tāḥ*, and *imāḥ* are in like manner, by ii. 41, converted into *say*, *tāy*, and *imāy*.

नाकाराद्वकारस्य ॥२२॥

22. But *v* is not dropped after *ā*.

That is to say, final *āv* before a vowel—the result of the change of an original *āu*, by iii. 40—remains *āv*, being subject to no farther change. This rule is uniformly observed in the *saṁhitâ* of the Atharvan, excepting in a couple of cases in book xix, which book the Prâtiçâkhya does not recognize as forming part of the Atharvan text: these are *pádâ ucyete* (xix. 6. 5), and *citrâ imâ vṛshabhâu* (xix. 13. 1). The commentator's examples are *dvâv imâu vâtâu vâtaḥ* (iv. 13. 2), *indravâyû ubhâv iha* (iii. 20. 6), and *ubhâv indrâgnî â bharatâm* (v. 7. 6).

The Vâj. Pr. teaches the loss of the *v* of *âv* as well as of *av* (iv. 124), but adds (iv. 125) that some would retain the *v* excepting when followed by *u*, *o*, and *âu*. The doctrines of the Tâitt. Pr. have been stated in full under the preceding rule. The Rik Pr. (ii. 9, 10, 11, r. 25, 28, 31, cxxix, cxxxii, cxxxv) holds the view referred to by the Vâj. Pr. in its latter rule: *o* and *âu*, according to it, become *av* and *âv* before any other than a labial vowel; before a labial, *a* and *â*.

गविष्टौ गवेषणा इति च ॥ २३ ॥

23. Nor in *gavishṭi* and *gaveshaṇa*.

These are the only words found in the Atharvan in which the diphthong *o* is the final of the first member of a compound before a following vowel, and in such a case, as we might expect, the fuller pronunciation is retained, and the *v* preserved. The commentator cites *ishumantaṁ gavishṭâu* (iv. 24. 5: p. *go-ishṭâu*), and *gaveshaṇaḥ sahamânaḥ* (v. 20. 11: p. *go-eshaṇaḥ*). Other like cases, as *gavâçir* and *gavish*, occur in the twentieth book of the text, but with that book the Prâtiçâkhya has nothing to do.

लेशवृत्तिरधिस्पर्शं शाकटायनस्य ॥ २४ ॥

24. According to Çâkaṭâyana, there takes place in these cases an attenuated utterance of *y* and *v*, as regards the contact.

The commentator gives us no help whatever as regards the interpretation of this difficult rule: he simply paraphrases it, as follows: *leçavṛttir bhavati adhisparçaṁ çâkaṭâyanasya*, and then proceeds to repeat all the illustrative citations given above under rule 21. The other treatises, however, throw a good deal of light upon its meaning. The word *leça*, 'diminution, attenuation, mutilation,' occurs in the same connection in the Tâitt. Pr., in a rule already quoted (under ii. 21), which states that Vâtsapra holds, not the omission, but the *leça*, of final *y* and *v* after *a* and *â*; and the commentary there explains *leça* by *luptavad uccâraṇam*, 'an utterance of them as if they were omitted.' In the Rik Pr., too, *leça* is once found, in the chapter treating of faulty pronunciation (xiv. 5), and is set over against *pîḍanam*—*leçena vâ vacanaṁ pîḍanaṁ vâ*, which Regnier translates "a pronunciation attenuated or pressed (i. e. too forcible)." Pâṇini (viii. 3. 18) attributes to Çâkaṭâyana the same doctrine as regards the pronunciation of final *y* and *v*—*vyor laghuprayatnataraḥ çâkaṭâyanasya*, 'the utterance of *y* and *v*, according to Çâkaṭâyana, is to be made with slighter effort.' Çâkaṭâyana, then, is to be understood as holding, like Vâtsapra, that the final semivowels are not to be omitted altogether, but slightingly and imperfectly uttered, the partial contact (i. 30) which is characteristic of them not being completely made. The citation by the commentator of the whole body of examples belonging to ii. 21 under this rule shows that he regards the latter as referring to all the cases included in the former; and its position after rules 22 and 23 would indicate that it applies to the combinations treated in those rules also. The scholiasts to Pāṇini restrict Çākaṭāyana's doctrine to *y* and *v* when preceded by *bho*, *bhago*, *agho*, and *a*: but the Vāj. Pr. (iv. 120) refers to him as exempting only the word *asāu* from the treatment prescribed for *y* and *v* in every other case—which treatment, however, it does not specify to be attenuation instead of omission.

पुमो मकारस्य स्पर्शे ऽघोषे ऽनूष्मपरे विसर्जनीयो ऽपुंश्चादिषु ॥ २५ ॥

25. The *m* of *pum* becomes *visarjanīya* before a surd mute not followed by a spirant, except in *puṅçca* etc.

This is a rule very hard to get along with. In the first place, it is altogether unnecessary and uncalled for, since, of all the words to which it is intended to apply, but a single one, *puṅçcalī*, is found in the Atharvan text, and that one is written by the *pada*-text precisely as in *saṁhitā*, and so requires no explanation from the Prātiçākhya. But we have noted, and shall have still to note, many cases in which the treatise deals with irregularities of derivation or combination, even though they are not reduced to regularity by the *pada*-text, so that we need not be much surprised to find the formation of *puṅçcalī* taught. Another difficulty is that, instead of simply disposing of the case which the text presents, the treatise gives to the rule a general form of statement, applicable to all possible cases. Yet even this is supported by its usage in several other instances, in which it affects a theoretic completeness suited to a general rather than to a special grammar; and the precise virtual accordance of our rule, with the exception of its last word, *apuṅçcādishu*, with one contained in Pāṇini's grammar (viii. 3. 6), is a sufficient explanation of the form of statement adopted. The addition of the word *apuṅçcādishu* remains the last and the worst difficulty, and I must confess myself unable to give a satisfactory solution of it. The commentator furnishes no help as regards it; his treatment of the whole rule is as follows: he first repeats it, inserting merely the omitted copula *bhavati* after *visarjanīyo*, and gives as illustrations *puṅskāma*, *puṅsputra*, and *puṅçcalī* (e. g. xv. 2. 1: the other words cited, here and hereafter, as already remarked, do not occur in AV.; these are all found, with *puṅskokila*, in the scholia to Pāṇini): he then asks "why does it say 'before a mute?'" and cites in reply *puṁyānam*; farther, "why 'before a surd mute?'" reply, because of *puṁdāna* (*puṁdāsa?* Pāṇ., *puṁdāsa* and *puṁgava*); again, "why 'before one not followed by a spirant?'" reply, because of *puṁkshura* (Pāṇ., *puṁkshīra* and *puṁkshura*); and finally, *apuṅçcādishu iti kim: puṅçcoraḥ*; 'why "excepting in *puṅça* etc.?" because of such cases as *puṅçcora*.' But *puṅçcora*, 'he-thief,' is as regular an instance of the application of the rule as *puṅskâmâ* or *puṅçcalî;* nor does it seem possible to find in *apuṅçcaḍḍishu* itself any form which constitutes an exception to the previous specifications. I can only conjecture that the reading is corrupt, and was corrupt before the commentator set himself at work upon it, and that his explanation was as unintelligible to himself as it is to us. The specification may have been intended for such words as *puṅkhyâna*, which constitutes an actual exception to the rule, and it is cited as such in Böhtlingk's note to Pâṇini viii. 3. 6, as from the Siddhânta-Kâumudî.

It deserves to be remarked that the introduction of the word *visarjanîya* into the next following rule tends strongly to show that the one now under discussion is an interpolation: otherwise the term should be understood in the rules which succeed, by implication from this, and should not require to be again specified.

The conversion of the *m* in *pum* into *visarjanîya* of course includes, by i. 68, the nasalization of the preceding vowel, and also the adaptation of the *visarjanîya* to the following consonant, by ii. 40, 62, etc.

नकारस्य चटतवर्गेष्वघोषेष्वनूष्मपरेषु विसर्जनीयः ॥२६॥

26. *N* becomes *visarjanîya* before surd palatal, lingual, and dental mutes not followed by spirants.

That is to say, virtually, a sibilant is inserted before the mute, of the same class with the latter, and the *n* itself is replaced by the nasalization of the preceding vowel. Here, again, the mention of linguals is superfluous, no cases arising in the text to which this part of the rule should apply. The commentator fabricates his whole series of examples illustrating the application of the rule, viz.: *bhavâṅç cinoti, bhavâṅç châdayati, bhavâṅsh ṭîkate, bhavâṅs tarati, bhavâṅs tatra.* To explain the reason of the specification "surd" contained in the rule, he cites two actual cases, *bṛhan dakshiṇayâ* (vi. 53. 1), and *nâi 'nân namasâ paraḥ* (vii. 7. 1), which show that no such conversion is made before a sonant or nasal mute. But farther, to explain the addition of the restriction "not followed by spirants," he resorts again to fabricated instances, *bhavân tsaru, mahân tsaru:* this time with good reason, since no such cases occur in our text, and the restriction, so far as concerns the Atharva-Veda, is superfluous, and is only inserted, like the specification of the lingual along with the palatal and dental mutes, in order to make the rule theoretically more complete.

The insertion of a sibilant between a final *n* and an initial *c* (as in *parvatâṅç ca*, i. 12. 3) is made in the Atharvan uniformly, without a single exception, and, owing especially to the frequency of the particle *ca* after a nominative or an accusative in *n*, the cases are very numerous: of *n* before *ch* the text affords no example. A like insertion of *s* before *t* (*th* never occurs as initial) is not rare (the text presents sixty-seven cases), but the exceptions—which the treatise notes in rule 30, below—are also tolerably numerous: they are all given in a marginal note farther on.

The doctrine of the Vâj. Pr. on the subject of these insertions corresponds precisely with that of our own treatise; its rules (iii. 133, 134), however, omit the unnecessary mention of the lingual mutes, and restriction to mutes not followed by spirants, although they retain the equally unnecessary mention of *ch* and *th*. The exceptions are given in detail (iii. 142–144); among them are to be found no cases of *n* before an initial *c*. The Tâitt. Pr. gives a general rule (v. 20) for the insertion of the sibilant before *c*, and then (v. 21) rehearses all the cases (seven in number) in which it does not take place. The insertion before *t* is noted in another place (vi. 14), and all the cases of its occurrence (only eighteen in number) are there enumerated. The Rik Pr. (iv. 32 etc.) catalogues all the words before which the sibilant is added, as well before *c* (iv. 32, r. 74, cccxiii), as before *t* (iv. 33, r. 76, cccxv): such words in the Rig-Veda are not very numerous; its usual method of *sandhi* is *ñ-c* and *n-t* simply. The Rik presents, on the other hand, a few cases (five) in which a sibilant, converted to *visarjanîya*, is inserted after *n* before an initial *p* (R. Pr. iv. 34, r. 78, cccxvii, cccxviii).

It is sufficiently evident that this insertion of a sibilant after a final *n* before a surd mute is no proper phonetical process: the combination of the nasal and following non-nasal is perfectly natural and easy without the aid of a transition sound, nor can any physical explanation be given of the thrusting in between them of a sibilant, which only encumbers the conjunction. Some other reason must be sought for the phenomenon; nor is such a reason difficult to discover. The historical rather than phonetical origin of the *r* which is appended (see rule 29, below) to a few accusatives plural in the Vedic language before a vowel has been long since pointed out by Bopp (see his shorter Sanskrit grammar, § 82[b]); and a kindred explanation of the conversion of *ân* into *âñ* before a vowel (see rule 27, below) was added by him in his Comparative Grammar (see the second edition, i. 468, 478, 479). He has refrained from tracing the insertion of a sibilant before *c* and *t* to the same cause, doubtless, because of the numerous instances in which the insertion is made after a word which is not entitled by origin to a final *s*. But nothing is more natural than that an insertion originally organic, but of which the true character was forgotten, and which had come to seem merely euphonic, should considerably extend its sphere of occurrence, and should be by degrees, and more and more, applied to cases to which it did not historically belong. Now a very large majority of the words ending in *n* are accusatives plural and nominatives singular,*

* That I might not seem to speak at random upon this point, I have looked through half of the Atharvan text, or books i–ix, and have noted the character of every word terminating in *n* which is to be found therein. The result is set forth in the following table:

Accusatives plural in	*ân*	520		Vocatives in	*an*	63	
	în	40			*in*	19	82
	ûn	62		Locatives in	*in*	64	
	ṝn	8	630		*an*	14	78
Nominatives singular in	*an*	143		Verbal forms in	*an*	135	
	ân	117	260		*ân*	8	143
Total			890	Total			303

It is thus seen that the forms to which a final *s* originally belongs outnumber the others almost precisely in the proportion of three to one, or constitute three-quarters of the whole number of words ending in *n*.

to both of which cases comparative grammar clearly shows that a final *s* belongs as case-ending; and I can entertain no doubt that the whole phenomenon of the insertion of the sibilant arose from its preservation in these forms, and from the inorganic extension of the same mode of combination, by analogy, to the much smaller classes of vocative, locative, and verbal forms. The same conclusion is favored by the aspect of the phenomenon of the insertion of *s* between *n* and *t*, as it presents itself in the text of the Atharva-Veda. Although the insertion is there made after other forms than those originally entitled to a final *s*, it is rare after such forms in a ratio four times greater than that of the rarity of the forms themselves: that is to say, while these are in number one-third of the others, the insertions after them are only one-twelfth as numerous. And, on the other hand, although the insertion is sometimes omitted after nominatives singular and accusatives plural, it is omitted five times as often, in proportion, after the final *n* of other forms than these. For a detailed and classified statement of all the passages in which the sibilant is either inserted or omitted after a final *n* before an initial *t*, see the appended marginal note.*

आकारोपधस्योपबद्धादीनां स्वरे ॥ २७ ॥

27. The final *n* of *upabaddha* etc., when preceded by *ā* and followed by a vowel, becomes *visarjanīya.*

This process includes two additional steps, taught elsewhere in the

---

* Cases of the *sandhi* with insertion of *s* between *n* and *t*: I. Accusatives plural. 1. in *ān*: i. 8. 4. ii. 12. 7; 25. 4. iii. 2. 5. iv. 19. 4; 22. 1; 36. 3. v. 8. 6. vi. 112. 2. vii. 97. 3. viii. 6. 7. x. 2. 15, 16. xi. 1. 6, 10, 28; 5. 2, 4, 7; 6. 17; 9. 22, 24; 10. 23. xii. 2. 40, 53. xviii. 1. 47; 2. 34; 3. 63; 4. 39, 66. 67. xix. 27. 4 (*ter*); 28. 2; 35. 3, 5; 36. 5; 49. 6; 66. 1. 2. in *īn*: iii. 21. 1. 3. in *ūn*: viii. 6. 8. x. 7. 42. xi. 1. 20. xix. 6. 14. 4. in *ṝn*: iv. 27. 2. II. Nominatives singular. 1. in *an*: vii. 18. 1; 18. 2. xiii. 1. 52, 59. xvii. 10. xviii. 2. 20. 2. in *ān*: ix. 2. 19–24. xii. 1. 18. xiii. 2. 29; 4. 44. xvii. 16. III. Vocatives singular in *an*: v. 22. 5. IV. Locatives singular in *in*: xi. 5. 10. V. Verbal forms in *an*: xix. 19. 10. xx. 135. 6, 7.

Cases of the *sandhi* without insertion of *s*: I. Accusatives plural. 1. in *ān*: vii. 30. 2. 2. in *īn*: xviii. 2. 16, 18. 3. in *ūn*: vii. 54. 2. II. Nominatives singular. 1. in *an*: xiii. 2. 36. xiv. 1. 6. xix. 28. 4. 2. in *ān*: iv. 32. 2. xviii. 2. 32. xx. 128. 14. III. Vocatives singular in *an*: i. 14. 3. vii. 9. 2. IV. Locatives singular in *in*: i. 15. 2; 35. 3. v. 26. 4. vii. 48. 1. x. 6. 17. xiv. 2. 48, 49. V. Verbal forms in *an*: i. 11. 2. iii. 9. 2; 22. 3. iv. 7. 7; 14. 1; 35. 2. x. 10. 24. xi. 5. 2. xiv. 2. 14.

That is, in tabular form:

		with *s*.		without *s*.	
Accusatives plural in	*ān*	40		1	
	īn	1		2	
	ūn	4		1	
	ṝn	1	46	0	4
Nominatives singular in	*an*	6		3	
	ān	10	16	5	8
Total			62		10
Vocatives singular in	*an*		1		2
Locatives singular in	*in*		1		7
Verbal forms in	*an*		3		9
Total			5		18

treatise, before the combination is complete, and the final *saṅhitā* form reached. The conversion of the *n* into *visarjanīya* itself implies, by i. 68, the nasalization of the preceding vowel, so that *upabaddhān* becomes *upabaddhāṅḥ;* then the *visarjanīya*, by ii. 41, becomes *y* before the following vowel: *upabaddhāṅy iha;* and lastly, by ii. 21, the final *y* is rejected, and we obtain *upabaddhāṅ iha*. This seems a cumbrous and artificial process, yet it is in part well-founded and correctly carried out. All the cases in which this loss of a final *n* occurs are accusatives plural or nominatives singular, which originally possessed a final *s* after the *n*, and the loss of the *n* before the sibilant, with accompanying nasalization of the preceding vowel, and then the disappearance of the sibilant itself, as in other cases after *ā* and before a vowel, are unquestionably the cause of the *sandhi* as it finally presents itself. Our treatise, then, by bringing in the *visarjanīya* as a step in the process, and treating of this combination in intimate connection with those related ones which form the subjects of rules 26 and 29, has a decided theoretic advantage over either of the other Prātiçākhyas. The Rik Pr. (iv. 26, r. 68, cclxxxiv) prescribes simply the omission of the final, excepting at the end of a *pāda*, afterwards (iv. 26, 27) specifying the cases in which the omission takes place even at the end of a *pāda*, and finally (iv. 30, 31) those in which it does not take place even within a *pāda* (there are only eleven such cases). The Vāj. Pr. (iii. 141) and the Tāitt. Pr. (ix. 20) come one degree nearer to the method of our treatise, by converting the *n* into *y* before its elision, and both give in detail (V. Pr. iii. 145–149, T. Pr. ix. 23–24) the exceptional cases in which the *n* remains unchanged.

The commentator cites only the first five instances which the text contains, viz.: *upabaddhāṅ iha " vaha* (i. 7. 7), *çūsa itthā mahāṅ asi* (i. 20. 4), *yo asmāṅ abhidāsati* (e. g. i. 19. 3), and *sarvān mac chupathāṅ adhi* (e. g. ii. 7. 1). More than a hundred cases occur in the Atharva-Veda, so that the *gaṇa upabaddhādayaḥ* must have been a tolerably stout one. I add in a marginal note a complete list of the cases, classified.*

To give with the same detail the exceptions to the rule, or the cases in which final *ān* remains unchanged before a vowel, would be quite useless. They are very frequent, by far outnumbering the instances of the loss of the *n*—thus, in the first four books of the text, against thirteen instances of *āṅ* before a vowel, we have forty-one of *ān*, and twelve of these between two *pādas*—and they are found indifferently in all possible situations, so that it is quite impossible to lay down any rule

* I. Accusatives plural: 1. before *a:* i. 19. 3; 21. 2. ii. 7. 1. iii. 8. 6. iv. 19. 5, 7. v. 5. 9; 18. 11; 20. 8. vi. 16. 1, 2; 41. 3; 54. 3; 69. 2; 72. 1; 75. 3; 76. 4; 77. 1; 112. 2; 121. 4; 129. 2. vii. 9. 2; 27. 1; 57. 1; 68. 1; 109. 4. viii. 3. 4, 20; 4. 14; 9. 24. ix. 1. 19; 2. 25; 4. 24. x. 2. 23, 23; 5. 41; 6. 19, 30; 7. 7; 10. 4. xi. 1. 30; 9. 17, 23, 24; 10. 23. xii. 1. 25; 2. 17; 3. 16 (*bis*), 18; 4. 31. xiii. 1. 63; 2. 5, 18, 31. xiv. 1. 43, 56; 2. 5, 10. xviii. 1. 45; 2. 11, 13, 16, 18; 4. 58, 61. xix. 6. 8; 13. 8; 26. 3; 52. 7; 56. 4; 60. 4. xx. 127. 7; 128. 4, 5; 136. 15. 2. before *ā:* ii. 25. 4. vi. 38. 2. xviii. 3. 55. xix. 59. 2. 3. before *i:* i. 7. 7. ii. 27. 5; 31. 1. v. 8. 1; 18. 6; 23. 8. vi. 37. 3. vii. 117. 1. 4. before *u:* iv. 34. 7. vi. 59. 2. viii. 9. 23. ix. 9. 15, 19 (*bis*). x. 8. 14, 14, 15. xii. 3. 10, 40. xviii. 2. 21. 5. before *ṛ:* viii. 8. 7. xviii. 1. 16. 6. before *e:* xi. 1. 4.

II. Nominatives singular: 1. before *a:* i. 20. 4. iii. 16. 5. vii. 91. 1. viii. 5. 22. xiii. 2. 39 (*ter*). xviii. 1. 24. xx. 128. 4, 5. 2. before *i:* vii. 92. 1. viii. 4. 2. 3. before *u:* xviii. 1. 32, 48 (*bis*).

respecting them. The loss of the *n* with nasalization of the vowel is evidently an old-style *sandhi*, going out of use, and no longer appearing except sporadically. It is interesting, as regards this *sandhi* and that taught in the preceding rule—which have both, as explained above, the same historical origin—to note the relations of the Rik and the Atharvan usage to one another and to the practice of the classical Sanskrit. The insertion of the *s*, which has become a necessary proceeding under the modern euphonic rules, is almost universal in the Atharvan, and comparatively rare in the Rik: the conversion of *n* into *anusvâra*, of which the general Sanskrit grammar knows nothing, is only infrequently observed in the Atharvan, while it is made in the Rik with but few exceptions.

वृक्षाँ वनानीति वकारे ॥२८॥

28. In the passage *vṛkshâñ vanâni*, *n* is converted into *visarjanîya* before *v*.

The commentator cites the passage, *vṛkshâñ vanâni sam cara* (vi. 45. 1), which is the only one of its kind in the text. A few such instances, of the loss of *n* before semivowels, with nasalization of the preceding vowel, are found in the Rik and White Yajus, and are noticed in their Prâtiçâkhyas (see R. Pr. iv. 28, r. 68, cclxxxvii, and V. Pr. iii. 135, 136).

The commentary, to explain why the rule does not read simply *vṛkshâñ iti vakâre*, says *uttarapadasya grahaṇam etâvattvârtham: iha mâ bhût: vṛkshân vâto vṛkshân vayâḥ*; 'the citation of *vṛkshân* along with its following word is for the purpose of restricting the action of the rule to this particular case: the conversion is not to be made in the passages *vṛkshân vâtaḥ* and *vṛkshân vayâḥ*.' These counter-examples, however, are fabricated: no such passages occur in the Atharvan. Nor is the citation of *vanâni* in the rule necessary, although excusable enough: a *v* follows *vṛkshân* in no other passage of the text, except in xii. 1. 51, where it is separated from it by an *avasâna*, and so exercises upon it no euphonic influence.

नाम्युपधस्य रेफ ऋतूँरुत्सृजते वशीत्येवमादीनाम् ॥२९॥

29. Preceded by an alterant vowel, *n* becomes *r* in the passages *ṛtûñr ut sṛjate vaçî* etc.

All the vowels except *a* and *â* are called *nâmin*, as tending to produce the *nati*, or conversion, of a following *s* into *sh*. The Rik Pr. (e. g. i. 17, 20) has the same term; see Regnier's note to i. 17 (r. 65, 66): the Vâj. Pr. uses instead *bhâvin*.

The Prâtiçâkhya is to be reprehended here for not treating the cases to which this rule applies in the same manner as those coming under the preceding rules, by prescribing the conversion of *n* into *visarjanîya*, and leaving it for rule 42, below, to change the latter into *r*. In fact, the first two words of the rule are superfluous, and might advantageously be omitted. The origin of this peculiar and rather uncommon *sandhi* is clearly the same with that of those which form the subject of rules 26 and 27. Only nine cases of it occur in the Atharvan: of these, three are cited by the commentary, viz.: *ṛtūṅr ut sṛjate vaçī* (vi. 36. 2), *mo shu paṇīṅr abhi* (v. 11. 7), and *dasyūṅr uta bodhi* (iv. 32. 6); the others are the word *ṛtūn* three times before *a* (vi. 61. 2, 3. vii. 81. 1), and *pitṝn* three times before *u* (xviii. 2. 4, 23; 4. 40).

The Rik Pr. (iv. 29, 30) prescribes the insertion of *r* after *īn* and *ūn* everywhere before a vowel, except at the end of a *pāda* (and once even there), and in a single instance after *ṝn*. The same *sandhi* is also made in half a dozen instances before *y*, *v*, and *h*. The Vāj. Pr. specifies (iii. 140) the few passages in its text where the conversion of *n* to *r* occurs after *ī* and *ū*; and the Tāitt. Pr. (ix. 20) puts the conversion of *ān* to *āṅ* and of *īn* and *ūn* to *īṅr* and *ūṅr* into the same rule together.

न समैरयन्तादीनाम् ॥ ३० ॥

30. Exceptions are the passages *sam āirayan tām* etc.

By the position of this rule, the *gaṇa samāirayantādayas* ought to include exceptions to all the preceding rules, beginning at ii. 26. Since, however, the rules 27–29 apply only to certain specified cases, it is difficult to see the necessity of specifying any exceptions to them, and we cannot help conjecturing that the present precept belongs to rule 26 alone, and should properly come in next after it, as rule 27. The first passage of the *gaṇa*, *sam āirayan tāṅ vy ūrṇuvantu* (i. 11. 2), is the first instance which the text presents of a *n* directly preceding *t* without the interposition of a sibilant, and the commentator goes on to cite the two next succeeding cases of the same character, viz.: *kulapā rājan tām u te* (i. 14. 3), and *asmin tishṭhatu yā* (i. 15. 2): the three happen to be typical examples of the three principal classes of cases—verbal forms, vocatives, and locatives—in which we should not expect to see the sibilant inserted, since the forms did not originally end in a sibilant. For a complete list of the exceptions to rule 26, see the final marginal note to the exposition of that rule.

मकारस्य स्पर्शे परसस्थानः ॥ ३१ ॥

31. *M*, before a mute, becomes of like position with the latter.

The Rik Pr. (iv. 3, r. 6, ccxxv) adds the restriction *visthāne*, 'before a mute of another class,' which is a matter of course, and does not need specification; and both it and the other treatises (V. Pr. iv. 11; T. Pr. v. 27) state distinctly what is implied in our rule by i. 93, that the sound into which the *m* is converted is the nasal of the same class with the following mute. The commentator gives the following instances, writing always an *anusvāra* for the nasal into which the *m* is converted: *saṁ kāçayāmi vahatum* (xiv. 2. 12), *udāgāṅ jīvaḥ* (xiv. 2. 44), *taṅ ḍayamānam* (fabricated: no such case in AV.), *san nas tebhiḥ* (ii. 35. 2), *saṁ tāiḥ paçubhiḥ* (iv. 36. 5), *san nashṭena* (vii. 9. 4), *san tvayā 'dhishṭhimahi* (xiv. 2. 17), and *mā tvā vṛkshaḥ sam bādhishṭa* (xviii. 2. 25). The manuscript reads farther *çāntas tān malā 'ntaḥpade tavarge prakṛtyā: durṇāmnīḥ sarvāḥ.* The beginning of this is probably an additional citation, but, if it be so, it is so corrupted in reading that I am unable to trace it out. The rest is a restriction applied by the commentator himself, *vārttika*-like, to the action of the rule: 'in the interior of a word, *m* remains unchanged before a dental: e. g. *durṇāmnīḥ sarvāḥ* (iv. 17. 5).' It is unnecessary to remark, however, that the Prâtiçâkhya has nothing to do with explaining the *m* of such a word, and that the commentator's emendation of his text is therefore impertinent; it is also bungling, since such a *vārttika*, if constructed at all, should be made to apply, not to a dental only, but to a lingual, in such words as *aryamṇā*.

अन्तःस्थोष्मसु लोपः ॥ ३२ ॥

32. Before semivowels and spirants, it is omitted.

This omission, by i. 67, carries with it the nasalization of the preceding vowel. The commentator's examples are *vṛkshaṁ yad gāvaḥ* (i. 2. 3), *pitaraṁ varuṇam* (i. 3. 3), *saṁrādhayantaḥ sadhurāḥ* (iii. 30. 5), *parā 'dya devā vṛjinaṁ çṛṇantu* (viii. 3. 14), *ny oshataṁ hatam* (viii. 4. 1), *saṁ subhūtyā* (iii. 14. 1), and *bhavasi saṁ samṛddhyā* (xii. 3. 21).

The Rik Pr. (iv. 5, r. 15, ccxxxiv) converts *m* into *anusvāra* before the spirants and *r*, but treats it before *y*, *l*, and *v* (iv. 3, r. 7, ccxxvi) in the same manner as our treatise (rule 35, below) before *l* alone. The Vāj. Pr. (iv. 1, 3, 9) teaches precisely the same doctrine, but refers (iv. 4) to Kāçyapa and Çākaṭāyana as holding that the *m* is dropped. The Tāitt. Pr. (xiii. 2) declares, like our own treatise, the *m* to be lost, but only before the spirants and *r*; before all the other semivowels it converts it (v. 28) into the nasalized semivowel, agreeing in this with the Rik Pr. and Vāj. Pr.; it also notices, however (xiii. 3), the view of the Ath. Pr. as held by some authorities.

ऊष्मस्वेवान्तःपदे ॥ ३३ ॥

33. In the interior of a word, it is omitted before spirants only.

As examples of the loss of *m* in the interior of a word before spirants, the commentary presents the whole list of examples—*dve ca me viṅçatiç ca* etc.—already given above, under i. 27, and repeated under i. 53 and i. 83. As counter-example, we have *patir yaḥ pratikāmyaḥ* (ii. 36. 8) alone. Instances of *m* before *r* in like position would not be hard to give—e. g. *tāmradhūmrāḥ* (x. 2. 11)—but it is found before *l* only in root syllables, as in *malimlucam* (viii. 6. 2), and before *v* only in the case which forms the subject of rule 37, below.

Both this rule and the next concern matters with which the Prâtiçâkhya properly has no concern. Accordingly, the Rik Pr. (iv. 3, r. 7, ccxxvi) disposes of them simply by specifying that *m* is altered before an initial semivowel, excepting *r* (in connection with which, in the later rule, it omits to repeat the specification), and the Tāitt. Pr. says nothing upon the subject. But the Vāj. Pr. (iv. 2) gives a precept which includes both the rule we are treating of and the one which follows it.

नकारस्य च ॥ ३४ ॥

34. As is also *n*.

The commentator's citations to illustrate this rule are those already once given, under i. 64, including the words *parûṅshi*, *yajûṅshi*, and *havîṅshi*, and, to show that *n* is not altered in the interior of a word before semivowels, he farther quotes *tâdî nâmâ 'ni kanyâ* (x. 4. 24). As instance of *n* before *v* within a word, we may take *tanvaḥ* (e. g. i. 1. 1): before *r* and *l* it is found only when final.

The Vâj. Pr. (iv. 2) is the only other treatise which contains a rule corresponding with this.

उभयोर्लकारे लकारो ऽनुनासिकः ॥ ३५ ॥

35. Both *m* and *n*, before *l*, are converted into a nasalized *l*.

The commentator quotes from the text, as instances of *m* before *l*, *tal̃l̃* lokam* (iii. 28. 5), *amĩl̃ lokena* (iii. 29. 3 etc), *pratimâl̃l̃ lokâḥ* (xviii. 4. 5); and, as instances of *n* before *l*, *duryandhîl̃l̃ lohitâsyân* (viii. 6. 12), and *sarvâl̃l̃ lokân* (e. g. iv. 38. 5).

It is perhaps to be regretted that the editors of the published text did not follow this rule of the Prâtiçâkhya with regard to both *m* and *n*. The manuscripts, however, are almost unanimous in reading only a single *l* after an original *m*, with a nasal sign over the preceding vowel (there are but two or three cases, if I recollect aright, of a doubled *l*), and their authority has in this respect been followed. Where an original *n* has disappeared, on the other hand, the manuscripts follow, not without some exceptions, the directions of the Prâtiçâkhya, and we have done the same, also without absolute uniformity.

The three other kindred works (see R. Pr. iv. 3, r. 7, ccxxvi; V. Pr. iv. 9; T. Pr. v. 26, 29) agree with one another, and disagree with our treatise, in converting *m* before all the three semivowels *y*, *l*, and *v* into those semivowels nasalized; as regards the treatment of the *n*, there

---

* The lack of suitable type renders it necessary to represent the *sandhi*, in transcribing the instances, in this imperfect way: properly, no *n* should be written, and the sign of nasality should be set above the first *l* itself. It will have been noticed, also, that (for the same reason) the general method of transcription adopted for the nasal sounds is not in accordance with the theory of the Prâtiçâkhya. The latter knows no *anusvâra*, and nothing intermediate between a nasal mute and a nasalized semivowel or vowel. We ought, then, in our transcription, to write, on the one hand, in every instance a nasal adapted in class to the following mute, as has been done in the examples under ii. 31—only, if we choose, taking the liberty to substitute a dotted *n* and *m* in case of the assimilation of those letters, according to rules ii. 10, 11, 31—and, on the other hand, in cases falling under rules ii. 27, 29, 33, etc., to write a vowel with a nasal sign above it. The distinction made in ordinary usage between the simple dot and the dotted crescent, as nasal signs, is purely arbitrary, founded on nothing in the theory of the Prâtiçâkhya, and having but a scanty and uncertain support from the Atharvan manuscripts: some of the latter occasionally, or even generally, attempt to use the dotted crescent for a nasalized vowel, and the dot for a nasal mute, but for the most part they employ the latter indiscriminately for both classes of cases.

is a universal accordance (compare R. Pr. iv. 4, r. 8, ccxxvii; V. Pr. iv. 13; T. Pr. v. 25, 26).

न समो राजति ॥ ३६ ॥

36. An exception is the *m* of *sam* before the root *râj*.

The only words coming under the action of this rule are *samrâj*, *samrâjñî*, and *sâmrâjya*: verbal forms from the root *râj* with the prefix *sam* are not found in the text. The commentary cites *samrâḍ eko vi râjati* (vi. 36. 3), *samrâjñy edhi çvaçureshu samrâjñy uta devṛshu*: *nanândaḥ samrâjñy edhi samrâjñy uta çvaçrvâḥ* (xiv. 1. 44). The derivative *sâmrâjya* (p. *sâm-râjya*) is found once only (xiv. 1. 43).

The other treatises duly notice the same exceptional case (see R. Pr. iv. 7, r. 23, ccxlii; V. Pr. iv. 5; T. Pr. xiii. 4); the Tâitt. Pr. alone attempting to give the rule a more general form, and declaring *sam* and *sâm* not liable to change when followed by *râ*: it is strange if the treatise do not thus lay itself open to the imputation of an error; our own text, at any rate, has such forms as *saṁrâdhayantaḥ* (iii. 30. 5).

संध्ये च वकारे ॥ ३७ ॥

37. As also, before a *v* which is the result of *sandhi*.

The passage here referred to, and cited by the commentator, is *sam v ânâ 'ha âyum* (vi. 56. 3), where the particle *u*, following *sam*, is converted into *v* by iii. 39. There are two closely analogous cases—*çam v astu*—in the nineteenth book (xix. 10. 7, 9), which this rule is not constructed to cover, since the Atharvan text recognized by our treatise consists only of the first eighteen books of the present Atharva-Veda.

वर्गविपर्यये स्फोटनः पूर्वेण चेद्विरामः ॥ ३८ ॥

38. In case of a combination in the inverted order of the mute-series, there takes place *sphoṭana*, provided the former is a final.

Weber (p. 207) regards *viparyaya* as signifying here simply 'difference,' but it does not seem to me possible to give the word so general and indefinite a meaning, and the whole treatment of the subject by the two Prâtiçâkhyas goes to show, at least by negative evidence, that the cases contemplated by them are only those in which a mute of one series (*varga*) enters into combination with one of a preceding series, so that in the group the natural order of the series appears inverted. The precept of the Vâj. Pr. (iv. 162) is to the effect that it either is or is not an error of pronunciation to utter a guttural after another mute with *sphoṭana*. This is in appearance a narrowing of the sphere of occurrence of the *sphoṭana* to no small extent, as compared with our treatise: but it is almost only in seeming; for, allowing the exception made in the next following rule, there are but two combinations requiring *sphoṭana* to be found in the Atharvan in which a guttural is not the second member, and each is represented by but a single case, and one of the two is in the nineteenth book of the text: they are *pṭh* (*trishṭupchandāḥ*, vi. 48. 3), and *bj* (*trishṭubjagatyāu*, xix. 21. 1). The commentator to the Vāj. Pr. (Weber, p. 266) defines *sphoṭana* to be "the separated utterance of a close combination of consonants" (*piṇḍībhūtasya saṁyogasya pṛthag uccāraṇam*); our commentator gives no such explanation, merely paraphrasing the rule as follows: *vargāṇāṁ viparyaye sphoṭanaḥ sandhyo bhavati: pūrveṇa ced virāmo bhavati*: but the text itself has already (see i. 103) defined *sphoṭana* to be a quarter or an eighth of a short *a*—doubtless a *saṁvṛta a*, or the neutral vowel. There can be no doubt, then, that the *sphoṭana* is that very brief unclosure of the organs which we often, if not ordinarily, allow to take place between two mutes standing in conjunction with one another, and of the former of which we desire to make clearer the pronunciation. In passing from a *t* to a *k*, for instance, while it is possible by an effort to make the release of the *t*-closure and the formation of the *k*-closure so truly simultaneous that nothing whatever shall escape from the mouth during the transfer, it is more natural to let so much breath slip out between as shall render audible the unclosure of the dental position, and so far relieve the imperfect or *abhinihita* utterance of the *t*, rendering it comparatively clear and distinct (*sphuṭa*). This insertion is then properly enough called *sphoṭana*, 'that which makes clear, distinct, or evident:' we have noticed above (under i. 103) that the commentator gives it also another kindred name, *vyañjaka*, 'manifester.' It is, under other circumstances of occurrence, very nearly the same with that release or separation of the passive and active organs of production which the Vāj. Pr. (i. 90) prescribes after the pronunciation of a final mute in the *pada*-text, so that the next word may begin with a new effort. That the Hindu theory allows *sphoṭana* in the combination of the phrase only in case two mutes meet in the inverse order of the *vargas* to which they belong has something of arbitrariness in it, yet is not without foundation; for it may be noted, I think, that it is perceptibly harder to change from a contact farther forward in the mouth to one farther back, than to make a like transfer in the contrary direction, without allowing any intervening escape of breath or sound: and the order of the *vargas* follows the advance in the mouth of the place of formation.

The commentator cites, as instances of the occurrence of *sphoṭana*, *vashaṭkāreṇa* (p. *vashaṭ-kāreṇa*, e. g. v. 26. 12), *avaṭkam* (p. *avaṭ-kam*, ii. 3. 1), *ejatkāḥ* (p. *ejat-kāḥ*, v. 23. 7), *trishṭub gāyatrī* (xviii. 2. 6), and *yad gāyatre* (ix. 10. 1). Of other combinations than these, the text presents *pk* (*anushṭup katham*, viii. 9. 20), *tkh* (e. g. *utkhidan* [p. *ut-khidan*], iv. 11. 10), and *dgh* (e. g. *padghoshāiḥ* [p. *pat-ghoshāiḥ*], v. 21. 8). Whether combinations of the dental nasal with a following guttural mute are to be regarded as coming under the rule, and admitting *sphoṭana*, is rendered at least doubtful by our commentator, who goes on to say: "why does the rule say *pūrveṇa*? because of such cases as *kramān ko asyāḥ* (viii. 9. 10)." It is evident from this that he would understand *pūrva* as equivalent here to *anuttama*, 'not last in a mute-series,' i. e. 'non-nasal.' This seems to me, however, a very forced interpretation, and unsupported by the usage of the word elsewhere, in this or in the other Prâtiçâkhyas. The Vâj. Pr. makes no such exception of the nasals, nor is it noticed in the verse—from the same metrical treatise, doubtless, which has often been found cited above—with which the commentary on the rule closes: *vargâṇâṁ viparîtânâṁ saṁnipâte nibodhata: vyavâyî sphoṭanâkhyas tu yad gâyatre nidarçanam;* 'know ye that in the collocation of the series in their inverted order there takes place an insertion called *sphoṭana: yad gâyatre* is an instance of it.' I am disposed, then, to look upon the exclusion of the nasals from the operation of the rule as a later gloss, foisted in upon the rule itself. There is by no means a lack of reason for making the exception; since the nasals are accompanied throughout their utterance by a free emission of intonated breath through the nose, and are by it made so distinctly audible that there is felt no impulse to give them additional clearness by the insertion of such a sound as *sphoṭana*. If the interpretation of the commentator be rejected, we shall have to add to the list of groups given above as coming under the action of the rule not only *nk*, of which an instance has already been cited, but also *nkh* (e. g. *keçân khâdantaḥ*, v. 10. 3), *ng* (e. g. *vidvân gandharvaḥ*, ii. 1. 2), and *ngh* (e. g. *devân ghṛtavatâ*, iii. 10. 11). To the specification of the rule that the consonant followed by *sphoṭana* must be a final, the commentary brings up the counter-example *reṇor adgâ iva* (i. 27. 3), where the group *dg*, although composed of a dental before a guttural, suffers no such interposition. The term *virâma*, which is used once or twice also in the technical language of the other Prâtiçâkhyas, has the same signification with *avasâna*, and denotes a pause accompanied with a suspension of euphonic influences; such as takes place in the ordinary text only where there is a sign of interpunction, or at the end of a sentence or paragraph, but in the *pada*-text is found after every word, and even between the two separated parts of a compound word.

न टवर्गस्य चवर्गे कालविप्रकर्षस्तत्र भवति तमाहुः कर्षणा इति ॥ ३९ ॥

39. But not in the case of a lingual before a palatal; here there takes place a prolongation of the time: and this they call *karshaṇa*.

That is to say, when a *ṭ* comes before a *c*, or a *ḍ* before a *j* (the only two cases which can occur under the rule), there is no separation of the two consonants by unclosure and reclosure of the organs, but the effect of the contact is merely to lengthen out the time employed in uttering the group: the name applied to this prolongation, *karshaṇa*, '*tractio*, drawing out, extension,' is not elsewhere met with in the grammatical literature. The commentator cites as examples *shaṭ ca 'mâḥ*. (iv. 20. 2), *shaṭ ca me shashṭiç ca* (v. 15. 6), and *shaḍ jâtâ* (viii. 9. 16): they are the only instances of these combinations to be met with in the Atharvan text, except one in the nineteenth book (*shaṭ ca*, xix. 47. 4).

It is easy to see the physical ground of this exception to the rule prescribing *sphoṭana*. The same close relationship with respect to place of utterance which causes the final palatal to pass often into a lingual, instead of reverting to the guttural out of which it originally grew, causes the lingual, in coming before the palatal, to virtually double it only. The transfer of position of the organs is too slight and easy to necessitate the emission of an intervening sound.

This is the last rule in the first section of the second chapter. The manuscripts this time omit to specify the number of rules contained in the section, and adds simply *dvitīyasya prathamaḥ pādaḥ*.

विसर्जनीयस्य परसस्थानो ऽघोषे ॥ ४० ॥

40. *Visarjanīya*, before a surd consonant, becomes of like position with the following sound.

That is to say, applying rule i. 95, it is converted into the spirant (*ūshman*) corresponding in position with the following letter. Thus, before *c* and *ch* it becomes *ç*; before *ṭ* and *ṭh*, *sh*; before *t* and *th*, *s*; before *ç*, *sh*, and *s*, it is changed into each of those letters respectively; before *k* and *kh* it becomes *jihvāmūlīya*, and, before *p* and *ph*, *upadhmānīya*—these last two spirants being, as already noticed, clearly implied in this rule, although nowhere referred to by name as belonging to the scheme of spoken sounds recognized by the treatise. *Visarjanīya* itself, then, would only stand, in *sanhitā*, before a pause. The theory of the Prātiçākhya, however, is not at all the practice of the manuscripts, and the latter, rather than the former, has been followed by us in the printed text. In none of the Atharvan codices is any attempt made to distinguish the *jihvāmūlīya* and *upadhmānīya* from the *visarjanīya*—and, as we cannot but think, with much reason: since the division of this indistinct and indefinite sound into three different kinds of indefiniteness savors strongly of an over-refinement of analysis. Nor do the manuscripts—except in a few sporadic cases, and without any agreement among one another as regards these—convert *visarjanīya* into a sibilant before a sibilant. In the final revision of the edited text, the rule of the Prātiçākhya in this respect was begun to be followed in the interior of a word (see ii. 3. 3, 5; iii. 21. 2; iv. 17. 2), but was soon neglected again, and the text in general shows *visarjanīya* before a sibilant in all situations. The rule that the *visarjanīya* is to be dropped altogether before a sibilant followed by a surd mute—a rule which is laid down by the Rik and Vāj. Prātiçākhyas, and not by our own, but which is rather more usually, although with very numerous and irregularly occurring exceptions, followed in the Atharvan manuscripts—has been uniformly carried out in the edition; although many will doubtless be inclined to think with me that, considering the varying usage of the manuscripts, it would have been better to follow the authority of the Prātiçākhya, and so to avoid the ambiguity occasionally arising from the omission of the final spirant.

The commentator's illustrative citations are as follows: before gutturals (*kavarge*: he prefixes in each case such a specification to his classes of examples), *antaḥkoçam iva* (i. 14. 4); before palatals, *yaç ca dvishan*

(i. 19. 4); before linguals, *vṛkshash ṭîkate* (a fabricated instance: no case of this conversion is to be found in AV.! the same example occurs under Pâṇ. viii. 3. 34); before dentals, *mayas tokebhyaḥ* (i. 13. 2), *avis tokâni* (v. 19. 2), *balhikân vâ parastarâm* (v. 22. 7), *yujas tuje janâḥ* (vi. 33. 1), *yathâ pumas tâyâdaram* (vi. 72. 2), *prâ 'vantu nas tujaye* (vii. 49. 1), *trayastrinçena jagatî* (viii. 9. 20), *makhas tavishyate* (xviii. 1. 23); before labials, *tataḥ pari prajâtena* (vi. 89. 1); before *s*, *vâtabhrajâs stanayan* (i. 12. 1: edition *-jâ stanayan*, and this time with the assent of all the MSS. except E.), *arussrâṇam* (ii. 3. 3: I. *aruḥsrâṇam*, and, in verse 5, I. and H. do.; all the others, in both cases, *arusrâṇam*; pada *aruḥ-srâṇam*), *virratâs sthana* (iii. 8. 5: all the MSS. except H., *virratâḥ sthana*), *ati durgâs srotyâḥ* (x. 1. 16). Instances for *ç* and *sh* are not given.

The Vâj. Pr. (iii. 8, 11) gives as taught by Çâkaṭâyana the doctrines of our treatise—namely, that *visarjanîya* becomes a sibilant before a sibilant, and *jihvâmûlîya* and *upadhmânîya* before gutturals and labials—while it states (iii. 9) that Çâkalya leaves *visarjanîya* unchanged before a sibilant, and itself, not deciding that point, maintains the *visarjanîya* before gutturals and labials. Before palatals and dentals, it prescribes (iii. 6, 7) the conversion into *ç* and *s*: of the hypothetical case of an initial lingual it takes no notice. Before a sibilant followed by a surd mute, it rejects the *visarjanîya* altogether (iii. 12), as already noticed. The Rik Pr. likewise treats at considerable length the changes which our treatise compresses into a single rule. It first (iv. 10, r. 31, 32, ccl, ccli) gives rules which agree in all points with our own, only excepting the case of a mute followed by a sibilant, and, later, that of a sibilant followed by a surd mute, before which (iv. 12, r. 36, cclv) the *visarjanîya* is to be struck out. But it then goes on (iv. 11, r. 33, 34, cclii, ccliii) to permit the retention of the spirant unchanged before gutturals, labials, and unaltered sibilants, and even, finally (iv. 12, r. 38, cclvii), to pronounce this the approved usage before gutturals and labials. The Tâitt. Pr. also (ix. 2, 3) agrees with our treatise, only excepting *ksh*, before which *visarjanîya* is to remain unaltered. It then rehearses the varying opinions of other authorities: Âgniveçya and Vâlmîki (ix. 4) hold that the spirant maintains its identity before gutturals and labials, while others (ix. 5) who allow it in these cases to become *jihvâmûlîya* and *upadhmânîya*, leave it unchanged before sibilants—it being specified, however, that of this number are not Plâkshi and Plâkshâyaṇa. The omission before a sibilant followed by a surd is mentioned (ix. 1) as the doctrine of Kâṇḍamâyana.

The discordance of opinion among the ancient Hindu grammarians as to the treatment of *visarjanîya* before surd letters is thus shown to have been very great, the only point upon which they all agree being its conversion into *s* and *ç* before dentals and palatals—or, more properly, the retention of the original sibilant in the former position, and its conversion into the nearly related palatal sibilant, by assimilation, in the latter. The assimilation to a following sibilant must, it should seem, be regarded as a more primitive mode of pronunciation than the retention of—or, more properly, conversion into—*visarjanîya*, which latter has become exclusively prevalent in the later language. It is possible, too, that the so-called guttural and labial spirants may have had more of the sibilant character than the mere breathing *visarjanîya*, and so have been intermediate steps between the latter and the original sibilant.

स्वरे यकारः ॥ ४१ ॥

41. Before a vowel, *visarjanîya* becomes *y*.

This is an intermediate step to the total disappearance of the spirant, by ii. 21, and it is very hard to say whether the conversion into y is a matter of grammatical theory only, or whether it gives account of an actual process of phonetic transition. The rule is limited by the one which follows it, and then farther by ii. 53, so that all which remains of it is that *visarjanîya* is lost when following *â* and preceding a vowel, and when following *a* and preceding any other vowel than *a*. The commentator's citations, illustrating these two cases, are *yasyâ upastha urv antariksham* (vii. 6. 4: p. *yasyâḥ : upa-sthaḥ*), *madhyandina ud gâyati* (ix. 6. 46), *abhipaçyata eva* (x. 8. 24), and *sa âpaḥ* (not found in AV.: perhaps the reading is corrupt, and *va âpaḥ* [iii. 13. 7] or *na âpaḥ* [xii. 1. 30] is the passage intended).

The Tâitt. Pr. (ix. 10) gives its general rule in a form closely corresponding with that of our own. The Vâj. Pr. (iv. 36) also makes the conversion of the spirant to y before elision, but restricts it formally as well as virtually to the case of a *visarjanîya* preceded by *a* and *â*. The Rik Pr. (ii. 9, 10, r. 24, 27, cxxviii, cxxxi) follows a peculiar method: it assumes no conversion into y, nor does it declare the spirant omitted, but teaches that when the latter is preceded by a long vowel, not subject to conversion into *r*, and followed by a vowel, it becomes *â*; and when in like circumstances but preceded by a short vowel, it becomes *a*.

नाम्युपधस्य रेफः ॥ ४२ ॥

42. If preceded by an alterant vowel, it becomes *r* before a vowel.

The alterant vowels, as already noted (under ii. 20), are the whole series excepting *a* and *â*.

The commentator's citations are *agnir âsînaḥ* (ix. 7. 19), *vâyur amitrâṇâm* (xi. 10. 16), *syâ 'ham manyor ava jyâm iva* (v. 13. 6), and *tâir amitrâḥ* (v. 21. 8).

The other treatises (R. Pr. i. 20, r. 76, lxxvii, and iv. 9, r. 27, ccxlvi; V. Pr. iv. 36; T. Pr. viii. 6) combine into one this rule and the following.

There is here another *lacuna* in the manuscript: immediately upon the citation *tâir amitrâḥ* follow *tasyâ agnir vatsaḥ* and the other illustrations of the conversion of *visarjanîya* preceded by an alterant vowel into *r* before a sonant consonant, and then follow the words *ghoshavati ca*, before the rule *âraḥ* etc. It is evident that the copyist has leaped over the rule *ghoshavati ca*, together with its own paraphrase, the final repetition of the preceding rule, and perhaps some of the illustrative citations belonging to one or both of them. There is no reason whatever to suppose that anything more than this is omitted, or that any rule is lost altogether.

घोषवति च ॥ ४३ ॥

43. As also before a sonant consonant.

The remaining citations of the commentator are *tasyâ agnir vatsaḥ* (iv. 39. 2), *agner bhâgaḥ stha* (x. 5. 7), *arâtîyor bhrâtṛvyasya* (x. 6. 1), and *tâir medino angirasaḥ* (x. 6. 20).

It has been already noticed that the other Prâtiçâkhyas unite this rule with the preceding.

आवः करकस्व वि वराबिभरसर्वनाम्नः ॥ ४४ ॥

44. Also is changed into *r* before a vowel or sonant consonant the *visarjanîya* of *âvaḥ*, *kaḥ*, *akaḥ*, *ca vi vaḥ*, and *abibhaḥ*—except in the case of a pronoun.

In this and the following rules, as far as the 49th inclusive, are treated the words whose final *visarjanîya* represents an original *r*, and not *s*, and in which, accordingly, the *r* is liable to reappear before a sonant initial, even though *a* or *â* precede. The Rik Pr. and Vâj. Pr. deal with this class of words in a somewhat different manner. The former, in the concluding part of its first chapter (i. 20–26) rehearses all the words of which the final spirant is *rephin* or *riphita*, 'liable to pass into *r*,' and then, in a later chapter (iv. 9), prescribes the conversion into *r* of the *riphita visarjanîya* before sonants. The Vâj. Pr. gives a like list (i. 160–168), and a like precept for the alteration (iv. 35). The Tâitt. Pr., like our own treatise, disposes of the whole matter at once (in viii. 8–15). The words of the class are quite differently combined in the different Prâtiçâkhyas, so that any detailed comparison is impracticable: thus, for instance, the words treated in this rule of ours are found scattered through Rik Pr. i. 21, 22, 23, 26, Vâj. Pr. i. 161, 164, 168, and Tâitt. Pr. viii. 8, 9.

The cases to which the rule refers are instanced by the commentator, as follows: *suruco vena âvaḥ: âvar ity âvaḥ* (iv. 1. 1), *sarasvati tam iha dhâtave kaḥ: kar iti kaḥ* (vii. 10. 1), *apaḥ nirṛtyâ akaḥ: akar ity akaḥ* (ii. 25. 1), *antaç ca yonim asataç ca vi vaḥ: var iti vaḥ* (iv. 1. 1), and *yaṁ parihastam abibhar aditiḥ putrakâmyâ* (vi. 81. 3). It will be noticed that the commentator repeats each word to which the rule applies, with *iti* interposed, except in the last case, where the *r* appears in *saṁhitâ*. This is in accordance with the usage of the *pada*-text of the Rig-Veda, but not with that of the Atharvan, which in no single instance* performs *parihâra* of a word ending in a *riphita visarjanîya*; and we must accordingly regard the repetitions as taken from the *krama*-text, which would give such a form to the words in question, as standing at the end of a line. In the case of *vi vaḥ*, we have the preceding word *ca* also extracted, in order to limit the rule to this particular passage, or, as the commentator has it, *[illegible]ârtham* (compare note to ii. 28). The cases

* Excepting in the twentieth book, whose *pada*-text is shown by this and other peculiarities to be merely a putting together of extracts from that of the Rik.

intended to be thus excluded must be such as *vi vo dhamatu* (iii. 2. 2), but they are sufficiently provided against by the final specification of the rule, "when the word is not a pronoun," and I do not see how the citation in the text of both the *ca* and the *vi* can escape the charge of superfluity. As counter-examples, illustrating the necessity of the final specification, the commentator cites *hiraṇyavarṇā ayam yadā vaḥ: va iti vaḥ* (iii. 13. 6), and *yatre 'dam veçayāmi vaḥ* (iii. 13. 7): he does not choose to notice the fact that these cases are also excluded by their lacking a preceding *ca vi;* and he gives no instances of *kaḥ* as a pronoun, as it was his duty to do. All the other treatises distinguish the *kaḥ* whose final is *riphita* by calling it *anudātta*, 'unaccented,' which compels them then farther to specify the cases in which the verbal form *kaḥ* (*kar*) happens to be accented.

The term *sarvanāman*, 'all-name,' used to denote a pronoun, is an ingenious and interesting one: it is not found in either of the other treatises, but is employed by Pāṇini. *Nāman*, 'name,' includes substantives, adjectives, and pronouns; but while the two former, being descriptive of quality, are restricted in their application to certain objects or classes of objects, a pronoun may be used of anything indifferently; it is a title of universal applicability.

द्वार्वारिति ॥ ४५ ॥

45. Also that of *dvāḥ* and *vāḥ*.

The commentator cites *prathamā dvāḥ: dvār iti dvāḥ* (ix. 3. 22), *tasmād vār nāma* (iii. 13. 3), and *divyam ghṛtam vāḥ: vār iti vāḥ* (xviii. 1. 32); repeating, as under the previous rule, the final words of the half-verses, as they would be repeated in the *krama*-text.

अजहातेरहाः ॥ ४६ ॥

46. Also that of *ahāḥ*, except it be from the root *hā*.

An equivalent and, one would think, preferable form for this rule would have been *harater ahāḥ*, '*ahāḥ* when coming from the root *har* (*hṛ*).' The commentator's examples are *indras tān pary ahār dāmnā* (vi. 103. 2, 3), *iha rāshṭram ā 'hāḥ* (xiii. 1. 4: the commentator, or the copyist, omits to add *ahār ity ahāḥ*), and *agnish ṭad ā 'hāḥ* (vii. 53. 3: here is added *ahār ity ahāḥ*, but it is out of place, the word not standing *in pausa;* perhaps the *parihāra* has slipped away from its proper place after the preceding citation to this: but then the word following *ahāḥ* should also have been quoted in the last passage, and it should read *agnish ṭad ā 'hār nirṛteḥ*). As counter-example, to show that *ahāḥ* from the root *hā* forms no exception to the general rule respecting a *visarjanīya*, the commentator cites *ahā arātim* (ii. 10. 7).

एकामन्त्रिते रोद्विवचनान्तस्य ॥ ४७ ॥

47. Also that of the vocative singular of a noun whose dual ends in *rāu*.

The commentator first cites three phrases, of which the first two are not to be found in the Atharvan, and the third belongs under the next following rule—viz. *dhātar dehi, savitar dehi, punar dehi* (xviii. 3. 70: but possibly the three phrases form a single passage together, and are a genuine citation from some other text)—and then adds two genuine and appropriate instances: *bhūme mātar ni dhehi* (xii. 1. 63), and *tvacam etāṁ viçastaḥ: viçastar iti vi-çastaḥ* (ix. 5. 4). He goes on to give counter-examples: first, to show that the conversion into *r* takes place only in a singular vocative, he cites a passage—*dāivyā hotāra ūrdhvam* (v. 27. 9)—containing a plural vocative from a theme of the same character; and second, to show that a vocative of such a theme only is treated in the manner described, he cites the vocative singular of a theme in *as*, which has *sāu* and not *rāu* in the dual, viz. *tavishasya pracetaḥ: praceta iti pracetaḥ* (iv. 32. 5); adding *pracetaḥ sāudvivacanāntam.*

Here, as in more than one other instance, our treatise shows a greater readiness than the others to avail itself of the help of grammatical categories in constructing its rules: all the other Prātiçākhyas laboriously rehearse in detail, one by one, the words which are here disposed of as a class, in one brief rule.

अन्तः पुनः प्रातः सनुतः स्वर्व्ययानाम् ॥ ४८ ॥

48. Also that of *antaḥ, punaḥ, prātaḥ, sanutaḥ,* and *svaḥ,* when indeclinables.

The final specification is intended only for the first and last words of the series, *antaḥ* being possible as nominative singular of *anta*, and *svaḥ* of *sva*. The commentator illustrates as follows: *antardāv juhuta* (vi. 32. 1), *punar māi 'tv indriyam* (vii. 67. 1), *prātar bhagam pūshaṇam* (iii. 16. 1), *sanutar yuyotu* (vii. 92. 1), *svar no 'pa tvā* (ii. 5. 2). As counter-examples, to show the necessity of the specification "when indeclinables," he gives *yo naḥ svo yo araṇaḥ sajātaḥ* (i. 19. 3), *samagraḥ samantaḥ: samagra iti sam-agraḥ: samanto bhūyāsam: samanta iti sam-antaḥ* (vii. 81. 4: the commentator thus gives the *krama*-text for the passage *samagraḥ samanta bhūyāsam*).

The other treatises exclude the noun *ánta* by defining the accent of *antáḥ*, and the Rik Pr. treats *sváḥ* in the same way—a method which renders necessary considerable additional limitation and explanation.

स्वर्षाश्च ॥ ४९ ॥

49. And that of *svaḥ*, also in *svarshāḥ*.

The commentator cites the passage, *çūsham agriyaḥ svarshāḥ* (v. 2. 8). The reason of the word *ca* in the rule, he says, is that the following letter is a surd; and he adds that the spirant becomes *r* only in *saṁhitā*, the *pada* form being *svaḥ-sāḥ*: this last is rather a gratuitous piece of information.

अहर्नपुंसकम् ॥ ५० ॥

50. Also that of *ahaḥ*, when neuter.

14

The examples quoted from the text are *yad aharahar abhigachâmi* (xvi. 7. 11), and *ahar mâ 'ty apiparaḥ* (xvii. 25). As counter-examples, to show that the final is liable to become *r* only when the word is neuter, we have *samaho vartate* (not in AV.), and *dvâdaçâho 'pi* (xi. 7. 12).

The passages in which the other Prâtiçâkhyas take note of this irregular change of *ahas* are Rik Pr. i. 26 (r. 103, civ), Vâj. Pr. i. 168, and Tâitt. Pr. viii. 8, 13.

The next rule furnishes exceptions to this one.

न विभक्तिरूपरात्रिरथंतरेषु ॥५१॥

51. But not before a case-ending, or the words *rûpa*, *râtri*, and *rathaṁtara*.

As examples of *ahaḥ* before case-endings, the commentator gives us *ahobhyâm* and *ahobhiḥ*, but the latter of them (xviii. 1. 55: p. *ahaḥ-bhiḥ*) is the only instance of the kind which the Atharvan text contains. For the compound *ahorâtre* he cites two cases, *ahorâtrâbhyâṁ nakshatrebhyaḥ* (vi. 128. 3), and *ahorâtre idam brûmaḥ* (xi. 6. 5): it is a word of frequent occurrence. For the combinations of *ahas* with following *rûpa* and *rathaṁtara* are quoted *yad aho rûpâṇi dṛçyante*, and *yadâ 'ho rathaṁtaraṁ sâma gîyate*, neither of which passages is to be found in the Atharvan. It is a very suspicious circumstance that a *vârttikâ* to a rule of Pâṇini's (viii. 2. 68) mentions the same three exceptions which our rule gives: and it is very probable that our treatise in this case, as in several others, has constructed its rule so as to include all the cases noted as occurring in general usage; and hence, that the two phrases quoted are not necessarily to be regarded as having constituted a part of the Atharvan text for which the Prâtiçâkhya was composed.

The Rik Pr. (iv. 13, r. 40, cclix) makes exceptions only of *ahobhiḥ* and *ahorâtre*; the Vâj. Pr. (i. 163) excepts cases in which *ahaḥ* is followed by *bh*; the Tâitt. Pr. (viii. 13, 14) teaches the conversion of the final of *ahaḥ* into *r* when it is not the final member of a compound, nor followed by *bhiḥ* or *bhyâm*.

ऊधोऽम्नोभुवसाम् ॥५२॥

52. Nor is the *visarjanîya* of *ûdhaḥ*, *amnaḥ*, and *bhuvaḥ* convertible into *r*.

This rule is utterly idle in our treatise, since no precept has been given which should in any way require or authorise the conversion into *r* of the final of these words. The original form of *ûdhas*, however, is *ûdhar*, as is clearly shown by the comparison of the kindred languages (οὖθαρ, *Euter*, udder), and by its treatment in the Rig-Veda; and the Rik Pr., accordingly (i. 22, r. 97, 98, xcviii, xcix), has to give rules respecting it. Neither of the other treatises takes notice of it or of either of the words here associated with it. All three, however, are noted by Pâṇini (viii. 2. 70, 71), as words which may or may not, in Vedic use, change their final into *r*; and the instance there cited for *bhuvaḥ*, *bhuvo viçveshu bhuvaneshu*, looks as if it were meant to be the same which our commentator gives, viz. *bhuvo viçveshu savaneshu yajñiyaḥ*, and which is not to be found in the Atharvan. The commentator farther cites for *bhuvaḥ* an actual Atharvan passage, *bhuvo vivasvân anvâtatâna* (xviii. 2. 32); but even here it would hardly be necessary to understand the word as having the same meaning as in the mystic trio *bhûr bhuvaḥ svar*, with which the later religious philosophy amuses itself. For *ûdhaḥ* and *amnaḥ*, the examples quoted are *yo asyâ ûdho na veda* (xii. 4. 18), and *ye amnâ jâtân mârayanti* (viii. 6. 19: the only case).

अकारोपधस्योकारो ऽकारे ॥५३॥

53. When preceded by *a*, *visarjanîya* becomes *u*, before a following *a*.

And this *u*, of course, combines with the preceding *a*, so that the *aḥ* becomes *o*, as is directly taught by the other treatises (R. Pr. ii. 12, r. 33, cxxxvii; V. Pr. iv. 42; T. Pr. ix. 7). The instances cited are *paro 'pe 'hy asamṛddhe* (v. 7. 7), and *paro 'pe 'hi manaspâpa* (vi. 45. 1). For the treatment of the following initial *a*, see iii. 53, 54.

This rule is much mutilated by the copyist, both in its first statement (*akâro 'kâre*) and in its final repetition (*akâropadhasyokâre*), so that its true form is only restorable from the commentator's paraphrase, which reads *akâropadhasya visarjanîyasyo 'kâro bhavati: akâre parataḥ.* Evidently the triple recurrence of the syllables *kâra*, *kâro*, *kâre* bothered the copyist's weak head, and he stumbled from the one to the other of them in an utterly helpless manner.

घोषवति च ॥५४॥

54. As also before a sonant consonant.

The commentator's illustrations are *tathâ saptarshayo viduḥ* (iv. 11. 9), *tad vâi brahmavido viduḥ* (x. 8. 43), and *tasyâm naro vapata bîjam asyâm* (xiv. 2. 14).

The corresponding rules of the other treatises are Rik Pr. iv. 8 (r. 25, ccxliv), Vâj. Pr. iv. 41, and Tâitt. Pr. ix. 8.

आकारोपधस्य लोपः ॥५५॥

55. When preceded by *â*, it is dropped.

That is to say, it is so treated in the position defined in the last rule, before a sonant consonant; the case of *âḥ* before a vowel was included in ii. 41, above. The commentator cites *anamîvâ vivakshavaḥ* (ii. 30. 3), *dhîrâ deveshu* (iii. 17. 1), and *ekaçatam tâ janatâ yâ bhûmiḥ* (v. 18. 12), which last passage contains three cases of the application of the rule.

The corresponding rule of the Vâj. Pr. is found at iv. 37, that of the Tâitt. Pr. at ix. 9. The Rik Pr. (iv. 8, r. 24, ccxliii) teaches that the *visarjanîya* (along with its preceding vowel, of course) in such a case passes into *â*—which is a peculiar way of saying the same thing.

शेपहर्षणीं वन्दनेव वृक्षम् ॥५६॥

56. As also in *çepaharshaṇîm* and *vandane 'va vṛksham*.

The commentator cites the two passages: *oshadhîṁ çepaharshaṇîm* (iv. 4. 1: p. *çepaḥ-harshaṇîm*) and *vandane 'va vṛksham* (vii. 115. 2: p. *vandanaḥ-iva*). The former is a striking case of arbitrariness in etymologizing on the part of the authors of the *pada*-text, for there is neither necessity nor plausibility in treating the compound as if made up of *çepas* and *harshaṇa*: the former member is evidently *çepa*, which in the Atharvan is much the more common of the two forms of this word. And as for the other case, of elision of the *visarjanîya* before *iva* and contraction of the two vowels into a diphthong, it is equally surprising to find this one singled out to be so written, from among the many in the text which are to be so read. For the contraction of a final syllable, ending either in an original *s* or *m*, with the following particle of comparison *iva*, so that the two together form but two syllables, is the rule rather than the exception in the Atharva-Veda. Out of 59 instances in the text, in which a final *aḥ* occurs before *iva*, there are only 13 in which the metre shows the *sandhi* to be regular: in 46 cases we are to read *e 'va*; *am iva* is contracted in the same manner 25 times out of 40; *âḥ iva*, only 4 times out of 19; *im iva*, 3 times out of 5; *iḥ iva*, 7 times out of 10; *uḥ iva*, 6 times, or in every instance the text contains; *um iva*, only once out of 3 times: and there are single sporadic cases of a similar elision after the terminations *eḥ*, *âs*, *ân*, *ad*, *ud*, which would pass without notice, as mere irregularities of metre, were it not for their analogy with the others I have mentioned, but which, considering these latter, are worth adverting to, as illustrations of the same general tendency.

एष स व्यञ्जने ॥५७॥

57. As also in *eshaḥ* and *saḥ*, before a consonant.

The instances selected by the commentator are *esha priyaḥ* (ii. 36. 4), and *sa enâṁ mahayatu* (iii. 1. 1).

All the other treatises (R. Pr. ii. 4, r. 11, 12, cxv, cxvi; V. Pr. iii. 15, 16; T. Pr. v. 15) include *syaḥ* in the same rules with *eshaḥ* and *saḥ*: the word, however, nowhere occurs in the Atharvan text.

न सस्पदीष्ट ॥५८॥

58. But not in the passage *sas padishṭa*.

The passage, *adharaḥ sas padishṭa* (vii. 31. 1), is cited by the commentator. It is one which occurs in the Rig-Veda also (iii. 53. 21), and is noticed by its Prâtiçâkhya (iv. 20, r. 58, cclxxvii).

दीर्घायुत्वायादिषु ॥५९॥

59. *Visarjanîya* is also dropped in *dîrghâyutvâya* etc.

Besides the word *dîrghâyutvâya* (e. g. i. 22. 2: p. *dîrghâyu-tvâya*), which is of frequent occurrence in the Atharvan, the commentary cites *atho sahasracaksho tvam* (iv. 20. 5: p. *sahasracaksho iti sahasra-caksho*), and *barhishadah* (xviii. 1. 45, 51: p. *barhi-sadah*). In all these cases, it will be noticed, the *lopa* of the *visarjanîya* is made in the *pada*-text, as well as in *sanhitâ*, as is directed in a later rule (iv. 100). In the two first, there is an actual substitution of the themes *âyu* and *cakshu* for the usual *âyus* and *cakshus*; in the other we are to assume, rather, that the final of *barhis* is lost in making the *sandhi*, and we have a right to be surprised that the *pada*-text does not give us *barhiḥ-sadaḥ*.

Here ends the second section of the second chapter: the signature is: 59: *dvitîyasya dvitîyaḥ pâdaḥ*.

दुर उकारो दाशे परस्य मूर्धन्यः ॥ ६० ॥

60. The *visarjanîya* of *duḥ* becomes *u* before *dâça*, and the following dental is replaced by a lingual.

That is to say, *duḥ* becomes *dû*, and *dâça*, *ḍâça*, making *dûḍâça*. The passage containing the word is cited by the commentator, as follows: *yenâ dûḍâçe asyasi* (i. 13. 1); and he adds *sanhitâyâm ity eva: durdâça iti duḥ-dâçe*; this is the form the word would assume in the *krama*-text: the *pada* reads simply *duḥ-dâçe*. The theme of the word is rather *dûḍâç* than *dûḍâça*.* The commentator says farther: *apara âha: dhânâçadâçadabhyeshu lupyeta upadhâyâç ca dîrghaḥ tavargîyasya ṭavargîya iti: dûḍâçaḥ: dûḍabhaḥ: dûḍhyaḥ: ava dûḍhyo jahi*; 'another says, before *dhâ*, *nâça*, *dâça*, and *dabha*, the *visarjanîya* is dropped, the preceding vowel is lengthened, and a lingual substituted for a dental: thus, *dûḍâçaḥ*, [*dûṇâçaḥ*], *dûḍabhaḥ*, *dûḍhyaḥ*; *ava dûḍhyo jahi* (Rig-Veda i. 94. 9).' Of these words, only the one mentioned in our rule is found in the Atharvan; the others occur in the Rik, and are the subject of a rule of its Prâtiçâkhya (v. 24, r. 55, ccclxxi). A part of them are also noted by the Vâj. Pr. (iii. 41, 42). The Atharvan has *duḥ-naça* (v. 11. 6), but treats it according to the regular methods of combination, making *durṇaça* in *sanhitâ*.

शुनि तकारः ॥ ६१ ॥

61. Before *çun*, it becomes *t*.

This is intended merely as an explanation of the mode of formation of the word *ducchunâ*, which is accordingly to be regarded as passing through the stages *duḥ-çunâ*, *dut-çunâ*, and hence (by ii. 13, 17) *ducchunâ*. Two instances of its occurrence are cited: *duchunâṁ grâmam* (v. 17. 4), and *tad râshṭraṁ hanti duchunâ* (v. 19. 8). As the *pada*-text does not analyze the word, but writes it simply *duchunâ*, this rule is properly superfluous, and we have a right to wonder that it was intro-

* It is quite probable, however, that *dâça* in the rule means, not 'the theme *dâça*,' but 'the root *dâç*.'

duced into our treatise, rather than, with Weber (p. 187, 188) to be surprised that nothing like it is found in the Vâj. Pr.

समासे सकारः कपयोरनन्तःसद्यःश्रेयश्छन्दसाम् ॥ ६२ ॥

62. In a compound, it becomes *s* before *k* and *p*, excepting in the case of *antaḥ*, *sadyaḥ*, *çreyaḥ*, and *chandaḥ*.

The citations given in illustration of the rule are *adhaspadam* (e. g. ii. 7. 2: p. *adhaḥ-padam*), *pibasphâkam* (iv. 7. 3: p. *pibaḥ-phâkam*), *namaskâreṇa* (iv. 39. 9: p. *namaḥ-kâreṇa*), and *yo viçvataspâṇir uta viçvataspṛthaḥ* (xiii. 2. 26: p. *viçvataḥ-pâṇiḥ; viçvataḥ-pṛthaḥ*). With regard to the second of these, I would remark that its treatment by the *pada*-text, and its citation under this rule, seem to depend upon a false etymology, inasmuch as its final member is plainly not *phâka*, but *sphâka*, a word allied with *sphâna* and *sphâti*, repeatedly met with elsewhere: in the combination *pibaḥ-sphâka*, then, the final of the first member has disappeared, according to the rule of the Rik Pr. and Vâj. Pr. (spoken of above, under ii. 40) for the loss of a *visarjanîya* before a sibilant followed by a surd mute. The commentator then cites in full the passages illustrating the exceptions, viz. *antaḥkoçam iva* (i. 14. 4), *antaḥpâtre rerihatîm* (xi. 9. 15), *sadyaḥkrîḥ* (xi. 7. 10), *çreyaḥketaḥ* (v. 20. 10), and *chandaḥpakshe* (viii. 9. 12). Next follows what has the appearance of being another rule, with its commentary: *paraḥparaḥ: para iti cá 'mreḍitasamâse na sakâro bhavati: tvat paraḥparaḥ*; '*paraḥ-paraḥ*: the *visarjanîya* of *paraḥ* also does not become *s* in a compound of repetition: e.g. *tvat paraḥparaḥ* (xii. 3. 39).' This is not, however, regarded by the commentator as a rule, since after it he gives, as final repetition before the next rule, our rule 62, *samâse .... chandasâm*. It is also evidently not to be reckoned as a rule, on account of its interrupting the *anuvṛtti*, or implication by inference from the preceding rule, of *visarjanîyaḥ sakâro bhavati*, which continues to the end of the section. It must be looked upon as a *vârttika*, or secondary limitation by another hand, of the rule under which it is introduced. Respecting the propriety of its introduction, moreover, there may be question. The only other case of the kind occurring in the text is *paruḥparuḥ* (e. g. i. 12. 3), which, as we shall see, is cited by the commentator under rule 80, below: as it ought not to be if it belongs under our present rule. It may be, then, that such cases of repeated words are not regarded as distinctly enough compounded to be entitled to the unqualified name *samâsa*, 'compound.'* They seem, however, to be treated as regular compounds by the other Prâtiçâkhyas, and our own *pada*-text makes no distinction between them and the rest, writing *paruḥ-paruḥ* precisely like *vâta-jâḥ*, for example.

Our manuscripts are not consistent or unanimous in their mode of treatment of the class of compounds to which this rule relates, one or more of them, in several instances, retaining the final *visarjanîya* of the

* The same thing appears from their separate mention in the fourth chapter (iv. 40), as if not included among regular compounds (iv. 9).

first member, instead of changing it into the sibilant: in a single case (*âyushprataraṇaḥ*, iv. 10. 4), they all agree in so doing: we have, however, regarded this coincidence as accidental, and adopted in the published text the reading which the Prâtiçâkhya requires.

Rule ii. 81, below, directs the conversion into *sh*, after an alterant vowel, of the dental sibilants prescribed by this and the following rules of the section.

The other treatises (R. Pr. iv. 14, r. 41, cclx; V. Pr. iii. 29; T. Pr. viii. 23) give the same general precept for the conversion of *visarjanîya* into a sibilant before *k* and *p*, and detail the exceptions in following rules.

निर्दुराविर्हविरसमासे ऽपि ॥ ६३ ॥

63. The *visarjanîya* of *niḥ*, *duḥ*, *âviḥ*, and *haviḥ* becomes *s* before *k* and *p*, even elsewhere than in a compound.

The particle *duḥ* never appears in the Atharvan text except as compounded with other words, but it would seem from this rule that the compounds which it forms are not entitled to the name *samâsa*. The commentator cites as examples *dushkṛtam* (e. g. iv. 25. 4) and *dushpîtam* (not found in AV.; take instead *dushpratigraha* [x. 10. 28], the only like case which the text affords): both are also given in illustration of the corresponding rule of Pâṇini (viii. 3. 41). *Dushkṛt* and *dushkṛta* are the only words in our text in which *duḥ* is followed by *k*. The preposition *niḥ* becomes *nish* before *k* only, and, excepting a single case (*nishkritaḥ*, ii. 34. 1), only in verbal forms and derivatives of the root *kar*: the commentator cites one of them, viz. *kushṭhas tat sarvaṅ nish karat* (v. 4. 10). But it occurs three times before *k* and *p* in the accidental combinations of the phrase (viz. *niḥ kravyâdam*, xii. 2. 16 [B. I. *nish kr°*]; do. xii. 2. 42; *niḥ pṛthivyâḥ*, xvi. 7. 6), and the manuscripts almost without exception read there *niḥ*, which has been adopted in the edition as undoubtedly the true reading. *Âviḥ* occurs only in connection with forms of the root *kar* (sometimes not immediately combined with them): the commentator instances *dvish kṛṇushva rûpâṇi* (e. g. iv. 20. 5), and *dvish kṛṇuta rûpâṇi* (not found in AV.). *Haviḥ* becomes *havish* but once, in the passage *havish kṛṇvantaḥ parivatsarîṇam* (iii. 10. 5), which the commentator cites: it evidently forms here a kind of half-compound with *kar*. For this word the commentator is himself obliged to instance an exception, as follows: *tato 'pa vadati: haviḥ puroḍâçam*; 'from this is to be made the exception *haviḥ puroḍâçam* (xviii. 4. 2).' The rule is evidently not entitled to much credit as a clear and complete statement of the phenomena with which it is intended to deal.

त्रिः ॥ ६४ ॥

64. As is also that of *triḥ*.

The only case in the text coming under the rule is *apâlâm indra trish pûtvî* (xiv. 1. 41): the commentator cites it, and adds also *trish kṛtvâ*, *trish prakārṇa*, not found in the Atharva-Veda. The Rik Pr. treats the same case in iv. 24 (r. 63, cclxxxii).

कुरुकरंकरत्कृणोतुकृतिकृधिष्वकर्णयोः ॥ ६५ ॥

65. As also a *visarjanīya*, except that of *karṇayoḥ*, before *kuru*, *karam*, *karat*, *kṛṇotu*, *kṛti*, and *kṛdhi*.

The cases to which this rule is meant to apply are of very different frequency of occurrence, and the rule itself is of very different degrees of accuracy as concerns the forms mentioned. For *kuru*, the commentator cites *pitṛbhyaç ca namas kuru* (xiv. 2. 20), the only instance in which this rare form (found elsewhere only at xi. 9. 1, and its repetitions in the same hymn) is preceded in the *pada*-text by *visarjanīya*. For *karam* we have cited *subuddhām amutas karam* (xiv. 1. 18): also the only instance. For *karat*, the instance *sammanasas karat* (vii. 94. 1) is given: the text also affords *jangiḍas karat* (xix. 34. 2, 10; 35. 5), and, besides this, only *nish karat* (e. g. ii. 9. 5). Under *kṛṇotu*, the commentator remarks *kṛṇotv ity atra tridhātv 'ti vaktavyam*, 'under *kṛṇotu* it should have been noted that the change occurs only in three cases:' and he proceeds to cite the three cases, viz. *dīrgham āyush kṛṇotu* (vi. 78. 3), *agnish kṛṇotu bheshajam* (vi. 106. 3), and *maṇish kṛṇotu devajāḥ* (x. 6. 31). In all these passages, however, the manuscripts read, without dissent, *visarjanīya* before the *k*, and the edition has followed their authority (except in vi. 106. 3, where, by some oversight, *sh* has been introduced). Other instances in which *kṛṇotu* has an unaltered *visarjanīya* before it are tolerably numerous,* and nowhere among them does a single codex read *s* or *sh*. The next word, *kṛti*, is one which, for a double reason, has no right to a place in the rule: in the first place, it occurs nowhere except in compounds; and secondly, it converts into a sibilant only the preceding *visarjanīya* of *niḥ* and *baviḥ*, and so would be sufficiently provided for by rule 63, even if not adjudged to fall under rule 62. The commentator cites for it *tasya tvam asi nishkṛtiḥ* (v. 5. 4). Finally, *kṛdhi* actually shows a marked tendency to preserve the original final sibilant of the preceding word, and does it in numerous instances:† the commentator cites two of them, viz. *anamitram puras kṛdhi* (vi. 40. 3), and *a 'mam nish kṛdhi pūrusham* (v. 5. 4: this belongs rather under rule 63); the only exception is that noticed in the rule, and cited by the commentator, viz. *mithunaṁ karṇayaḥ kṛdhi* (vi. 141. 2). Besides these, we have, of forms from the root *kar*, *tiras karaḥ* (iv. 20. 7), which the commentator cites under rule 80, below, but which has as good a right to be specially noted in this rule as one or two other of the cases the latter contains. Not much can be said in praise of the way in which the rule is constructed.

The other Prātiçākhyas (R. Pr. iv. 15, r. 43, cclxii; V. Pr. iii. 22, 28, 31; T. Pr. viii. 25, 26) treat these cases in nearly the same way: whether with no greater accuracy, I cannot say.

---

* They are vi. 40. 1, 2; 53. 3; 73. 3; 80. 1; 104. 3. vii. 32. 1; 33. 1; 51. 1; 91. 1. viii. 5. 4. ix. 2. 7; 4. 2. xi. 1. 6. xii. 1. 1, 42.

† They are i. 13. 2; 26. 4; 34. 2. v. 6. 4 (H. I. ḍk). vi. 40. 3; 74. 3; 136. 2. vii. 20. 2; 96. 3. viii. 5. 17. xix. 6. 6.

ततस्परी ब्रह्मपरे ॥ ६६ ॥

66. Also the *visarjanîya* of *tataḥ* before *pari*, when the latter is followed by *brahma*.

The case referred to, and cited by the commentator, is *tatas pari brahmaṇâ* (i. 10. 1). As counter-example, to show that it is only before *brahma* that the change takes place, is quoted *tataḥ pari prajâtena* (vi. 89. 1); one other such case is afforded by the text, but in the nineteenth book (xix. 57. 6). A similar case, in which the suffix *taḥ* becomes *tas* before *pari*, is *sindhutas pari* (iv. 10. 4 and vii. 45. 1); the Prâtiçâkhya takes no notice of it, if it be not intended to be included in the *gaṇa* with which the section concludes (ii. 80).

पञ्चम्याश्चाङ्गेभ्यःपर्यादिवर्जम् ॥ ६७ ॥

67. Also the *visarjanîya* of an ablative before *pari*, except in *angebhyaḥ pari* etc.

The Rik Pr. (iv. 15) and Vâj. Pr. (iii. 80) give the additional specification that the *pari* must be at the end of a *pâda*, or before a pause, and the addition of that restriction to our own rule would have made it accurate, and obviated the necessity of the *gaṇa*. The instances and counter-instances are both tolerably numerous, and are detailed in a marginal note.* The commentator cites, as instances, *kushṭho himavatas pari* (xix. 39. 1), *jâtaḥ himavatas pari* (iv. 9. 9 and v. 4. 2), and *vidyuto jyotishas pari* (iv. 10. 1); and, as counter-instance, the passage heading the *gaṇa*, *prâṇam angebhyaḥ pary âcarantam* (ii. 34. 5). The instance first cited is the only one anywhere to be found, in the text or in the commentary of our treatise, which seems to come from the nineteenth book of the present Atharvan text: but I do not regard its occurrence as by any means to be taken for an evidence that that book constituted a part of the commentator's Atharva-Veda; it is to be explained rather as a slip of his memory in quoting, or as a reading of one of his *kushṭha* hymns, differing from that of our text.

दिवस्पृथिव्यां सचतिवर्जम् ॥ ६८ ॥

68. Also that of *divaḥ* before *pṛthivî*, except when the latter is followed by the root *sac*.

The commentator cites two of the passages to which the rule relates, viz. *divas pṛthivyâ antarikshât samudrât* (ix. 1. 1), and *divas pṛthivîm abhi ye sṛjanti* (iv. 27. 4). The text affords three others, viz. vi. 100. 3;

* Cases of an ablative in *s* before *pari* at the end of a *pâda*: i. 10. 4. iv. 9. 9; 10. 1; 15. 10. v. 4. 2. vi. 111. 3. vii. 38. 1; 53. 7. viii. 4. 5. x. 1. 32. xi. 2. 4. xiv. 2. 44. xix. 39. 1, 5.

Cases of an ablative in *ḥ* before *pari* not at the end of a *pâda*: ii. 34. 5. vi. 126. 2 (*bis*). vii. 64. 1. viii. 9. 4. ix. 4. 16. x. 7. 25. xiii. 1. 26. xix. 3. 1; 35. 4 (*bis*); 44. 8, 9; 45. 9; 57. 6.

128. 2. xix. 3. 1. The only counter-instance is that mentioned in the rule, and given in full by the commentator, viz. *â yanti divaḥ pṛthivîm sacante* (xii. 3. 26).

The Ṛik Pr. (iv. 20, r. 57, cclxxvi) adds the restriction that the conversion into the sibilant occurs only when *divaḥ* begins a *pâda*. This would be correct also, if made a part of our own rule. The other two treatises do not apparently note any such cases as occurring in their texts.

पृष्ठे च ॥ ६९ ॥

69. As also before *pṛshṭha*.

The commentator cites a single case, *divas pṛshṭhe dhâvamânam suparṇam* (xiii. 2. 37). The others are iv. 14. 2. xi. 5. 10. xii. 2. 12. xiii. 4. 1. xviii. 1. 61. To show that only *divaḥ* is subject to this change of its final before *pṛshṭha*, the commentator instances *bhûmyâḥ pṛshṭhe vada* (v. 20. 6).

The original sibilant of *divas* also maintains itself before *p* in two other cases, viz. *divas putrâu* (viii. 7. 20) and *divas payaḥ* (xix. 44. 5). With the latter our treatise has nothing to do: the former it lets fall, apparently, into the *barathrum* of the *gaṇa* which closes the subject and the section (rule 80).

Compare Ṛik Pr. iv. 22 (r. 61, cclxxx), and Vâj. Pr. iii. 23.

यः पतौ गव्यामस्याःपरवर्जम् ॥ ७० ॥

70. Also that of *yaḥ* before *pati*, except when *gavâm* and *asyâḥ* precede.

Nearly all the passages of the text to which the rule relates are cited by the commentator; they are *divyo gandharvo bhuvanasya yas patiḥ* (ii. 2. 1), *mṛḍâd gandharvo bhuvanasya yas patiḥ* (ii. 2. 2), and *dhâtâ vidhâtâ bhuvanasya yas patiḥ* (v. 3. 9): to be added are only *bhavishyad bhuvanasya yas patiḥ* (xiii. 3. 7), and *yâni cakâra bhuvanasya yas patiḥ* (xix. 20. 2). The exceptions are also cited, as follows: *gavâm yaḥ patiḥ* (ix. 4. 17), and *dîrghâyur asyâ yaḥ patiḥ* (xiv. 2. 2). One cannot but think that a better form for the closing restriction of the rule would have been "whenever *bhuvanasya* precedes."

These cases are not distinguished by the Ṛik Pr. and Vâj. Pr. from those coming under our next rule.

षष्ठ्याश्चाशच्याः ॥ ७१ ॥

71. Also the *visarjanîya* of a genitive, excepting that of *çacyâḥ*, becomes *s* before *pati*.

The cases coming under this rule are almost innumerable, and it would be a waste of labor to specify them in full. The commentator cites four, viz. *vâcas patiḥ* (e. g. i. 1. 1), *ushas patiḥ* (xvi. 6. 6), *brahmaṇas patiḥ* (e. g. vi. 4. 1), and *jagatas patiḥ* (vii. 17. 1). The only exception is that which the rule mentions; the commentator cites it: *arâtyâḥ paryâḥ patiḥ* (xiii. 4. 47).

The other treatises bring together all the cases of conversion into a sibilant before *pati*, and give their rules a more empirical form (see R. Pr. iv. 15, r. 42, cclxi; V. Pr. iii. 34; T. Pr. viii. 27).

इडायास्पदे ॥ ७२ ॥

72. Also that of *iḍâyâḥ* before *pada*.

The passage is *iḍâyâs padam* (iii. 10. 6). The commentator gives a counter-instance—*hastinyâḥ padena* (vi. 70. 2)—to show that only the genitive *iḍâyâḥ* undergoes this change before *pada*.

That the rule is not so framed as to include also the closely analogous case *iḍas pade* (vi. 63. 4), the only other one in the text where an original final sibilant is preserved before *pada*, gives reason to suspect that the verse containing it was not in the commentator's Atharvan: a suspicion which is supported by the peculiar mode of occurrence of the verse, at the end of a hymn with the subject of which it has nothing to do. It looks as if it had been thrust in at the end of vi. 63, because in the Rik text (x. 191) it preceded the verses of which vi. 64 is composed.

Compare Rik Pr. iv. 17 (r. 49, cclxviii), and Vâj. Pr. iii. 22, which note both the cases.

पितुः पितरि ॥ ७३ ॥

73. Also that of *pituḥ* before *pitar*.

The commentator cites *yas tâni veda sa pitush pitâ 'sat* (ii. 1. 2), and a similar phrase is found once more in the text (at ix. 9. 15). On the other hand, we have three cases in the eighteenth book (xviii. 2. 49; 3. 46, 59) in which *pituḥ* stands before *pitaraḥ*, and, by the unanimous authority of the manuscripts, maintains its *visarjanîya*. We must suppose either that the Prâtiçâkhya and its commentator overlooked these passages, or that they did not stand in the text contemplated by them, or that they stood there with the reading *pitush pitaraḥ*.

The Rik Pr. notes a similar case at iv. 25 (r. 64, cclxxxiii).

द्योश्च ॥ ७४ ॥

74. As also that of *dyâuḥ*, in the same situation.

The commentator instances *dyâush pitar yâvaya* (vi. 4. 3*), and

---

* The manuscripts vary somewhat in their reading of these words, both as regards the sibilant and the accentuation: only I. gives the *sh* which the Prâtiçâkhya requires; the rest have *ḥ*. Hp. and I. accent *dyâ'ush*, the others *dy'âush*. There can be no question that the latter is the true method: the word must be divided into two syllables in reading, and the vocative accent of an initial syllable belongs only to the former of the two: thus, *dí·âush*; which, when written together as a single syllable, becomes, of course, *dy'âush*. One or two other like cases are found in the text.

dyaush pitar nyañcaṁ adharāṅ (not found in AV.). At iii. 9. 1, where the two words occur again in connection, all the MSS. excepting I. and H. give *dyâush*, and the edition reads the same. At iii. 23. 6, every codex presents *dyâuḥ*, which was accordingly received into the edited text: and the same reading was adopted at viii. 7. 2, where the same line occurs again, although two of the MSS. (W. and I.) there have *dyâush*. It might have been better, considering the discordance of the manuscripts, and the consequent inferior weight of their authority, to allow the Prâtiçâkhya to determine the reading of all these passages.

Like cases occurring in the Rik and Vâjasaneyi are treated in their Prâtiçâkhyas (R. Pr. iv. 23, 24; V. Pr. iii. 33).

आयुः प्रथमे ॥ ७५ ॥

75. Also that of *âyuḥ* before *prathama*.

The passage is cited by the commentator: *âyush prathamam prajâm posham* (iv. 39. 2, 4, 6, 8), but, in every case of its occurrence, the manuscripts read without dissent *âyuḥ*. The edition, however, has in this instance followed the authority of the Prâtiçâkhya.

प्रे मुषिजीव्यपरे ॥ ७६ ॥

76. As also before *pra*, when followed by the roots *mush* or *jîv*.

The two passages to which the rule relates are *mâ na âyush pra moshîḥ* (viii. 2. 17), and *dîrgham âyush pra jîvase* (xviii. 2. 8). In both passages, however, all the manuscripts read *âyuḥ*—as does our own commentary, in citing them—and the printed text does the same. As counter-example, the commentator brings forward *jîvâtum âyuḥ pra tira* (xii. 2. 45); other cases are viii. 2. 2 (where P. reads *âyush* both times) and xix. 32. 3.

परिधिः पताती ॥ ७७ ॥

77. Also that of *paridhiḥ* before *patâti*.

The passage is *yathâ so asya paridhish patâti* (v. 29. 2, 3), and the manuscripts are unanimous in supporting the reading prescribed by the Prâtiçâkhya.

निवतस्पृणाती ॥ ७८ ॥

78. Also that of *nivataḥ* before *pṛṇâti*.

That is, in the passage *yâ viçvâ nivatas pṛṇâti* (vi. 22. 3), as is read by all the MSS.

मनस्पापे ॥ ७९ ॥

79. Also that of *manaḥ* before *pâpa*.

The commentary cites the passage: *paro 'pe 'hi manaspâpa* (vi. 45. 1). The *pada*-text regards *manaspâpa* as a compound, writing it *manaḥ-pâpa*. Its separate mention by the Prâtiçâkhya would seem to indicate that the latter regards the two words as independent; since, as a compound, it would fall under rule 62, and would need no special notice. The accentuation does not help to settle the question, and the sense is nearly as good one way as the other.

रायस्पोषादिषु च ॥ ८० ॥

80. Also that in *râyasposha* etc.

Under this rule, the commentator instances only three cases, viz. *râyas posham* (e. g. i. 9. 4), *parush paruḥ* (e. g. i. 12. 3), and *mâ piçâcañ tiras karaḥ* (iv. 20. 7): the latter has been already remarked upon, as not less entitled to be included in rule 65 than some of the cases to which that rule relates. There are to be found in the text quite a number of other like cases, not provided for in any of the foregoing rules; they are as follows: *divas putrâu* (viii. 7. 20) and *divas payaḥ* (xix. 44. 5), already spoken of under rule 60; *iḍas pade* (vi. 63. 4), referred to under rule 72; *adhamas padîshṭa* (viii. 4. 16: see R. Pr. iv. 20); *dvishatas pâdayâmi* (xi. 1. 12, 21); *apas putrâsaḥ* (xii. 3. 4) and *mahas putrâsaḥ* (xviii. 1. 2), of which the latter is a Rik passage, and noted in its Prâtiçâkhya (iv. 21); *rajas pṛthu* (xiii. 2. 28: see R. Pr. iv. 19); and *çiras kṛtam* (xiii. 4. 40). In all these passages, the testimony of the manuscripts is unanimous in favor of the sibilant: in iv. 34. 8, a part of them (P. M. W. E.) read *dhenush kâmadughâ;* and in more than one instance elsewhere, one or two manuscripts give a *s* or *sh*, instead of *visarjanîya*, before an initial *p* or *k*. Unfortunately, it is impossible to tell what is the teaching of the Prâtiçâkhya with regard to any such cases; we do not even know how accurately it or its commentators had noticed and noted the instances which their text contained. There is no apparent reason why the single cases noted in rules 66, 72, 77, 78, 79 should not have been left to go into the *gaṇa*, if a *gaṇa* was to be established, and neither the accuracy nor the method of the treatise, in dealing with this class of phenomena, is worthy of unqualified commendation.

The eightieth rule ends the section, of which the signature is: 80: *dvitîyasya tṛtîyaḥ pâdaḥ*.

अत्र नाम्युपधस्य षकारः ॥ ८१ ॥

81. In all these cases, *s* becomes *sh*, when preceded by an alterant vowel.

The commentator says: *yad etat: samâse sakâraḥ kapayor ananta ity anukrântaḥ: atra nâmyupadhasya sakârasya shakâro bhavati: etâny eva 'dâharaṇâni: nâmyupadhasye 'ti drashṭavyam: ita uttaraṁ yad anukramishyâmaḥ;* 'the meaning is that, from the rule "In a compound" etc. [ii. 62] onward, in every case, a *s* preceded by an alterant vowel becomes *sh:* the illustrative instances are those already given:

the specification "when preceded by an alterant vowel" continues in force, as we go on farther from this point.' That is to say, the action of the present rule is retrospective as well as prospective, and extends to all the cases in which the conversion of *visarjanîya* to *s* takes place according to the rules of the preceding section, as also to the cases which are now farther to be specified; and that, whether the *s* to which the rules relate is original, or comes from *visarjanîya* by rule ii. 40 etc. The subject of this whole section is the *nati* of the dental sibilant, or its conversion into the lingual, *sh*. The same phenomenon is treated in Rik Pr. v. 1–19, Vâj. Pr. iii. 53–82, and Tâitt. Pr. vi. 1–14. The grouping of the cases is so different in the different treatises that any detailed comparison of rule with rule is only occasionally and partially practicable.

सहेः साड्भूतस्य ॥ ८२ ॥

82. Also in the root *sah*, when it takes the form *sâṭ*.

The commentator cites, as cases coming under this rule, *turâshâṭ* (ii. 5. 3), *ṛtâshâṭ* (not in AV.), *pṛtanâshâṭ* (e. g. v. 14. 8), *çatrûshâṇ nîshâṭ* (v. 20. 11), *abhîshâḍ asmi viçvâshâṭ* (xii. 1. 54). As counter-example, to show that it is only when *sah* becomes *sâṭ* that the change of sibilant takes place, he instances *prasahanam*, which is not found in our text. That *sâḍbhûta* means 'when it becomes *sâṭ*,' and not 'when it becomes *sâh*,' appears from the instances *amitrasâha* and *satrâsâha* (see under iii. 23), in which, although the vowel of the root is lengthened, the sibilant remains unaltered. If *ashâḍha* occurred in any earlier book than the nineteenth (it is found only at xix. 7. 4), the rule would have to be altered, or else *sâḍ* in *sâḍbhûta* would have to be understood as meaning both *sâḍ* (*sâṭ*) and *sâḍh*. There is no real necessity for any such rule as this, since all the words to which the commentary regards it as relating have precisely the same form in *pada* as in *saṁhitâ*. But there is a graver objection to the rule than its dispensability: it is quite out of place where it stands. In the first place, it treats of an initial *s*, while the treatise otherwise puts off such cases until after all those of a final *s* are disposed of; and, much worse, it interrupts the *anuvṛtti* of *nâmyupadhasya*, which must necessarily take place from rule 81 to those that follow; since, in the majority of the cases which it concerns, the sibilant is preceded by long *â*. Either there is here an unusual degree of awkwardness and inconsistency of method on the part of the author of the treatise, or the rule is an interpolation.

The later rules iii. 1 and iv. 70, which deal with the same irregularly formed words from different aspects, are to be compared.

तद्धिते तकारादौ ॥ ८३ ॥

83. Also before a *taddhita*-suffix beginning with *t*.

As instances, the commentator first gives *sarpishṭaram*, *yajushṭaram*, *vapushṭaram*—not one of which words occurs in the Atharvan, while the first two are found as examples under the corresponding rule of

Pâṇini (viii. 3. 101)—and then *vapushṭamam* (*vapushṭame*, p. *vapuḥ·tame*, v. 5. 6: I have noted no other similar case in the text). As counter-example, to show the necessity of the restriction "before a *taddhita*-suffix," he cites *agnis takmânam* (v. 22. 1); to show that of "beginning with *t*," he gives *sarpishâ, yajushâ, vapushâ*, which are not in the Atharvan, while the first of them, again, is an example under Pâṇini's rule just referred to.

The corresponding rule of the Rik Pr. is at v. 16 (r. 31, ccclviii), and Tâitt. Pr. vi. 5 includes one or two similar cases. Neither, however, gives a grammatical definition of the phenomenon, like that of our treatise.

युष्मदादेशे तेस्त्वमादिवर्जम् ॥ ८४ ॥

84. Also before forms of the second personal pronoun, excepting in *tais tvam* etc.

Those forms used as "substitutes for *yushmat*," or as cases of the pronoun of the second person, before which the conversion of final *s* into *sh* takes place in the Atharvan, are *tvam, tvâ*, and *te*: the cases are enumerated below.* The commentator cites, as instances, five of them, viz. *barhish te astu* (i. 3. 1 etc.), *gîrbhish ṭvâ vayam* (i. 35. 4), *dyâush ṭvâ pitâ* (ii. 28. 4), *tâbhish ṭvam asmân* (ix. 2. 25), and *tâish ṭe rohitaḥ* (xiii. 1. 35). As examples from the *gaṇa* of exceptions, he offers *tâis tvam putram* (iii. 23. 4), *vadhris tvam* (iv. 6. 8), and *pravastâis tvâ* (iv. 7. 6). This *gaṇa* I have not thought it worth while to take the trouble to fill up, deeming it of more interest to give the complete list of the cases in which the change of the sibilant did, rather than of those in which it did not, take place. The former are, I believe, the more numerous of the two classes.

तत्तानग्रादिषु च ॥ ८५ ॥

85. Also before *tat, tân agra*, etc.

The forms of the third personal, or demonstrative, pronoun before which a final *s*, after an alterant vowel, is converted into *sh*, are *tam, tat*, and *tân*. The cases, which are not numerous, are detailed below.† The commentator cites four of them, viz. *agnish ṭad dhotâ* (e. g. vi. 71. 1), *agnish ṭân agre* (ii. 34. 3), *vâyush ṭân agre* (ii. 34. 4), and *nish ṭam bhaja*

---

* Before *tvam*: ix. 2. 25. xi. 9. 6. Before *tvâ*: i. 22. 3; 35. 4. ii. 28. 4. iii. 29. 8. v. 26. 3, 12. xiv. 2. 59–62. xviii. 4. 9. xix. 27. 1 (*bis*); 34. 6; 37. 4; 46. 1. Before *te*: i. 3. 1–5. ii. 13. 4; 29. 5. iv. 6. 6. v. 25. 9; 28. 5. vi. 92. 3; 111. 2. vii. 88. 2; 74. 2. viii. 2. 12. ix. 4. 10. x. 9. 2. xii. 1. 18. xiii. 1. 35. xiv. 2. 8. xviii. 4. 9. 15. xx. 133. 2. At iii. 10. 10. all the *saṃhitâ* MSS., without exception, give *gîrbhyash ṭvâ*, which was deemed, however, much too anomalous and unsupported a reading to be received into the edited text.

† Before *tam*: iv. 32. 2. Before *tat*: i. 32. 2. vi. 71. 1, 2. vii. 58. 3. x. 9. 26. xviii. 3. 55. xix. 59. 2. Before *tân*: ii. 34. 3, 4. xviii. 2. 28. There is a single case, moreover, in which all the *saṃhitâ* MSS. read *sh* after *a*: viz. *nash ṭrâbhiḥ*, ii. 35. 2; but this reading has been rejected in the edition, as an evident blunder, apparently growing out of a confusion with the participle *nashṭebhiḥ*.

(iv. 22. 2). He also adds two examples of another class, viz. *dushṭano* (p. *dustano iti duḥ tano:* iv. 7. 3), and *nishṭakvarim* (p. *niḥ-takvarim:* v. 22. 6). The rule must be meant also to include *gobhish ṭarema* (vii. 50. 7). The word *dushṭara* (vi. 4. 1) would seem to come properly under it, but its treatment by the *pada*-texts (it is written *dustara*, not *duḥ-tara*) indicates, I should think, that the Hindus regarded it as an irregular compound of *duḥ* and *stara*, from the root *star* (स्तृ); hence it would fall under the next rule, or else under rule 98.

स्तृतस्वस्वपिषु ॥ ८६ ॥

86. Also before *stṛta*, *sva*, and the root *svap*.

But three cases occur under this rule, one for each of the words mentioned in it: they are *anishṭṛtaḥ* (p. *aniḥ-stṛtaḥ:* vii. 82. 3), *nishva* (p. *niḥ: sva:* vi. 121. 1 and vii. 83. 4), and the frequently occurring *dushvapnyam* (p. *duḥ-svapnyam:* e. g. vi. 46. 3), with which goes its derivative *dâushvapnyam* (p. *dâuḥ-svapnyam:* iv. 17. 5). The commentator cites them all, excepting the last: the second of them he gives in its connection, thus: *duritam nishvâ 'smat*. All these words* have in the edited text been written in a similar manner, with but a single sibilant, as I have here cited them, and as they are given by the commentary in our manuscript. This does not, however, appear to be the way in which the Prâtiçâkhya intends that they should be written, for it prescribes that the final *visarjanîya* or sibilant should be converted into *sh* before the initial *s*; not that there should be a dropping out of either sibilant. Yet the Prâtiçâkhya also is defective as regards its treatment of them; for, while it has directed above (ii. 16) that a dental mute (*tavargîya*) be converted into a lingual after final *sh* in the preceding word, it has given no such rule respecting the dental sibilant. If we follow our treatise, then, implicitly, we shall write *anishstṛtaḥ*, *nish svâ*, *dushsvapnyam*, which are barbarous and impossible forms. The manuscripts write, without dissent, *anishṭṛtaḥ* and *nishva;* as regards *dushvapnya*, their usage is very irregular; they vary with the utmost inconsistency between that form and *duḥshvapnya*, in no single instance writing *dushshvapnya*. While, therefore, we are compelled to look upon *anishshṭṛtaḥ*, *nish shva*, and *dushshvapnyam* as the forms which the Prâtiçâkhya intends to sanction, we cannot but hold the editors justified in following for the two former cases the unanimous authority of the MSS., and in making the third conform to them. To *dushṭara* reference has been made under the preceding rule, as a case akin with these, but differently treated, in that one of the two sibilants has been rejected: on account of this irregularity, doubtless, it is treated as an anomalous case by the *pada*-text, and left undivided.

The Vâj. Pr. (iii. 71) adopts and sanctions the form *duḥshvapnya:* the Rik Pr. (v. 1, r. 1, cccxviii) requires, like our treatise, *dushshvapnya*, although the manuscripts, as noticed by Müller, usually read *dushvapnya*.

* Except in the passage vi. 121. 1, where the edition, by a reprehensible inconsistency, reads *niḥ shva*.

नामिकरेफात्प्रत्ययसकारस्य ॥ ८७ ॥

87. Also the *s* of a suffix, after an alterant vowel, *k*, or *r*.

This rule, like the corresponding one in the Vâj. Pr. (iii. 57), is not precisely in place in a Prâtiçâkhya, which has nothing to do with the processes of derivation in connection with which its application must be made: hence the other two treatises present nothing analogous to it. The commentator illustrates it by citing *phâlâj jâtaḥ karishyati* (x. 6. 2), *iyakshamâṇâ bhṛgubhiḥ* (iv. 14. 5), and *havishâ* " *'hârsham enam* (iii. 11. 3). He explains *ka* in the rule by *kavargât*, 'after a guttural,' probably in view of the requirement of some authorities (see under ii. 6) that the *k* should become *kh* before the sibilant.

स्त्रैषूयम् ॥ ८८ ॥

88. Also that of *strâishûya*.

This word occurs but once in the text, in a passage cited by the commentator: *strâishûyam anyatra* (vi. 11. 3: p. *strâisûyam*). Why, among the words mentioned in iv. 83, it should be singled out to be made thus the subject of a special rule, is not at all clear. The position of the rule, too, thrust in between the two closely related rules 87 and 89, and disturbing their connection, is in a high degree awkward, and calculated to inspire suspicions of an interpolation.

नलोपे ऽपि ॥ ८९ ॥

89. Even when a *n* has been lost.

This rule attaches itself immediately and closely to rule 87, from which it has been blunderingly separated by the intrusion of rule 88. It is intended to apply to such cases as *yajûṅshi*, *havîṅshi*, where, by ii. 34, there has been a loss of *n* before the ending *si*, accompanied, by i. 67, with nasalization of the preceding vowel, when the ending itself is converted into *shi* after the alterant vowel, although the latter is nasal. Among the other treatises, the Vâj. Pr. (iii. 56) alone gives a similar precept. The illustrative citations of the commentator are the same which he has already twice before given, under i. 84 and ii. 34.

उपसर्गाद्धातोः ॥ ९० ॥

90. Also that of a root, after a preposition.

This is a very general precept, and the instances of its application in the text, in forms of conjugation and of derivation, are quite numerous. The commentator selects as illustrations but two: *vṛkshaṁ yad gâvaḥ parishasvajânâ anushphuram* (i. 2. 3: p. *pari-sasvajânâḥ*; *anushphuram* is an exception to the rule, akin with those detailed in rule 102, below), and *vishitaṁ te vastibilam* (i. 3. 8: p. *vi-sitam*). As counter-examples, to show that it is only after a preposition that the initial *s* of a root is regularly converted into *sh*, the commentator fabricates a couple of cases, viz. *dadhi siñcati*, *madhu siñcati*; the former of them appears also among the counter-examples under the corresponding rule of Pāṇini (viii. 3. 65). The proper exceptions to the rule are detailed below, in rules 102–107.

The Tāitt. Pr. (vi. 4) has a general rule like this of our own treatise, for the change of an initial *s* after a preposition: the other two Prātiçākhyas rehearse the cases in detail (see R. Pr. v. 4–10; V. Pr. iii. 58–70).

अभ्यासाच्च ॥ ९१ ॥

91. As also after a reduplication.

The commentator is more than usually liberal in his citations under this rule; he gives us *sushūdata* (i. 26. 4), *abhi sishyade* (v. 5. 9), *ā sushvayanti* (v. 12. 6; 27. 8), *sishāsavaḥ sishāsatha* (vi. 21. 3), *tat sishāsati* (xiii. 2. 14), and *sushuve* (xiv. 1. 43). In all these cases, as in all others of the same kind which the text affords, the *pada*-text gives the dental sibilant unchanged; thus, *susūdata*, *sisyade*, etc.

This class of cases is not treated by itself in the other Prātiçākhyas.

स्थासहिसिचीनामकारव्यवाये ऽपि ॥ ९२ ॥

92. And that of the roots *sthā*, *sah*, and *sic*, even when an *a* is interposed.

There is, owing to the imperfection of our manuscript, a slight doubt as to the precise reading of this rule, the copyist, as in one or two other cases which we have already had occasion to notice, having skipped a line of his original, or from one *kāra* to another and later one, whereby we have lost part of the original statement of the rule and nearly the whole of its paraphrase; the final repetition of the rule before the one following being also slightly defective. I restore the mutilated passages conjecturally as follows, noting within brackets the parts supposed to be omitted: *sthāsahisicīnām akāra*[*vyavāye 'pi: sthāsahisicīnām upasargasthān nimittād akāravyavāye 'pi dhātusakāra*]*sya shakāro bhavati*: ......*sthāsahisicīnām akāravyavā*[*ye*] *'py abhyāsavyavāye 'pi sthaḥ*.

Of the cases to which the rule relates, the commentator instances three; viz. *abhy ashṭhāṁ viçvāḥ* (x. 5. 36 and xvi. 9. 1), *tena devā vy ashahanta* (iii. 10. 12), *yenā 'kshā abhyashicyanta* (xiv. 1. 36). For the root *sthā* the text affords us two other examples, *adhy ashṭhāt* (x. 10. 13) and *adhy ashṭhām* (xii. 1. 11). These are actually all the cases occurring in the Atharvan in which the three roots named in the rule are preceded by prepositions ending in alterant vowels, with interposition of the augment—except the anomalous form *vy āsthan* (xiii. 1. 5), where the irregular initial *ā* is read in *pada* as well as in *saṁhitā*, and which does not come under the present rule, since there is an interposition of *ākāra*, not *akāra*.

Similar cases are noted by the other treatises (see V. Pr. iii. 64; T. Pr. vi. 3).

अभ्यासव्यवायेऽपि स्थः ॥ ९३ ॥

93. And that of the root *sthâ*, even when the reduplication is interposed.

Two cases are cited by the commentator under this rule, viz. *sapta sindhavo vitashṭhire* (iv. 6. 2), and *brahma pururûpam vi tashṭhe* (ix. 10. 19). In the latter passage, the edition gives erroneously *vi tasthe:* two of the manuscripts (W. and E.) read *vi cashṭe;* the others have, correctly, *vi tashṭhe* (or, by a carelessness very common in the codices, *vi tashṭe:* E., for instance, never distinguishes *shṭh* and *shṭ* from one another): the *pada*-text presents *vi : tasthe.* We have in two other passages (ix. 9. 2. xiv. 2. 9) *adhi tasthuḥ* (not *tashṭhuḥ*); this apparently constitutes an exception to the rule which has escaped the notice both of the treatise and of the commentator: possibly, however, the *adhi* is not in these passages regarded as standing in the relation of *upasarga* to the root *sthâ*, since it does, in fact, belong rather, in a prepositional relation, to preceding ablative cases, than to the verbal form as its prefix: and this is the more clearly indicated by its retaining its independent accent before the accented verb.

परमेभ्योऽनापाके ॥ ९४ ॥

94. As also after *parama* etc.; but not after *âpâka.*

The commentator's explanatory paraphrase is as follows: *paramâdibhyaḥ pûrvapadebhyaḥ anâpâke uttarapadasthasya sakârasya shakâro bhavati;* 'after *parama* etc., as former members of a compound, excepting *âpâke*, the *s* of the second members of the compound becomes *sh.*' This does not, in terms, restrict the rule to cases of the root *sthâ* in composition, implying an *anuvṛtti* of *sthaḥ* from the preceding rule: yet we can hardly doubt that it is properly to be so restricted, and the commentator himself gives examples only from the root *sthâ:* they are *parameshṭhî* (e. g. iv. 11. 7: p. *parame-sthî*), *bhuvaneshṭhâḥ* (ii. 1. 4: p. *bhuvane-sthâḥ*), *madhyameshṭhâḥ* (ii. 6. 4: p. *madhyame-sthâḥ*), and *añgeshṭhâḥ* (vi. 14. 1: p. *añge-sthâḥ*). The exception, as noted by him, is *âpâkesthâḥ prahâsinaḥ* (viii. 6. 14: p. *âpâke-sthâḥ*). These are all the words in which *sthâ* is compounded with a locative ending in *e;* and, considering the form of the rule, it is probable that only such compounds were intended to be included under it: if the other compounds in which the *s* of *sthâ* is lingualized (viz. *rayishṭhâ*, *rayishṭhâna*, *girishṭhâ*, *pathishṭha*, *goshṭha*, and *gavishṭhira*—of which the last is read in *pada* as in *saṁhitâ*, while the others are separated, with restoration of the dental sibilant) had also been aimed at, the exception *bhûristhâtra* (iv. 30. 2: p. *bhûri-sthâtra*) would likewise have required notice.

The form of statement of the *gaṇa*, *paramebhyaḥ* instead of *paramâdibhyaḥ*, is quite peculiar.

अपसव्याभ्यां च ॥ ९५ ॥

95. As also after *apa* and *savya.*

There is still *anuvṛtti* of *sthaḥ:* the *s* of the root *sthā* becomes *sh* after *apa* and *savya*. The cases are separately noticed, because in them the change takes place irregularly after *a*, instead of after an alterant vowel. The commentator cites the two passages: *apāshṭhāc chṛṅgāt* (iv. 6. 5: p. *apāshṭhāt*), and *savyashṭhāç candramāḥ* (viii. 8. 23: p. *savya-sthāḥ*).

अग्नेः स्तोमसोमयोः ॥ ९६ ॥

96. Also that of *stoma* and *soma* after *agni*.

The commentator instances *yāvad agnishṭomena* (ix. 6. 40: p. *agni-stomena*), and *agnīshomāv adadhuḥ* (viii. 9. 14: p. *agnīshómāu*). As was the case with the last rule, the two words to which the precept relates are of different character, the one necessarily requiring the rule, in order to determine its *saṅhitā* reading, while the other might have been safely left unnoticed by the Prātiçākhya. There is yet another case in the Atharvan text, which would seem to call for inclusion in this rule: it is *agnishvāttāḥ* (xviii. 3. 44: p. *agni-svāttāḥ*). We can hardly suppose that it was intentionally omitted here, to be included in the *gaṇa* of rule 98, below: either it must have been overlooked by the maker of the treatise, or the verse which contains it (it is also a Rik verse; see RV. x. 15. 11) was not in his Atharva-Veda: that it was, however, contained in the text recognized by the commentator, is shown by the fact that he several times (under i. 80, 84 and ii. 34) cites the phrase *atto havīṅshi*, which forms part of its second line.

The commentator gives, as counter-example, *abhi somo avīvṛdhat* (i. 29. 3).

सुञः ॥ ९७ ॥

97. Also that of *su*.

The commentary furnishes the following examples: *idam ū shu* (i. 24. 4), *tad ū shu* (v. 1. 5), *mahīm ū shu* (vii. 6. 2), *anyā ū shu* (xviii. 1. 16), *stusha u shu* (xviii. 1. 37), and *tyam ū shu* (vii. 85. 1). Other cases are: after *ū*, v. 6. 4; after *u* (the same particle not lengthened), vii. 73. 7; after *mo*, v. 11. 7. xviii. 3. 62; after *evo*, vi. 84. 3; after *o*, vii. 72. 2; after *vidmo*, i. 2. 1. These are all the instances in which *su* follows in the Atharvan the particle *u*, or a word whose final is combined with the latter. On the other hand, in the only passage in the text (*pṛthivi su:* xviii. 3. 51) in which it follows an alterant vowel of another character, it remains unchanged. Our rule, then, is defective, and should have been restricted either by the specification of the alterant vowels to which the effect upon *su* is limited, or by a mention of the exception. The other treatises are less general, and hence, it may be presumed, more accurate, in their treatment of the change of this particle (see R. Pr. v. 2, 3; V. Pr. iii. 59, 60, 61; T. Pr. vi. 2).

त्र्यादिभ्यः ॥ ९८ ॥

98. Also after *tri* etc.

Here is another of those convenient *gaṇas*, set as a catch-all for whatever cases may not have been otherwise provided for, and rendering it impossible for us to ascertain the precise degree of accuracy with which the authors of the treatise examined and excerpted their text. The commentator cites three passages, *ye trishaptâḥ* (i. 1. 1: p. *tri-saptâḥ*), *goshedhâm* (i. 18. 4; p. *go-sedhâm*), and *raghushyado 'dhi* (iii. 7. 1: p. *raghu-syadaḥ*): he also, in his paraphrase, limits the application of the rule to cases of this character, in which an alterant vowel at the end of the first member of a compound comes before an initial *s* of the following member. Of such cases, besides those falling under rule 90, above, and those which are specially referred to in the rules preceding and following this, or which are mentioned in connection with them, I have noted in the Atharvan text the following: *dhṛshṇushena* (v. 20. 9: p. *dhṛshṇu-sena*), *sushṭuti* (e. g. vi. 1. 3: p. *su-stuti*), *purushṭuta* (vi. 2. 3: p. *puru-stuta*), *ṛshishṭuta* (vi. 108. 2: p. *ṛshi-stuta*), *gobhishak* (vii. 7. 1: p. *gobhi-sak*), *pṛthushṭuka* (vii. 46. 1: p. *pṛthu-stuka*), *sushûman* (vii. 46. 2: p. *su-sûman*), *anushṭup* (e. g. viii. 9. 14: p. *anu-stup*), *trishṭup* (e. g. viii. 9. 14: p. *tri-stup*), *trâishṭubha* (ix. 10. 1: p. *trâistubha*), *trishandhi* (e. g. xi. 9. 23: p. *tri-sandhi*), *râtishâc* (e. g. xviii. 3. 20: p. *râti-sâc*), and *divishṭambha* (xix. 32. 7). Exceptions will be given below, under rule 103.

ऋकारान्तात्सदेः ॥ ९९ ॥

99. Also that of the root *sad*, after a word ending in *ṛ*.

The commentator instances *hotṛshadanam* (vii. 99. 1: p. *hotṛ-sadanam*), and *pitṛshadanâḥ pitṛshadane tvâ* (xviii. 4. 67: p. *pitṛ-sadanâḥ* etc.). To these may be added *pitṛshad* (xiv. 2. 33: p. *pitṛ-sad*); and in *nârshada* (iv. 19. 2: p. *nârsada*) is also implied *nṛshad*.

बर्हिःपथ्यप्सुदिविपृथिवीति च ॥ १०० ॥

100. As also after *barhi*, *pathi*, *apsu*, *divi*, and *pṛthivî*.

The instances are, as cited in the commentary, *barhishadaḥ pitaraḥ* (xviii. 1. 51: p. *barhi-sadaḥ*), *pathishadî nṛcakshasâ* (xviii. 2. 12: p. *pathisadî iti pathi-sadî*), *apsushado 'py agnîn* (xii. 2. 4: p. *apsu-sadaḥ*), *ye devâ divishadaḥ* (x. 9. 12: p. *divi-sadaḥ*), and *pṛthivishadbhyaḥ* (xviii. 4. 78: p. *pṛthivisat-bhyaḥ*).

We have reason to be surprised that the root *sad* is treated in this manner, being made the subject of these two separate rules. If the compounds into which it enters as final member are to be excepted from the general *gaṇa* of rule 98, we should expect to find it directed that the *s* of *sad* should always be lingualized after an alterant vowel, as is actually the case. Not only is there, by the method adopted, a loss of that brevity which treatises of the *sûtra* class are wont to aim at almost as their chief object, but there is also a loss of completeness: the only remaining compound of *sad* of this class, *sushad* (e. g. ii. 36. 4), is left out, to be provided for in the general *gaṇa*. Or is it possible that *su* is regarded as falling under rule 90, as if a proper *upasarga* or preposition? If so, the forms into which it enters would be sufficiently provided for; since, excepting in the cases noted in the later rules (102 etc.), it always lingualizes the initial *s* of a root, while it has no effect upon that of a preposition or adverb, as in *susaha* (vi. 64. 3: p. *su-saha*) and the numerous compounds in which it is followed by *sam*, as *susaṁrabdha*.

ह्रिदिविभ्यामस्तेः ॥ १०१ ॥

101. Also that of the root *as* after *hi* and *divi*.

The commentator cites two of the cases falling under this rule, viz. *âpo hi shṭhâ* (i. 5. 1), and *ye devâ divi shṭha* (i. 30. 3): to which I add *divi shan* (xvii. 12 and xviii. 4. 59). The commentator then notes an exception which had escaped the authors of the treatise—prefacing it with *tato 'pa vadati*, 'from this rule is made the exception'—*vimuco hi santi* (vi. 112. 3): it is, in fact, the only case of the kind which the text affords—unless *hi satyâḥ* (i. 10. 1) is to be regarded as also falling under the rule, *satya* being an evident and acknowledged derivative from the root *as*.

Thus ends the Prâtiçâkhya's tale of the conversions of final or initial *s* into *sh*; what remains of the chapter is only a rehearsal in detail of exceptions to the rules already given. But there are still left in the Atharvan text a few instances of the same conversion, which can hardly be regarded as included in any of the preceding rules, since they are analogous with none of the other cases there treated of: unless something has been lost from this final section of the chapter—of which there are no indications—the treatise-makers and their commentator must lie under the imputation of having been careless enough to overlook them. The passages referred to are as follows: *âd u shṭenam* (iv. 3. 4), *tam u shṭuhi* (vi. 1. 2), *ni sha hiyatâm* (viii. 4. 10), and *cid dhi shmâ* (xviii. 1. 33). There would be little plausibility in a claim that the verses containing these passages were not included in the Atharva-Veda accepted by the school to which the treatise belonged, or that the readings of the school were different. And certainly, neither of these things could be maintained with regard to *svarshâḥ* (v. 2. 8: p. *svaḥ-sâḥ*), since the conversion of the final *visarjanîya* of its *svaḥ* into *r* has already been made the subject of a special rule, while nevertheless the Prâtiçâkhya contains no precept directing us to read it otherwise than *svarsâḥ*. The word would fall under the analogy of rule 87, but its final syllable could by no means be reckoned as a suffix (*pratyaya*).

न सृपिसृजिस्पृशिस्फूर्जिस्वरतिस्मरतीनाम् ॥ १०२ ॥

102. The *s* of the roots *sarp*, *sarj*, *sparç*, *sphûrj*, *svar*, and *smar* is not changed into *sh* according to the preceding rules.

This is evidently a rule of kindred sphere with rule 106, below, and the two might well enough have been combined into one, which should teach that a root containing a *r*, either semivowel or vowel, was not liable to the changes prescribed in this section. The corresponding rules in the other treatises have nearly this form (R. Pr. v. 11, r. 23, cccxl; V. Pr. iii. 81; T. Pr. vi. 6). As so stated, it would require the notice of but a single exception, *vi shparat* (vi. 56. 1 and x. 4. 8). As the rules now stand, they are slightly inexact, for in neither of them are included *anusphuram* (i. 2. 3), *atisara* (v. 8. 2 etc.), and *pratisara* (e. g. ii. 11. 2), although other forms of the root *sar* are contemplated in rule 106.

The commentator's illustrative examples are as follows: *vi sṛpo virapçin* (not in AV.; take instead *parisarpati* [v. 23. 3]; there are an abundance of such cases in the actual text), *atisṛshṭo apâm vṛshabhaḥ* (xvi. 1. 1), *visprçaḥ* (perhaps a corrupted reading for *uparisprçaḥ* [v. 3. 10], the only case our text contains), *mṛçyamânâ 'bhi sphûrjati* (xii. 5. 20), *vidathâ 'bhisvaranti* (ix. 9. 22), *nirṛtho yaç ca nisvaraḥ* (xii. 2. 14), and *prati smarethâṁ tujayadbhiḥ* (viii. 4. 7).

गोसन्यादीनां च ॥ १०३ ॥

103. Nor that of *gosani* etc.

The instances which the commentator has chosen to give from this *gaṇa* are *gosanim* (iii. 20. 10), *vi simataḥ* (iv. 1. 1), *abhi sishyade* (v. 5. 9), and *anu sûtaṁ savitave* (vi. 17. 1–4). We cannot but be surprised that the first of these words was chosen to head the *gaṇa*; it is no proper exception to any of the foregoing rules; the only one under which it would have any claim to come is rule 98, and there its simple exclusion from the *gaṇa* to which alone the precept is calculated to apply would be sufficient warrant for its reading. The third instance is a fair exception to rule 90, besides being an instance under rule 91. The second and fourth are, like the first, no legitimate cases for a rule like this, since *vi* and *simataḥ*, *anu* and *sûtum*, are disconnected words, which only accidentally come together in the arrangement of the sentence: if all such cases are to be taken note of, the *gaṇa* will be considerably and unnecessarily extended. Of actual cases having claim to constitute together a *gaṇa* of exceptions, the text does not furnish a great number: I have noted, besides the three words mentioned under the last rule, *antisumne* (vii. 112. 1), *pratispâçanam* (viii. 5. 11), *visalyaka* (e. g. ix. 8. 2), *abhisatvâ* (xix. 13. 5), and *prâtisutvanam* (xx. 129. 2: the reading is very doubtful). As good a right as *gosani* to inclusion in the *gaṇa* have also *bhûristhâtrâm* (iv. 30. 2), and *bahusûvarî* (vii. 46. 2).

अध्यभिभ्यां स्कन्देः ॥ १०४ ॥

104. Nor that of the root *skand*, after *adhi* and *abhi*.

The cited instances are *adhi skanda vîrayasva* (v. 25. 8), and *abhiskandam mṛgî 'va* (v. 14. 11). As counter-instance, the commentator brings forward *ekaçataṁ vishkandhâni* (iii. 9. 6), which is a blunder—unless, indeed, the commentator's grammatical system derives *skandha*, 'shoulder,' from the root *skand*. An actual example of the kind he seeks to give is *parishkanda* (xv. 2. 1 etc.).

परेः स्तृपातेः ॥ १०५ ॥

105. Nor that of the root *star*, after *pari*.

The commentator cites *pari stṛṇīhi pari dhehi vedim* (vii. 99. 1), and *paristaraṇam id dhaviḥ* (ix. 6. 2). As counter-example, he can find only *vishṭārī jātaḥ* (iv. 34. 1). *Vishṭārin* doubtless comes from the root *star*; yet, as the *pada*-text does not analyze it, but writes it in its *saṁhitā* form, it might have been neglected, and the root *star* added to those rehearsed in rule 102, with which it evidently belongs.

रेफपरस्य च ॥ १०६ ॥

106. Nor one that is followed by *r*.

The examples offered in the commentary are *sisratāṁ nārī* (i. 11. 1), *parisrutaḥ kumbhaḥ* (iii. 12. 7), and *pra bhānavaḥ sisrate* (xiii. 2. 46): the first and third are exceptions to rule 91, the second to rule 90. The text furnishes a number of other cases, which it is unnecessary to rehearse here, as there are no counter-exceptions.

अभि स्याम पृतन्यतः ॥ १०७ ॥

107. Nor in *abhi syāma pṛtanyataḥ*.

The passage, as cited by the commentator, is *vayam abhi syāma pṛtanyataḥ* (vii. 93. 1*): as a quite peculiar case, it is properly enough made the subject of a special rule. To show the necessity of citing in the rule the following word, *pṛtanyataḥ*, the commentator brings forward *viṣvāḥ pṛtanā abhi shyāma* (xiii. 1. 22).

The signature of the chapter is as follows: 16: *iti dvitīyo 'dhyāyaḥ samāptaḥ*. The number which should inform us how many rules are counted in the chapter is again unfortunately corrupt, and we are left to conjecture as to how it should be amended. I see no reason to suspect the loss of a rule or rules in the manuscript.

CHAPTER III.

CONTENTS:—SECTION I. 1–25, lengthening of final and other vowels in *saṁhitā*.

SECTION II. 26–38, doubling of consonants when final or in combination with other consonants; 29–32, exceptions; 33–36, vowels exempt from euphonic combination; 37, nasals do.; 38, method of combination of *ā* between two vowels; 39, conversion of final vowels into semivowels; 40, do. of final diphthongs into vowel and semivowel; 41–52, fusion of final and initial vowels; 53–54, absorption of initial *a* after final *e* and *o*.

---

* All the MSS. except W. read *shyāma*, which has accordingly been received into the edited text.

Section III. 55–64, different kinds of *svarita* accent; 65–74, occurrence and modifications of the several accents in the combinations of the phrase.

Section IV. 75–85, conversion of the dental nasal *n* into the lingual *ṇ*; 86–95, exceptions; 96, anomalous insertion of a sibilant in a single case.

सहावाडन्ते दीर्घः ॥ १ ॥

1. Before the root *sah*, when it ends in *âḍ*, the vowel is lengthened.

In this rule, *âḍanta* has virtually the same meaning as *sâḍbhûta* in rule ii. 82. It would not do to say "before *sah* when it becomes *sâh*," because of the words *amitrasâha* and *abhimâtishâha*, in which, though the vowel of the root is lengthened, the preceding final remains unchanged. The illustrative citations of the commentator are precisely those already given, under ii. 82, including the two words, example and counter-example, *prâshâṭ* and *prasahanam*, which are not found in the Atharva-Veda.

This rule also belongs in the category of the supererogatory, since in none of the words to which it relates does the *pada*-text afford a different reading from that of the *sanhitâ*. There would be just as much reason, so far as we can see, for a rule prescribing the prolongation of the *a* in the root *sah* itself—and that, in fact, is what the Vâj. Pr. (iii. 121) does, while it takes no notice of the change of the preceding vowel.

The Rik Pr. devotes three chapters (vii–ix) to the subject of the irregular prolongation of vowels. In the Vâj. Pr., the same subject occupies the sixth section of the third chapter, and one rule in the seventh (iii. 95–128); in the Tâitt. Pr., the third chapter: the latter treatise inverts the form of statement adopted by the others, and details the cases in which a vowel which is long in *sanhitâ* must be shortened in *pada*. The method in which the different works combine and put forth the phenomena of prolongation is so different, and so little would be gained by any detailed comparison of their teachings, that I shall for the most part content myself with this general reference.

अष्ट पदयोगपक्षपर्णदंष्ट्रचक्रेषु ॥ २ ॥

2. Also is lengthened the *a* of *ashṭa*, before *pada*, *yoga*, *paksha*, *parṇa*, *danshṭra*, and *cakra*.

Compounds of *ashṭa* with *parṇa* and *danshṭra* are not to be found in the present Atharva-Veda, nor are we necessarily to conclude, from their being mentioned in the rule, that any such occurred in the text recognized by the makers of our treatise: it is more likely that they have here, as in some other cases, detailed all the instances of the prolongation which they had noticed, without being particular as to their source. The rule, moreover, is an unnecessary one, since the *pada*-text everywhere offers the same reading with the *sanhitâ*, as is expressly directed by a later rule (iv. 94).

The citations of the commentary are *ashṭāpadī caturakshī* (v. 19. 7), *ashṭāpakshām* (ix. 3. 21), *ashṭāyogaiḥ* (vi. 91. 1), *ashṭāparṇaḥ, ashṭādanshṭram, ashṭācakrā navadvārā* (x. 2. 31), and *ashṭācakram vartate* (xi. 4. 22).

व्यधावप्रत्यये ॥ ३ ॥

3. Also a vowel before the root *vyadh*, when it is without a suffix.

The commentator's instances are *çvāvit* (v. 13. 9), and *hṛdayāvidham* (viii. 6. 18); to these is to be added only *marmāvidham* (xi. 10. 26), which, under iv. 66, is also cited in the commentary. By the latter rule, the *pada* in all these cases reads precisely like the *sanhitā*, without any division of the words, and without restoration of the short vowel. As counter-example, to show that, when the root takes a suffix, the vowel preceding it is not lengthened, we have a form of verbal inflection, *pravidhyanto nāma* (iii. 26. 4), brought forward.

उञ इदमूषादिषु ॥ ४ ॥

4. The particle *u* is lengthened in *idam ū shu* etc.

Of the passages in which *u* is thus made long, the commentator cites six, viz. *idam ū shu* (i. 24. 4), *tad ū shu* (v. 1. 5), *mahim ū shu* (vii. 6. 2), *anya ū shu* (xviii. 1. 16), *stusha ū shu* (xviii. 1. 37), and *tyam ū shu* (vii. 85. 1); the other cases afforded by the text are *pary ū shu* (v. 6. 4), and *pare ū te* (xviii. 3. 7). Were it not for this last case, the rule of our treatise might have been constructed like that of the Vāj. Pr., which says (iii. 109) that *u* before *nu* is lengthened.

ओषधेरपञ्चपद्याम् ॥ ५ ॥

5. Also the final vowel of *oshadhi*, except in the strong cases.

Those of the strong cases of *oshadhi* which the rule would except are, of course, only the nominative and accusative singular, since the others would, by the rules of declension, show a gunated or a lengthened vowel, or a semivowel, in its place. The commentator cites no actual passages in illustration of the rule, but merely catalogues the forms in which the long vowel would appear, viz. *oshadhībhiḥ* (e. g. ii. 10. 2), *oshadhībhyām* (not found in AV.), *oshadhībhyaḥ* (e. g. vi. 20. 2), *oshadhīnām* (e. g. iii. 5. 1), and *oshadhīshu* (e. g. i. 30. 3): as counter-example, he adds *iyam ha mahyam tvām oshadhiḥ* (vii. 38. 5). The *pada*-text, in all these cases, reads precisely like the *sanhitā*.

Since the rule does not restrict itself to forms of declension, it is guilty of an oversight in taking no account of the compound *oshadhija* (x. 4. 23: p. *oshadhi-ja*) as a farther exception. In the only other compounds which the text affords—viz. *oshadhīsamçita* (x. 5. 32: p. *oshadhi-samçita*), and *oshadhīmant* (xix. 17. 6; 18. 6)—the rule of the Prātiçākhya is observed.

जीवन्तीमोषधीम् ॥ ६ ॥

6. And except in the phrase *jîvantîm oshadhîm*.

The commentator quotes the passage a little more fully, *jîvantîm oshadhîm aham* (viii. 2. 6; 7. 6), and adds that the inclusion of the accompanying word in the rule is intended to limit the exception to this particular passage; citing, as counter-examples, *imâm khanâmy oshadhîm* (iii. 18. 1), and *oshadhîm çepaharshanîm* (iv. 4. 1).

साढः ॥ ७ ॥

7. The vowel of *sâḍha* is long.

The commentator cites for us the only passage in which this participle occurs, *vâcâ sâḍhaḥ parastarâm* (v. 30. 9). The rule is one of the most utterly superfluous presented by our treatise, which, of course, has nothing to do with the mode of formation of such words. Moreover, if it was inclined to do a work of supererogation as regards them, it should not have omitted to notice also *rûḍhvâ*, *rûḍha*, *mûḍha*, *gûḍha*, and other like forms which the text contains. Probably the reason why this particular one was noticed, and not the others, is that the regular form, according to the rules of the general grammar, is *soḍha*. Pâṇini (vi. 3. 113) remarks the occurrence in specific cases of forms like *sâḍha*. The compound *ashâḍha* is found but once in the Atharvan, and that in the nineteenth book (xix. 7. 4).

बहुलं रात्रेः ॥ ८ ॥

8. As to the final vowel of *râtri*, diversity of usage prevails.

This is rather a discreditable confession on the part of our treatise, whose business it is to settle authoritatively the reading of its school in all cases admitting of any doubt, that it does not feel equal to dealing with the irregularities of the word in question. Nothing like it has hitherto met us, but we shall find several instances in that which follows. It is also a very unnecessary acknowledgment; for, in the first place, there was no such rule as this absolutely called for, since the *pada*-text everywhere reads all the forms of *râtri* like the *saṃhitâ*; and, in the second place, there is no great perplexity in the phenomena. In the nominative we always meet with *râtrî*, except in a single case (xiii. 4. 30), where *râtris* occurs; as accusative, only *râtrîm* is found, and *râtrim*, which the Rig-Veda has (e. g. i. 35. 1), is never read; as vocative, we have only *râtri*, never *râtre*; and the other forms are, with the exception of *râtraye* (viii. 2. 20), such as would come from the theme *râtrî*.

The commentator, as under rule 5, gives the series of cases *râtribhiḥ* (xviii. 1. 10), *râtribhyâm*, *râtribhyaḥ*, *râtrîṇâm* (e. g. iv. 5. 4), and *râtrishu*, only two of which are to be found in our text. As example of the short vowel, again, he cites an actual case, *vrâtya ekâṃ râtrim* (xv. 13. 1).

विश्वस्य नरवसुमित्रेषु ॥ ९ ॥

9. Also as to that of *viçva*, before *nara*, *vasu*, and *mitra*.

Here are quite heterogeneous cases, mixed together in one rule. The noun *viçvā́nara* and its derivative *vāiçvānara* always show the long vowel, and moreover are read in *pada* precisely as in *saṁhitā*. *Viçvā́vasu* the *pada*-text divides, restoring the short vowel: thus, *viçva-vasu*; but the long vowel invariably appears in *saṁhitā*. We also find *viçvā́mitra* three times in the text (iv. 29. 5. xviii. 3. 15, 16), and it is each time written *viçvā́mitra*, without division, by the *pada*-text. But in a half-verse which occurs twice in the eighteenth book (xviii. 3. 63; 4. 54), we meet with *viçvamitrā́ḥ*, which the *pada* divides, *viçva-mitrā́ḥ*.* It is only, then, in regard to this last word that we need in our rule the implication of *bahulam* by inference from the one preceding, and it is so very difficult to justify the implication, with no *ca* in the rule to indicate it, and with nothing in any following rule to denote its cessation, that I am inclined to think that the passage containing *viçamitrāḥ* was overlooked by the authors of the treatise, or did not occur in the text they recognized, and that the interpretation of the rule has been modified by the commentator in order to bring it in.

The commentator cites, as instances of the long vowel, *viçvā́nare akramata* (iv. 11. 7), *yó viçvā́vasum* (ii. 2. 4), and *viçvā́mitra jamadagne* (xviii. 3. 16); as example of the short vowel, *tam arcata viçvamitrā́ḥ* (xviii. 3. 63; 4. 54).

शुनः पदे ॥ १० ॥

10. Also as to that of *çvan* before *pada*.

The commentator cites all the instances of occurrence of the compound of these two words which the text contains, three of them as examples of the long vowel, and one of the short; they are as follows: *atho sarvaṁ çvā́padam* (xi. 9. 10), *çvā́pado makshikā́ḥ* (xi. 10. 8), and *uta vā çvā́padaḥ* (xviii. 3. 55); and, on the other hand, *vyāghraḥ çvapadā́m iva* (viii. 5. 11 and xix. 39. 4). All these forms admit of being derived from a theme *çvapad*, instead of *çvapada*, and the last of them must necessarily come from *çvapad*. It would be possible, then, to get rid of the necessity of implying an *anuvṛtti* of *bahulam* in this rule, as the commentator does, by regarding it as relating only to the cases in which *çvan* precedes *pada*, and not to that in which it precedes *pad*. There is the same strong objection to the inference of *bahulam* here as in the preceding rule: that nothing in the rule indicates it, and that the next one implies not *bahulam*, but simply *dīrghaḥ*, without anything to point out the cessation of the former and the resumption of the latter. Such ambiguity is quite foreign to the usual method of the treatise.

The *pada*-text reads, in each of the passages cited, precisely like the *saṁhitā*, without division of the compound, so that the rule might be omitted altogether without practical loss.

---

* The first time, all the manuscripts, without exception, accent *viçvā́mitrāḥ*, and the edition follows their authority: in the repetition of the verse, Bp. and M. and the edited text have *viçvamitrā́ḥ*, B. and P. *viçvā́mitrāḥ*; this part of the eighteenth book has been lost in E., and is unaccented in I. The word is evidently a vocative, and the true reading is *viçvamitrāḥ*, without accent, in both passages.

उपसर्गस्य नामिनो दस्ति ॥ ११ ॥

11. A final alterant vowel of a preposition is lengthened before *t* of the root *dâ*.

The only two words in the text falling under this rule are *apratîttam* (vi. 117. 1) and *parîttaḥ* (vi. 92. 2), in which the final *i* of *prati* and *pari* becomes *î* before the *t* which is all that remains of the root *dâ* before the participial suffix *ta*. The commentator mentions both, and likewise *nîttâ*, *vîttâ*, and *parîttiḥ*, no one of which is to be found in the Atharvan; nor are his counter-examples, *prattam* and *avattam*, Atharvan words. The rule has a more general form of statement than would be required if it were constructed only to fit the cases which our text presents: and we may also, indeed, recognize in the fact of its presence at all the influence of the general grammar: the words to which it relates are read alike in *pada* and in *saṁhitâ*, and none of the other treatises has anything corresponding to it: compare Pâṇini, vi. 3. 124.

वर्तादिषु ॥ १२ ॥

12. As also before *varta* etc.

What words we are to assume to be implied in this rule, by inference from those which precede it, is not entirely clear. The commentator's understanding of it we are unable to arrive at, for there is here another slight *lacuna* in the manuscript: the copyist has jumped carelessly from the *vartâdishu* of the first statement of the rule to that of the paraphrase, so that the greater part of the latter is lost. The instances given in the commentary are *abhîvartena* (i. 29. 1: p. *abhi-vartena*), and *viçvam anyâm abhîvâra* (i. 32. 4: p. *abhi-vâra*). We may with plausibility conclude from this that we are to imply in the rule not merely the *dîrghaḥ*, 'conversion into a long vowel,' which belongs to the whole section, but the specific limitation to a preposition ending in an alterant vowel, given in the last rule; and that the commentary would read, if restored, as follows: *vartâdishu* [*: upasargasya nâmyantasya vartâdishu*] *parataḥ dîrgho bhavati.* The words, then, to which the rule relates, would be, besides those already cited: *vîbarha* (ii. 33. 7: p. *vi-barha*), *abhîvarga* (e. g. iii. 5. 2: p. *abhi-varga*), *parîçâsa* (v. 14. 3: p. *pari-çâsa*), *pratîbodha* (e. g. viii. 1. 13: p. *prati-bodha*), *pratîvarta* (e. g. viii. 5. 4: p. *prati-varta*), *anûvṛj* (ix. 4. 12: p. *anu-vṛj*), *pratîkâça* (ix. 8. 6: p. *prati-kâça*), *abhîvṛta* (e. g. ix. 10. 7: p. *abhi-vṛta*), *parîvṛta* (e. g. x. 8. 31: p. *pari-vṛta*), *samparîvṛta* (x. 2. 33: p. *sam-parivṛta*), *pratîhâra* (xi. 7. 12: p. *prati-hâra*), *nîvid* (xi. 7. 19: p. *ni-vid*), *abhîmodamud* (e. g. xi. 7. 26: p. *abhimoda-mud*), *abhîlâpalap* (xi. 8. 25: p. *abhilâpa-lap*), *anûrâdha* (xix. 15. 2), *parîṇah* (xix. 48. 1), and *nînadha* (xix. 57. 4)—all which are separated by the *pada*-text (except in the nineteenth book, which has no *pada*-text), with restoration of the original short vowel of the preposition. In the same category would belong *anûjahire* (p. *anu-jahire*), which is the reading of all the Atharvan manuscripts at xviii. 3. 46, but which in the published text is altered to *anûhire*, to accord with the Rik reading of the same passage (x. 15. 8), for which the other seems a blundering substitution. In a single word, *nîhâra* (e. g. vi. 113. 2), the *pada* does not restore the theoretically correct form, but reads with the *saṁhitâ*: possibly *nînâha*, were there a *pada*-text for the passage, would be treated in the same way. There are a few cases where a final *a* of a preposition is also lengthened before a root, but in these the *pada*-text attempts no restoration of the regular form, and their omission from the rules of the Prâtiçâkhya would therefore be of no practical importance: they are *prâṇâha* (ix. 3. 4), *prâvṛsh* (e. g. xii. 1. 46), *prâvṛta* (e. g. xii. 5. 2); and *upânah* (xx. 133. 4) doubtless belongs to the same class.

There are, however, still remaining a few compounds in the Atharvan text, the final vowel of the first member of which is lengthened in *saṁhitâ*, and which are not treated of in any of the rules which follow; so that, if the rule now in hand is to be so interpreted as to exclude them, no provision would appear to have been made for them in our treatise; they are *saṁdhanâjit* (e. g. v. 20. 3: p. *saṁdhana-jit*), *ukthâmada* (v. 26. 3: p. *uktha-mada*), *tardâpati* (vi. 50. 3: p. *tarda-pati*), *sahasrâposha* (e. g. vi. 79. 3: p. *sahasra-posha*; at vi. 141. 3 we have *sahasraposha*), *âhutîvṛdh* (vii. 32. 1: p. *âhuti-vṛdh*), *svâvasum* (vii. 50. 3: p. *sva-vasum*: RV. reads in the corresponding passage *svavasum*), *naghârisha* (e.g. viii. 2. 6: p. *nagha-risha*), *pavînasa* (viii. 6. 21: p. *pavi-nasa*), *purîtat* (e. g. ix. 7. 11: p. *puri-tat*), *vishûvṛt* (x. 2. 11: p. *vishu-vṛt*), *purûvṛt* (x. 2. 11: p. *puru-vṛt*), *purûvasu* (xiv. 2. 47: p. *puru-vasu*), and *urûṇasa* (xviii. 2. 13: p. *uru-nasa*).

अकारस्याभ्यासस्य बहुलम् ॥ १३ ॥

13. The *a* of a reduplication is or is not lengthened.

As instances of the prolongation of *a* in a syllable of reduplication, the commentator gives us *dâdhṛshuḥ* (i. 27. 3: p. *dadhṛshuḥ*), *abhivâvṛdhe* (i. 20. 1: p. *abhi-vavṛdhe*), *vâvṛdhete* (v. 1. 5: p. *vavṛdhete*), and *jîtasya vâvṛtuḥ* (v. 19. 13: p. *vavṛtuḥ*). The same prolongation takes place in the Atharvan in *sâsahe* (xix. 34. 5) and *sâsahânaḥ* (iii. 6. 4), *câklpat* (vi. 35. 3), *câklpuḥ* (ix. 10. 10), and *câklpe* (e. g. vii. 87. 1), and *tâtṛshuḥ* (xviii. 3. 47); and also, in the twentieth book (xx. 127. 3), in *mâmahe*. As examples of the short *a* in the same position, the commentator cites *anena viçvâ sasahe* (i. 16. 3) and *sasahe çatrûn* (ii. 5. 3). The root *sah* is the only one in which, while the *pada*-text gives always the short vowel to the reduplication, the *saṁhitâ* sometimes prolongs it and sometimes leaves it unchanged. Elsewhere we have in *saṁhitâ* either always the long *â* (and especially often in the forms of *vâvṛdh*), or always the short *a*.

There are also two or three roots in the reduplications of which other vowels than *a*, short in the *pada*-text, are lengthened in *saṁhitâ*: they are *rûrupaḥ* (iv. 7. 5), *rîrishaḥ* (e. g. v. 3. 8), and *çûçucaḥ* (xviii. 2. 4). The Prâtiçâkhya may intend to include these forms in the *gaṇa* of rule 21, below, but they would much more properly have been provided for in the present rule.

जीहीडाहम् ॥ १४ ॥

14. Note *jîhîḍâ 'ham*.

Or, as the commentator expounds it, there is in this passage a lengthened vowel—viz., that of the first syllable of *jihîḍa*. The passage is cited: *akratur jihîḍâ 'ham** (iv. 32. 5: p. *jihîḍa*). The commentator regards the word *bahulam* as still in force from the preceding rule, and adds, as an instance in which a short vowel appears in the reduplication of this root, *yad vâ pitâ 'parâddho jihîḍe* (vi. 116. 2). But it is evident that there is no need here of any implication of *bahulam*, and that all cases but one of the occurrence of *jihîḍa* are excluded from the rule by the citation in the latter of the accompanying word *aham*.

Compare farther rule iv. 67, which teaches *samâpatti* of *jihîḍa* in the *pada*-text.

साह्याम ॥ १५ ॥

15. And *sâhyâma*.

The commentator quotes from the text: *sâhyâma dâsam âryam* (iv. 32. 1: p. *sahyâma*). He does not attempt to prove the implication of *bahulam* by *anuvṛtti* from rule 13, although there is just as good reason for doing it here as under the preceding rule. Compare the converse of this rule in the next chapter (iv. 88).

There are in the Atharvan text a few causative forms from verbal roots which show in the first or radical syllable a short *a* in *pada* and a long *â* in *saṁhitâ*, and which are not specially noted in this section, being left, apparently, to fall into the *gaṇa* of rule 21, below, although no reference is there made to them by the commentator. They are *yâmaya* etc. (e. g. i. 20. 3), from *yu*; *cyâvayati* etc. (e. g. x. 1. 13), from *cyu*; *rânayantu* (vi. 9. 3), from *van*; *yâmaya* (vi. 137. 3), from *yam*; and *ylâpayantu* (ix. 9. 10), from *glâ*. Directions for the shortening of their first syllables in *pada* are given in the next chapter (iv. 91–93).

विद्मादीनां शरादिषु ॥ १६ ॥

16. The final vowels of *vidma* etc. are lengthened before *çara* etc.

This rule, together with two later ones of this section (19 and 25)—of which the one relates to the final of an instrumental case, and the other to that of the particle *adha*—makes up the sum of all that our treatise has to say respecting the frequent and important phenomenon of the prolongation in *saṁhitâ* of a final vowel. The other Prâtiçâkhyas treat the subject at great length and apparently with exhaustive fullness (see R. Pr., chapters vii and viii; V. Pr. iii. 96–128; T. Pr. iii). As regards our own treatise, we must confess that we can hardly help questioning the actuality of all its *gaṇas*, when we find set up in the rules such as would have to be of so immense extent as the two here presented us, which must contain hundreds of words each.† It were

---

* The edition reads erroneously *jihîḍâ 'ham*, with the corresponding Rik passage. All the *saṁhitâ* manuscripts of the Atharvan give *jihîḍa*, and in the *pada*-text the word is followed by a figure 4, the usual sign of a *samâpanna* word, or one which the *pada* has reduced from an irregular to a theoretically regular form.

† The longest *gaṇa* belonging to Pâṇini's grammar, *ardharcâdayaḥ*, contains, in Böhtlingk's edition, 232 words.

almost as well, we should think, to turn off the matter with a *kvacit*, as is done below, in rule 54, openly confessing inability to master its intricacy and vastness, as to dispose of it thus.

The commentator does not feel called upon to give himself any more trouble than the authors of the treatise have taken, and he leaves the two *gaṇas* to take care of themselves, after citing three passages by way of examples, as follows: *vidmā çarasya pitaram* (i. 2. 1), *evā rogaṁ cā ’srāvam* (i. 2. 4), and *evā me prāṇa mā bibheḥ* (ii. 15. 1 etc.). In filling out the *gaṇa*, and giving a complete account of the usage of the Atharvan text with reference to the prolongation of a final vowel, I shall put together all the cases, including those which belong under rules 19 and 25, since the same principle evidently governs them all.

The prolongation is so prevailingly a metrical phenomenon in the Atharva-Veda, called out by the exigencies of the verse, that I shall arrange my exhibition of it accordingly. There are certain points in the *pāda*, whether of eight, of eleven, or of twelve syllables, at which the long vowel is especially liable to be called forth: these are, 1st, toward the beginning of the *pāda*, of whatever length, the second syllable; 2nd, toward the end, the sixth syllable in a *pāda* of eight syllables, and the eighth or the tenth in one of eleven or twelve syllables: the protraction evidently tending in the former case to give an iambic movement to the commencement of the verse, and, in the latter case, to impress upon it an iambic cadence—which, however, is in the 11-syllable *pāda* made trochaic by the addition of an odd syllable. A long syllable at these points, then, I shall regard as regular; elsewhere, as irregular.

I. The *pāda* of eight syllables (rarely lengthened to ten), usually forming *anushṭubh* verses, but, less often, combined into *gāyatrī*, *paṅkti*, or *bṛhatī* stanzas: these do not require to be distinguished from one another, since the prolongation depends solely upon the interior construction of the *pāda* itself, and not upon the mode of combination of the latter.

1. Protraction of a final vowel in the second syllable of the *pāda*, as in the example *vidmā çarasya pitaram* (i. 2. 1):

a. Of verbal forms: *vidmā* (i. 2. 1; 3. 1–5), *pibā* (ii. 5. 1), and *tishṭhā* (iv. 7. 5).

b. Of forms of declension: *tenā* (i. 3. 1–5. iii. 7. 3;* 14. 1. iv. 5. 1; 7. 1. vi. 7. 1, 2, 3; 12. 1, 2; 24. 3; 30. 1, 3; 82. 3; 91. 1. vii. 38. 2. xviii. 2. 30), and *yenā* (i. 13. 1. iii. 9. 4. vii. 36. 2. ix. 5. 17. xiii. 2. 21).

c. Of particles: *evā* (i. 2. 4; 3. 6–9; 11. 6. ii. 15. 1–6; 30. 1; 36. 4. iii. 6. 3, 6. v. 21. 4–6. vi. 8. 1, 2, 3; 17. 1–4; 46. 3; 58. 2; 70. 1–3; 85. 3; 102. 1; 105. 1–3; 138. 5; 139. 4, 5; 141. 3. vii. 13. 1; 50. 5. ix. 1. 11, 12, 13, 16, 17. x. 1. 13; 3. 13–15, 17–25; 6. 33. xi. 4. 19. xii. 4. 34; 5. 65. xiv. 1. 43. xviii. 4. 55. xix. 50. 4; 57. 1), *adhā* (i. 28. 4. iii. 20. 1. vi. 65. 1. x. 4. 25. xiii. 1. 30. xiv. 2. 20. xviii. 2. 23), *yatrā* (iii. 28. 6), and *ghā* (vi. 1. 3).

2. Protraction in the sixth syllable, or the third from the end of the *pāda*, as in *imaṁ vardhayatā giraḥ*:

a. Of verbal forms: *vardhayatā* (i. 15. 2. xix. 1. 1, 2), *janayathā* (i. 5.

* The edition, following the authority of a part of the MSS., reads

3), *ilayatâ* (i. 17. 4), *yâvayâ* (i. 20. 3; 21. 4. iv. 19. 7. xii. 1. 32), *gamayâ* (i. 21. 2), *nâçayâ* (i. 23. 2, 3), *kṛṇutâ* (iii. 9. 1. xii. 2. 34), *anadatâ* (iii. 13. 1), *jayatâ* (iii. 19. 7), *vardhayâ* (iii. 20. 1. vi. 5. 3; 54. 1), *tânayâ* (iv. 4. 6. vi. 101. 2), *shvâpayâ* (iv. 5. 7), *kalpayâ* (iv. 12. 5), *nayathâ* (iv. 13. 1), *jîvayathâ* (iv. 13. 1), *châçayâ* (iv. 18. 4), *dûshayatâ* (vi. 100. 2), *dyâ* (vi. 103. 2, 3: 104. 2), *cakṛmâ* (vi. 114. 1; 115. 1. x. 3. 8), *mâdayâ* (vi. 130. 4), *shyâ* (vii. 18. 1), *bharatâ* (vii. 60. 7), *jaghnimâ* (x. 4. 12), *bhajâ* (xiv. 1. 25), *vâpayâ* (xviii. 3. 6), *carâ* (xx. 127. 11).

b. Of forms of declension: *sahasyenâ* (iv. 5. 1), and *bhadreṇâ* (vii. 60. 7).

c. Of particles: *ivâ* (vi. 37. 2).

3. Besides cases of the two kinds already noted, we have a few in which the protraction still favors the iambic movement of the verse, although not at its two cardinal points:

a. In the fourth syllable of the *pâda*, as in *hariṇasyâ bhiyam kṛdhi:* of verbal forms, *parehâ* (iv. 33. 8), and *çṛṇotâ* (xx. 127. 7); of forms of declension, *dhâmâ* (vi. 31. 3), and *hariṇasyâ* (vi. 67. 3); of particles, *angâ* (ii. 3. 2), and *achâ* (iii. 20. 2).

b. In the final syllable of the *pâda:* of this class we have but two cases, viz. *kalpayâ* (iv. 12. 5), and *angâ* (ii. 3. 2); and in each passage the same word occurs in another position, protracted according to the usual analogies, so that we may regard the irregular protractions in the final syllable as the effect of attraction.

4. Protraction of a final vowel in such a position that it seems to obstruct, rather than assist, the regular movement of the verse:

a. Protraction in the third syllable of the *pâda*, as in *çrathayâ sûshanne tvam:* of verbal forms, *çrathayâ* (i. 11. 3), *mṛḍayâ* (i. 13. 2; 26. 4), *itâ* (iii. 10. 7), *sunotâ* (vi. 2. 3), *juhotâ* (xviii. 2. 2); of particles, *smâ* (x. 4. 6).

b. Protraction in the fifth syllable, or in the fourth from the end: only a single case, *ivâ* (iv. 4. 7, third *pâda*).*

A summary view of the cases of protraction in the 8-syllable *pâda* (including also the very rare 10-syllable *pâda*) is as follows:

Syllable,	Regular. 2nd.	6th.	Indifferent. 4th.	5th.	Irregular. 3rd.	5th.
Verbal forms,	8	40	2	1	6	0
Forms of declension,	26	2	2	0	0	1
Particles,	77	1	2	1	1	0
Sum,	111	43	6	2	7	1
Total,	154		8		8	

II. In the *pâda* of eleven syllables, with trochaic close; usually forming regular *trishṭubh* verses, but not unfrequently irregularly combined, especially with *jagatî pâdas*, of twelve syllables:

1. Protraction at the commencement of the *pâda*, in the second syllable: e. g. *vidmâ tam utsam yata âbabhûtha.*

a. Verbal forms: *vidmâ* (iv. 31. 5. x. 1. 20. xiii. 3. 21), *yukshvâ* (xviii.

* The edition reads, with a part of the MSS., *iva.*

1. 25), *vahā* (xviii. 1. 30), *mṛḍā* (xviii. 1. 40), *açyā* (xviii. 1. 52), *bhavā* (xix. 24. 5), and *çrudhī* (ii. 5. 4. xviii. 1. 25).

b. Forms of declension: *tenā* (iii. 16. 5. vii. 20. 4; 79. 1), *yenā* (vii. 12. 1. xviii. 1. 54; 4. 44), and *kshāmā* (xviii. 3. 21).

c. Particles: *evā* (iv. 39. 1, 3, 5, 7. vi. 72. 1; 74. 3. xii. 2. 25), *adhā* (iii. 4. 4. iv. 32. 7. v. 22. 2, 2. vii. 73. 11. viii. 4. 15. x. 2. 7. xii. 3. 2, 9. xviii. 1. 16, 51; 2. 11; 3. 21; 4. 48, 70), *yatrā* (iii. 28. 5. vi. 22. 2; 120. 3. ix. 9. 22. xviii. 1. 50), *atrā* (v. 1. 5. ix. 10. 12. xii. 2. 26, 27), *adyā* (viii. 4. 15. ix. 10. 9), *ghā* (xviii. 1. 11), *achā* (vi. 39. 2), and *smā* (xii. 3. 3).

2. Protraction in the cadence of the *pāda*. Here we have two classes of cases to distinguish, viz., those in which the eighth syllable, or the fourth from the end, suffers protraction, as in *divaṁ gacha prati tishṭhā çarīrāiḥ*; and again, those in which the tenth syllable, or the last but one, is made long, as in *mā vaḥ susroc camaso dṛṅhatā tam*.

α. Protraction in the eighth syllable.

a. Verbal forms: *viveçā* (i. 12. 3. xi. 4. 20), *tishṭhā* (ii. 34. 5. xviii. 2. 7), *bhajā* (iii. 4. 2, 4), *avā* (iii. 16. 3), *mādayathā* (iv. 21. 6), *bharā* (iv. 32. 3), *svadayā* (v. 12. 2), *sṛjā* (v. 27. 11), *juhutā* (vi. 32. 1), *rakshā* (viii. 3. 19), *sahyā* (x. 9. 1), *taratā* (xii. 2. 26, 27), *nudatā* (xii. 2. 30), *pacatā* (xii. 3. 27), *bhavatā* (xii. 3. 29), *sṛjatā* (xii. 3. 46), *cakṛmā* (xviii. 1. 51), *dīyā* (xix. 13. 8), and *avatā* (xix. 13. 11).

b. Forms of declension: *aryā* (i. 12. 2), *janimā* (ii. 28. 2. iv. 1. 3. xviii. 3. 22), *amṛtenā* (iii. 12. 8), *kāvyenā* (v. 1. 5), and *martyenā* (ix. 10. 8, 16).

c. Particles: *evā* (vii. 4. 1. x. 8. 12), *adyā* (vii. 82. 6), and *utā* (vii. 97. 1).

β. Protraction in the tenth syllable. This case is comparatively rare, and is nearly confined to verbal forms, of which we have *mṛḍatā* (i. 20. 1. xviii. 3. 16), *bharā* (ii. 6. 3. iv. 32. 7), *sṛjā* (v. 2. 3), *hantanā* (vii. 77. 2), and *dṛṅhatā* (xix. 58. 4): besides these, we find only *ihā* (xix. 56. 6).

3. In the *trishṭubh pāda*, as in the *anushṭubh*, we have in a few odd cases the fourth syllable lengthened, as in *tiraḥ purū cid arṇavaṁ jaganvān*; they are as follows: verbal form, *tishṭhatā* (xii. 2. 27); form of declension, *purū* (xviii. 1. 1); particle, *ghā* (xviii. 1. 3).

4. The irregular protractions are found to take place in the third, the fifth, or the seventh syllable of the *pāda*.

a. Protraction in the third syllable, as in *urushyā ṇa urujmann apraγuchan*: but two cases occur, viz. *urushyā* (vi. 4. 3), and *vyathayā* (xiii. 1. 31), and in the latter passage the metre is hopelessly irregular.

b. Protraction in the fifth syllable, as in *mitraç cid dhi shmā juhurāṇo devān*: of this class, we have only cases of particles, viz. *prā* (ii. 5. 5. vii. 26. 1*), and *shmā* (xviii. 1. 33).

c. Protraction in the seventh syllable: an example is *na yat purā cakṛmā kad dha nūnam*. The words of which the final is lengthened in this position are, with a single exception, verbal forms, viz. *çṛṇuthā* (iv. 21. 6), *bharā* (iv. 22. 6. vii. 73. 9), *khidā* (iv. 22. 7), *çṛtā* (vi. 63. 2; 84. 3), *suvā* (vii. 14. 3), *nudā* (vii. 34. 1), and *cakṛmā* (xviii. 1. 4, 33). Of forms of declension, we have *janimā* (v. 11. 5).

---

* In both these passages the printed text reads *pra*, without any support from the manuscripts.

The tabular summary for the 11-syllable *pâda* is as follows:

Syllable,	Regular. 2nd.	6th.	10th.	Indifferent. 4th.	Irregular. 3rd.	5th.	7th.
Verbal forms,	10	23	7	1	2	0	10
Forms of declension,	7	8	0	1	0	0	1
Particles,	36	4	1	1	0	3	0
Sum,	53	35	8	3	2	3	11
Total,	96			3	16		

III. In the *jagatî pâda*, or that of twelve syllables.

1. Protraction at the beginning of the *pâda*, in the second syllable, as in *çikshâ ṇo asmin puruhûta yâmani*. Here we have, of verbal forms, *çikshâ* (xviii. 3. 67); of forms of declension, *purâ* (vi. 49. 3); of particles, *evâ* (iv. 23. 2. vi. 97. 1), *adhâ* (vii. 83. 3. xviii. 4. 63), and *yadî* (xviii. 1. 21).

2. Protraction in the cadence of the *pâda*, taking place, as in the *trishṭubh pâda*, at two different points, either at the eighth syllable or at the tenth; that is, at the fifth or the third from the end.

α. At the eighth syllable, as in *asmâkam an̄çam ud avâ bhare-bhare*: of such cases, the text affords us the verbal forms *mukshâ* (ii. 35. 3), *kṛṇutâ* (vi. 55. 3), *ruhemâ* (vii. 6. 3), *avâ* (vii. 50. 4), and *ichâ* (xviii. 1. 16); and the form of declension *dharmâ* (vi. 51. 3).

β. At the tenth syllable, as in *tâḥ saptagṛdhrâ iti çuçrumâ vayam*: here we have only the verbal forms *siñcathâ* (vi. 22. 2), *dhârayâ* (vii. 82. 3), *çuçrumâ* (viii. 9. 18), *veçayâ* (ix. 2. 25), and *sîdatâ* (xi. 1. 12).

3. Of the protraction in the middle of the verse, or at the fourth syllable, there is to be found but a single case, *yad ejathâ maruto rukmavakshasaḥ* (vi. 22. 2).

4. Protraction of a final against the requirements of the metre, in the seventh syllable, or the sixth from the end. Only one unquestionable case can be found, viz. *pary û shu pra dhanvâ vâjasâtaye* (v. 6. 4); with which may be classed *gṛṇatâ*, at v. 27. 9, in a verse of irregular character, and perhaps rather belonging under the 8-syllable *pâda*.

The cases of the 12-syllable *pâda* may be thus summed up:

Syllable,	Regular. 2nd.	6th.	10th.	Indifferent. 4th.	Irregular. 7th.
Verbal forms,	1	5	5	1	2
Forms of declension,	1	1	0	0	0
Particles,	5	0	0	0	0
Sum,	7	6	5	1	2
Total,	18			1	2

There thus appear to be, in the whole text, 268 cases of the protraction of a final vowel to help the metrical movement in the opening or the cadence of the *pâda*, and 12 which favor the movement in the middle of the *pâda*, against 26 which contravene the orderly flow of the metre. To point out the cases in which protraction does not take place at the two important points at which it is thus shown usually to occur, and to establish the laws, if there be any, which determine in each instance the retention or the change of the short vowel, cannot, of course, be attempted here.

It will be noticed that the vowel which is lengthened is almost always *a*: the text furnishes us, indeed, but three examples of the protraction of a final *i* (ii. 5. 4. xviii. 1. 21, 25), and two of that of *u* (vi. 49. 3. xviii. 1. 1)—except the particle *u*, as taught in rule 4 of this chapter.

बहुलं मतौ ॥ १७ ॥

17. Before the suffix *mant* a vowel is or is not lengthened.

The term *matu* is treated by the commentary as covering both the suffix *mant* and its equivalent *vant*: in fact, he cites instances only for the latter, as follows: *çâle 'çvâvati* (iii. 12. 2), *açvâvatîr gomatîḥ* (iii. 16. 7), and *açvâvatîm pra tara* (xviii. 2. 31); and farther, as examples of the short vowel before the suffix, *vîravatîḥ sadam* (iii. 16. 7), and *ghṛtavatî payasvaty uc chrayasva* (iii. 12. 2).

The complete list of words in our present Atharvan text which exhibit in *sanhitâ* a prolongation of the final vowel of a theme before the possessive suffix *vant* is as follows: *açvâvant* (e. g. iii. 12. 2), *varaṇâvant* (iv. 7. 1), *madâvant* (e. g. iv. 7. 4), *samâvant* (iv. 18. 1), *priyâvant* (iv. 18. 4), *uttarâvant* (e. g. iv. 22. 5), *vîryâvant* (e. g. iv. 37. 5), *vṛshṇyâvant* (v. 25. 8), *bhaṅgurâvant* (vii. 71. 1), *açitâvant* (ix. 6. 38), *rocanâvant* (xiii. 3. 10), *ishṭâvant* (xviii. 3. 20), *hlâdivant* (vii. 90. 3), and *vishûvant* (ix. 3. 6). In all these words, the *pada*-text restores the final vowel of the theme to its short form, and (by iv. 17) separates the theme and the suffix by *avagraha*.* For the suffix *mant* we have but a single word, *tvishîmant* (e. g. iv. 19. 2 : p. *tvishi-mant*): and so also for the suffix *van*—viz. *satyâvan* (p. *satya-van*: iv. 29. 1, 2)—respecting which I do not know whether it should be regarded as included under the technical designation *matu*. There are a few words in which the long vowel before the possessive suffix is properly regarded as rightfully belonging to the theme, and so is left unshortened in the *pada*-text; such are *dakshiṇâvant*, *çîtikâvant*, *hlâdikâvant*, *utkrushîmant*, and *jyotishîmant*.

Of the words mentioned above, only two—viz. *açvavant* (vi. 68. 3. xviii. 3. 61) and *vîryavant* (viii. 5. 1. xviii. 4. 38)—ever show in *sanhitâ* forms having the vowel short. The former of them is specially noted in the Vâj. Pr. (iii. 97) as doing so in a single instance.

इकायां च यकारादौ ॥ १८ ॥

18. As also before a suffix beginning with *y*, in a desiderative form.

In this rule, the *anuvṛtti* of *bahulam* is duly indicated, by the insertion of *ca*. As examples of desiderative forms exhibiting the lengthened vowel before *y*, the commentator cites *adhvarîyatâm* (i. 4. 1 : p. *adhvari-yatâm*), *vṛshâyamâṇaḥ* (ii. 5. 7 : p. *vṛsha-yamânaḥ*), and *çatrû*-

---

* Our *pada* MS. does, indeed, read *rocanavant* (xiii. 3. 10), without separation: but this is, it can hardly be doubted, a mere error of the scribe.

yatīm abhi (iii. 1. 3: p. *çatru-yatīm*): as examples of the short vowel, he gives *arātīyāt* (iv. 36. 1: p. *arāti-yāt*), *janīyanti* (xiv. 2. 72: p. *jani-yanti*), *putrīyanti* (xiv. 2. 72: p. *putri-yanti*), and *mṛgayuḥ* (x. 1. 26: p. *mṛga-yuḥ*)—adding to the last word *prabhṛtāni ca*, which I take to be, not a part of this or of any other citation, but (with amendment to *prabhṛtīni ca*) a simple expression for 'et cetera;' although the commentator does not anywhere else, I believe, give us such an intimation that more examples might be had for the seeking. The only ones of this class which our text farther presents are *sukshetriyā* and *sugātuyā* (both at iv. 33. 2: p. *su-kshetriyā : su-gātuyā*), besides *amitrayu*, in the twentieth book (xx. 127. 13). Of cases of the long vowel, we have also *aghāyant* (e. g. x. 4. 10: p. *agha-yant*) and *aghāyu* (e. g. i. 20. 2: p. *agha-yu*: in *abhyaghāyánti* [v. 6. 9 and vii. 70. 3*] the *pada*-text leaves the vowel long, writing *abhi-aghāyánti*), *vasūyā* (iv. 33. 2: p. *vasu-yā*), *çapathīyant* (e. g. v. 14. 5: p. *çapathi-yant*), *janīyant* (vi. 82. 3: p. *jani-yant*), *amitrāyant* (vii. 84. 2: p. *amitra-yant*: the Rik, in the corresponding passage [x. 180. 3], has the short vowel), *kavīyamāna* (ix. 9. 18: p. *kavi-yamāna*), and *nipriyāyate* (xii. 4. 11 etc.: p. *ni-priyayate*): *satvanāyant* (v. 20. 1) seems to belong to the same class, but it is written by the *pada* with the long vowel, *satvanā-yan*. From the themes *amitra* and *jani*, it will be noticed, come desiderative or denominative forms of either class, or with both the short and long vowel.

तृतीयान्तस्य ॥ १९ ॥

19. As also the final vowel of an instrumental case.

In the form of this rule there is nothing which continues the implication of *bahulam*, but such an implication is, of course, unavoidably necessary, and is made by the commentator. As instance of the long vowel, he cites *yenā sahasraṁ vahasi yenā 'gne sarvavedasam* (ix. 5. 17); as instance of the short vowel, *kena çrotriyam āpnoti* (x. 2. 20). All the cases occurring under this rule have been detailed above, in the note to rule 16: excepting *tenā* and *yenā*, which are tolerably frequent (*tenā* occurs 24 times, and *yenā* 8 times), we have, of instrumentals with lengthened finals, only a few sporadic instances, viz. *sahasyenā*, *bhadreṇā*, *amṛtenā*, *kāvyenā*, and *martyenā*, each in a single passage. Of other forms of declension which undergo a like prolongation, the text affords us two genitives, *asyā* and *kariṇasyā*; and, as accusative singular, *puru* is twice lengthened into *purū*. Besides these, we find only such forms as *janimā* for *janimāni*, in which the long vowel may be more properly regarded as thematic and not metrical. This latter class of cases, however, has been reckoned in with the rest under rule 16, because it is so treated by the *pada*-text, which writes the final vowel short.† In a single instance (*brahma*: v. 2. 8) the *saṁhitā* preserves the short vowel.

---

* Amended in the published text to *abhyaghāyati*.

† Excepting in two cases, viz. *varimā* (iv. 25. 2), and *sadmā* (ix. 9. 3). I do not at all understand the reason of these exceptions, and they may possibly be misreadings of our *pada* MSS.; the *pada*-text reads *sadma* at v. 1. 3, and in the Rik passage (i. 164. 9) corresponding with ix. 9. 3, both *pada* and *saṁhitā* give *sadma*.

रलोपे ॥ २० ॥

20. When *r* is dropped, the final vowel is lengthened.

The other treatises (R. Pr. iv. 9, r. 29, ccxlviii; V. Pr. iv. 34; T. Pr. viii. 17), with better reason, give this rule in connection with that for the omission of the final *r*, which takes place (by ii. 19) only before a following initial *r*. The commentator repeats once more the same series of quotations which he has given already twice before, under i. 28 and ii. 19, only excepting the first, *çaradaḥ puruci rāyaḥ* (ii. 13. 3): he then, as if in surprise at his own audacity, asks himself why he has omitted this; and makes reply that, although it offers an instance of the loss of a final *r*, it shows no protraction of the vowel, which was long already.[1]

नारकादीनां प्रथमस्य ॥ २१ ॥

21. Of *nāraka* etc., the first vowel is lengthened.

The commentator cites only three cases under this rule, viz. *nārakam* (xii. 4. 36: p. *narakam*), *sādanam* (e. g. ii. 12. 7: p. *sadanam*), and *āsata indra* (viii. 4. 8: p. *asataḥ*). The first word occurs only once in the Atharvan; the second is found several times, but *sadana*, with short antepenult, still oftener; for *āsat* we have also two other passages in the same hymn with the one quoted (viii. 4. 12, 13). Besides these, the word of most frequent occurrence, belonging to the same class, is *purusha*, which usually* becomes *pūrusha* at the end of a *pāda* (as noted by the Vāj. Pr., iii. 118), or where its first syllable has that place at which a long vowel is especially needed in the cadence of the *pāda*. Moreover, the text offers us *sūyamān* (iv. 27. 1: p. *su-yamān*†), and *sūyavasa* (e. g. iv. 21. 7: p. *su-yavasa*), with its compound *sūyavasād* (vii. 73. 11: p. *suyavasa-at*). Causative forms, such as *yāvaya* (p. *yavaya*), which the treatise perhaps meant to include in this rule, have been spoken of above, under rule 15.

दीदायादीनां द्वितीयस्य ॥ २२ ॥

22. Of *didāyat* etc., the second vowel.

The commentator's examples are *didāyat* (iii. 8. 3: p. *didayat*), *ushāso vīravatīḥ* (iii. 16. 7: p. *ushasaḥ*), and *ushāsānaktā* (e. g. v. 12. 6: p. *ushasānaktā*). The latter compound occurs several times in our text: from the theme *ushas* we have also once (xiii. 2. 46) the accusative *ushāsam* (p. *ushasam*). The only other word of like character which I have noted in the Atharvan is *çrathāya* (vii. 83. 3: p. *çrathaya*). A part of the compounds exhibiting protraction in the final syllable of the first member, and of which a detailed list has been given above, under

[1] *kim artham idaṁ nodāhriyate: puruci rāyaḥ: yady api ralopo dīrgha evāsaḥ.* The reading is very corrupt, but the thing aimed at is, I believe, clear.

* In the Atharvan only usually, and not universally: exceptions are v. 30. 2, viii. 7. 2. xi. 8. 32. xii. 4. 13. xix. 6. 1, and one or two others.

† The edition reads, with I. and II., *suyamān*.

rule 12, might be regarded as falling under this rule; but as a part of them also would not, since it is their third syllable that is prolonged, and not their second, I preferred to give them all together in that place.

सात्रासाहादीनामुत्तरपदाद्यस्य ॥ २३ ॥

23. Of the compounds *sâtrâsâha* etc., the first vowel of the second member.

The instances cited by the commentator are *sâtrâsâhasya* (v. 13. 6: p. *sâtrâ-sahasya*), *amitrasâhaḥ* (e. g. i. 20. 4: p. *amitra-sahaḥ*), and *vishâsahiḥ* (e. g. i. 29. 6: p. *vi-sasahiḥ*); all of them from the root *sah*. The text furnishes another derivative from the same root belonging under this rule, viz. *abhimâtishâhaḥ* (iv. 32. 4: p. *abhimâti-sahaḥ*): the only other case which I have found is *nyâyanam* (vi. 77. 2: p. *ni-ayanam*). The word *ukthaçâsaḥ*, which the *pada*-texts of the Rik and White Yajus write *uktha-çasaḥ*, and which therefore receives attention from their Prâtiçâkhyas (R. Pr. ix. 10; V. Pr. iii. 122), is read in our *pada* (xviii. 3. 21) *uktha-çâsaḥ*.

ऋत वृधवरीवानेषु ॥ २४ ॥

24. Of *ṛta*, the final vowel, before *vṛdh*, *varî*, and *vân*.

The instances cited by the commentator are *ṛtâvṛdhaḥ* (e. g. xi. 6. 19: p. *ṛta-vṛdhaḥ*), *ṛtâvarî yajñiye* (vi. 62. 1: p. *ṛta-varî*), and *ṛtâvânam vâiçvânaram* (vi. 36. 1: p. *ṛta-vânam*): the same words occur elsewhere, in a few passages which it is unnecessary to specify; they always show a long vowel in *saṁhitâ* and a short in *pada*, while the other numerous compounds of *ṛta* have everywhere the short vowel only.

अध त्यंधीःपरवर्जम् ॥ २५ ॥

25. Also that of *adha*, excepting when followed by *tyam* and *dhîḥ*.

The commentator's illustrative citations for *adhâ*, with lengthened final, are *adhâ yathâ naḥ* (xviii. 3. 21), and *adhâ pitṝ̂ṅr upa drava* (xviii. 2. 23): he also quotes the exceptions mentioned in the rule, as follows: *adha tyaṁ drapsam* (xviii. 1. 21), and *adha dhîr ajâyata* (xviii. 1. 21). There is, however, yet another case in the text in which the final vowel is left short, and which has been overlooked both by treatise and commentator: it is *adha syâma* (xviii. 3. 17). All the passages in which *adhâ* occurs have been given above, in the note to rule 16. Except in the single case in which it is followed by *dhîḥ*, the word always stands at the beginning of a *pâda*. The commentator adds from his metrical authority a verse containing a virtual repetition of the rule: *adhe 'ti vyañjane dîrgho varjayitvâ tyadhîparam: svarâdâv api*[1] *sarvatra vyañjane hrasva eva tu*; '*adha* is long before a consonant, excepting the cases in which it is followed by *tyam* and *dhîḥ*; but before a consonant preceded by a vowel (?) it is everywhere only short.'

---

[1] ?—MS. *svadârdavyya*.

Very little can be said in praise of the manner in which our treatise, in this section, deals with the intricate and numerous phenomena of the irregular prolongation of vowels in the Atharvan text; its statements are greatly wanting in accuracy, in completeness, and in systematic construction and arrangement. The form of its general rules, which embrace a great number of cases, is objectionable from indefiniteness: the cases which are made the subject of its special precepts are chosen arbitrarily and with little judgment, and in part are such as required no notice; while, on the other hand, it is doubtful whether one or two classes of cases are provided for at all: and finally, in several instances it abdicates altogether the office of a Prâtiçâkhya, and, instead of determining the usage of its school as to the points upon which it touches, leaves them as unsettled as it found them.

As elsewhere in the signature of the separate sections of this chapter, no statement is made respecting the number of rules which the section contains: the manuscript says simply *tṛtîyasya prathamaḥ pâdaḥ*.

पदान्ते व्यञ्जनं द्विः ॥ २६ ॥

26. At the end of a word, a consonant is pronounced double.

The subject of the duplicated pronunciation of consonants, or of the *varṇakrama*, as it is sometimes called, is one of the most peculiar in the whole phonetical science of the Hindus. It is also the one, to my apprehension, which exhibits most strikingly their characteristic tendency to arbitrary and artificial theorizing; I have not succeeded in discovering the foundation of fact upon which their superstructure of rules is based, or explaining to myself what actual phonetic phenomena, liable to occur in a natural, or even a strained, mode of utterance, they supposed themselves to have noted, and endeavored thus to reduce to systematic form. The *varṇakrama*, however, forms a not inconspicuous part of the phonetic system of all the Prâtiçâkhyas, and is even presented by Pâṇini (viii. 4. 46–52), although the latter mercifully allows us our option as to whether we will or will not observe its rules. To present and compare in full detail the systems of the other authorities in connection with that of our own treatise would take a great deal of room, and, moreover, could be done at best but imperfectly, since our manuscript, as will be shown below, exhibits a *lacuna* of some extent and importance in the midst of its treatment of the subject. I shall accordingly only refer under each of our own rules to those precepts of the other treatises which are most nearly related to it.

If the first rule of the second chapter is still to be strictly applied, we must conclude that the makers of the Prâtiçâkhya recognized the duplicated methods of pronunciation as of force only in the *saṅhitâ-pâṭha*, and not in the utterance of the disjoined text, or the *padapâṭha*. This interpretation is somewhat supported by the fact that both the Rik Pr. (vi. 3, r. 14, cccxc) and Pâṇini (viii. 4. 51) attribute to Çâkala or Çâkalya, the teacher to whom the invention of the *padapâṭha* is generally ascribed, a denial of all duplicated utterance.

As regards our first rule, it is directly in contravention with the doctrine of the other treatises (R. Pr. vi. 2, r. 7, ccclxxxiv; V. Pr. iv. 114; T. Pr. xiv. 15), which unanimously teach that a consonant is not duplicated *in pausa*. The commentator's instances are again *godhuk, virâṭ, dṛshat, trishṭup*, the same words which we have had adduced so many times before (see i. 8 etc): they are accordingly to be pronounced *godhukk, virâṭṭ, dṛshatt, trishṭupp;* but the manuscript omits, as in almost all the examples given under the following rules, to write the duplicated letter double.

ङणना ह्रस्वोपधाः स्वरे ॥ २७ ॥

27. As are also *ṅ*, *ṇ*, and *n* before a vowel, when final and preceded by a short vowel.

This is a rule familiar to all students of Sanskrit, as being obligatory in the euphony of the later classical dialect, and not in the older language of the Vedas alone. It is equivalently stated by all the treatises (R. Pr. vi. 4, r. 15, ccexci; V. Pr. iv. 101; T. Pr. ix. 18, 19), except that the others omit the needless mention, along with the other two nasals, of *ṇ*, which never occurs as a final. Pâṇini's *pratyâhâra* (viii. 3. 32) includes all the three. Pâṇini and the Tâitt. Pr. very properly treat this doubling of a final nasal as something apart from and unconnected with the phenomena of the *varṇakrama*, by teaching it in a different part of their texts from that which deals with the latter subject; and in the Rik Pr., also, the rule rather follows next after, than is introduced among, those which prescribe the other duplications.

The commentator cites, as examples of a final nasal doubled, *pratyaṅṅ eshi* (not in AV.), *pratyaṅṅ ud eshi* (xiii. 2. 20), *udyann âdityaḥ* (ii. 32. 1), and *sugaṇṇ âste* (no such case in AV.: the instance is also given by Pâṇini's scholiasts). To illustrate the necessity of the restrictions "when preceded by a short vowel" and "before a vowel," he cites *arvâṅ âkṛtyâ cara* (iii. 2. 3), and *udaṅ jâtaḥ* (v. 4. 8). Finally, he quotes from his metrical authority a verse which restates the rule, with examples: *ṅaṇanâs tu padântâ ye hrasvapûrvâḥ svarodayâḥ: teshâṁ dvirbhâvam ichanti pratyaṅṅ udyann sugaṇṇ iti.*

संयोगादि स्वरात् ॥ २८ ॥

28. Also the first consonant of a group, after a vowel.

In all the other treatises (R. Pr. vi. 1, r. 1, ccclxxviii; V. Pr. iv. 97; T. Pr. xiv. 1), this is put at the head of the subject of the *varṇakrama*, as the fundamental and most important rule.

The commentator gives as instances the two indifferent words *agniḥ* (e. g. i. 7. 4) and *vṛkshaḥ* (e. g. iv. 7. 5), which are to be pronounced *aggniḥ* and *vṛkkshaḥ*. Then follows a *lacuna* in the manuscript, of some extent and importance, since it certainly includes one or more rules. After the two quoted examples, namely, follows *visarjanîyaḥ sasthâne ca*, of which the two last words constitute a rule which the commentary goes on to expound in full, while the first, *visarjanîyaḥ*, is the final repetition of the rule next preceding: and in both of them there is *anuvṛtti* of *na*, 'not;' that is to say, the text has passed from giving rules for the occurrence of the duplication, to giving those for its non-occurrence. As we have found several times before, where there were lesser *lacunæ*, that the copyist had skipped carelessly from a word to a like word farther on, so we may suppose the same to have taken place here: *agniḥ* and *vṛkshaḥ* were very probably quoted again as examples under the rule *visarjanîyaḥ*, and, the copyist's eye falling upon them, he overleaped all that intervened. It may be, however, that this conjecture is erroneous, and that the *lacuna* is of greater extent than would fairly admit of such an explanation. How many rules it includes, there are no means of determining: of this chapter we appear to have remaining ninety-six rules, while its signature states a hundred and five to be the number contained in it: but, on the one hand, we have not hitherto found reliable the numbers given in the signatures to the chapters; and, on the other hand, there is still another *lacuna*, of undetermined extent, in the fourth section (see under rule 80); and yet once more, we cannot be absolutely certain that the commentator does not, in one or two cases, state and expound two or more rules together, as once or twice in the first chapter (rules 12–13, 14–16). The treatment of the general subject by the other Prâtiçâkhyas varies so much, as regards fullness of detail as well as the doctrines held on minor points, that I do not venture to attempt to fill up, by their guidance, the gap which the carelessness of our copyist has left, and I continue without break the enumeration of the rules which still remain to us.

* * * * * * * * * *

[न] विसर्जनीयः ॥ २९ ॥

29. *Visarjanîya* is not doubled.

The other treatises also exempt *visarjanîya* from duplication: see Rik Pr. vi. 1 (r. 1, ccclxxviii), Vâj. Pr. iv. 112, and Tâitt. Pr. xiv. 15.

As already explained, in the preceding note, it is probable that the commentator gave again, in order to show that *visarjanîya* is not doubled when final (by iii. 26), like any other consonant, the instances *agniḥ* and *vṛkshaḥ*.

सस्थाने च ॥ ३० ॥

30. Nor a consonant which is followed by another of the same class.

The Rik Pr. makes no such exception as this: the other two treatises, however, do so, and each divides the precept into two, the one (V. Pr. iv. 108; T. Pr. xiv. 23) prohibiting the doubling of a consonant when followed by the same consonant, the other (V. Pr. iv. 113; T. Pr. xiv. 23, last half), when followed by a mute of the same series; the Vâj. Pr. farther specifying that the following mute must not be a nasal.

The commentator cites as instances a number of words, evidently without any particular reference to the Atharvan text, although two or three of them happen to occur there: they are *indraḥ* (e. g. i. 9. 1), *candrah* (e. g. ii. 15. 3), *mandrah* (xviii. 1. 30), *ushṭrah*, *kroshṭrah* (*kroshṭre*, xi. 2. 2), *bhrâshṭram*, *neshṭram*, and *râshṭram* (e. g. iii. 4. 1). Several of them are found also in the scholia to Pâṇini, as illustrations of his rule (viii. 4. 50) that, according to Çâkaṭâyana, no duplication takes place in a group of more than two consonants. The instances are wanting in variety, as illustrating our text, since they all present groups of three consonants, while we must suppose our rule to apply no less to groups of two, and to forbid duplication in such words as *antah*, *asti*, *ashṭa*, etc.

रेफहकारौ परं ताभ्याम् ॥ ३१ ॥

31. Nor *r* and *h*—but the consonant following those two letters is doubled.

The commentator's examples are those which have been already given, and in part twice, under i. 58 and i. 100, and they need not, therefore, be repeated here.

The Rik Pr. (vi. 2, r. 4, ccclxxxi) subjects only *r* to this rule, leaving *h* to meet the same treatment with the other spirants; the Tâitt. Pr. (xiv. 4) does the same; the precept of the Vâj. Pr. (iv. 98) is to the same effect with ours, and so is also that of Pâṇini (viii. 4. 46), except that the latter here, as elsewhere, merely allows, and does not require, the duplication.

शषसाः स्वरे ॥ ३२ ॥

32. Not, however, *ç*, *sh*, and *s*, before a vowel.

This is an exception, of course, to the latter part of the preceding rule, since the sibilants would not, by any other precept, be subject to duplication before a vowel. The illustrations given in the commentary are none of them from the Atharvan, although a part of them are to be met with in the *scholia* to the corresponding rule of Pâṇini (viii. 4. 49); they are *karshati*, *âdarçah*, *akshaturçah*, and *tatarsha*[1] *puroḍâçam*. As counter-example, to show that the sibilant is exempt from duplication only before a vowel, we have given us *sdrshhyodakena yajeta*, which is also no citation from the Atharvan text.

The Rik Pr. (vi. 2, r. 10, ccclxxxvii) exempts from duplication any spirant, when followed either by a vowel or by another spirant. The Tâitt. Pr. (xiv. 16) and Pâṇini (viii. 4. 49) precisely agree with our treatise. The Vâj. Pr. fails to make any corresponding exception.

The manuscripts of the Atharva-Veda, so far as known to me, do not, save in very infrequent and entirely sporadic cases, follow any of the rules of the *varṇakrama* proper (rule 27, as already remarked, is really of another character), excepting the one which directs duplication after a *r*; and even in this case, their practice is as irregular as that of the manuscripts of the later literature. See Weber, pp. 246–248, for interesting statements respecting the usages of the codices of the Vâjasaneyi-Sanhitâ.

---

[1] *t*—MS. *tatarçam*.

प्रगृह्याश्च प्रकृत्या ॥ ३३ ॥

33. The *pragṛhya* vowels remain unchanged.

As was already remarked above, under i. 73, the designation of certain vowels as *pragṛhya*, made in the first chapter (rules 73–81), is not enough to exempt them from the operation of the rules for the combination in *saṁhitâ* of final and initial vowels: it is deemed necessary to add here that the vowels so designated maintain under all circumstances their own proper form. The method of the Rik Pr. and Vâj. Pr. is the same: see R. Pr. ii. 27 (r. 50, 51, clv, clvi); V. Pr. iv. 84.

The commentator's examples are *kena pârshṇî âbhṛte: pârshṇî iti* (x. 2. 1), *indravâyû ubhâu: indravâyû iti* (iii. 20. 6), and *ubhâv indrâgnî â bharatâm: indrâgnî iti* (v. 7. 6). The text offers a single case in which a final *pragṛhya* vowel is combined with a following initial: it is *nṛpatî 'va* (viii. 4. 6). The same passage is found in the Rig-Veda (vii. 104. 6), exhibiting the same anomalous *sandhi*, and such exceptional cases are duly noted by the Rik Pr. (ii. 27, r. 54, clix), as is one of the same character by the Vâj. Pr. (iv. 86). That no reference is made to the passage in our treatise is possibly to be taken as an indication that the true Atharvan reading is *nṛpatî iva*, as is actually given by E. and I.

एना एहा आदयश्च ॥ ३४ ॥

34. Also *enâ ehâḥ* etc.

The passage cited in the rule as heading the *gaṇa* is found at xii. 3. 33, where both *saṁhitâ* and *pada* read *enâ' ehâ'ḥ pári* etc., the establishers of the *pada*-text evidently regarding *enâ* as the instrumental of the pronominal root *a*. To me, however, it seems more plausible to take the word as accusative plural feminine of the pronoun *ena*, which is usually enclitic, but in one or two instances (see the Böhtlingk-Roth lexicon, *sub verbo*) is accented, when standing at the head of a *pâda*. The form then would be *enâ'ḥ*, and the *sandhi* perfectly regular, and its treatment as an irregularity would be due only to a misapprehension on the part of the author of the *pada*. The other cases cited by the commentator, as composing the rest of the *gaṇa*, are *yathâ man nâ 'pagâ asaḥ* (i. 34. 5. ii. 30. 1. vi. 8. 1–3), and *pṛthivî uta dyâuḥ* (xviii. 1. 5). The latter is found also in the Rig Veda (x. 10. 5), and is noticed by its Prâtiçâkhya (ii. 39). The other is a somewhat intricate case. As regards, first, the accent of the word—all analogy requires that, as containing a root for its final member, it should be accented upon the last syllable, *apagâ'*. Thus, indeed, the *pada*-text actually reads where the passage first and last occurs; but at ii. 30. 1 it gives *ápa-gâ*, and with this accentuation agree all the *saṁhitâ* manuscripts in every instance, so that this reading has been received into the printed text. Second, as regards the form—there is not, so far as I can see, any reason why we should not regard *apagâ* as the theme of the word, and not *apaga*, and so consider the form as found in the text to be *apagâs*, and the *sandhi* to be entirely regular. It is true that most of the Atharvan compounds into which the root *gam* or *gâ* enters as final member exhibit it in the shortened form *ga* (as *durgá*, *sugá*, *svargá*), but we have once *purogâ* (v. 12. 11), and in like derivatives from other similar roots, as *jan* and *pá*, the short and long forms exchange with one another quite irregularly (e. g. *prathamajâ'ḥ*, iv. 35. 1, and *prathamajáḥ*, iv. 4. 5). I should be inclined to accuse the *pada*-text of a similar misapprehension in this passage with that exhibited in the other. There are one or two other cases in the Atharvan text which belong more or less clearly under this rule. In iv. 16. 1, all the *sanhitá* MSS., without exception, read *adhishṭhâtá antikâd iva* (p. *adhi-sthâtá*): the edition treats this as a blunder, and amends to *adhishṭhâtá 'ntikâd iva*, but it might be possible to regard the passage as offering a case of anomalous *sandhi*. The theory of an error in this case, in which all the *sanhitá* MSS. chance to coincide, is supported by the analogy of the quite similar passage *rocaná'*: *asyá*, at vi. 31. 2, where P., M., and I. read *rocaná' asyá* in *sanhitá*, while W., E., and H. give *rocaná' 'syá*, with the Rik, Sâman, and White Yajur Vedas. At v. 26. 6, where the *sanhitá* manuscripts read *rûpá' asmín*, the *pada* has *rûpâ'ḥ* : *asmín*. Unless authority for *rûpá* as a feminine noun can be found elsewhere, it will probably seem easier to regard *rûpá* as a briefer form of *rûpâṇi*, and the *sandhi* as an anomalous one. A like case is vii. 97. 4, *sádanâ akarma*, where Bp. is amended by a second hand from *sâdanâ* to *sâdanâḥ*. An evident instance of pretty gross blundering is to be seen at xviii. 4. 58, where, instead of *pratárito 'shásâm*, as the sense and metre require, and as is read by the Rik and Sâma Vedas (RV. ix. 86. 19; SV. i. 559), all our *sanhitá* manuscripts present *pratáritá ushásâm*, which the *pada* also supports by giving *pra-táritáḥ*.

यवलोपे ॥ ३५ ॥

35. Where *y* or *v* has been dropped, the preceding vowel remains unchanged.

That is to say, wherever, by the loss of a final *y* or *v* according to the phonetic rules of the second chapter (ii. 21), a hiatus takes place, and two vowels are brought into juxtaposition with one another, they are not combined, but the hiatus remains. Two vowels can be thus brought together, according to the rules of our treatise, only by the loss of *y* and *v*, a final *visarjanîya* being converted into *y*, by the theory here taught, before its final disappearance. The same prohibition against applying the rules of combination twice over to the same case is given by the other treatises (R. Pr. ii. 2, r. 5, cix; V. Pr. iii. 3), in the form of a general precept, governing and restricting the application of its special rules.

As instances, the commentator cites again the whole series of passages given under ii. 21, and which I refrain from repeating here.

Although this is a rule of universal application as regards the mode of writing the text, the metre shows that it was not always observed by the authors of the hymns: see, for example, ix. 4. 19, 23, where we have to read *brâhmaṇebhya ṛshabhaṁ dattvâ* and *asmin goshṭho 'pa pṛñca naḥ*, instead of *brâhmaṇebhya ṛshabham* and *goshṭha upa*. Such cases are not infrequent. In a single instance, too (x. 1. 15), our *saṁhitā* MSS. make the double combination, reading *ayam panthāḥ kṛtye 'ti tvā nayāmaḥ*, instead of *kṛtya iti* (p. *kṛtye : iti*);* but the edited text has restored the latter reading.

केवल उकारः स्वरपूर्वः ॥ ३६ ॥

36. Also an *u* forming a word, when it is preceded by a vowel.

That is to say, of course, the particle *u*—whenever, by the operation of the euphonic rules, a hiatus is produced before it. There are found but three such cases in the Atharva-Veda; two of them are cited by the commentator, as follows: *sa u eva mahāyamaḥ* (xiii. 4. 5), and *sa u açmānam asyati* (xiii. 4. 41); the third is *ayaṁ vā u agniḥ* (xv. 10. 7).

The corresponding rules of the other treatises are Rik Pr. ii. 28 (r. 55, clx), Vāj. Pr. iv. 87, and Tāitt. Pr. ix. 16, 17: the Rik Pr. also leaves the *u* unchanged after a *y* arising from conversion of an original *i*, one such case occurring in its text (*praty u adarçi*, vii. 81. 1), while the Tāitt. Pr. inserts a transition *v* between the *u* and the following vowel.

नमौ संधौ ॥ ३७ ॥

37. Also *n* and *m*, when the results of euphonic processes.

The commentator fabricates his examples, instead of deriving them from the Atharvan text: they are *nadīn tarati* and *triṣṭum nayati*. The former is intended to show that a *n* which is the result of the assimilation of a final *m*, by ii. 31, before an initial *t*, is not liable to a farther insertion of a sibilant before the *t*, by ii. 26; the latter, that a *m* which grows out of the assimilation of a final labial to a following initial dental nasal, by ii. 5, is not then, by ii. 31, convertible into *n* by a second assimilation.

This rule is of the same character with the last but one, and is replaced, or rendered unnecessary, in the other treatises, by the general precepts there referred to.

आकारः केवलः प्रथमं पूर्वेण ॥ ३८ ॥

38. An *ā* forming an entire word is first combined with the preceding vowel.

An instance will best explain the meaning of this rule. In the passage which the *pada*-text writes *dhiyā : ā : ihi*, if *ā* is first combined with the following word, it will form *e 'hi*, and the combination of this with the preceding word will give *dhiyāi 'hi*: but if the combination of *ā* with *dhiyā* be first made, producing *dhiyā*, the addition of *ihi* will give, as final result, *dhiye* " *'hi*. The latter is the true method of making the two successive *sandhis*, as we are taught by this rule, and by corresponding rules in the other treatises (R. Pr. ii. 2, r. 7, cxi; T. Pr. v. 3);

* P. only has, by a copyist's error, *kṛtyāi 'ti* in both its copies of the tenth book.

which, however, express themselves in a more general manner, declaring that all *sandhis* must be made in the order of their occurrence.

The commentator is this time conscientious enough to cite all the passages illustrating the rule which the text contains: they are *dhiya* " 'hi (ii. 5. 4), *juhasva* " 'ndra (ii. 5. 4), *stanayitnava* " 'hi (iv. 15. 11), *krushṭha* " 'hi (v. 4. 1), *udakena* " 'hi (vi. 68. 1), and *avapaçyata* " 'ta (xviii. 4. 37).

स्वरे नामिनो ऽन्तःस्था ॥ ३९ ॥

39. Before a vowel, an alterant vowel becomes a semivowel.

Instead of citing actual examples from the text, the commentator prefers to fabricate his illustrations, which are *dadhy atra*, *madhv atra*, *mâtrartham*, *pitrartham*: a part of them are identical with those given in the *scholia* to the corresponding rule of Pâṇini (vi. 1. 77).

The other treatises have corresponding rules: that of the Vâj. Pr. (iv. 45) being precisely like our own; that of the Rik Pr. (ii. 8, r. 21, 22, cxxv, cxxvi) being more elaborately stated; and that of the Tâitt. Pr. (x. 15) restricting the conversion into a semivowel to *i*, *î*, and *u*—a restriction which might with the same propriety have been made by all, since final *û* is always *pragṛhya*, and final *ṝ* nowhere in the Vedas, so far as I am aware, comes to stand before an initial vowel.

संध्यक्षराणामयवायावः ॥ ४० ॥

40. The diphthongs, in the same situation, become respectively *ay*, *av*, *ây* and *âv*.

And then farther, by ii. 21, 22, the final semivowels are dropped, except in the case of *âv*, so that of *e* and *o* is left before an initial only *a*; of *âi*, only *â*—which vowels are then exempt, by iii. 35, from farther combination with their successors. The absorption of initial *a* by final *e* and *o*, and its retention without change after them in some cases, is taught by rules 53 and 54, below.

The commentator's illustrations are again of his own devising, for the most part; they are *agna âsâm*, *vâya âsâm*, *agna ûtaye*, *vâya ûtaye* (iv. 25. 6), *asmâ u dhâra*, *asâv âdityaḥ* (xv. 10. 7), *çrayanam*, *câyakaḥ*, *lavanam*, *lâyakaḥ*, *pavanam*, *pâvakaḥ* (e. g. vi. 47. 1). The last six are examples of applications of the rule which the Prâtiçâkhya does not contemplate. A few of the instances are identical with those given under the corresponding rules of Pâṇini (viii. 3. 18, 19. vi. 1. 78).

The Rik Pr. (ii. 9, 10, 11, r. 25, 28, 31, cxxix, cxxxii, cxxxv) converts *âi* and *âu* directly into *â*, and *e* and *o* directly into *a*, adding that after the *a* and *â* which come from *o* and *âu* a *v* is inserted except before a labial vowel. The Vâj. Pr. (iv. 46) and Tâitt. Pr. (ix. 11–15) precisely agree with our treatise.

पूर्वपरयोरेकः ॥ ४१ ॥

41. In the following rules is taught the fusion of a preceding and a following vowel into a single sound.

This is a general heading or *adhikāra* for that which is to follow, or a rule governing the interpretation of the remaining rules in the section. The technical language of the Prātiçākhyas has no recognised method of indicating the fusion of two sounds into one, and the form of the following rules is ambiguous, since rule 44, for instance, literally means, according to the usual phraseology of the treatise, that *a* before *i* becomes *e*, and not *a* with *i*. Hence the necessity of this special rule of interpretation: it has its correspondents in the Vāj. Pr. (iv. 49), and the Tāitt. Pr. (x. 1); while the Rik Pr. (ii. 6 etc.) attains the desired end by a fuller or less technical mode of statement.

समानाक्षरस्य सवर्णे दीर्घः ॥ ४२ ॥

42. A simple vowel, with one of like quality, becomes long.

The commentator's illustrations are again of his own making: they are *daṇḍāgram*, *dadhīndraḥ*, *madhūshṇam*, *hotṝçyaḥ*, and *pitṝçyaḥ*. For the last case, indeed, the combination of two ṛ's, no Vedic example could be found.

The corresponding rules of the other treatises are Rik Pr. ii. 8 (r. 15, cxix), Vāj. Pr. iv. 50, Tāitt. Pr. x. 2.

सीमन्ते ह्रस्वः ॥ ४३ ॥

43. In *sīmanta*, the resulting vowel is short.

A most blundering and superfluous rule! The Atharva-Veda contains no such theme as *sīmanta*. In the passage which the commentator cites in illustration of the rule—viz. *jinato vajra tvaṁ sīmantam* (vi. 134. 3)—the theme is evidently *sīmant*, from which we find also a plural accusative, *sīmataḥ*, at iv. 1. 1; it is a parallel form with, and equivalent to, *sīman*, of which the text affords us an accusative singular, *sīmānam*, at ix. 8. 13. The rule evidently assumes *sīmanta* as the theme, and regards it as composed of *sīman* and *anta*. Our *pada*-text, as might be expected, makes no attempt to analyze the word. The commentator, after his illustrative citation, adds to the rule a restriction of his own, quite in the style of a *vārttika* to Pāṇini, as follows: *sīmante keçaveshṭe 'ti vaktavyam: yo hi sīmno antaḥ sīmāntaḥ saḥ;* 'it should have been said, "in *sīmanta*, when it means the parting of the hair;" for the extremity (*anta*) of a boundary (*sīman*) is *sīmānta*.' Since, however, *sīmānta* does not occur in the Atharvan, the limitation is just as impertinent as the original rule: more so, it could not well be. Compare *vārttika* 3 to Pāṇ. vi. 1. 94.

अवर्णस्येवर्णे एकारः ॥ ४४ ॥

44. *A* and *ā*, with *i* and *ī*, become *e*.

The commentator's illustrations, as given by our manuscript, are *ravadgomālendraḥ*, which, however, a comparison of the examples under the next rule and under the corresponding rule of Pāṇini (vi. 1. 87) shows to require amendment to *khaṭvendraḥ*, *mālendraḥ*.

The corresponding rules of the other treatises are Rik Pr. ii. 6 (r. 16, cxx), Vāj. Pr. iv. 52, and Tāitt. Pr. x. 4.

उवर्णे ओकारः ॥ ४५ ॥

45. With *u* and *ū*, they become *o*.

The commentator, as so generally in this portion of his work, makes his own illustrations, viz. *khaṭvodakam*, *mālodakam*: compare under Pāṇ. vi. 1. 87.

See the identical rules in the other treatises: Rik Pr. ii. 7 (r. 17, cxxi), Vāj. Pr. iv. 52, and Tāitt. Pr. x. 5.

There is a single instance in the text, in which this rule is not observed, and *a* + *ū* are not combined into *o*, but into *āu*: it is the word *prāuḍhaḥ* (xv. 15. 4: p. *pra-ūḍhaḥ*). B., indeed, reads *proḍho*, but doubtless only by an error of the copyist. We must suppose, either that the authors and commentator overlooked this word, or that its *pada* as well as *sanhitā* reading in their text would be *prāuḍhaḥ*, or that the passage containing it was not in their Atharva-Veda—of which suppositions, I should regard the first as the most plausible, and the last as the least likely.

अरमृवर्णे ॥ ४६ ॥

46. With *ṛ* and *ṝ*, they become *ar*.

The commentator's examples are *tasya ṛshabhasyā 'ṅgāni* (ix. 4. 11), *yajñartaḥ* (viii. 10. 4: p. *yajña-ṛtaḥ*), *kāmartaḥ* (not in AV.), and *nāi 'nān avartiḥ* (iv. 34. 3: the *pada*-text always writes the word *avartiḥ*, without separation).

The Tāitt. Pr. (x. 8) makes the *sandhi* in the same manner as our treatise: the Rik Pr. (ii. 11, r. 32, cxxxvi) and Vāj. Pr. (iv. 48), however, treat it very differently, merely prescribing that both *a* and *ā* become *a* before *ṛ*, without requiring the conversion of the latter into *r*. The usage of the *sanhitā* manuscripts of the Atharva-Veda is in conformity with neither rule; they follow a method of their own, in which is to be recognized the influence of a doctrine agreeing with or resembling that of our Prātiçākhya respecting the *svarabhakti*, or fragment of vowel sound, assumed to be thrust in between *r* and a following consonant (see i. 101, 102). Where the phonetical theory requires the insertion of the longer *svarabhakti*, or where a sibilant follows, there the manuscripts usually and regularly give the vowel *ṛ* instead of *r*, reading *iva ṛshabhaḥ* (iii. 6. 4), *svasu ṛshīṇām* (vi. 133. 4), etc.; before any other consonant, or where our treatise and the Rik Pr. interpose the shorter *svarabhakti* after the *r*, and the other Prātiçākhyas require no insertion at all (see the note to i. 101, 102), there our manuscripts regularly make the combination according to the rule now under discussion, writing *ṛtasya rtena* (vi. 114. 1), *iva rbhuḥ* (x. 1. 8), *sa rcām* (x. 8. 10), etc. These rules are not, however, altogether without exceptions: there are a number of passages in which one or more of the manuscripts read the semivowel *r* instead of the vowel *ṛ* before a *sh* (viz. iv. 4. 6. ix. 8. 14,

15, 16. x. 7. 14*a*; 10. 10. xi. 1. 1, 3; 3. 58. xii. 1. 6. xiii. 1. 55. xv. 2. 4, first time), and even a few (viz. x. 7. 14*c*. xi. 6. 11. xv. 2. 4 (*bis*); 14. 4. xix. 9. 18) in which they all agree in so doing; and, on the other hand, while in the very great majority of cases the ṛ is changed to *r* before any other consonant (it is found so changed, in the Atharvan text, before *k*, *g*, *c*, *j*, *ch*, *t*, *d*, *n*, *dh*, and *bh*), there are a very few instances (viii. 10. 4. xviii. 2. 31; 3. 24) in which one or more manuscripts leave it unaltered, and even two (x. 1. 12; 5. 30, before *g* and *k*) where they unanimously read ṛ.* As regards the orthography of the *sandhi* in the published text, accordingly, three courses were open to the editors: first, to follow the rule of the Prâtiçâkhya, and to convert the initial vowel everywhere into the semivowel; second, to carry out consistently the general principle derivable from the practice of the manuscripts, writing always ṛ before a sibilant, and *r* before any other consonant; and third, to be governed everywhere by the authority of the manuscripts where they were unanimous, and, where they disagreed, to give due weight to the principle just referred to, in choosing between their discordant readings. Unfortunately the edition has adopted none of these courses, but, while adhering with tolerable closeness to the manuscript readings through the early part of the text, gives everywhere only ṛ from the beginning of the eighth book onward, thus introducing the rule of the Rik and White Yajur Vedas, and following neither the Prâtiçâkhya nor the manuscripts of the Atharvan. The details given above, however, will show what are the readings of the manuscripts in any given passage.

It is worthy of remark that the manuscript of our commentary, like those of the Atharvan text, writes ṛ in the first instance cited (*tasya ṛshabhasya*), and *r* in all the rest.

There is a single passage of the text requiring special notice, as exhibiting in the *sanhitâ* manuscripts an entirely irregular *sandhi* of final *â* with initial ṛ: it is at xviii. 2. 31, where the *â* of *suçevâ* is left unshortened before *ṛkshâkam*, B. writing *suçevâ ṛkshâkam*, and all the others *suçevâ ṛkshâkam*. Probably the reading is corrupt, or the words wrongly analysed by the *pada*-text: perhaps we have to correct and divide *suçevâ : ârkshikâm*.

उपर्षन्त्यादिषु च ॥ ४७ ॥

47. Also in *uparshanti* etc.

The words and forms contemplated by this rule are exceptions to the one next following, according to which we should have *upârshanti* etc. The commentator cites in illustration the passages *yâ hṛdayam uparshanti* (ix. 8. 14), *yâḥ pârçve uparshanti* (ix. 8. 15), and *yâs tiraçcîr uparshanti* (ix. 8. 16); and these are the only cases of the kind pro-

* The lingual sibilant, *sh*, is the only spirant before which a *sandhi* of final *a* or *â* with initial ṛ is made in the Atharvan text: the text does, indeed, contain a single passage in which such a combination should properly take place before ṛ—viz. *krsnasa ṛçya iva rohitam* (iv. 4. 7)—but the tradition has most palpably and grossly misunderstood and blundered over the phrase, and the *pada* writes it *krsna : asi : ṛçyah-iva : rohitam*, instead of *krsnasara : ṛçyah-iva : rohitam*.

sented by the text, so that the "etc." at the end of the rule is quite superfluous as regards the Atharvan. In the passages cited, the *pada* reads *upa-ṛshanti*, and the *saṁhitâ* manuscripts, as already noticed in the last note, vary between *upârshanti* and *upaṛshanti*, W. even giving, in the second and third cases, *upârishanti*.

उपसर्गस्य धात्वादावारम् ॥४८॥

48. The *a* or *â* of a preposition, with the initial *ṛ* or *ṝ* of a root, becomes *âr*.

The commentator's illustrations are of his own fabrication, and in part are to be found under the corresponding rule of Pâṇini (vi. 1. 91): they are *upârshati*, *prârshati*, *upârchati*, *prârchati*, *upârdhnoti*, and *prârdhnoti*. The only case arising under the rule in the Atharva-Veda is *â ṛchatu*, at ii. 12. 5. Our treatise might, then, like the Vâj. Pr. (iv. 57), have restricted the operation of the rule to the preposition *â*. The Tâitt. Pr. (x. 9) states the principle in the same general form in which it is here given.

भूतकरणस्य च ॥४९॥

49. As does also that of the augment.

This rule, of course, in a treatise whose subject is the *saṁdhyapadyâu guṇâu* of words (i. 1), is out of place and superfluous. It has no correspondent in any of the other treatises, and its chief interest and value to us lies in its presenting a term for 'augment'—*bhûtakaraṇa*, 'maker of past meaning'—which is elsewhere unknown, at least in the Prâtiçâkhya literature.

The commentator cites, in illustration of the rule, *sa ârdhnot* (iv. 39. 1 etc.); and also, as counter-example, showing that it applies only to the augment, *katamâ sa ṛcâm* (x. 8. 10).

एकारैकारयोरैकारः ॥५०॥

50. With *e* and *âi*, *a* and *â* become *âi*.

Again the commentator gives us only fabricated illustrations, which, with the help of the *scholia* to the corresponding rule of Pâṇini (vi. 1. 88), are readable as follows: *khaṭvâirakâ*, *mâlâirakâ*, *khaṭvâitikâyanaḥ*, *mâlâitikâyanaḥ*.[1]

The corresponding rules in the other treatises are Rik Pr. ii. 7 (r. 18, cxxii), Vâj. Pr. iv. 55, Tâitt. Pr. x. 6.

ओकारौकारयोरौकारः ॥५१॥

51. With *o* and *âu*, they become *âu*.

The commentator this time presents us two actual citations from the

[1] *khaḍvâirakâḥ : mâlâirakâḥ : khaḍvâitikâyanânaḥ : mâlâitikâyanânaḥ.*

text, viz. *brahmâudanam pacati* (xi. 1. 1 : p. *brahma-odanam*), and *tasyâu 'danasya* (xi. 3. 1); but then adds a fictitious case, *brahmâupagavaḥ*, which occurs also in Pâṇini's *scholia* (to rule vi. 1. 88).

The corresponding rules in the other treatises are Rik Pr. ii. 7 (r. 19, cxxiii), Vâj. Pr. iv. 55, and Tâitt. Pr. x. 7.

शकल्येष्यादिषु पररूपम् ॥ ५२ ॥

52. In *çakalyeshi* etc., the result has the same form with the latter constituent.

The commentator cites under this rule the following cases: *çakalyeshi yadi vâ te janitram* (i. 25. 2 : p. *çakalya-eshi*), *anamîvâ upetana* (iii. 14. 3 : p. *upa-itana*), *arvâcî gâur upe 'shatu* (vi. 67. 3), and *upeshantam udumbalam* (viii. 6. 17 : p. *upa-eshantam*). Of these cases, the first would equally admit of being regarded as a case of regular *sandhi*, and analyzed as *çakali-eshi*: the second is analogous with the combinations to which rule 38 of this chapter relates, the preposition *â* being in *sanhitâ* combined with *upa*, and then the resulting *upâ* with *itana*. Of this kind, the text presents one additional instance, in *upeyimá* (x. 1. 10 : p. *upa-eyimá*; it is made up of *upa-â-iyimá*): it is the only passage falling under the rule which the commentator does not give.

Similar cases are noted by the Rik Pr. at ii. 36, 37, by the Vâj. Pr. at iv. 53, 54, and by the Tâitt. Pr. at x. 14.

एकारौकारान्तात्पूर्वः पदादेरकारस्य ॥ ५३ ॥

53. After a word ending in *e* or *o*, an initial *a* becomes one with the preceding vowel.

The commentator cites a few instances of this exceedingly common *sandhi* (the occurrence of which will be more particularly treated of under the next rule), as follows: *te 'vadan* (v. 17. 1 : the instance, however, may perhaps be given as one fabricated, and not as a citation from the Atharvan text; it is found in the *scholia* to Pâṇ. vi. 1. 115), *te 'kravan* (as is read both here and under iii. 55; perhaps we are to amend to *te 'kṛṇvan*, but that also is not to be found in the Atharvan), *so 'bravît* (xv. 3. 2), *yo 'sya dakshiṇaḥ karṇaḥ* (xv. 18. 3), and *so 'rajyata* (xv. 8. 1).

The physical explanation of this combination is exceedingly difficult. The Rik Pr. (ii. 12, 13, r. 33, 34, cxxxvii, cxxxviii) and Vâj. Pr. (iv. 58), as well as Pâṇini (vi. 1. 109), treat it in the same manner as our treatise, as a union of *a* with the preceding diphthong, or its absorption by the latter. The Tâitt. Pr. alone (xi. 1) teaches an actual loss or omission of the *a*.

क्वचित्प्रकृत्या ॥ ५४ ॥

54. Sometimes the *a* remains unabsorbed.

The commentator quotes from the text, in illustration, the passage *ye agnayaḥ* (iii. 21. 1), and adds *sahasravarsam ide aira*, which is not found in the Atharvan text.

With this rule and the preceding our treatise makes short shrift of a subject which occupies long passages of the other Prâtiçâkhyas (R. Pr. ii. 13–28; V. Pr. iv. 58–82; T. Pr. xi. 1–xii. 8), and has cost their authors a vast deal of labor. The saving is made, however, at the expense of its reputation and value as an authority for the readings of its text, since it does not determine the *sanhitâ* form of one of the many hundred passages in which initial *a* comes in contact with final *e* or *o*. There is not in the whole work another so discreditable confession of unwillingness or inability to cope with the difficulties of an intricate subject.

In endeavoring to make some systematic exhibition of the usage of the Atharvan text with reference to this *sandhi*, I have been able, after more than one trial, to devise no better scheme of presentation than one founded upon a comparison of the actual written usage of the text with the requirements of the metre. If there is any rule or system of rules, of a more formal character, underlying and determining the very various phenomena—which I cannot but seriously doubt—I have been unable to discover any trace of it. The tabular conspectus, then, is as follows—the lines distinguishing the cases in which the metre appears to require the retention of the *a* unabsorbed, as a separate syllable, from those in which its absorption is demanded, in order to make the verse of proper length; and the columns showing how often the *a* is by the manuscripts omitted and retained respectively:

	In written text:				Total.
	omitted.		retained.		
I. Where metre requires omission,		252		41	293
II. Where metre requires retention:					
a, at beginning of *pâda*,	198		39		
b, elsewhere in *pâda*,	102		965		
		300		1004	1304
Total in metrical part of text,		552		1045	1597
III. In unmetrical passages,		192		28	220
Total in whole text,		744		1073	1817

Upon examining this table, it will be seen, in the first place, that in the unmetrical portions of the Atharvan text the greatly prevailing method of making the *sandhi* is that which is followed in the Sanskrit literature proper, viz. by omission of the *a*: the proportion of omissions to retentions is that of 7 to 1. In the metrical portions, on the other hand, the more common custom is to retain the *a*, the retentions being to the omissions nearly as 2 to 1. When we come to inquire farther what was the usage of the makers of the hymns, we find that the proportion in favor of the retention of the *a* as a separate syllable is considerably greater, or almost as 4½ to 1. There is, then, considerable discordance between the written and spoken usage in the metrical part; and yet this discordance appears in great measure at a single point, or where the final *e* or *o* of a *pâda* precedes the initial *a* of another *pâda*. In this situation—where, if ever, we should expect the traditional and written reading to correspond with the original spoken form of the verse—the recorded text usually leaves out the *a*, and mars as much as it can the metrical form of the verse: the proportion of omissions to retentions is here as 5 to 1; and in the Rig-Veda, so far as I have observed, it is still larger: there can be but very few instances in the earlier portions, at least, of that text, where the custom of omission of *a* at the beginning of a *pâda* is not followed. Making exception of this special case, it may be said that the usage of the written text follows in the main the requirements of the metre—although with not infrequent exceptions, which in the case of the required omissions make somewhat less than a sixth of the whole number, and in the cases of required retention, considerably less than one-ninth.

There are, of course, a number of doubtful cases, where the metre is irregular and obscure, or where it might be restored either with the omission or the retention of the *a* as a separate syllable: but, rather than form of them a separate class, I have determined and ranked each case according to my best judgment; and the general relations and bearings of the scheme are not, I am sure, perverted by any errors I may have committed.

Here, at the end of the second section of the chapter, the manuscript says again simply *tṛtîyasya dvitîyaḥ pâdaḥ*.

The proper subject of the next section is the calling forth or modification, in connection with the combinations of the phrase, of the accents already laid down and defined in the first chapter (i. 14–17). With this, however, is also connected a distinction and nomenclature of the different kinds of *svarita* or circumflex accent which the theory of the school recognizes: and the latter subject is even allowed in part to take precedence of and overlie the former, in such a manner as to render their joint presentation confused and imperfect, as will be pointed out in detail below. By way of introduction to the section, and before stating and explaining its first rule, the commentator gives us the following four verses:* *shaḍ eva svaritajâtâni lakshaṇajñâḥ pratijânate: pûrvaṁ pûrvaṁ dṛḍhataraṁ mṛdîyo yad yad uttaram:—abhinihitaḥ prâçlishṭo jâtyaḥ kshâipraç ca tâ ubhâu: tâirovyañjanapâdavṛttâv ity etat svaritamaṇḍalam:—sarvatîkshṇo 'bhinihitas tataḥ prâçlishṭa ucyate: tato mṛdutarâu svarâu jâtyaḥ kshâipraç ca tâv ubhâu:—tato mṛdutaraḥ svâras tâirovyañjana ucyate: pâdavṛtto mṛdutara iti svârabalâbalam*; 'those skilled in distinctions recognize six kinds of circumflex accent, and no more. Of these, each preceding one is harder, each succeeding one is softer: viz., the *abhinihita*, the *prâçlishṭa*, and the *jâtya* and *kshâipra*, these two; farther, the *tâirovyañjana* and *pâdavṛtta*: this is the series of circumflex accents. The *abhinihita* is entirely sharp; next is ranked the *prâçlishṭa*; the next pair, of softer character, are the *jâtya* and *kshâipra*, these two; the *tâirovyañjana* is called softer than these; the *pâdavṛtta* is still softer: thus are laid down the relative strength and weakness of the circumflex accents.' We have here evidently the schemes of two different authorities, which accord quite closely with one another; the only difference being that the former seems to rank as equal the two accents last mentioned. Indeed, the commentator goes on to add, in accordance with this, *apara âha: tâirovyañjanapâdavṛttâu tulyavṛttî iti*; 'another says, "the *tâirovyañjana*

* The last two of these verses are also cited in Uvaṭa's commentary to the Vâj. Pr.: see Weber, p. 189.

and *pâdavṛtta* are of like quality."[1] Other authorities, however, construct the scale somewhat differently: thus the Vâj. Pr. (i. 125) makes the order run as follows: *abhinihita*, *kshâipra* (with which the commentator declares the *jâtya* to agree in rank), *praçlishṭa*, *tâirovyañjana*, *tâirovirâma* (see below, under rule 62), and *pâdavṛtta*; while the Tâitt. Pr. (xx. 9–12) declares the effort of enunciation (*prayatna*) of the *kshâipra* and *jâtya*, together with the *abhinihita*, to be harder, that of the *praçlishṭa* and *prâtihata* (see under rule 62) to be softer, and that of the *tâirovyañjana* and *pâdavṛtta* to be yet less (*alpatara*). The Rik Pr., like our own treatise, takes no notice of these alleged differences of utterance among the different kinds of circumflex. It is not, however, without good reason that our commentator gives himself the trouble to state them, since their recognition can hardly have been without its important influence upon the division of the *svarita* into its numerous forms. The three arrangements quoted above agree, it will be noticed, in ranking the forms of the independent *svarita* above those of the enclitic, but are discordant as regards the relative position of the members of each class; and this may serve to us as a significant indication that the differences of secondary rank are of but trifling consequence. Precisely what is meant by "sharp" (*tîkshṇa*) and "hard" (*dṛḍha*) on the one hand, and "soft" (*mṛdu*) on the other, is not very clear: but that the proper circumflex, which arises upon the combination into a single syllable of an original acute and an original grave element, is more strongly marked and distinct in its quality of double pitch than that circumflex which is only enclitic, need not be doubted.

After this preliminary exposition, the commentator goes on to add *udâttaḥ pûrvaḥ: paro 'nudâttaḥ: svaritaḥ sandhiḥ*; 'an acute preceding; a grave following: their combination circumflex.' I am not altogether confident that this is not the first rule of the section, since, as we shall see, the two rules which follow are defective in form, and need some such predecessor. Considering, however, the faulty construction of the whole section, the limited applicability of the words in question as an *adhikâra* or heading for that which follows, their inconsistency with rule 66 below, and the absence of the paraphrase and repetition which ought to follow them, if they are a rule, I have not ventured to regard them as a part of the treatise; they are more probably an addition of the commentator, intended to supply the deficiency of the next two rules.

एकारौकारौ पदान्तौ परतो ऽकारं सो ऽभिनिहितः ॥५५

55. When an *a* is absorbed by a preceding final *e* or *o*, the resulting circumflex is *abhinihita*.

This is by no means a close version of the rule as it stands in the text; literally translated, it reads as follows: 'final *e* and *o*; following them, an *a*: that is *abhinihita*.' The construction presents a grammatical difficulty. If *akâra*, 'the sound *a*,' is not here used as a neuter—and such words are elsewhere only masculine—the form *akâram* must be understood as an accusative, and can only be construed as dependent upon *parataḥ*, used prepositionally, and taken as meaning 'before' instead of 'after,' so that we must translate 'final *e* and *o* before an *a*: that is *abhinihita*:' and to treat *parataḥ* thus seems to me hardly admissible.* The commentator does not help us much, but, if I rightly apprehend his meaning, he treats the word as a neuter nominative; his paraphrase reads *ekārāukārāu padāntāu udāttāu parataḥ akāraḥ*[1] *padādi anudāttaḥ sa abhinihitaḥ svaro bhavati*; '*e* and *o*, final, with acute accent; after them, *a*, initial, unaccented; that becomes an *abhinihita* accent (or vowel).' But passing over this difficulty, as of inferior consequence, since the virtual meaning of the phraseology is clear, we find another and a graver one in the fact that the form of the rule seems to imply that the occurrence of this *svarita* has been already sufficiently taught, and that nothing remains but to give it a name; while nevertheless the treatise nowhere informs us under what circumstances a circumflex accent arises in connection with the meeting of a final *e* or o and an initial *a*, or even that it arises at all. Its doctrine must be, of course, the same which is taught in all the other treatises; namely, that when an initial unaccented or grave *a* is elided after or absorbed into a final diphthong which itself has an acute accent, its own accent is represented in that of the resulting diphthong, reducing the latter from acute to circumflex. This case of circumflex, as well as that which forms the subject of the next rule, is an exception under rule 66 below, which teaches that a vowel resulting from the fusion of elements whereof one is acute, is itself acute: it ought, accordingly, to be specifically described and taught as such an exception. The admission as a rule of the words referred to above as used by the commentator before the statement of the precept now under discussion—viz. 'an acute preceding; a grave following: their combination circumflex'—would not satisfactorily relieve the difficulty, because this would be equivalent to setting up over against rule 66 another general rule opposed to it, without establishing in any way the relation between them. We can hardly avoid supposing that the constructors of this part of the treatise have not been skilful enough, or careful enough, to combine the two subjects of the section in such a manner as to give completeness to both. The Vāj. Pr. (iv. 59) and Tāitt. Pr. (xii. 9) give rules for the occurrence of the *abhinihita* circumflex in connection with those for the absorption of the initial *a*, and define and name the accent elsewhere (V. Pr. i. 114; T. Pr. xx. 4), when treating of the general subject of accent: the Rik Pr. deals with both matters together, but with clearness and precision, first prescribing the *svarita* (iii. 7, r. 12, cxcix), and then later (iii. 10) giving it its distinctive appellation.

The names of the different kinds of *svarita* are chiefly derived from those belonging to the euphonic combinations in connection with which they arise. These latter, however, are not expressly given in all the treatises. Thus, the Rik Pr. alone (ii. 13, r. 34, cxxxviii) calls the absorption of initial *a* into preceding final *e* and *o* the *abhinihita sandhi*

* The commentator uses *parataḥ* very often, in paraphrasing the locative of precedence, but always puts it after the locative: thus, in the first rule of this chapter, *sahāu*, 'before the root *sah*,' is explained by *sahāu parataḥ*; and so in scores of other cases.

[1] *akāra*.

while the Vâj. Pr., as well as our own treatise, agrees with it in applying to the resulting circumflex the title of *abhinihita*. The Taitt. Pr. (xx. 4) has for the same accent the slightly different name *abhinihata*, which is palpably an artificial variation of the other.

As examples of the *abhinihita* circumflex, the commentator gives us precisely the same series of phrases as under rule 53 above, viz. *té 'vadan, té 'kravan, só 'bravît, yó 'sya dákshinah kárnah, só 'rajyata.* In a few cases (which are detailed below, in a marginal note*), our Atharvan manuscripts fail to give the circumflex to an *e* or *o*, originally acute, which has absorbed an unaccented *a*, and leave it acute; but these are evidently to be explained simply as perpetuating original errors of transcription, and as requiring at our hands the emendation which they have not received from the native copyists.

इकारयोः प्राश्लिष्टः ॥ ५६ ॥

56. The circumflex arising from the fusion of two short *i*'s is *prâçlishṭa*.

Praçlishṭa or *praçlesha* is the name given by the Rik Pr. (ii. 7, r. 20, cxxiv) to all those cases of combination in which two vowels, or a vowel and diphthong, are fused together into a single vowel or diphthong: that is to say, to those of which our treatise treats in the latter half of the preceding section (rules 42–51). A *svarita* accent arising in connection with such a combination is by all the other treatises called *praçlishṭa*. The manuscript of our own treatise, both text and commentary, varies between the two forms *prâçlishṭa* and *prâkçlishṭa*, more often reading the latter; which, however, has seemed to me too anomalous, not to say too monstrous, a term to be permitted to stand. The Rik Pr. (iii. 6, r. 13, cc) informs us that a single teacher, Mâṇḍukeya, held that the *praçlishṭa svarita* arose in all cases of a *praçlesha* combination where the former element was acute and the latter grave, and it is well known that the Çatapatha Brâhmaṇa follows this rule of accentuation throughout. Pâṇini (viii. 2. 6) also permits it, whenever the unaccented latter element is the initial of a word—that is to say, everywhere in the combinations of the phrase. But the predilection of the Sanskrit for the circumflex accent is much too weak to allow of so frequent an occurrence of it as the general acceptance of this rule would condition, and all the Prâtiçâkhyas lend their authority to the usage prescribed in our rule 66 below, that a combination into which enters an *udâtta* vowel is itself *udâtta*, the acute element raising the grave to its own pitch. All, however, allow the exception which forms the subject of the last rule,

* The passages are x. 10. 10 (*bis*). xi. 2. 49; 10. 28. xii. 3. 58; 4. 36, 47 (here, however, I. gives *sé* instead of *sá*, and B. has been amended to the same reading). xv. 14. 9 (H. and P. *spd*). xvi. 4. 8. xviii. 4. 15. The edition has generally corrected the accentuation in these cases; but in three passages—viz. xi. 10. 28. xii. 3. 58. xviii. 4. 16—the erroneous reading of the manuscripts remains. Once, by a contrary error, the codices generally agree in giving the circumflex to a final *e*, while leaving the *a* unabsorbed after it: thus, *yajñè ajâyata* (xiii. 1. 48), but I. and E. (the latter by emendation) give the consistent reading *yajñó 'jâyata*, which has been received into the edited text.

and all but the Tâitt. Pr. allow also that which is treated of in this rule: if i and i, both short, are fused together into a long vowel, this vowel has the *prâçlishṭa svarita:* thus, î̂. The illustrations cited by the commentator are *abhî́ 'hi manyo* (iv. 32. 3), *bhindhî́ 'dám* (vii. 18. 1), and *diçî́ 'tâḥ* (xi. 2. 12 etc.).* But the arising of the circumflex is expressly restricted to the case in which both the i's are short: if the former of the two is long, it is very natural that, as the more powerful element, it should assimilate the weaker grave vowel, and make the whole compound acute. Thus *enî́ iva* becomes *enî́ 'va*, not *enî̂ 'va* (v. 14. 11); *mahî́ : iyám* becomes *mahî́ 'yám* (ix. 10. 12), etc. Such cases, especially of *iva* following an acute final î́, are not uncommon.† The cases in which a long unaccented î, on the other hand, is preceded by a short accented í, are exceedingly rare; there is but a single one in the whole Atharvan text, and it is cited by the commentator as a counter-example under the present rule, as follows: *mā́ vanim mā́ vā́cam no ví ''rtsîḥ* (v. 7. 6: p. *ví : îrtsîḥ*); he adds, *paro dîrghaḥ: iha asmât prâçlishṭo na bhavati;* 'the latter of the two i's is long: hence here the *prâçlishṭa* accent does not arise.' We should, however, expect that in such a compound, especially, the circumflex would not fail to appear; for if, in the fusion of í and i, the grave accent of the second element is represented in the accentuation of the resulting long vowel, by so much the more should this be the case in the fusion of í + î, where the second element is the stronger. The teachings of accentual theory are so obvious and explicit upon this point that it is hardly possible to avoid the conclusion that the Hindu grammarians, in establishing their system, overlooked or disregarded the combination í + î, on account of its rarity, and that the accent of the cases later noted was made to conform to the rule, instead of the rule being amended to fit the cases. The Vâj. Pr. (iv. 133), indeed, makes a special exception of the word *vî̂kshita* (p. *vi-îkshita*), allowing it the *praçlishṭa* circumflex which all such compounds palpably ought to have: whether the text of the White Yajus contains any other examples of the class, besides the one cited under the general rule (iv. 132: *hî́ ''m*, from *hí : îm;* the same passage is the only one given under the corresponding rule in the Rik Pr. [iii. 7, r. 12, cxcix]), Weber does not inform us. It is not easy to see any reason in the nature of things why a combination of two u's should not be subject to the same law of accent as that of two i's. This, however, is another very rare case; in the whole Atharvan not a single example occurs, nor have I happened to meet with any in the Rig-Veda; that this is the reason why the Prâtiçâkhyas generally take no notice of any *praçlishṭa* accent arising from such a combination is altogether probable. It is not a little remarkable, then, that the Tâitt. Pr. takes no note of the fusion of two i's as giving rise to a *svarita*, but (x. 17) prescribes it for the case in which, by a *praçlesha* combination, ô is formed, and applies (xx. 5) to this alone the name *praçlishṭa:* the instances cited in

* The other instances which the text affords are to be found at iii. 11. 2. v. 23. 7. vi. 92. 3; 123. 2; 126. 2. vii. 26. 7; 73. 7. xi. 3. 18. xii. 3. 34, 41. xv. 2. 2. xviii. 2. 41. xix. 44. 7.

† In the Atharvan, we have them at iv. 33. 6. v. 14. 11 (*bis*); 20. 11. vi. 8. 3. vii. 62. 1. ix. 2. 6; 4. 2; 10. 12. x. 1. 14, 32. xi. 5. 1. xiv. 2. 31, 44.

its commentary are *sú 'nnīyam iva*, *sú 'dgātā́*, *mā́sú 'ttishṭhan*, and *dikshú 'padadhāti*.

Our commentator discourses upon this rule at more than his usual length. After the citation of the examples and counter-example, with the remark upon the latter, which have already been given, he goes on as follows: *atī 'va yaḥ: atī 've 'ty atī-iva: tāirovyañjana ity eshaḥ: īkāraḥ prākçlishṭo yadā syād udāttaḥ pūrvaḥ paro 'nudāttaḥ sa prākçlishṭaḥ svaryata eva nityaṁ sandhijaṁ svaritaṁ nā 'nyad āhuḥ: divī 'va cakshuḥ: divī 'va jyotiḥ: divī 've 'ti divi-iva*; 'in the passage *átī 'va yáḥ* (ii. 12. 6)—where the *krama*-text would read *átī 've 'ty átī-iva* —the circumflex of the *ī* is *tāirovyañjana*' (see rule 62, below). 'When an *ī* is the result of *praçlesha*, the former element being acute and the latter grave, that result of *praçlesha* is always made circumflex. No other circumflex accent is declared to arise from the *sandhi*. Instances are *divī̀ 'va cákshuḥ* (vii. 26. 7), *divī̀ 'va jyótiḥ* (vi. 92. 3), where the *krama*-text reads *divī̀ 'vé 'ti divi-iva*.' I am not quite sure that I have correctly interpreted all of this, but its significance is evidently of the smallest.

Precisely the same objection lies against the form of this rule as against that of the preceding: that, whereas it ought to be a definition and a prescription, it is in fact merely nomenclatory.

अनुदात्तपूर्वात्संयोगाद्यवान्तात्स्वरितं परमपूर्वं वा जात्यः ॥५७॥

57. A circumflex which follows a conjunction of consonants ending with *y* or *v* and preceded by an unaccented vowel, or which has no predecessor, is the *jātya*.

The meaning of the term *jātya* is 'natural, original, primitive:' the circumflex syllables to which it is applied are those which have that accent in their own right and always, independently of the combinations of the sentence. The long, lumbering, and awkward account of it which the rule offers may be divided into two parts: that which is necessary to its distinction from the enclitic *svarita*, which, by rule 67 below, ordinarily follows any acute syllable, and that which is added to describe the kind of syllable in which it is invariably found to occur. The former part is contained in the words "preceded by an unaccented vowel, or having no predecessor," the enclitic circumflex being only possible as succeeding an acute. The other part is "after a conjunction of consonants ending with *y* or *v*:" that is to say, no syllable in Sanskrit has an independent circumflex accent except as it results from the conversion of an original accented *i* or *u* (short or long) into its corresponding semivowel *y* or *v* before a following dissimilar vowel; thus *kanyā̀* represents an earlier *kaní-ā*, *svàr* an earlier *sú-ar*, and the like. The *jātya svarita*, then, precisely corresponds in origin and in quality with the *kshāipra*, the one next to be described, and differs from it only in period, arising in connection with the combination of syllables into words, rather than of words into a sentence.

The definition or description of the *jātya* circumflex given by our treatise is after all imperfect, since it fails properly to distinguish the *jātya* from the *kshāipra*. Such *kshāipra* accents as are instanced by *abhyàrcata* (vii. 82. 1), *nv èténa* (v. 6. 5), and the like, answer in every particular to the defined character of the *jātya*. The word *pade*, 'in an independent or uncombined word,' or something equivalent, needs to be added to the rule. Such a limitation is not omitted from the description of any of the other treatises. The Rik Pr. (iii. 4, r. 7, cxciv) defines all the other kinds of *svarita* first, and describes this as the one which remains, and which occurs in an uncombined word; the Vāj. Pr. (i. 111) gives a definition nearly corresponding to our own, but much more concisely expressed, and omitting the specification corresponding to our *apūrvaṁ vā*, 'or which has no predecessor,' which the commentator is therefore obliged to supply. Finally, the Tāitt. Pr. (xx. 2) agrees quite closely with our treatise in the form of its definition, only adding the item noticed above as omitted here; but it calls the accent *nitya*, 'constant, persistent,' instead of *jātya*.

The commentator, after a simple repetition of the rule with the appendix of *svaro bhavati* to fill out its ellipsis, adds in illustration the same series of words which he has given us once before, under i. 17: they are, as instances of the *jātya* circumflex preceded by an unaccented vowel, *amāvāsyā̀*, *kanyā̀*, *dhānyàm*, *ācāryàḥ*, and *rājanyàḥ*; of the same in an initial or unpreceded syllable, *nyàk*, *kvà*, *svàḥ*.

अन्तःस्थापत्तावुदात्तस्यानुदात्ते क्षैप्रः ॥५८॥

58. The circumflex arising upon the conversion into a semivowel of an acute vowel before a grave is the *kshāipra*.

The name *kshāipra* is given by the Rik Pr. (ii. 8) to the combinations taught in our rule 39, above, or to those in which *i*, *ī*, *u*, *ū*, and *ṛ* become respectively *y*, *v*, and *r* before a following dissimilar vowel: the term comes from *kshipra*, 'quick, hasty,' and marks the *sandhi* as one in which there is a gain of time, or a hastened, abbreviated utterance of the semivocalized vowel. All the treatises (R. Pr. iii. 7; V. Pr. iv. 47; T. Pr. x. 16) teach that in such a case, when the former element of the compound is acute and the latter grave, the resulting syllable is circumflex; and all (R. Pr. iii. 10; V. Pr. i. 115; T. Pr. xx. 1) apply to the circumflex thus arising the name of the combination, *kshāipra*. Our own rule is this time free from the ambiguities which we have had occasion to notice in the definitions of the *abhinihita* and *prāçlishṭa* accents, and would admit of being interpreted as a precept as well as a definition, as follows: 'in the case of the conversion into a semivowel of an acute vowel before a grave, there arises the circumflex called *kshāipra*.'

The commentator cites two actual cases of the *kshāipra* circumflex, viz. *abhyàrcata* (vii. 82. 1: p. *abhi : arcata*) and *vidvàñgaḥ* (vi. 125. 1: p. *vidū-aṅgaḥ*), and fabricates two others, viz. *mātrarthàm*, *pitrarthàm* (i. e. *mātṛ-arthaṁ* etc.).

अन्तःपदे ऽपि पञ्चपद्याम् ॥५९॥

59. And even in the interior of a word, in a strong case.

It may be questioned whether this rule is merely nomenclatory, or also prescriptive; whether its meaning is that the *svarita* which appears in the finals of the strong cases of certain words whose themes are oxytone is to be accounted as *kshâipra* and not *jâtya*, or that a circumflex of the *kshâipra* variety arises when the accented final vowel of a theme, in the strong cases, is converted into a semivowel before the case-ending. The same question comes up also in connection with the two following rules. But I presume that they are all to be understood as precepts, and to be reckoned along with the other cases in which our Prâtiçâkhya turns aside to meddle with matters lying without its proper sphere. Not one of the other treatises offers anything corresponding; they would all, apparently, class as *jâtya* the circumflex accents here treated of, not distinguishing them from the others which occur within the limits of a word, or in the uncombined text. The rules, however, are not without some interest, as showing that the authors of our work appreciated the entire analogy which the circumflex accents with which they deal have with the ordinary *kshâipra*. Thus *nadyàs* is equivalent to *nadî'-as*, as *nadyàsti* would be to *nadî' asti*, while *nadyâ'i*, *nadyâ's* represent *nadî-â'i*, *nadî-â's*; the terminations of the strong cases showing no trace of that tendency which is exhibited by the other case-endings to draw away upon themselves the accent of the final vowel of the theme: compare *tudántam*, *tudántah*, *tudántas*, with *tudatâ'*, *tudatás*, *tudatás*.

The commentator cites from the text, by way of illustration, *nadyò nâ'ma stha* (iii. 13. 1), *pippalyàḥ sám* (vi. 109. 2), and *rudatyàḥ púrushe hatê* (xi. 9. 14); and also, as counter-example, to show that the circumflex arises only in a strong case, *táyâ sahasraparṇyâ' hṛ'dayam* (vi. 139. 1). Instances of both kinds are of not infrequent occurrence. In a small number of cases—viz. *karkaryàḥ* (iv. 37. 4), *pṛdâkvàm* (x. 4. 17), and *vilipyàm* (xii. 4. 41)—all the manuscripts give an acute accent to endings of the class to which the rule refers; these are, however, evident errors, and should properly have been amended in the edited text.

The commentator closes his exposition, as so often elsewhere, with a verse which is a virtual re-statement of the rule, but its form is so corrupt that I refrain from attempting to restore and translate it.[1]

ऊकारस्य सर्वत्र ॥ ६० ॥

60. Or also throughout the declension, if the final of the theme is *û*.

The manuscript reads in this rule *ukârasya*, 'if the final is *u*,' but the facts seem to require the amendment to *û*, and the method of writing of our copyist is too careless to make his authority of much weight against it. The rare termination *û* has power usually to hold its own accent, even before the ending of a weak case, and the resulting final syllable thus becomes circumflex. The commentator's instances are *tanvâ'* (e. g. i. 33. 4), *tanvè* (e. g. i. 3. 1), *vitândyoç camvòḥ* (ix. 10. 12),

[1] It reads: *antodâttâ nadî syâd [illegible] cet tathâ? [illegible] [illegible] kshâipra ucyate.*

and *vadhvàç ca vástram* (xiv. 2. 41). The only other cases afforded by the text are *tanvàs* (gen. or abl.: e. g. ii. 29. 1), *tanvà'm* (at i. 18. 3, and one or two doubtful places in the nineteenth book), and *aṣṭhīvàs* (x. 10. 23). But there are also sundry exceptions to be found in the Atharvan, which the commentator has not failed to notice and record; he says: *tato 'pavadati*, 'from this rule one must make the exceptions,' *urvārvā' iva* (vi. 14. 2), *pṛdākvà'ḥ* (x. 4. 5), *çvaçrvā'i*[1] (xiv. 2. 26), and *çvaçrvā'ḥ* (xiv. 1. 44); to which is to be added *vadhvā'i* (xiv. 2. 9, 73). All these exceptional forms, it will be remarked, have a heavy ending, while of those which exhibit the circumflex accent the ending is light in every instance but one (*tanvà'm*). The words *bāhvòs* (e. g. vii. 56. 6) and *ūrvòs* (xix. 60. 2) are instances—and, if my search has been thorough, the only ones which the text presents—of like forms from themes in *u*, which are not to be regarded as contemplated by the rule.

ओण्योश्च ॥ ६१ ॥

61. Also in *oṇyoḥ*.

That is to say, in the single word *oṇyòḥ* the final syllable has a *kshāipra svarita*, though the form is a weak case, and not from a theme in *ū*. The commentator cites the passage *oṇyòḥ kavikratum* (vii. 14. 1), the only one in which the word occurs. The Atharvan affords one other like case, viz. *kalyāṇyā'i* (vi. 107. 3), unless we are to assume there an error of the tradition represented by our manuscripts, which seems to me more likely.

व्यञ्जनव्यवेतस्तैरोव्यञ्जनः ॥ ६२ ॥

62. A circumflex between which and the preceding acute vowel consonants intervene, is the *tāirovyañjana*.

Literally, 'one separated by consonants is *tāirovyañjana*.' There is here a notable change of subject and of implication. We have passed, without any warning, from considering the necessary or independent circumflex to treating of that which is enclitic only, arising, according to following rules (rules 67–70), in an unaccented syllable which is preceded by an acute, and not again immediately followed by an acute or circumflex. Our treatise and the Rik Pr. (iii. 9, 10) subdivide the enclitic circumflex into two forms only, the *tāirovyañjana*, where the circumflexed syllable is separated from the acute by one or more consonants, and the *pādavṛtta* (the Rik Pr. calls it *vāivṛtta*), where a hiatus intervenes. The Vāj. Pr. (i. 117, 119) and the Taitt. Pr. (xx. 6, 7) also teach the same accents; but the former distinguishes under the *tāirovyañjana* a sub-form, *tāirovirāma* ('having a pause between'), as occurring when the acute is parted from its enclitic circumflex not only by consonants but by the *avagraha*, or pause which separates the two parts of a compound word: thus, in *prajā'-vat*, for instance, the enclitic accent of *vat* would be the *tāirovirāma*, while in *pra-jā'nām* that of *nām*

---

[1] 1—MS. *çvaçurvāḥ*.

would be the *tâirovyañjana* simply. The *tâirovirâma*, then, can occur only in the *pada*-text. The Tâitt. Pr. takes no notice of this *pada* accent, but allows the name *tâirovyañjana* only to a circumflex which follows an acute in the same word: if the acute syllable is a final, and the circumflex an initial, the latter is to be denominated *prâtihata* (xx. 3): thus, in *tátra*, the enclitic *svarita* of *tra* would be *tâirovyañjana*; in *tát te*, that of *te* would be *prâtihata*.* The practical importance of these numerous and varying subdivisions of an enclitic accent must be, as we cannot but think, very insignificant.

The commentator's examples of the *tâirovyañjana* accent are *idáṁ devâḥ* (ii. 12. 2) and *idám indra* (ii. 12. 3): it is, in both instances, the initial syllable of the second word which is made circumflex by the influence of the preceding acute. According to the Tâitt. Pr., both would be cases of *prâtihata*.

विवृत्तौ पादवृत्तः ॥ ६३ ॥

63. Where there is a hiatus, the circumflex is *pâdavṛtta*.

As was noticed in the last note, the Rik Pr. calls this accent *vâivṛtta*, 'arising in connection with a hiatus.' The term *pâdavṛtta* is evidently a mutilated substitute for *pâdavivṛtta* or *pâdavâivṛtta*, 'arising in connection with a hiatus between two words.'†

The commentator illustrates from the Atharvan text with *yâ'ḥ kṛtyâ' âṅgirasî'r yâ'ḥ kṛtyâ' âsurî'r yâ'ḥ kṛtyâ'ḥ svayáṁkṛtâ yâ' u câ 'nyébhir â'bhṛtâḥ* (viii. 5. 9): here are three cases of the *pâdavṛtta* circumflex, viz. in the syllables *âṅg* and *âs*, following the first and second occurrence of *kṛtyâ'*, and in the particle *u*, following the last *yâ'*.

अवग्रहे सविधः ॥ ६४ ॥

64. Where there is a division between the two parts of a compound word, the accent is of the same character.

This rule is far from possessing all the explicitness that could be desired; two or three different interpretations of it seem admissible. In the first place, it may be understood to apply only to a class of cases falling under the preceding rule, the implication of *vivṛttâu* being continued; it would mean, then, that when in the division of a compound word a hiatus is made between the acute final of the former member and the grave initial of the latter member, the enclitic circumflex accent of the latter is to be ranked as a *pâdavṛtta*, just as if the hiatus caused by the *avagraha* had been due to the operation of the ordinary rules of euphony. This interpretation is supported by the character of the citations made by the commentator to illustrate the rule; they are as follows: *ukshâ-annâya*: *vaçâ'-annâya* (iii. 21. 6), *yajñâ-ṛtaḥ* (viii. 10.

* Roth (preface to his Nirukta, p. lxv) and Weber (p. 136) regard the *tâirovirâma* and *prâtihata* as identical, but I do not see how this is possible.

† The definition of the Tâitt. Pr. (xx. 6) brings out this derivation more distinctly than our own; we read there *padavivṛttyâm pâdavṛttaḥ*.

4),* *çatá-çaradá* (e. g. x. 9. 1), *çatá-áyushá* (iii. 11. 3, 4), and *dirghá-áyushá* and *dirghá-áyushah* (not to be found in AV.: we have, however, the nominative *dirghá-áyuḥ*, at xiv. 2. 2, 63): in all these compounds, the enclitic *svarita* of the vowel following the sign of division is *pádavṛtta*. But the rule as thus interpreted seems of very little use, since such cases might be regarded as falling under the preceding rule without any special direction to that effect. The commentator does not include the word *vivṛttáu* in his paraphrase, and the fact that his citations are all of one class is far from conclusive against the intended comprehension of the other classes also under the same precept. If the implication of *vivṛttáu* be rejected, and *avagrahe* be taken to mean 'in any case of the separation of the two parts of a compound,' whether accompanied by a hiatus or not, there will, however, still remain a question as to the signification of *savidhaḥ*, 'of the same character.' Does it refer only to *pádavṛttaḥ*, and shall we assume that the enclitic circumflex of an initial syllable after a pause of separation, or *avagraha*, is always to be reckoned as *pádavṛtta*, the pause having the same effect in all cases as a hiatus—so that in *çatá-vṛshṇyam* (i. 3. 1 etc.), *sám-çrutam* (i. 3. 6), *á'-bhṛtáḥ* (i. 6. 4), and the like, the syllables *vṛ*, *çru*, and *bhṛ* would be *pádavṛtta*? Or does it refer also to *táirovyañjana*, and shall we understand that, notwithstanding an *avagraha*, the accent of a following syllable remains just what it would be were there no such pause; a hiatus conditioning a *pádavṛtta*, and the intervention of consonants (as in the examples last quoted) a *táirovyañjana*? Of these three possible interpretations, I am inclined to favor the last; and especially, as it is supported by the authority of the Rik Pr., which lays down the general principle (iii. 15, r. 23, ccx) that where syllables are separated by *avagraha*, their accentuation is the same as if they were connected with one another according to the rules of *sandhi*.

अभिनिहितप्राश्लिष्टजात्यक्षैप्राणामुदात्तस्वरितोदयानाम-
णुमात्रा निघाता विकम्पितं तत्कवयो वदन्ति ॥ ६५ ॥

65. Of the *abhinihita*, *práçlishṭa*, *játya*, and *kshâipra* accents, when followed by an acute or a circumflex, a quarter-mora is depressed: this the wise call *vikampita*.

The reason of this rule cannot be made evident without a somewhat detailed exposition of the laws laid down by the Hindu grammarians as regulating the rise and fall of the voice in connection with the consecution of the accents. In the first chapter (i. 14–17) we had merely a brief definition of the three tones of voice in which a syllable may be uttered: the low or grave (*anudátta*), belonging to unaccented syllables, the high or acute (*udátta*), which is the proper tone of an accented syllable, and the circumflex (*svarita*), combining a higher and a lower

* The *pada* manuscript reads *yajña-ṛtaḥ*, but such an accentuation is contrary to all analogy, and would in itself be in a high degree suspicious; and it is fully convicted of falsity by the citation of the word as an instance under this rule.

pitch within the limits of the same syllable, and, as we have seen, always resulting, as an independent accent, from the fusion of two originally separate elements, of which the one was acute and the other grave. If this were the whole story, the subject of accent in Sanskrit would be of no more intricacy and difficulty than in Greek: nor even of so much, since in Sanskrit neither of the accents is restricted as regards the place which it may occupy in the word; and we should only have to note and learn upon which syllable, and with which accent, each word in the language was uttered, and what were the few simple rules which govern the combinations of accented and unaccented syllables in the phrase. A great complication, however, is introduced into the system, in the first place, by the rule, taught by all the Hindu authorities (see our rule 67, below), that an originally grave syllable, when it follows an acute, receives an enclitic circumflex: that is to say, that the voice, when once raised to the pitch of acute, does not ordinarily come down with a leap to the level of the grave, but makes its descent in the course of the next following syllable; or, to illustrate by an instance, that we do not say *a*·^{mit}·*trân*, but *a*·^{mit}·*trân*.* To this rule is made the important exception (rule 70, below), that the syllable which would otherwise receive the enclitic circumflex maintains its character of grave, in case an acute or circumflex comes next after it: the theory being, apparently, that the voice prepares itself for rising to the acute pitch by sinking before it: it must, if possible, mount from the station of a syllable wholly grave. Thus we have, as the mode of utterance of *amitrân pári* and *amitrân kvà*, *a*·^{mit}·*trân*·^{pa}·*ri*, *a*·^{mit}·*trân*·^{k}*va*. Now comes the farther complication, in which all the Prâtiçâkhyas agree (see rule 71, below), that the unaccented syllables which follow a circumflex, although regarded as having the value of grave, are yet pronounced at the pitch of acute: that is to say, that, in pronouncing *pṛshadâjyápraṇuttânâm*, we say *pṛ·sha·dâj*·$^{yap·pra·ṇut·tâ·nâm}$, and not *pṛ·sha·dâj*·$^{yap·pra}$·*ṇut·tâ·nâm*. This grave accent with the tone of acute is in the Rik Pr. (iii. 11) and Tâitt. Pr. (xxi. 10) called the *pracaya* (the word means 'accumulation'): its theoretical ground I find it exceedingly difficult to discover. But it evidently stands in close relation—whether as cause or as effect, I would not attempt to say too confidently—with a somewhat different description of the character of the circumflex. The first portion of the latter accent, namely, is by the Rik Pr. (iii. 2, 3) declared to be uttered, not at acute pitch, but with a yet higher tone, and its later portion at acute pitch. The Tâitt. Pr. (i. 41–42) gives the same account of a circumflex that immediately follows an acute, although, as we have seen (in the note to i. 17), liberally citing the discordant opinions of other authorities. These two treatises, then, would require our pronunciation to be *pṛ·sha·dâj*·$^{yap·Pra·ṇut·tâ·nâm}$. Neither our own work nor the Vâj. Pr. gives such a definition of the circumflex; and yet the theory of the

* In writing these instances, I follow the rules for the division of the syllables given in the first chapter (i. 55–58); and also, in order not to misrepresent them, I make the duplication of the *varga-krama* (iii. 26–32), but omit any attempt to designate *abhinidhâna*, *yama*, etc.

pracaya accent, to my apprehension, so manifestly recognizes and implies it, that I cannot believe otherwise than that its statement is omitted by them, and that it really forms a part of their system. If the voice has already, in the utterance of the enclitic *svarita*, sunk to the actual grave pitch, it can scarcely be believed that it should be called upon to rise again to the level of acute for the utterance of the following unaccented syllables: while, on the other hand, if the circumflex be removed bodily to a higher place in the scale, and made to end at acute pitch, the following grave syllables might naturally enough be supposed to run on at the same level. Hence I regard the form of the word last given as representing the mode of its pronunciation which must be assumed to be taught by the theory of our treatise, as well as by that of the others. If, now, the grave syllables succeeding a circumflex are uttered at acute pitch, how shall an actual acute, occurring after them, be distinguished from them? Provision for this case is made in the rule, common to all the treatises (see our rule 74, below), that the grave which next precedes an acute or circumflex is not of acute tone, but remains grave. Thus, putting an acute syllable after the word which has been employed in illustrating the *pracaya* accent, we should have *prshadājyápraṇuttānām mā'* pronounced as *prshadāj*-yap-Pra-ṇut-tā-nām-mā. Thus is assured to the voice a low syllable from which to rise to the following acute, just as where the enclitic *svarita*, before an acute or circumflex, was given up for a grave pronunciation. Analogous with these two cases is that which forms the subject of the rule at present under discussion. It is constantly happening that an acute syllable follows one which has an independent circumflex, which cannot, of course, like the enclitic, be converted to grave out of complaisance to its successor. If, however, it were left unaltered, the distinction of the following acute from a *pracaya anudātta* would be endangered. If *yè 'syā́ṁ sthá pratī́cyāṁ diçí* should be uttered ye-syāṁ-sthap-pra-tīc-yāṁ-di-çi, it might be understood as *yè 'syāṁ stha pra°* etc.; while the sinking of the circumflex syllable *yè* to the level of the *anudātta* pitch—as ye-syāṁ etc. —would mark the following syllable as truly *udātta* or acute. But that the avoidance of such ambiguities was the sole, or even the principal, reason for the depression of tone taught in the rule is rendered improbable by the fact that the same is prescribed also before an independent *svarita*, which latter could not, even without any alteration of tone in the preceding syllable, be confounded with an enclitic *svarita* or with any other accent. The depression is more probably owing to the theoretical requirement that the voice should, when possible, always rise to the utterance of a real acute or circumflex from the lowest or *anudātta* pitch: which is satisfied by the retention of the *anudātta* quality before an *udātta* or *svarita* in a syllable which would otherwise become enclitic *svarita* or *pracaya anudātta*, and by the lowering of the final portion of an independent *svarita* in the same position.

The equivalent rule of the Rik Pr. (iii. 3, r. 5, cxcii) is given in connection with the first definition of the *svarita* accent: this is to be of the pitch of *udātta* in its latter portion, unless an *udātta* or *svarita* follows, in which case it is *anudātta*. The commentary informs us that the depression to *anudātta* pitch is called *kampa*, a term connected with the *vikampita* of our rule (both come from the root *kamp*, 'to tremble'). An interpolated verse at the end of the third chapter of the Rik Pr. (iii. 19) restates the same precept, in terms closely corresponding with those of our treatise. The Vāj. Pr. (iv. 137) says, in like manner, that before an *udātta* or *svarita* the latter portion of a *svarita* is further depressed. It is upon the authority of the Vāj. Pr. (i. 60) that the term *aṇumātrā*, literally 'minute measure,' used in our text, is interpreted to signify the definite quantity of a quarter-mora. The same phenomenon of *kampa* is treated in the Tāitt. Pr. (xix. 3 etc.), but with peculiar complications of theory which it is not necessary to explain here.

The commentator offers instances of each of the kinds of circumflex mentioned in the rule; they are as follows: of the *abhinihita*, *yò 'bhyā́taḥ* (xi. 2. 13), *yè 'syā́m* (iii. 26. 1 etc.), *so 'rtham* (the Atharvan contains no such phrase, nor can it be a genuine instance, as *artha* has the acute on the first syllable, and the accentuation of the two words combined would be *sò 'rtham*; it is altogether probable that the reading is corrupt, and that the phrase intended to be cited is *sò 'bhrám* [xiii. 4. 25]: this is the nearest approach to the other which our text furnishes, and is moreover an instance of a circumflex before a circumflex, which the commentator would be likely to seek); of the *praçlishṭa*, *bhindhī́ 'dám* (vii. 18. 1), *diçī́ 'táḥ* (xi. 2. 12 etc.); of the *jātya*, *amāvāsyā̀ svàḥ* (these two words do not occur in juxtaposition in the Atharvan: we have *amāvāsyā̀ mā́m* at vii. 79. 2, and e.g. *svàr ṇá* at ii. 5. 4); and of the *kshāipra*, *nadyò nā́ma stha* (iii. 13. 1), *pippalyàḥ sám* (vi. 109. 2), and *rudatyàḥ púrushe hatè* (xi. 9. 14): they are to be pronounced

ru-dat-ya-pu-ru-she-ha-te, *bhin-dhī-dam*, *yo-bhi-yā-taḥ*, etc.

Whether the Hindu grammar is much the gainer by this intense elaboration of the accentual theory may fairly be questioned: whether, indeed, it has not lost more than it has gained by the exaggeration, and even the distortion, in more than one particular, of the natural inflections of the voice. To me, I must acknowledge, it seems clear that those ancient grammarians might better have contented themselves with pointing out in each word the principal accent and its character, leaving the proclitic and enclitic accents, the claimed involuntary accompaniments of the other, to take care of themselves; or, if they could not leave them unnoticed, at least stating them in a brief and general way, as matters of nice phonetic theory, without placing them on a level with the independent accents, and drawing out a complete scheme of rules for their occurrence. The obscurity and false proportion given by them to the subject of the Sanskrit accent has availed to confuse or mislead many of its modern investigators: and we find, for instance, our modern Sanskrit grammarians explaining the independent circumflex as originated by the fusion of an acute with an enclitic circumflex, in which fusion the former accent gives way to the latter, the substance to its own shadow! The Prātiçākhyas, it will be noticed, countenance no such explanation, but describe the real circumflex as arising from the combination of an acute with a following grave element.

The designation of the accents in the Atharvan manuscripts is somewhat various, and requires a brief explanation. The Rik method of designation is now familiar to all students of the Vedic department of the Sanskrit literature, and is perfectly adapted to the theory of the accent as above set forth; all syllables uttered at grave or *anudātta* pitch have a horizontal mark below them: a *svarita* or circumflex syllable, whether its circumflex be independent or enclitic, has a perpendicular stroke above; all syllables spoken with acute or *udātta* tone are left unmarked, whether they be proper *udātta* or accented syllables, or only *pracita anudātta*, grave in value but acute in pitch. An example is the verse (xi. 10. 19) from which some of the illustrations given above have been drawn:

त्रिषन्धे तमसा त्वममित्रान्परि वारय ।

trishandhe támasā tvám amítrān pári vāraya,

पृषदाज्यप्रणुत्तानां मामीषां मोचि कश्चन ॥

pṛshadājyápraṇuttānām mā́'mī́'shām moci káç caná.

The agreement between theory and method of designation here is, indeed, so close as reasonably to awaken suspicion whether the latter may not have exercised some influence upon the former. This mode of marking the accented syllables, now, has been adopted in the edited text of the Atharvan, although not followed throughout by a single one of our Atharvan manuscripts. In these, the circumflex, whether independent or enclitic, which follows an acute is usually marked within the syllable itself, sometimes by a dot, sometimes by a horizontal line; the independent circumflex after a grave, generally by an oblique line drawn upward and across the syllable, but often by a convex line below it. The grave syllable is marked as in the Rik, or, quite as often, by a dot instead of a horizontal line below. The different methods are interchanged in several cases within the limits of a single manuscript, and as some of their features are incapable of being represented in printing without complete suits of type prepared expressly for the purpose, no one can call in question the right of the editors to substitute the Rik method.* But there is one other case, namely that which forms the subject of the rule to which this note is attached, which gives trouble in the designation. A *svarita* immediately preceding an *udātta* cannot receive simply the usual *svarita* sign, lest the following syllable be deemed a *pracaya* instead of *udātta*. The method followed in such a case by the Rik is to append to the circumflexed vowel a figure 1 or 3 —1 if the vowel be short, 3 if it be long—and to attach to this figure

* Lesser and occasional peculiarities of the manuscript usages are passed over without notice: it may be farther remarked, however, that E., throughout a great part of its text, marks the acute syllables with the perpendicular line above, in addition to all the other usual signs of accent. The peculiar *svarita* signs of the White Yajus (see Weber, p. 138) nowhere appear.

the signs both of *svarita* and of *anudâtta*. Instances, in part from the examples already given, are:

दिशी३तः । नद्यो३ नामं । रुदत्य१ः पुरुषे ।
diçî́ 'tâḥ *nadyò nấma* *rudatyàḥ púrushe*

देव्यु१षसः । घर्मो३ अभीन्धे । भागो३ऽप्स्व१न्तः ।
devy' ushásaḥ (x. 8. 30), *gharmò 'bhî́ 'ndhe* (xi. 3. 18), *bhâgò 'psv àntáḥ* (x. 5. 15).

What is the reason of this style of writing the *vikampita* syllable, we are left to find out for ourselves; the Prâtiçâkhyas teach us only the modes of utterance. In seeking to explain it, we may first note the method pursued in the text of the Sâma-Veda, which is always to protract the vowel of the syllable, lengthening it if short, and adding the usual sign of protraction or *pluti*, the figure 3. This suggests to us, as not wanting in plausibility, the conjecture that the two Rik signs have a similar meaning, and are marks of protraction, the 1 indicating the mora or part of a mora by which the short vowel is regarded as increased, and the 3 the protracted or *pluta* value, to or toward which the long vowel is raised in pronunciation; the cause of the prolongation lying in the necessity of carrying the vowels concerned to a lower pitch of voice, which leads to an extension of their quantity—even though the theory of the Prâtiçâkhyas known to us does not recognize any such extension. The attachment to the figure of the signs of both *svarita* and *anudâtta* tone of course denotes that the syllable, although circumflex in its general character, descends, unlike the other circumflex syllables, to the full level of *anudâtta* pitch, indicated by the lower horizontal mark. This Rik method of notation of *vikampita* syllables has also been followed in the published Atharvan text, along with the rest of the system to which it belongs. As to the Atharvan manuscripts, they are not infrequently careless enough to omit the figure altogether, and when they write it, it is in almost all cases a 3, whether the vowel to which it is appended be long or short.* In about twenty passages,† they follow the method of the Sâma-Veda, and prolong the vowel of the syllable: this has, however, been restored to its short form in the edition, except in three instances (x. 1. 9. xiii. 1. 15; 3. 16). It will, I presume, be generally acknowledged that, in this condition of the manuscript authorities, the editors followed the safest course in accepting and carrying out consistently the Rik method of designation of the class of cases under discussion.

---

* In the second half of the text, or in books x–xx, I have noted but a single passage where all the MSS. read 1 after a short vowel, and but three others in which that figure is given by more than a single authority: its occurrence is in general entirely sporadic; it occasionally appears also, in place of 3, after a long vowel.

† The details are as follows: all lengthen the vowel at vi. 109. 1. x. 1. 9. xii. 4. 4; 5. 21. xiii. 1. 15; 3. 16. xix. 44. 5; one or more make the same prolongation at ii. 13. 5; 33. 6. vi. 97. 1; 109. 2; 120. 2. viii. 4. 15. x. 8. 30. xii. 2. 38. xvi. 6. 5. xviii. 1. 5; 2. 24. xix. 5. 2.

एकादेश उदात्तेनोदात्तः ॥ ६६ ॥

66. A vowel produced by combination with an acute is itself acute.

That is to say, when two simple vowels, or a vowel and a diphthong, coalesce and form a single vowel or diphthong (by rules 42-53, above), in case either of the two was acute, the resulting syllable is acute. The rule is a general one, and suffers only the two exceptions which form the subject of rules 55 and 56, above: namely, that *é* and *ó*, when they absorb a following *a*, become *è* and *ò*, and that *í* + *i* become *ī̀*. The corresponding rules of the other treatises are Rik Pr. iii. 6 (r. 10, cxcvii), Vâj. Pr. iv. 131, and Tâitt. Pr. x. 10 and xii. 10.

The series of passages given by the commentator in illustration of the rule is the same which was furnished under rule 38, above: viz. *dhiyé* " *'hi* (*dhiyā́ : ā́ : ihi*), *jushasvé* " *'ndra* (*jushasva : ā́ : indra*), *stanayitnúné* " *'hi* (*stanayitnúnā : ā́ : ihi*), *kúshṭhé* " *'hi* (*kúshṭha : ā́ : ihi*), *udakéné* " *'hi* (*udakéna : ā́ : ihi*), and *áva paçyaté* " *'ta* (*áva : paçyata : ā́ : ita*). The instances are ill chosen, so far as regards variety of combination; but they illustrate sufficiently the fact that, whether the acute element is the former or the latter of the two combined, the accent of the result of fusion is alike acute. It might have been well to offer also examples of the extreme cases in which a final acute *á* assimilates and renders acute a following diphthong, such as *çatấudanā* (*çatá-odanā*: e. g. x. 9. 1) and *ihấi 'vá* (*ihá : evá*: e. g. i. 1. 3): such combinations with *âi* and *âu* the text does not contain.

The other treatises give the rule (R. Pr. iii. 6, r. 11, cxcviii; V. Pr. iv. 130; T. Pr. x. 12) that when a circumflex is combined with a following grave, the result of the combination is circumflex. A like rule is needed here also, in order to determine the accentuation of such cases as *tanvā̀ 'ntárikSham* (xvii. 13: *tanvā̀ : antárikSham*), *pathyè 'va* (xviii. 3. 39: *pathyā̀ : iva*), etc., and its omission must be regarded as an oversight.

उदात्तादनुदात्तं स्वर्यते ॥ ६७ ॥

67. A grave syllable following an acute is circumflexed.

This is the rule prescribing the enclitic *svarita*, the position of which in the accentual system has been sufficiently explained in the last note but one. It is, as we have seen above (rules 62, 63), subdivided into the two kinds called *tâirovyañjana* and *pâdavṛtta*, according as one or more consonants, or only a hiatus, intervene between the acute vowel and its successor. The commentator gives here only the two instances of the *tâirovyañjana* which he had already cited under rule 62.

The corresponding rules of the other treatises are Rik Pr. iii. 9 (r. 16, cciii), Vâj. Pr. iv. 134, and Tâitt. Pr. xiv. 29, 30.

व्यासे ऽपि समानपदे ॥ ६८ ॥

68. And even in the disjoined text, within the limits of the same word.

The term *vyâsa*, excepting here and in rule 72, is not met with anywhere in the Hindu grammatical language. Our commentator, according to his usual custom, spares himself the trouble of giving any explanation of it, or even of replacing it in his paraphrases by a less unusual synonym. The instances adduced, however, in illustration of the rules, and the general requirements of the sense, show clearly that it means the disjoined or *pada* text. By their *adhikâra* (ii. 1), all rules in the second and third chapters should apply only to the *sanhitâ*, or combined text; hence it must here be specifically taught that in *pada*, as well as in *sanhitâ*, the syllable following an acute is enclitically circumflex, if the latter be in the same word with the former, and so not separated from it by a pause or *avasâna*. The examples given under the rule are *ayútam* (e.g. viii. 2. 21), *amṛ́tam* (e.g. i. 4. 4), and *antáriksham* (e.g. ii. 12. 1); in these words, the syllables *tam*, *tam*, and *rik* have the *táirovyañjana* variety of the enclitic circumflex, and they are accordingly written अयुतम् । अमृतम् । अन्तरिक्षम्, and not अयुतम् । अमृतम् । अन्तरिक्षम्.

A corresponding rule is to be found in the Rik Pr. at iii. 4 (r. 6, cciii).

अवग्रहे च ॥ ६९ ॥

69. As well as where there is a separation of a compound into its constituents.

That is to say: although, in the *pada*-text, the pause which separates each independent word from the one following it breaks the continuity of accentual influence, so that a final acute of the one does not render circumflex the initial grave of the other, yet the lesser pause of the *avagraha*, which holds apart the two members of a compound word, causes no such interruption; on the contrary, an acute at the end of the former member calls forth the circumflexed utterance in the first syllable of the latter member. The commentator offers us rather a monotonous series of illustrations, namely *sú-saṃçitaḥ* (vi. 105. 2), *sú-yataḥ* (vi. 111. 1), *sú-çṛtam* (vii. 72. 3), *sú-dṛḍham* (x. 2. 3), *sú-bhṛtam* (e.g. vi. 30. 1), and *sú-hutam* (e.g. vi. 71. 1): these are to be pronounced and written सुऽसंशितः । सुऽयतः etc., and not सुऽसंशितः । सुऽयतः etc.

The Rik Pr. (iii. 15, r. 23, ccx) and Vâj. Pr. (i. 148) lay down the principle that *avagraha* makes no difference in the accentuation of the syllables which it separates; both, also (R. Pr. iii. 16, V. Pr. i. 148), except the rare cases in which each of the parts of a compound has an acute accent; such as are, in the Atharvan, *pári-dhâtavấi* (ii. 13. 2) and *tánû-nápât* (v. 27. 1). In such words as the latter, the Vâj. Pr. (i. 120) calls the circumflex of the syllable preceding the pause by a special name, *tâthâbhâvya*.

नोदात्तस्वरितपरम् ॥ ७० ॥

70. Not, however, when an acute or circumflex syllable succeeds.

A syllable originally grave remains grave before a following *udātta* or *svarita*, even though preceded by an *udātta*, and hence, by the last rules, regularly entitled to the enclitic circumflex. The proclitic accent thus appears, in the estimation of the Hindu phonetists, to be more powerful than the enclitic, and the law which requires the voice to plant itself upon a low pitch in order to rise to the tone of acute or independent circumflex to be more inviolable than that which prescribes a falling tone in the next syllable after an acute. The commentator illustrates by citing *çáṁ na ā́paḥ* (i. 6. 4), *yó asyá viçvájanmanaḥ* (xi. 4. 23), and *asyá sutásya svàḥ* (ii. 5. 2): the syllables *na*, *as* and *viç*, and *su* and *syas*, which by rule 67 would be circumflexed, are by this rule reinstated in their *anudātta* character, and must be written with the *anudātta* sign below: thus, शं न आपः । यो अस्य विश्वजन्मनः । अस्य सुतस्य स्वः.

The corresponding rules of the other treatises are Rik Pr. iii. 9 (r. 16, cciii, last part), Vāj. Pr. iv. 135, and Tāitt. Pr. xiv. 31. Cases of occurrence of the accent called by the Vāj. Pr. *tāthābhāvya* (as noticed under the last rule) constitute in the other systems an exception, which is apparently not admitted by the school to which our Prātiçākhya belongs.

स्वरितादनुदात्त उदात्तश्रुतिः ॥७१॥

71. A grave following a circumflex has the tone of acute.

The position and relations of this rule in the accentual system have been sufficiently treated of in the note to rule 65. All the other treatises (R. Pr. iii. 11, r. 18, ccv; V. Pr. iv. 138, 139; T. Pr. xxi. 10) lay down the same principle, stating also distinctly what must be regarded as implied in our precept, that not only the single grave syllable which immediately follows the circumflex receives the acute utterance, but those also which may succeed it, until, by rule 74, the proximity of an acute or circumflex causes the voice to sink to the proper *anudātta* tone. The Rik Pr. and Tāitt. Pr. use the term *pracaya*, 'accumulation, indefinitely extended number or series,' in describing this accent, the latter employing it in its ordinary sense, the former giving it as the name of the accent.

The commentator cites from the text, as instances, *devī́r dvā́ro bṛhatīr viçvaminvā́ḥ* (v. 12. 5), and *mā́dhvī dhartā́rā vidathasya satpatī* (vii. 73. 4): each passage presents a whole *pracaya*, or accumulated series, of syllables having the accent prescribed by the rule. Such syllables are, as has been already pointed out, left unmarked with signs of accentuation in the written texts, like the proper acute syllables whose tone they share: thus, देवीर्द्वारो बृहतीर्विश्वमिन्वाः.

Next follow two rules, identical in form with rules 68 and 69 above, and, like them, prescribing the application of this principle in the *pada*-text also. They are covered by the same rules of the other treatises which have already been cited.

व्यासे ऽपि समानपदे ॥७२॥

72. And even in the disjoined text, within the limits of the same word.

That is to say, in *pada* as well as in *saṁhitâ*, those unaccented syllables which follow in the same word a circumflex, whether independent or enclitic, are uttered at the pitch of acute; and they are correspondingly marked in the written texts. The commentator's examples are *uru gū́'lhāyāḥ* (v. 13. 8) and *kakā́'ṭikām* (x. 2. 8): these are uttered and written उरु ऽगूल्हायाः । ककाटिकाम्, and not उरु ऽगूल्हायाः । ककाटिकाम्.

अवग्रहे च ॥७३॥

73. As well as where there is a separation of a compound into its constituents.

That is to say, again, the *avagraha*, or pause of division, does not interfere with the influence of a circumflex, any more than (by rule 69) with that of an acute, upon the following unaccented syllables. The commentator gives us the examples *çvā̀n-vatīḥ* (xi. 9. 15), *svàḥ-vatī* (xviii. 1. 20), and *áçman-vatī* (xii. 2. 26), which we are to read and write श्वन्ऽवतीः । स्वःऽवती । अश्मन्ऽवती, and not श्वन्ऽवतीः । स्वःऽवती । अश्मन्ऽवती.

स्वरितोदात्ते ऽनन्तरमनुदात्तम् ॥७४॥

74. But the syllable immediately preceding a circumflex or acute is grave.

This rule applies only to those originally *anudâtta* syllables which would otherwise, under the action of rule 71, be spoken with the *udâtta* tone, as following a *svarita*. It is, as has been already pointed out, closely analogous in character with rules 65 and 70, above, and has a like theoretic ground. The commentator illustrates it by citing the passages *ajā́s tā́d dadṛçe kvà* (x. 8. 41), *idáṁ devāḥ çṛṇuta yé* (ii. 12. 2), and *idám indra çṛṇuhi somapa yát* (ii. 12. 3), where the syllables *çe*, *ta*, and *pa*—which, though properly unaccented, would be pronounced at acute pitch, like their predecessors, by rule 71—are depressed to the level of grave, in preparation for the succeeding circumflex or acute. We write, accordingly, अजास्तद्ददृशे क्व । इदं देवाः शृणुत ये । इदमिन्द्र शृणुहि सोमप यत्.

This rule is common to all the systems: compare Rik Pr. iii. 12 (r. 20, ccvii), Vâj. Pr. iv. 140, and Tâitt. Pr. xxi. 11.

As, at the beginning of this section, the commentator gave us an introduction to it, composed mainly of citations from unnamed sources, so here, at the end, he appends a postscript, chiefly made up of the *dicta*, upon points connected with accentuation, of authorities to whom he refers by name. He first says: *asvarāṇi vyañjanāni svaravantī 'ty āṅyatareyaḥ;* 'the consonants are destitute of accent: "they are accented," says Āṅyatareya.' Upon this point our treatise nowhere distinctly declares itself, but, as already noticed (under i. 55), its rules of syllabication may be naturally interpreted as implying that the consonant which is assigned to a particular syllable shares in the accentuation of its vowel. The Vāj. Pr. (i. 107) states this explicitly. Next we have: *kiṁ saṁdheḥ svaritaṁ bhavati: pūrvarūpam ity āṅyatareyaḥ: uttararūpaṁ çāṅkhamitriḥ;* 'what part of a combination is circumflexed (or accented)? "the former constituent," says Āṅyatareya; "the latter constituent," says Çāṅkhamitri.' In the absence of any illustrations, I am at a loss to see to what kind of combinations this question and its answers are to be understood as applying. Next follows a passage which we have had once before, in the commentary on i. 93 (see the note to that rule); it reads here as follows: *kim aksharasya svaryamāṇasya svaryate: ardhaṁ hrasvasya pādo dīrghasya 'ty eke sarvam iti çāṅkhamitrir aksharasyāi 'shā vidhā na vidyate: yad yad viçvaribhara.* A renewed consideration affords me no new light upon this passage. Finally, we read *ṛgardharcapadānlanāvagrahavivṛttishu mātrākālakālaḥ,* which appears to me to have to do with the determination of the length of the different pauses occurring in the recitation of the Veda; namely, the pauses at the end of a half-verse, between two words in the *pada*-text, between two parts of a divisible compound (also in *pada*-text), and where a hiatus occurs in *saṁhitā;* but I have not succeeded in restoring any intelligible and consistent reading of the passage. The Vāj. Pr. (v. 1) and Rik Pr. (i. 6, r. 28, xxix) declare the pause of division of a compound, or the *avagraha*, to have the length of a mora; the Tāitt. Pr. (xxii. 13) recognizes four pauses (*virāma*): that at the end of a verse, that at the end of a *pada* or disjoined word, that of a hiatus, and that of a hiatus within a word (as *praügam*), declaring them to have respectively the length of three moras, two moras, one mora, and a half-mora.

The signature of the *pāda* or section is *tṛtīyasya tṛtīyaḥ pādaḥ.*

ऋवर्णरेफषकारेभ्यः समानपदे नो णः ॥७५॥

75. After ṛ and ṝ, *r*, and *sh*, within the limits of the same word, *n* is changed to *ṇ*.

This rule is an *adhikāra*, or heading, indicating the subject of the section, and making known what is to be implied in the following rules. It might properly, then, have been left by the commentator without illustration, like ii. 1. He prefers, however, to cite from the text the passages *pari tṛṇḍhi pari dhehi vedim* (vii. 99. 1) and *paristaraṇam id dhaviḥ* (ix. 6. 2), which offer instances of the lingualization of the nasal; and he also adds *kushaṇam* and *toshaṇam*, which are not Atharvan words. As counter-examples, to show that the nasal is converted only if the preceding cerebral is found within the same word, he gives *svar nayati, prātar nayati,* which are also fabricated cases; compare the similar ones in the scholia to Pāṇ. viii. 4. 1.

The Rik Pr. introduces the same subject with a precept (v. 20, r. 40, ccclvii) which also includes our next rule and a part of 89 below. The leading rules of the Vâj. Pr. (iii. 83) and Tâitt. Pr. (xiii. 6) are in close agreement with ours.

पूर्वपदाद्द्रुघणादीनाम् ॥ ७६ ॥

76. In *drughaṇa* etc., the same effect takes place after a cause which is contained in the former member of a compound.

The commentator paraphrases *pûrvapadât* by the expression which, for the sake of clearness, has been substituted for it in translating, viz. *pûrvapadasthân nimittât.* His cited illustrations are *drughaṇaḥ* (vii. 28. 1 : p. *dru-ghanaḥ*), *sûtâ grâmaṇyaḥ* (iii. 5. 7 : p. *grâma-nyaḥ*), *rakshohaṇaṁ vâjinam* (viii. 3. 1 : p. *rakshaḥ-hanam*), *bṛhaspatipraṇuttânâm* (viii. 8. 19 : p. *bṛhaspati-pranuttânâm*), *pṛshadâjyapraṇuttânâm* (xi. 10. 19 : p. *pṛshadâjya-pranuttânâm*), and *durṇihitâishiṇîm* (xi. 9. 15 : p. *durnihita-eshiṇîm*). The latter case, we should think, is one of somewhat ambiguous quality, since in the form of the word, as given by the *pada*-text, there is nothing to show that *dur* stands in the relation of *pûrvapada*, or former member of a compound, to *nihita*, they being unseparated by *avagraha*. The same objection lies against the two preceding instances; but also the much more serious one that they are examples properly belonging under rule 79, below, the converted n being that of a root after a preposition.

The other examples of the action of this rule afforded by the Atharvan text are *parâyaṇa* (e. g. i. 34. 3 : p. *parâ-ayana*), *vṛshâyamâṇa* (ii. 5. 7 : p. *vṛsha-yamâna*; the *uttarapada* is here a suffix of derivative conjugation), *paripâṇa* (e. g. ii. 17. 7 : p. *pari-pâna*), *vṛtrahaṇam* etc. (e. g. iv. 28. 3 : p. *vṛtra-hanam*), *durṇaça* (v. 11. 6 : p. *duḥ-naça*), *triṇâman* (vi. 74. 3 : p. *tri-nâman*), *puruṇâman* (vi. 99. 1 : p. *puru-nâman*), *urûṇasa* (xviii. 2. 13 : p. *uru-nasa*), and *sahasraṇîtha* (xviii. 2. 18 : p. *sahasra-nîtha*). We have also a few cases of a class analogous with the last one given by the commentator, where the principle is precisely the same, although, in the actual division of the words, the *avagraha* falls elsewhere than between the converting lingual and the nasal: they are *suprapâṇa* (iv. 21. 7 : p. *su-prapâna*; our *pada*-manuscript, to be sure, reads here, but doubtless only by an error of the copyist, *su-prapâṇa*), *suprâyaṇa* (v. 12. 5 : p. *su-prâyana*), and *anuprayâṇa* (vii. 73. 6 : p. *anu-prayâna*). Some other words, which would otherwise have to be noted under this rule, are made the subject of special precepts later in the section (rules 82–85).

The general rule of the Rik Pr., as already noticed, includes this of ours as well as the preceding. By the Vâj. Pr. and Tâitt. Pr., the cases are stated in detail.

अकारान्तादह्नः ॥ ७७ ॥

77. The n of *ahan* is changed after a former member of a compound ending in *a*.

Pāṇini's rule, viii. 4. 7, is precisely coincident with this, and the illustrative citations of its scholiasts are in good part those which our commentator gives us, and which are all strange to the Atharvan: they are, as examples of the rule, *prāhṇaḥ*, *pūrvāhṇaḥ*, and, as counter-examples, *nirahṇaḥ*, *paryahṇaḥ*, and *durahṇaḥ*. Our text has only the two examples *aparāhṇaḥ* (ix. 6. 46: p. *apara-ahnaḥ*) and *sahasrāhṇyam* (e. g. x. 8. 18: p. *sahasra-ahnyam*), and furnishes no counter-examples at all, so that the rule evidently finds its justification in the observed phenomena of the general language, and not in those of the Atharva-Veda.

विभक्त्यागमप्रातिपदिकान्तस्य ॥७८॥

78. Also is liable to be changed the *n* of a case-ending, that of an *āgama*, and the final *n* of a *prātipadika*.

This rule is the exact counterpart in form of Pāṇini's rule viii. 4. 11, and the technical terms which it contains are undoubtedly identical in meaning with those there given: *āgama* is an augment or inorganic insertion;* *prātipadika* is a theme of regular derivation, ending in a *kṛt* or *taddhita* suffix. The commentator's instances are as follows: for the case-ending *ina*, *svargeṇa lokena* (not in AV.), *varāheṇa pṛthivī saṁvidānā* (xii. 1. 48); for the *āgama n*, *ati durgāṇi viçvā* (vii. 63. 1: p. *duḥ-gāni*); for the final of a theme, *nāi 'nam ghnanti paryāyiṇaḥ* (vi. 76. 4: p. *pari-āyinaḥ*).

The other treatises have nothing corresponding to this rule, which is, indeed, an unnecessary one, as a Prātiçākhya usually takes the words of its text in their *pada*-form, without going farther back to enquire how they came to assume that form. Such a word as *varāheṇa*, where *pada* and *saṁhitā* read alike, is not regarded by the others as calling for any notice: those analogous with the other instances cited might have been ranked as falling under the preceding rule. *Paryāyiṇaḥ* is, it may be remarked, the only word of its class which the text presents, excepting *pravāhiṇaḥ*, in book xx (xx. 127. 2), and *durgāṇi* also stands alone in its class; nor have I noted a single instance of such a compound form as would be *svaḥ-gena* or *duḥ-gena*, where the alteration of the case-ending in the second word would be made in the reduction of *pada* to *saṁhitā*.

उपसर्गाद्धातोर्नानापदे ऽपि ॥७९॥

79. Also that of a root after a preposition, even in a separate word.

That is to say, even when the words are not connected together as parts of a compound. The commentator gives us a single instance where the cause of conversion stands *nānāpade*, and two in which it stands *pūrvopade*; they are *apaḥ pra ṇayati* (ix. 6. 4), *yā eva yajña āpaḥ praṇīyante* (ix. 6. 5: p. *pra-nīyante*), and *jīvām ṛtebhyaḥ pariṇīyamānām*

* The Böhtlingk-Roth lexicon, upon the authority of this rule, erroneously makes it signify 'suffix.'

(xviii. 3. 3: p. *pari-nîyamânam*). Instances of a somewhat different character, where the preposition lingualizes the initial *n* of the root in *saṅhitâ* and not in *pada*, although in the latter text no *avagraha* separates the two words, have been already given above, under rule 76. The text presents us *praṇutta* in like combinations also after *vâibâdha* (iii. 6. 7) and *sâyaka* (ix. 2. 12); and we have farther, in *pada*, *su-praṇîti* (e. g. v. 11. 5), and *parâṇayât** (xviii. 4. 50). The initial *n* of a root is almost always cerebralized by the preceding preposition in the Atharvan, even when (as at ii. 7. 1, ix. 2. 17, x. 4. 26, etc.) the augment intervenes: the only exceptions are the combinations of *nabh* with *pra* (vii. 18. 1, 2), and of *nṛt* with *pari* (e. g. iv. 38. 3) and *pra* (e. g. viii. 6. 11). It is unnecessary to detail, therefore, all the rather numerous instances of the change.

The cases forming the subject of this rule are not classified together by the other Prâtiçâkhyas.

प्रपराभ्यामेनः ॥ ८० ॥

80. Also that of *ena*, after *pra* and *parâ*.

The commentator cites nearly all the examples which the text affords: they are *prâi 'ṇân chṛṇihi* (x. 3. 2), *prâi 'ṇân vṛkshasya* (iii. 6. 8: the same verse has, in its first *pâda*, *prâi 'ṇân nude*), and *parâi 'ṇân devaḥ* (viii. 3. 16). As counter-example, to show that it is only after the two prepositions mentioned in the rule that *ena* exhibits the lingualization of its nasal, is farther cited *pary enân prâṇaḥ* (ix. 2. 5).

Here follows a *lacuna*, apparently of considerable extent. Where this rule should be repeated, before the one next succeeding, we read *praparâbhyâmerṇayâmasi navateç ca;* and the sequel shows that *navateç ca* is a rule by itself, while what precedes is the mutilated remnant of another. This, aided by the implication in *navateç ca*, and by the text, which offers us the passage to which the rule was evidently intended to refer, we are enabled to restore with tolerable certainty to its true form, as *punar ṇayâmasi*: what has become lost in the interval, we can only conjecture. Perhaps the treatise next took note of another case which the text affords of the lingualization of the nasal of *ena*, viz. *â jabhârṣi 'ṇâm* (v. 31. 10). Possibly there followed also a mention of the passage *asṛjan nir eṇasaḥ* (ii. 10. 8); but this is very questionable, as the reading itself is doubtful.† But it is beyond question that a part of the omitted passage had reference to the not infrequent change of the *n* of *naḥ* in *saṅhitâ* into *ṇ* after a lingual near the end of the preceding word: this is much too common to have been passed over without notice, and the class of cases is too large and distinct to have been thrown

* This is a case of entirely anomalous division and accentuation. We should expect *upa-sampárâṇayât*, like *anu-sampráyâhi* (xi. 1. 36) etc.; but the *pada* reads *upa-sám : parâṇayât*, and all the *saṅhitâ* MSS. agree with it as regards the accent: it can hardly be otherwise than an error of the tradition: see below, under iv. 2.

† It is given by M. W. H. and I.; but P. (if I have not been careless enough to omit to note its reading) and E. have *enasaḥ*, and the printed text has followed their authority.

under any of the other rules of the section. The statement might be put into the form of two rules, as follows:

प्रपरिभ्यां नः ॥

आशीरुरुष्यगृहेषुशिक्षेभ्यश्च ॥

'The *n* of *naḥ* is lingualized after *pra* and *pari*. As also, after *âçîr*, *urushya*, *gṛheshu*, and *çiksha*.'

Under the first rule, the cases would be i. 2. 2; 7. 5. ii. 4. 2, 6; 7. 3, 4. iii. 16. 3; 20. 2. 3. iv. 10. 6. v. 7. 3. vi. 37. 2. vii. 2. 1; 5. 5. xi. 2. 20. xii. 2. 13; 3. 55–60. xiv. 2. 67. xix. 34. 4, 5. Under the second, the passages are *âçîr ṇa ûrjam* (ii. 29. 3), *urushyâ ṇa urujman* (vi. 4. 3: E. *na*), *asamâtiṁ gṛheshu ṇaḥ* (vi. 79. 1: E. *naḥ*), *upahûto gṛheshu naḥ* (vii. 60. 5: E. *naḥ*), and *çikshâ ṇo asmin* (xviii. 3. 67). Where *naḥ* follows *gṛheshu*, the edition reads both times *naḥ*, without conversion, although the manuscript authority for the lingual nasal is precisely what it is for the same after *urushyâ*, E. alone dissenting. At iv. 31. 2, a part of the manuscripts (P. M. W.) read *sendrâir ṇaḥ*, but the edition properly follows the prevailing authority of the others (E. I. H.), and gives, with the Rig-Veda (x. 84. 2), *naḥ*. I have noted a single case where the Atharvan reads *naḥ*, while the Rik, in the parallel passage, has *ṇaḥ*: it is vii. 97. 2 (RV. v. 42. 4).

It is altogether probable that a whole leaf, or a whole page, of the original of our copy of the text and commentary (or possibly, of the original of its original), is lost here, with as many as three or four rules. Fortunately, it is in the midst of the rehearsal of cases of a certain kind, which rehearsal can be made complete without the aid of the treatise: so that the loss is not of essential consequence.

* * * * * * * *

पुनर्णयामसि ॥ ८१ ॥

81. Also that of *nayâmasi*, after *punaḥ*.

The passage referred to is *taṁ tvâ punar ṇayâmasi* (v. 14. 7): all our *saṁhitâ* manuscripts agree in giving the lingual nasal. Whether I have given the form of the rule correctly is not quite certain, a portion of it being lost altogether, as was pointed out in the last note.

नुवतेश्च ॥ ८२ ॥

82. As also that of the root *nu*.

The word to which alone the rule relates is *punarṇava* (p. *punaḥ-nava*), for which the commentator cites three passages, viz. *candramâç ca punarṇavaḥ* (x. 7. 33), *yâ rohanti punarṇavâḥ* (viii. 7. 8), and *punar â 'gâḥ punarṇavaḥ* (viii. 1. 20). The authors of our treatise, then, must have derived *nava*, 'new,' from the verbal root *nu*, 'to praise,' instead of from the pronominal word *nu*, 'now.'

पूर्याणाः ॥ ८३ ॥

83. Also in *pûryâṇa*.

The commentator instances but a single phrase in illustration of the rule, viz. *pathibhiḥ pûryâṇaiḥ* (e. g. xviii. 1. 54 : p. *pûḥ-yânaiḥ*). There is small reason to be seen for singling out this word in order to make it the subject of a special rule, and the same is true of those treated in the two following rules: they might all have been as well left to fall into the *gaṇa* of rule 76.

दुर्णाम्नः ॥ ८४ ॥

84. Also that of *durṇâman*.

The commentator extracts from the text three of the passages in which this word occurs, viz. *durṇâmnîḥ sarvâḥ* (iv. 17. 5), *durṇâmâ tatra mâ gṛdhat* (viii. 6. 1), and *durṇâmâ ca sunâmâ ca* (viii. 6. 4). The *pada* writes *duḥ-nâman*.

अवग्रहादृकारात् ॥ ८५ ॥

85. Also after an *ṛ* at the end of the former member of a compound.

The commentator's examples are *devayânâḥ pitṛyâṇâḥ* (vi. 117. 3: the *pada* form of the word is everywhere *pitṛ-yâna*), *pitṛyâṇaiḥ saṁ va â rohayâmi* (xviii. 4. 1), and *nṛmaṇâ nâma* (xvi. 3. 5 : p. *nṛ-manâḥ*). The text furnishes but a single other word falling under the rule, and that in the nineteenth book; viz. *nṛpâṇa* (xix. 58. 4).

It is worthy of note that Pâṇini has a rule (viii. 4. 26) which precisely corresponds with this, and that his scholiasts quote the same two words in illustration of it.

न मिनाति ॥ ८६ ॥

86. But not that of the root *mî*.

The commentator brings forward all the illustrations of the rule which the text contains—they are *pra minîj janitrîm* (vi. 110. 3), *pra minanti vratâni* (xviii. 1. 5), and *pra minâti saṁgiraḥ* (xviii. 4. 60)—excepting one in the nineteenth book, *praminâma vratâni* (xix. 59. 2). The rule itself is to be understood, it may be presumed, as giving exceptions to rule 79 above: yet the latter would seem to apply only to conversions of the nasal of a root itself, and not of the appended conjugational syllable.

The manuscript reads *minanti* instead of *minâti*, and the final repetition of the rule before its successor is wanting.

भानोश्च ॥ ८७ ॥

87. Nor that of *bhânu*.

This rule is entirely superfluous. Of the two cases cited under it by the commentator, the first, *citrabhâno* (iv. 25. 3), could fall under no rule for lingualizing the dental nasal excepting 76, and from that it would be excluded by absence from the *gaṇa* to which alone the precept applies; the other, *pra bhānoḥ sierate* (xiii. 2. 46), cannot be forced under any rule that has been laid down.

The Rik Pr. (v. 22, r. 49, ccclxvi) and Vaj. Pr. (iii. 91) also note *bhānu* as a word whose nasal is not subject to be changed to a lingual.

परेर्हिनोतेः ॥ ८८ ॥

88. Nor that of the root *hi* after *pari*.

The Atharvan text furnishes but one such case, which the commentator quotes: it is *parihinomi medhayā* (viii. 4. 6). As counter-example, the commentator brings up *pra hiṇomi dūram* (xii. 2. 6); but here, as well as in the other cases where the forms of the same verb exhibit a lingualized nasal after *pra*, the *pada*-text also (by iv. 95) shows the same. A strict application of rule 79, then, to the nasal only of a root itself, would render this rule also unnecessary.

The Rik Pr. (v. 22, r. 50, ccclxvi[b]) has a corresponding precept.

पदान्तस्पर्शयुक्तस्य ॥ ८९ ॥

89. Nor a final *n*, nor one conjoined with a mute.

The commentator's illustrative instances are *pūshan tava vrate* (vii. 9. 3), *saṁkrandanaḥ* (v. 20. 9), and *pāço granthiḥ* (ix. 3. 2). To the first part of the rule would need to be made the exceptions noted at iv. 99, but that, by the operation of that precept, they are made to read in *pada* as in *saṁhitā*, and so are withdrawn from the ken of the Prātiçākhya.

The first part of this rule is included in the general precept for the conversion of *n* as given by the Rik Pr. (v. 20, r. 40, ccclvii); which adds later (v. 22, r. 47, ccclxiv) that the *n* is not altered if combined with *y* or a mute. The Vaj. Pr. also divides the two parts of our precept (iii. 88, 92), but specifies only a dental mute as preventing the conversion of the nasal by combination with it. The Taitt. Pr. (xiii. 15) includes in one rule this of ours and also 91, 93, and 94 below.

नशेः षान्तस्य ॥ ९० ॥

90. Nor that of the root *naç*, when it ends in *sh*.

This rule is precisely the same with one of Pāṇini (viii. 4. 36), and it belongs rather to the general grammar than to a Prātiçākhya of the Atharvan, since our text does not furnish a single case to which it should apply. The examples which the commentator gives are in part those which are found also in Pāṇini's scholia: they are *pranashṭaḥ*, *parinashṭaḥ*, *nirnashṭaḥ*, and *durnashṭaḥ*. A counter-example, *durṇaçaṁ cid arvāk* (v. 11. 6), he is able to bring up from the Atharvan.

स्वरलोपे हन्तेः ॥ ९१ ॥

91. Nor that of the root *han*, when its vowel has been omitted.

The commentator offers the two following examples: *vṛtraghnaḥ stomāḥ* (iv. 24. 1), and *indreṇa vṛtraghnā medī* (iii. 6. 2); and the counter-example *rakshohaṇaṁ vājinam* (viii. 3. 1), which has already figured as example under rule 76 above. Unless *sparçayukta*, in rule 89, meant only 'combined with a following mute,' which is very unlikely, the present precept is superfluous, as merely specifying a case already sufficiently provided for elsewhere.

Pāṇini (viii. 4. 22) looks at this matter from the opposite point of view, and teaches that the *n* of *han* is lingualized whenever it is preceded by *a*. The Tāitt. Pr. (xiii. 15) mentions the case along with others, in a comprehensive rule.

क्षुभ्नादीनाम् ॥ ९२ ॥

92. Nor that of the root *kshubh* etc.

This, again, is coincident with one of Pāṇini's rules (viii. 4. 39), and, so far as *kshubh* is itself concerned, is out of place in the Prātiçākhya of the Atharva-Veda: for not only does this Veda contain no derivatives from the root to which it should apply (we find only *vicukshubhe* [vii. 57. 1] and *kshobhaṇa* [xix. 13. 2]), but also, if such forms as *kshubhnāti* (which the commentator gives as an example under the rule), *kshubhnītaḥ*, etc., did occur, their reading would be sufficiently determined by rule 89, above. The commentator fills up the *gaṇa* with *parinṛtyantyor iva* (x. 7. 43), *madhunā prapīnāḥ* (xii. 3. 41), and *pari nṛtyanti keçinīḥ* (xii. 5. 48): to these are to be added other forms of the root *nart* after *pari* and *pra*, and forms of *nabh* after *pra*—as already noted, under rule 79.

व्यवाये शसलैः ॥ ९३ ॥

93. Nor when there is intervention of *ç*, *s*, or *l*.

The instances cited in the commentary are *kaḥ pṛçniṁ dhenum* (vii. 104. 1), *garbhe antar adṛçyamānaḥ* (x. 8. 13), and *savitā prasavānām* (v. 24. 1). For the intervention of *l*, no case is brought up, nor do the Rik Pr. and Tāitt. Pr. make any account of this semivowel as ever coming in to hinder the conversion of the nasal. The Vāj. Pr., however, does so, and cites an instance, *nirjarjalpena* (in which, however, there is intervention also of a palatal). The latter treatise (iii. 94) and the Tāitt. Pr. (xiii. 16) throw together into one this rule of ours and the one next following: the Rik Pr. gives a separate precept answering to each (R. Pr. v. 21, r. 44, 42, ccclxi, ccclix).

चटतवर्गेश्च ॥ ९४ ॥

94. Or of palatal, lingual, or dental mutes.

The commentator gives the examples *upa 'ho 'paparcanā 'smin goshṭha upa pṛñca naḥ* (ix. 4. 23), *reshayāi 'nān* (xi. 1. 20: this, however, is no example under the rule), *yathā 'so mitravardhanaḥ* (iv. 8. 6), and *taṁ vartaniḥ* (vii. 21. 1).

The corresponding rules of the other Prâtiçâkhyas have been referred to above (under rule 93).

The physical explanation of the effect of the sounds mentioned in these two rules to prevent the lingualization of the nasal is obvious: they are all of them such as cause the tongue to change its position. When this organ is once bent back in the mouth to the position in which the lingual sibilant, semivowel, and vowels are uttered, it tends to remain there, and produce the next following nasal at that point, instead of at the point of dental utterance; and it does so, unless thrown out of adjustment, as it were, by the occurrence of a letter which calls it into action in another quarter.

पदेनावर्जिते च ॥ ९५ ॥

95. Or of a word, unless it be *â*.

As an example of prevention of the lingualization of *n* by the interposition of a word or words, even though composed only of such sounds as would not in the same word produce such an effect, the commentator gives us *pari 'me gâm aneshata* (vi. 28. 2). As an illustration of the specified exception, that *â* may so intervene, and the conversion yet take place, he gives *paryâṇaddham* (xiv. 2. 12: p. *pari-ânaddham*), which is, I believe, the only case of the kind afforded by the text.

The construction of the other rules relating to this general subject in the remaining Prâtiçâkhyas is not such as to require them to make the restriction here taught. Pâṇini, however, takes due note of it (viii. 4. 38), but omits to except the preposition *â*, so that (unless he makes the exception by some other rule which I have not observed) he would read *paryânaddha*.

तुविष्टमः ॥ ९६ ॥

96. Note *tuvishṭamaḥ*.

This word occurs only once in the Atharvan, in a passage cited by the commentator, as follows: *indraḥ patis tuvishṭamaḥ* (vi. 33. 3). The *pada*-text reads *tuvi-tamaḥ*, so that there takes place, as the commentator says, an inorganic insertion of *s* (*sakârâgamaḥ*). The same word is found more than once in the Rig-Veda, but is written by the *pada*-text *tuviḥ-tama*, so that there is nothing irregular in the *sanhitâ* form, and it requires and receives no notice from the Rik Prâtiçâkhya. It is a legitimate matter for surprise to find the rule thrust in in this place, in connection with a subject to which it stands in no relation whatever: we should expect to meet it in the second chapter, along with rules 25 and 26 of that chapter, or after rule 30, or elsewhere. Its intrusion here, and the indefiniteness of its form, cannot but suggest the suspicion of its being an interpolation, made for the purpose of supplying an observed deficiency in the treatise.

The commentator, after citing the passage containing the word, goes on to say: *sanhitâyâm ity eva: tuvitama iti tuvitamaḥ:*[1] *anadhikâro*

[1] The MS. writes, in every case, *tuvittama* in the commentary, but doubtless only by a copyist's error.

sûtranirdeçaḥ: sûtrârthas tâvadyâçaç ca carcâparihârayor vacanam mâ bhûd iti; 'this is the form only in *saṁhitâ*; the *krama* reads *turîtama iti turi-tamaḥ*: in the absence of an explanatory heading, the rule simply points out the form; and the significance of the rule is . . . (?): in *carcâ* and *parihâra* [repetitions of *krama*] the reading is not to be so made: that is the meaning.'

The signature of the chapter is as follows: 105: *iti tṛtîyo 'dhyâyaḥ*. If its enumeration is to be trusted, our two *lacunæ* (unless some parts of the introduction and postscript of section iii are to be accounted as rules) have cost us nine rules.

CHAPTER IV.

CONTENTS:—SECTION I. 1–2, combination of prepositions in *pada*-text with following verb; 3–6, exceptions; 7, separation by *avagraha* of such combinations; 8–12, do. of the constituents of compound words; 15–30, do. of suffixes of derivation from primitive words; 31–34, do. of case-endings from themes; 35–40, do. of other suffixes and constituents of compounds; 41, do of *iva* from the preceding word; 42–46, do. of the constituents of words doubly compounded.

SECTION II. 47–48, absence of *avagraha* before suffix *mant* etc. in certain cases; 49–50, absence of division by *avagraha* of certain copulative compounds; 51–54, do. of other compounds; 55, do. of *vṛddhi* derivatives from compound words; 56, do. of compounds with the negative prefix; 57–72, do. of other compounds and derivatives.

SECTION III. 73–77, general rules for restoration in *pada*-text of original or normal forms of words; 78, their application in *krama*-text also; 79–93, rules for restoration in certain cases and classes of cases; 94–100, exceptions.

SECTION IV. 101–109, necessity of the *krama*-text and of its study; 110–126, rules for construction of *krama*-text.

Our three preceding chapters have covered the whole ground which a comparison of the other treatises shows it to have been the bounden duty of a Prâtiçâkhya to occupy, and in this final chapter are brought up matters which might have been left unhandled without detriment to the character of the work as a complete and comprehensive phonetic manual for the school to which it belonged. Its first three sections, namely, teach the construction of the *pada*-text: whereas we have hitherto assumed this text as established, and have been taught how to construct the *saṁhitâ* upon its basis, we now look upon the body of traditional scripture from just the opposite point of view, and, assuming the *saṁhitâ*, receive directions for forming the *pada* from it. No other of the kindred treatises thus includes in its plan the construction of the *pada*-text; the Vâj. Pr. is the only one which takes up the matter at all: devoting, indeed, the whole of one of its chapters, the fifth, to an exposition of the rules determining the use or omission of the *avagraha*, or pause of separation between the two parts of a compound word, which is the subject of our first two sections, but leaving untouched the subject of our third section, or the restoration of words to their normal form in *pada*, which is not less indispensable than the other to the formation of the text. As regards the fourth section and its theme, the *krama*-text, their correspondences and relations will be set forth when we arrive at the place.

As was the case with the third section of the foregoing chapter, our commentary offers us here a long introduction, containing about twenty *çlokas*, to the subject of the chapter. It is prefaced with the following words: *samâsâvagrahavigrahân pade yatho 'vâca chandasi çâkaṭâyanaḥ: tathâ vakshyâmi catushṭayaṁ padaṁ nâmâkhyâtopasarganipâtânâm;** 'as Çâkaṭâyana has set forth for the Veda the combination, division, and disjunction of words in *pada*, so will I set forth the quadruple word —noun, verb, preposition, and particle.' Next follows a definition of each of these four classes of words, and then an exposition of the rules according to which they are to be regarded as compounded with one another, as they occur in the connection of continuous text, illustrations of the principles stated being drawn from the Atharvan text. Finally is given a list of the twenty *upasargas* or prepositions, and a designation of their accentuation, which is also followed by a list of the *upasargavṛttini*, or words which are treated as if they were prepositions—such as *achâ*, *tiraḥ*, *puraḥ*, *kiṅ*, etc. The verses are in one or two places very corrupt, and their precise meaning is sometimes doubtful: hence, in order not to interrupt the progress of our treatise by too long an interlude, I defer to an additional note, at the end of the work, a presentation of their text and an attempt to translate them.

उपसर्ग आख्यातेनोदात्तेन समस्यते ॥ १ ॥

1. A preposition is compounded with a verb when the latter is accented.

This is the well-known usage of all the Vedic *pada*-texts, at least so far as they have been brought to general knowledge. With a true appreciation of the slightness of the bond which connects a verb with its prefix, the constructors of the disjoined text have ordinarily treated the two as independent words: unless, indeed, by the laws of accentuation of the sentence, the usually enclitic verb retains its accent, in which case the preceding preposition in turn loses its accent and becomes proclitic; and the two are then written together as a compound. The commentator cites, as instances of verbs thus compounded, *pari-yánti* (i. 1. 1), *sam-ábharaḥ* (i. 9. 3), and *sam-srávanti* (i. 15. 3). He adds, *upasargavṛttibhiç ca*, 'the same is the case with the words which are to be treated as if prepositions,' and cites *yám : arâte : puraḥ-dhatsé* (v. 7. 2), and *yám : amí' íti : puraḥ-dadhiré* (v. 8. 5). That our treatise itself, in mak-

* With the slight alteration of *yatho 'vâca* to *yathâ 'ha*, we should have here three equal successive *pâdas* of a metrical verse: but the impossibility of forcing the last compound into any such metrical form, as a fourth *pâda*, renders it very doubtful whether this is anything more than a curious coincidence, and whether the words are not meant for simple prose.

ing no special reference to such ambiguous words, means to regard them as to all intents and purposes actual *upasargas*, is altogether probable. As counter-example, to show that the preposition is not compounded with the verb when the latter is unaccented, the commentary offers *yáta-dhā́'nān : vi : lápaya* (i. 7. 2).

The rule of the Vāj. Pr. (v. 16) is to the effect that *avagraha* is used between a verb and a preceding preposition, when the latter is unaccented. This is in some degree a better form of statement, since the loss of accent in the preposition is rather the cause of its combination with the verb than the latter's acquisition of a tone.

अनेको ऽनुदात्तेनापि ॥ २ ॥

2. If there be more than one of them, they are compounded even with an unaccented verb.

If more prepositions than one are compounded with an unaccented verb, only one of them, the one next the verb, is accented, the others becoming proclitic. In such a case, the constructors of the *pada*-text have very properly combined all with the verb, instead of simply putting the prepositions together, since it is not the relation of the former to the latter preposition that costs the former its accent, but rather their common relation to the verb: we have not a compound preposition, but a duplicate verbal compound. A later rule (rule 7, below) teaches us that in such a combination the first of the prepositions is separated by *avagraha* from the rest.

The commentator gives as illustrations the compounds *ut-ā́nayati* (ix. 6. 54), *sam-ā́'cinushva : anu-samprayā́hi* (xi. 1. 36), and *upa-sampárcanayāt** (xviii. 4. 50). He adds, as under the last rule, *upasargavṛttibhiç ca*, and illustrates with *acha-ā'vadāmasi* (e. g. vii. 38. 3) and *abhi-hiṅkṛṇota* (xii. 3. 37).

I do not find any corresponding precept in the Vāj. Pr., although the cases which it concerns are not such as would properly fall under the rule of that treatise already referred to.

अनर्थकर्मप्रवचनीयान्ययुक्तैर्वियुक्तो ऽभिवितन्वादिषु ॥ ३

3. Disjoined from the verb, however, are such as are used without significance, or to set forth the object, or such as are otherwise connected—namely, in the cases *abhi vi tanu* etc.

The Sanskrit language, much more than any other of the Indo-European family, has, throughout its whole history, maintained the *upasargas* or prepositions in their original and proper character of adverbial prefixes, directing the action of the verb itself, and not belonging especially to the object of that action, or immediately governing its case-relation. Even in the Vedic dialect, where the preposition admits of being widely

---

* The citation of this word here and under rule 7 shows that its true *pada*-form is as here given, and not as it has been noticed above (under iii. 79) that our *pada*-MS. actually reads.

separated from its verb, it yet, in the great majority of cases, belongs distinctly to the verb, and not to any noun. But, while this is true as a general rule, there are yet cases, in the Vedic as well as in the more modern classical Sanskrit, where the preposition has detached itself from the verb, and is to be construed more intimately with the object of the action. Even here, it more often follows the noun, as auxiliary to its case-ending, and so occupies an intermediate position between adverb and preposition, something like the German adverbs of direction in such phrases as *aus dem Walde heraus*, *in den Wald hinein*, or like the German *an* in *ich blicke ihn an*, as compared with the *at* in our nearly equivalent expression "I look at him." Whenever it happens that a preposition thus attached to a noun comes, in the construction of the sentence, to stand before an accented verb, or before another preposition which is connected with a verb, there arises an exception to the two foregoing rules, and such exceptions are made the subject of this and the two following rules: the first of them deals with such cases as *gṛhā́n : úpa : prá : sīdāmi* (iii. 12. 9), where the preposition is followed by another accented preposition and an unaccented verb, so that, by iv. 2, 7, we ought to have *upa-prásīdāmi*; the second, with such as *yā́ḥ : viçvā́ : abhí : vi-páçyati* (vi. 34. 4), where the following preposition loses its accent before the verb, and the same rules would require *abhi-vipáçyati*; the third, with passages where a single preposition comes before an accented verb, and so ought to lose its own accent and enter into combination with it, so that we should have, instead of *yé : ántaḥ : pári : jajñiré* (x. 7. 25), *pari-jajñiré*. The description which our rule gives of such uses of the prepositions is in near accordance with that of Pāṇini, who also (i. 4. 83–98) calls by the name *karmapravacanīya* ('concerned with the setting forth of the object of the action') such prepositions as are used otherwise than in immediate connection with a verb. He likewise uses in the same connection (i. 4. 93) the term *anarthaka*, 'non-significant,' applying it, according to the scholiast's illustrations, to *adhi* and *pari* when used after an ablative adverb—thus, *kutaḥ pari*, 'whence'—where they are unessential to the completeness of the sense. Whether the same term would be applied to the same prepositions when following a case, as an ablative or locative, I do not know; nor precisely how it is to be understood in our rule: the commentator gives no explanation of it, nor of *anyayukta*, nor does he assign his illustrations to the several items of specification which his text furnishes him. The term *anyayukta* probably means 'belonging to another verb,' but such cases are quite rare in the text: an instance of the kind intended is perhaps *niḥ stuvā́nasya pātaya* (i. 8. 3), where the preposition *niḥ* belongs to the verb *pātaya*, and not to the intervening participle, to which it would otherwise be attached, with loss of its own accent. Pāṇini's *karmapravacanīya* is comprehensive enough to include all the cases to which our rules apply.

In filling up the *gaṇas* of our treatise, and giving all the cases of a preposition preceding a verb, but not placed in accentual and compositional relations with it, I shall include together all that would fall under this and the two following rules, since they evidently form a single class, and are only formally distinct from one another:

Of *adhi*, with an ablative case (or, rarely, an ablative adverb), ii. 7. 8. viii. 9. 4 (*bis*). ix. 5. 6; 9. 18. xiii. 1. 42; 3. 2. xix. 56. 1; with a locative case (or locative adverb), i. 3. 6; 32. 4. ii. 1. 5. viii. 9. 19. ix. 5. 4, 8; 9. 2; 10. 7. x. 7. 1, 12; 8. 41. xi. 7. 8, 9, 14. xii. 3. 36. xiii. 1. 37; 3. 6, 18. xiv. 1. 1; 2. 48. xviii. 4. 3: *anu* with an accusative, ii. 34. 3. vi. 97. 3; 122. 1. viii. 9. 12. x. 5. 25–35. xi. 8. 11, 19–22, 24, 27. xii. 2. 21. xiii. 2. 40; 3. 1. xv. 6. 1–9; 9. 1; 14. 1–12. xviii. 4. 28. xix. 13. 6; 44. 10: *antar* with a locative, i. 13. 3: *abhi*, with an accusative, iii. 21. 5. iv. 1. 3. v. 19. 4. vi. 34. 4. viii. 2. 4; 3. 9. ix. 10. 6. xii. 1. 29, 33; 3. 8, 12, 30, 52. xviii. 3. 2;* with an ablative, viii. 6. 22;† with a locative, xviii. 3. 40:‡ *ā* with a locative, xviii. 1. 59; *upa* with an accusative, iii. 21. 1, 9. xix. 56. 3; *pari* with an ablative, ii. 34. 5. x. 7. 25. xii. 3. 53.

But these prepositional or quasi-prepositional uses of the *upasargas* are of less importance to give in detail, because they are liable to occur in any part of the sentence, and their treatment as exceptions to the first rules of our chapter is a result of their accidental position in contact with a verb. There are other passages, considerably less numerous, where the prefixes, although evidently belonging to the verb, have an adverbial signification which is so far independent that they maintain their separate accent before an unaccented verb, or before another verbal prefix. The one most often thus treated is *abhi*, which is found before *pra* at iii. 1. 2; 2. 5. iv. 8. 2; 32. 7. xviii. 3. 73, and before other *upasargas* at i. 1. 3. viii. 4. 21. ix. 9. 3: *upa* occurs only before *pra*,§ at i. 28. 1. iv. 31. 1. vi. 37. 1. xviii. 2. 53: *ā*, also before *pra* alone, at iii. 4. 5. vi. 35. 1. xviii. 4. 49: *apa*, at iv. 31. 7; 32. 5: *pari*, at iii. 2. 4: *ava*, at vi. 65. 1 (p. *áva : á-yatā : áva* etc.): *anu*, at xiii. 4. 26: *sam* (perhaps to be connected with the following instrumentals), at xviii. 2. 58: and *ud*, at xii. 1. 39—where, however, it is difficult not to believe the manuscript reading erroneous, and requiring amendment to *ut-dṛçúḥ*.

In a single phrase, *sáṁ sáṁ sravantu* (i. 15. 1. ii. 26. 3. xix. 1. 1), the preposition *sam*, being repeated for emphasis before the verb, is both times accented, and so is left uncombined. At vi. 63. 4, in a like repetition, there takes place a combination, with accentuation only of the former word—thus, *sáṁ-sam : it*, etc.; and, at vii. 26. 3, the repetition of *pra* is treated in the same manner.

A briefer, and, we should have supposed, a more acceptable manner of disposing of all the cases to which these three rules relate, would have been to prescribe that when an *upasarga* maintained its own accent before an accented verb or another *upasarga*, it did not undergo combination with them. Such exceptions to the general rules for combination are treated by the Vāj. Pr. in rules 5 to 10 of its sixth chapter.

The commentator's cited illustrations are *ihá : evá : abhí : ví : tanu* (i. 1. 3), *sáṁ : sáṁ : sravantu* (e. g. i. 15. 1), *sá : prá : sādhaya* (i. 24. 4),

---

* In some of these passages—viz. iii. 21. 5. xii. 3. 12, 30—the special connection of *abhi* with the noun is but the faintest, and the cases are hardly to be reckoned as belonging in this class.

† Here, too, the preposition belongs rather with the verb than with the noun.

‡ This is a combination unsupported by other passages, and hardly to be borne: for *abhi* is doubtless to be read *adhi*, with the Rig-Veda (x. 18. 8).

§ Except in the anomalous combination *úpa : vandyáḥ*, at xviii. 4. 65.

and *úpa : prá : agât* (i. 28. 1). The third is a case having no proper analogy with the others, since *sa* is not at all a verbal prefix; I have taken no account of it in drawing out the above statement.

पूर्वेणाभिविपश्याम्यादिषु ॥ ४ ॥

4. In *abhi vipaçyâmi* etc., the former preposition is disjoined.

The cases falling under this rule—those of a preposition retaining its accent and independence before another preposition which is itself made proclitic and combined with a following accented verb—have been detailed in the preceding note. The commentator quotes four of them, viz. *yá'vat : te : abhí : vi-páçyâmi* (xii. 1. 33), *mánasâ : abhí : sam-vidúḥ* (iii. 21. 5), *yá'vat : sá' : abhí : vi-jáṅgahe* (v. 19. 4), and *yáḥ : viçvâ : abhí : vi-páçyati* (vi. 34. 4). The examples, as in sundry cases elsewhere, are wanting in variety.

योनावध्यैरयन्तादिषु च ॥ ५ ॥

5. In *yonâv adhy âirayanta* etc., the preposition is also disjoined from the verb.

This rule applies to such of the cases detailed in the note to rule 3, above, as show an accented and independent preposition immediately before an accented verb. The commentator instances *samânê : yónâu : ádhi : â'irayanta* (ii. 1. 5), *ádhi : tasthúḥ* (ix. 9. 2), *yé : ásataḥ : pári : jajñiré* (x. 7. 25), *samudrâ't : ádhi : jajñishé* (iv. 10. 2), and *pári : bhû'ma : jâ'yase* (xiii. 2. 3). The citation of the last passage seems to imply that the commentator regarded *bhûma* as a verbal form, from the root *bhû*; but he can hardly, except in the forgetfulness of a moment, have been guilty of so gross a blunder.

आशीर्बभूवेति प्लुतस्वरस्य सिद्धत्वात् ॥ ६ ॥

6. *Âçîḥ* and *babhûva* are disjoined, owing to the determination of the protracted vowel.

That is to say, if I do not misapprehend the meaning of the rule, owing to the recognition of the final syllable of each word as a protracted one. To what end the precept is given, unless the words referred to (x. 2. 28 and xi. 3. 26, 27) have an irregular accent on the protracted syllable, I do not see. If accented, they would have a right, by the first rule of this chapter, to combination with the preceding preposition; but, the present rule virtually says, they are seen to lose this right upon a recognition of the fact that the accented vowel is protracted, and that its accent is therefore of an anomalous character. It has been already noticed (under i. 105) that a part of our manuscripts accent *babhûvâ'3n* in the latter of the two passages referred to: not one gives an accent to *âçî3ḥ*, in either case of its occurrence.

पूर्वेणावग्रहः ॥ ७ ॥

7. The former preposition is separated by *avagraha*.

The *avagraha*, or pause of separation between the two parts of a compound word, is defined by two of the Prâtiçâkhyas (as has been already remarked, in the note following iii. 74) as having the length of a mora. From here to the end of section II (rule 72), the treatise is occupied with rules for its employment or omission. And, in the first place, with however many prepositions a verbal form may be compounded, it is always the first of them that is separated from the rest of the compound by *avagraha*. The commentator gives us as examples the same series of words which we had under rule 2, above, only prefixing to them *upa-ávditi* (ix. 6. 53).

यातुमावत् ॥ ८ ॥

8. In *yâtumâvat*, also, the former constituent is separated by *avagraha*.

I interpret this rule according to the explanation of the commentator, who regards *pûrvasya* as implied in it, by inference from the preceding rule. It comes in rather awkwardly here, as only prepositions have been contemplated, thus far in the chapter, as former constituents of compounds. The commentator adds an exposition of the matter, which is, however, too much corrupted and mutilated for me to restore and translate it: it reads *matvarthe: vâyom mâvacchabdo manupo mahâra-sya vakârah : âkârâgamaḥ*. The word is apparently regarded as being *yâtu-mant*, with an added suffix *vant*, and the rule is designed to teach us that, instead of being divided *yatumá-vat*, as we might expect, it is to read *yâtu-mâvat*—as our *pada* manuscripts do in fact present it to us. The word occurs only at viii. 4. 23.

समासे च ॥ ९ ॥

9. Separation by *avagraha* takes place also in a compound.

The *ca* in the rule evidently continues the implication simply of *ava-grahaḥ* from rule 7, and the connection of the text casts upon *yâtumâ-vat* the suspicion of being an interpolation. A corresponding precept, *samâse 'vagrahaḥ*, is by the Vâj. Pr. set at the head of its chapter upon the use of *avagraha* (v. 1).

The commentator cites, as examples of separable compounds, *upa-hûtaḥ* (e. g. i. 1. 4), *bhûri-dhâyasam* (i. 2. 1), *bhûri-varpasam* (i. 2. 1), and *bhûri-dhanâḥ* (vii. 60. 4). Whether such words as the first of these, or the participles of compounded verbs, should be regarded as falling under the designation *samâsa*, appears to me doubtful, as they present the closest analogies with the verbs from which they come. I have included them with verbal forms in filling up the *gaṇas* of rules 3 to 5.

उपजाते परेण ॥ १० ॥

10. When a compound is farther compounded with an appended member, the latter constituent is separated.

The instance which the commentator selects for illustrating this rule is *prajāpatisṛshṭaḥ* (x. 6. 19). The word *prajā* is itself divisible as a compound—thus, *pra-jā* (e. g. vii. 35. 3); upon farther adding *pati*, the former division is given up in favor of that between the old compound and its added member, and we have *prajā-pati* (e. g. ii. 34. 4); and a similar addition and removal of the pause of separation gives us *prajāpati-sṛshṭaḥ*: while we might have, did the words occur, the yet farther change *prajāpatisṛshṭaḥ-iva*, or *prajāpatisṛshṭi-bhiḥ*, and *prajāpatisṛshṭibhiḥ-iva*. In no compound is the separation by *avagraha* made at more than one point, and it is always the member last appended which is entitled to separation.

The form of the corresponding rule in the Vāj. Pr. (v. 7) is vastly preferable to that of our own. That treatise says "in the case of a compound composed of several members, separation by *avagraha* is made of the member last added." This puts the matter upon its true basis, and accounts for the usage of the *pada*-text-makers both where they separate the latter member, and where they separate the former member, from the rest of the compound. We shall see below (rule 12) that the treatment by our Prātiçākhya of the separation of a former member is very obscure and imperfect.

सुप्राव्या च ॥ ११ ॥

11. Also in *suprāvyā*.

That is to say, in the word specified the last member is separated from the rest of the compound, and not the first, as would be more in accordance with the general analogies of the system of separation. The passage, the only one in the Atharvan where the word occurs, is quoted by the commentator: *suprā-avyā* : *yájamanāya* (iv. 30. 6). *Suprāvī* is divided in the same manner by the *pada*-text of the Rig-Veda (e. g. i. 34. 4): it is of obscure derivation and meaning, and whether the etymology of it which is implied in its analysis as made by the Hindu grammarians is correct, is at least very doubtful. But whether composed of *su-pra-avī* or *su-pra-vī*, we should expect the *pada*-text to write it *su-prāvī* or *su-pravī*, and it is the recognition of its anomalous division which has caused it to be made the subject of a special rule. The commentator adds a verse about it, which, however, appears to deal rather with its accentuation than its division: *asaiçh prapūrvasya* [*suprapūrvasya*?] *tāçabdaḥ* [*yaçabdaḥ*?] *svaritaḥ paraḥ* : *suprāvī 'ti tṛtīyāyāḥ kshāipraḥ chandasi svaryate*.

The Atharvan reading *suprāvyā* is at any rate established by this rule, against *suprāvye*, which the Rik (x. 125. 2) offers, and which the connection also appears to require. Possibly the form implies an explanation of the word which seems suggested by the first line of the verse just quoted, as if from the root *av*, with the prefixes *su* and *pra*, and with the added desiderative suffix *yā*, 'with desire to show propitious favor.' Such an explanation, of course, would be futile, being sufficiently disproved by the accent alone.

अनिङ्गेन पूर्वेण ॥ १२ ॥

12. If the appended member is indivisible, the former member is separated.

This rule is very obscure, and I am far from feeling confident that my translation rightly expresses its meaning. The manuscript readings of its first word, in text and in comment, vary between *aniñgena*, *atiñgena*, and *anigena*. If the word really means 'immovable,' i. e. 'indivisible, inseparable,' we should expect rather *aniñgyena* (compare *iñgya* in rule 76, below); and possibly the latter may be the true reading: but as *iñga* also is an acknowledged word, having the meaning 'movable,' I have not ventured to alter the form presented by the manuscript. As I have rendered it, the rule would appear to mean only that when to a word already compounded an inseparable appendix, for instance a suffix, was added, the division would remain as before—as in *su-vîratâyâi*, *pra-paddbhyâm*, and the like—but this is a perfectly simple case, and one which hardly calls for especial attention and determination. The commentator's exposition is as follows: *aniñgeno 'pajâte: aniñgena viçeshalakshaṇena avikṛshitena: dvayoḥ saṁçaye jâte pûrveṇa 'vagraho bhavati;* 'when a word is farther compounded with an indivisible—that is to say, with a modificatory appendage which is not taken apart—and there arises a doubt between two, separation is made of the former.' My translation of the rule is founded upon my (somewhat questionable) interpretation of this paraphrase. The cited illustrations, however, do not at all support it; they are *su-kshetriyâ : su-gâtuyâ* (iv. 33. 2), *saha-sûktavâkaḥ* (vii. 97. 6), *su-antardeçâḥ* (ix. 5. 37), and *su-prajâḥ* (iv. 11. 3). The last three of these are plain cases of separation of the constituent last added from the rest of the compound: the first two are less unequivocal, since we should rather regard the suffix *yâ* as added to *sukshetra* and *sugâtu*, and the more natural division as being *sukshetri-yâ*, *sugâtu-yâ*;* but neither is *yâ* an *aniñgya* suffix, as is shown by the next following word, *vasu-yâ*, and the others detailed in rule 80, below. The commentator adds a verse of farther exposition, but this also throws no additional light upon the matter in hand: it is *dve yatrâ 'vagrahasthâne pûrveṇe 'ti pareṇa vâ: pûrveṇa 'vagrahas tatra sukshetriyâ sântardeçâḥ suprajâç ca nidarçanam;* 'where there are two places for separation by *avagraha*, either of the former or of the latter member of a compound, separation is there to be made of the first member: instances are *sukshetriyâ*, *sântardeçâḥ*, and *suprajâḥ*.' I do not see how this statement can be accepted as a correct one; for, of the compounds consisting of more than two members, the last is even more often separated from the first two than the first from the last two: the point of division being, except in a very few cases of which the treatise takes special note, determined by the history of the double or triple compound, upon the principle distinctly laid down in the Vâj. Pr., that the member last added is the one which must be separated. Thus, in

* The Rik *pada* (i. 97. 2) actually reads *sugâtu-yâ*, although it divides *su-kshetriyâ* like our own text.

the first four books of the text, we have, upon the one hand, *ṛta-prajāta*, *madhu-saṁdṛça*, *vi-āyāma*, *prati-abhicaraṇa*, *mushka-ābarha*, *brahma-saṁçita*, *su-saṁnata*, *svapna-abhikaraṇa*, *ā-utsūryam*, *ā-vyusham*, *āyuḥ-prataraṇa*, *çiva-abhimarçana*, *aksha-parājaya*, and *açva-abhidhānī*; and, on the other hand, *sarūpa-kṛt*, *sarūpam-karaṇī*, *sapatna-kshayaṇa*, *viskandha-dūshaṇa*, *sapatna-han*, *abhimāti-jit*, *abhiçasti-pā*, *saṁkalpa-kulmala*, *agnihotra-hut*, *ākūti-pra*, *āçāra-eshin*, *vijesha-kṛt*, *abhibhūti ojas*, and *abhimāti-sahas*. And in the rare cases where three independent words are fused into a compound by a single process, the last one is separated from the other two: such are *agha-visha* and *iliha-dam* (iv. 6. 4). It will be difficult, I think, to find any interpretation for our rule which shall make it other than a bungling and inaccurate account of the phenomena with which it professes to deal. To connect *aniṅgena* in construction with *pūrveṇa*, and translate 'the former member is separated from the rest when it is an indivisible word,' although it would satisfy well enough the requirements of the instances given by the commentator, would only throw us into new difficulties, for it would require us to read *sa-rūpakṛt* as well as *sa-antardeça*, *su-parṇasuvana* (v. 4. 2) as well as *su-kshetriyā*, and the like.*

तद्धिते धा ॥ १३ ॥

13. *Dhā* is separated, when a *taddhita*-suffix.

As instances of the separation of the secondary suffix *dhā* from the themes to which it is attached, the commentor cites *catuḥ-dhā : retaḥ* (x. 10. 29), *ashṭa-dhā : yuktaḥ* (xiii. 3. 19), *nava-dhā : hitāḥ* (xiii. 4. 10), and *dvādaça-dhā* (vi. 113. 3): in the same manner is treated *mitra-dhā*, at ii. 6. 4, for which the Vājasaneyi-Saṅhitā, in the corresponding passage (xxvii. 5), has *mitra-dheye*. On the other hand, the text offers a single exception to the rule, *viçvádhā* (vi. 85. 3), which neither the Prātiçākhya nor its commentary notices: it is accented on the penult, while all the other compounds with *dhā* accent the suffix itself.

The commentator adds: *vyatyayasvaçraddīrghebhyo dhāpratyaye na avagraho bhavati*; 'the suffix *dhā* does not suffer separation after . . . (?), *sva*, *çrat*, and a long vowel.' The words *svadhā* and *çraddhā*, into which the root *dhā* enters as last member, are here referred to, and

* The best way, it seems to me, of saving the credit of our Prātiçākhya as regards its treatment of the subject of double composition in these two rules, will be to regard rule 10 as equivalent to Vāj. Pr. v. 7; understanding *upajāte* as meaning simply 'added to,' whether by prefixion or suffixion, and *parvan* as signifying 'the later (i. e. the last added) constituent;' and then farther, taking rule 12 to be added in limitation of 10, and to mean: 'when, however, the added constituent is incapable of being separated, the division remains as before.' It might well enough be thought that, in such cases of prefixion as *avīra-han* (from *vīra-han*), or in such cases of suffixion as *su-vīratā*, *vidhā-ya*, *pari-vatsarīṇa*, *vi-irtad*, etc., the addition of another element virtually fused the prior compound into one word, and would be understood as annulling its division by *avagraha*, unless some direction was given to the contrary. This interpretation, however, would be contrary to the authority of the commentator, would require us to understand *parvan* and *pūrveṇa* in a different from their usual sense, and would convict rule 11 of being an interpolation, made since the misinterpretation of rule 10.

perhaps *gadhā* (iv. 3. 6); but to what the first item in the enumeration refers, I have not succeeded in discovering.

The kindred suffix *dā* remains always attached to the theme to which it belongs.

The Vāj. Pr. (v. 27) forbids the separation of *dhā* from a numeral, but allows it in other cases: it would read *caturdhā*, *ashṭadhā*, etc., in *pada*. The usage of the Rik *pada*-text also does not entirely correspond with that of the Atharvan in regard to the same suffix: thus the former has *bahudhā*, while the latter separates *bahu-dhā*.

त्राकारान्ते ॥ १४ ॥

14. Also *trā*, when it ends in *ā*.

The commentator's examples are *deva-trā : ca : kṛṇuhi* (v. 12. 2), and *puru-trā : te : vanvatām* (vi. 126. 1); and his counter-examples, of *tra* inseparable, are *yatra : devāḥ : amṛtam* (ii. 1. 5), and *tatra : amṛtasya : cakshaṇam* (v. 4. 3).

The Vāj. Pr. (v. 9) declares *trā* separable, and, as our treatise might just as well have done, regards *tra* as excluded by the designation of the form of the separable suffix as *trā*. The usage of the Rik *pada* is also the same with that taught in our rule. Doubtless it is the character of the forms to which *tra* is attached, as being pronominal roots, that prevents its separation from them, rather than anything in the suffix itself. The ablative suffix *tas* is not separated, even when it follows a word having an independent *status* in the language, as in *abhitas*.

थानेकाक्षरेण ॥ १५ ॥

15. Also *thā*, when it is combined with a polysyllable.

The commentator's examples are *ṛtu-thā : vi : cakshate* (ix. 10. 26), *nāma-thā : sa : manyeta* (xi. 8. 7); and his counter-examples are *adha : yathā : naḥ* (xviii. 3. 21), and *tathā : tat : agne* (v. 29. 2). Here, again, it is evidently not the length of the words to which the suffix is appended, as monosyllables or polysyllables, that determines its separability, but the character of the former as pronominal roots and of the latter as nominal themes.

The Vāj. Pr. (v. 12) details the words after which *thā* is separable.

तरतमयोः ॥ १६ ॥

16. Also *tara* and *tama*.

The commentator cites, as instances of these suffixes with separable character, *mádhoḥ : asmi : mádhu-taraḥ : madúghāt : mádhumat-taraḥ* (i. 34. 4), *út-tamaḥ : asi : oshadhīnām* (e. g. vi. 15. 1), *ahám : asmi : yaçáḥ-tamaḥ* (vi. 39. 3), and *nṛṇā́m : ca : bhágavat-tamaḥ* (ii. 9. 2). He adds, according to his usual method of introducing counter-examples: *taratamayoḥ iti kim artham*, 'why does the rule say *tara* and *tama*?' and gives the counter-examples *açvatarásya* (iv. 4. 8) and *açvataryā̀ḥ* (viii. 8. 22). The citation of these words in this manner, as if they were excluded by the very form of the rule itself from falling under its operation, suggests as the true reading and interpretation of the rule *taratamapoḥ*, '*tara* and *tama* when unaccented,' giving to the indicatory letter *p* the same force which it has as appended to the same suffixes by Pâṇini (e. g. v. 3. 55, 57). My copy of the manuscript, indeed, gives me everywhere *taratamayoḥ;* but, considering the small difference between *y* and *p* when hastily formed, I cannot be confident that the Hindu scribe did not mean to write the latter letter. But, in the first place, I find it very hard to admit that our Prâtiçâkhya would thus use an indicatory letter as an essential and determinative part of one of its rules, without giving anywhere any explanation of its value. Other such appendages to a suffix, corresponding with those which Pâṇini employs, are, it is true, elsewhere found in the treatise: thus we have (iv. 20) *tâtil*, where the *l* indicates that the syllable preceding the suffix has the accent; also *matu*, *vatu*, and *vasu*, whose appended *u* is intended to show that the suffix receives an augment (*âgama*) *n* in the strong cases, and takes the feminine ending *î;* and the particles *u* and *m* are called, with Pâṇini, *uñ* and *muñ*, to distinguish them from the exclamation *u* and the case-ending *su:* but the appended letters are nowhere used as significant. Again, we should expect that the *p*, if used at all, would be applied to each suffix, and that the rule would read *tarop-tamapoḥ* (compare Pâṇ. i. 1. 22), which is certainly not its form in the manuscript. Finally, the admission of the indicatory letter, with its Paninean signification, would not make the rule complete and accurate, as stating the usage of our *pada*-text with regard to the suffixes in question; for, on the one hand, we have *ratham-tará* (e. g. viii. 10. 13), and the prepositional comparatives *pra-tarám* (e. g. v. 1. 4), *vi-tarám* (v. 12. 4), and *sam-tarám* (vii. 16. 1); and, on the other hand, there are cases in which the unaccented endings are not separated from the themes to which they are attached, and one of these cases is even noted and specified by the commentator. The latter's discussion of the rule is fuller than usual, as he seems, for once, to feel the necessity of doing something to supply the deficiencies of his text; but his effort is only partially successful, and moreover, his language is so mutilated by the manuscript that I can make it out but imperfectly. He first asks why the separation of *tara* and *tama* is not made also in *katará* and *katamá*, *yatará* and *yatamá* (to which we may add *ítara* and *ántara*), and answers *netâuche* [*nâi 'tâu staḥ?*] *taratamâu anyâu etâv akârâdî pratyayâu: an̄gasyâ 'trâ ''dimâtram u çishyate lupyate param: svarâdî pratyayâv etâu padatvaṁ nâ 'tra çishyate;* 'these are not *tara* and *tama*, but other suffixes, commencing with *a* [viz. *atara*, *atama*]: in the derivatives in question, the first portion of the theme remains, but the last is dropped [i. e. *yatara* = *y* + *atara* etc.]: these are two suffixes with initial vowel: capability of standing as separate *padas* is not taught of them.' This distinction of the suffixes as applied to pronominal roots from those applied to other themes is evidently artificial and false: the difference is that the roots themselves are not, like derivative themes, detachable from the suffixes appended to them—as we have seen to be the case under the two preceding rules. The commentator, changing his subject, then goes on to say *gotamaḥ pratishedho vaktavyaḥ;* 'the word *gotama* must be noted as an exception to the rule;' and he cites the passage in which it occurs: *yá'u : gótamam : ávathaḥ* (iv. 29. 6); adding, by way of explanation, *saṁjñâyâṁ rûḍhiçabdo 'hâ tamâ 'trâ 'natiçâyane: asmânaḥ samudrâdis tasmân netyati gotamaḥ.* I have not succeeded in restoring this verse so as to translate it, but so much of it as applies to *gotama* may be pretty clearly understood: the word, as a proper name, is one of common currency, a *saṁjñâ*, or specific appellation employed without reference to its etymology, and its suffix *tama* has no superlative signification; hence there is a propriety in treating it otherwise than as an ordinary superlative.

There yet remains one word in the Atharvan, viz. *uttara*, whose treatment by the *pada*-text requires an exposition which the Prâtiçâkhya omits. While *uttama* is always divided—thus, *ut-tama*—the comparative is variously treated, being sometimes divided and sometimes left without *avagraha*. The Vâj. Pr. (v. 2) takes special note of this irregularity, declaring a word formed with *tara* or *tama* not separable when opposed in meaning to 'south;' that is, when meaning 'north'—this being, as we may suppose, another case of *saṁjñâ*. This principle is so far followed in our text that the word is never divided when it has the meaning 'north;' but it is also left without *avagraha* in quite a number of passages* where it has its own proper signification 'upper,' or the naturally and regularly derived ones 'superior,' 'remoter,' or 'later.' I can only suppose that the true principle which should determine the separation or non-separation was misunderstood and misapplied by the constructors of our *pada*-text.

मतौ ॥ १७ ॥

17. Also *mant*.

The illustrations chosen by the commentator from among the very numerous examples of this rule presented in the Atharvan text are *madhu-mat* (e. g. i. 34. 3) and *go-mat* (xviii. 3. 61). Exceptions are noted farther on, in rule 47.

The Vâj. Pr. (v. 9) states the principle more broadly, including together all possessive suffixes; among them, most of those which form the subject of our next rule.

वकारादौ च ॥ १८ ॥

18. Also a *taddhita* beginning with *v*.

The commentator cites as examples *atri-vat : vaḥ : krimayaḥ : hanmi : kaṇva-vat : jamadagni-vat* (ii. 32. 3), *ṛtu-vânam* (vi. 36. 1), *satya-vânam* (iv. 29. 1, 2), *açva-vân* (vi. 68. 3), *añji-vam* (viii. 6. 9), *keça-vâḥ* (viii. 6. 23),† *mârta-vatsam* (viii. 6. 26), *â-vayam* (viii. 6. 20), and *vádhû-yam*

* They are as follows: iii. 6. 5. iv. 22. 6. v. 28. 10. vi. 16. 4; 118. 3; 134. 2. viii. 2. 15. xi. 8. 16. xii. 1. 54.

† The MS. next gives *râṣṭvataḥ*, which I have not succeeded in identifying with any word in the Atharvan text.

(xiv. 1. 29). He must have been nodding when he added the last three words, of which the third has no suffix beginning with *v*, and the two others are not formed by suffixes, but by composition. He goes on to say *vijño pratishedho vaktavyaḥ*, but what is to be understood in, or from, *vijña*, I do not see: the cases of irregular absence of separation by *avagraha* which he adduces are *dravayaḥ : vi-baddhaḥ* (v. 20. 2), *ubhayávinam* (v. 25. 9), and the three words, of kindred character with the latter, *amayávi*, *mekhalávi*, *medhávi*, no one of which is found in the Atharvan, although we once have an accusative of the last of them, *medhávinam* (vi. 108. 4).

शसि वीप्सायाम् ॥ १९ ॥

19. Also *ças*, with distributive meaning.

The instances given in the commentary are *paru-çaḥ : kalpaya : enam* (ix. 5. 4), and *dhāma-çaḥ : sthātre : rejante : vi-kṛtāni : rūpa-çaḥ* (ix. 9. 16); the counter-examples, showing that *ças* is only separable when distributive, are *aṅkuçaḥ* (vi. 82. 3) and *kīnāçāḥ* (e. g. iii. 17. 5)—cases which it was very unnecessary to cite, since their suffix, if they have one, is *ça*, not *ças*.

The Vāj. Pr. (v. 9) marks *ças*, along with other secondary suffixes, as separable.

तातिलि ॥ २० ॥

20. Also *tāti*.

Pāṇini (e. g. iv. 4. 142) calls the suffix *tāti* by the same name, *tātil*, the appended *l* signifying, as has been already noticed, that the syllable preceding the suffix is accented. The Vāj. Pr., in its corresponding rule (v. 9), calls it simply *tāti*.

The commentator illustrates with the two passages *mahyái : ariṣṭa-tātaye* (iii. 5. 5), and *havishmantam : mā : vardhaya : jyeshṭha-tātaye* (vi. 39. 1).

The related suffix *tā* is never separated from the theme to which it is appended: *tva* forms the subject of rule 28, below.

उभयाद् द्युभि ॥ २१ ॥

21. Also *dyu*, after *ubhaya*.

The commentator cites the examples *ubhaya-dyuḥ : abhi-eti* (i. 25. 4) and *ubhaya-dyuḥ : upa : haranti* (viii. 10. 21), and the counter-example *yaḥ : anyedyuḥ* (i. 25. 4); which are the only cases (except a repetition of the phrase in i. 25. 4 at vii. 116. 2) presented in our text of derivatives—or, more properly, of compounds—formed with *dyu* or *dyus*. The name *dyubh* or *dyubhi*, which our treatise gives to the latter, is a strange one, and not supported by anything in Pāṇini: indeed, the latter seems never to use *bh* as an indicatory letter; the general grammar forms *ubhayadyus* with the suffix *dyus*, and *anyedyus* and its numerous kindred (see the Böhtlingk-Roth lexicon, under *dyus*, or Pāṇ. v. 3. 22) with the suffix *edyuas*: one is tempted to conjecture that the authors of our system may have regarded *dyus* in these compounds as a contraction for the instrumental plural *dyubhis*. The reading of the word is well assured, not only by the text and comment, but also by a cited verse with which the commentator closes his exposition: it reads *anyasyâ dyubhi tv etvam syâd anyo vâ dyahbhir ishyate: lopa edyubhi câ 'nyasya siddho vâ 'yam punar dyubhi.* This evidently has to do with the formation of *anyedyus*, accounting for the *e* which precedes the suffix: but I can offer no entirely satisfactory restoration of the text.

मात्रे च ॥२२॥

22. Also *mâtra.*

This is most palpably a rule which has its ground in the observed phenomena of the general language, and not in those of the Atharva-Veda; for although, in the later language, *mâtra* came to be used in such a mode and sense as to give some ground for its treatment as a suffix, it is in the Atharvan nothing but a noun, and even enters into composition only with *ati*, forming the adjective *atimâtra*, 'above measure, excessive.' The commentator cites, in illustration of the rule, the two passages in which this compound occurs, namely *ati-mâtram : avardhanta* (v. 19. 1) and *ye : âtmânam : ati-mâtram* (viii. 6. 13).

विश्वाद्दानीमि ॥२३॥

23. Also *dânîm*, after *viçva.*

The commentator cites, as example and counter-example, *viçva-dânîm* (e. g. vii. 73. 11) and *idânîm* (e. g. x. 8. 39), the only two Atharvan words which are formed with this suffix. Here, again, is an instance of a suffix remaining attached in *pada* to a pronominal root, while it is separated from a nominal theme (compare under rules 14–16).

मये ऽसकारात् ॥२४॥

24. Also *maya*, excepting after *s.*

A single example of the separation of the suffix *maya* is cited in the commentary, viz. *çaka-mayam : dhûmam* (ix. 10. 25); and also a single example of its non-separation, when following a theme ending in *s*, viz. *anaḥ : manasmayam* (xiv. 1. 12).

के व्यञ्जनात् ॥२५॥

25. Also *ka*, after a consonant.

Words in which the suffix *ka* is appended to a consonant are not at all frequent in the Atharvan: the commentator brings up two cases, viz. *avat-kam* (ii. 3. 1) and *ejat-kâḥ* (v. 23. 7), and I have noted but two others, viz. *manaḥ-kam* (vi. 18. 3) and *antyaḥ-kam* (x. 8. 25). As counter-examples, where the same suffix, following a vowel, is left attached in *pada* to its theme, he gives us *tuṇḍikaḥ* (viii. 6. 5) and *çipavitnubdḥ* (v. 23. 7). Such formations occur by scores in our text.*

*त्वे चान्तोदात्ते ॥२६॥

26. Also *tva*, in a word accented on the final syllable.

The instances cited by the commentator of the occurrence of this common suffix are *mahi-tvá' : kámāi* (iv. 2. 4), *amṛta-tvám : ânaçuḥ* (ix. 10. 1), and *çúcayaḥ : cuci-tvám* (xii. 3. 28). As counter-example, to show that the *tva* is separated only when it receives the accent, is cited *áditiḥ : jánitvam* (vii. 6. 1: the Rik *pada*, in the corresponding passage [i. 89. 10], has *jáni-tvam*); and this is the only word of the kind which the text contains, for at ii. 28. 3, where the edition reads *jánitváḥ*, all the manuscripts have *janitváḥ*. The commentator adds a verse respecting his counter-example, as follows: *janitvam aditeḥ paraṁ na 'ṅgyate kṛijanaparataḥ: itvo vā syāj janas tena padatvaṁ nā 'tra çishyate:* this informs us that *janitva* following *aditi* is not to be treated as separable, as being formed from the root *jan* by the suffix *itva*, which is not taught to be an ending capable of constituting an independent *pada*. He then proceeds to ask the question *iha kasmāt samāso na bhavati : ekaja : tvam : mahi : tvam;* 'why is there no combination in the passages *ekaja tvám* (iv. 31. 3 : p. *eka-ja : tvám*) and *mahi tvám* (not found in AV.); and he answers by a verse, from the authority, doubtless, which had suggested to him the query: *ekaja tvam mahi tvaṁ ca tad ubhayaṁ samasyate* [*tū 'bhayaṁ na samasyate!*]: *āmantritaṁ tayoḥ pūrvaṁ yushmada*[*s!*] *tvam paraṁ padam;* 'in neither of the phrases *ekaja tvam* and *mahi tvam* is there a combination; the former word is there a vocative, and the latter is *tvam* from *yushmad*.' It is clearly a work of supererogation on the part of the commentator to explain such self-evident matters. But he is not content even with this; he continues "why is not *agrepitva* separated?"—that is to say, I presume, why is it not divided *agrepi-tva*, instead of *agre-pitva?*—and he again cites a verse: *taddhite 'vagrahaḥ çishṭaḥ padatvaṁ nā 'tra çishyate: pibates taṁ nibodhata itvaṁ chāndasam ishyate;* 'separability is taught only of *taddhitas;* division into separate *padas* is not taught of this case; note that the word comes from the root *pā*, 'to drink,' with the Vedic suffix *itva*.' But, even were this exposition in itself worth giving, the word to which it relates does not occur in the Atharvan, nor—judging from its non-appearance in the Böhtlingk-Roth lexicon—in any other of the known Vedic texts. We could wish that our commentator had reserved his strength for points where its exertion would have done us some service.

The suffix *tra*, which appears in the single word *saṁskṛtatrá* to fill the office of *tva*, is in our *pada*-text (iv. 21. 4) left inseparable, while the Rik, in the corresponding passage (vi. 28. 4), interposes the *avagraha* before it. *Taya*, in *catushṭaya* (x. 2. 3), is not separated from its theme. Of *tā*, notice has been taken under rule 20.

---

* For example, in the first eight books, from which alone I have excerpted them, at i. 3. 2; 5. 6–9, 9; 11. 5; 25. 4; 34. 2. ii. 3. 1; 24. 1, 2; 26. 5. iii. 11. 2; 22. 4. v. 16. 6. vi. 29. 2; 43. 1; 83. 3; 121. 4. vii. 56. 5. viii. 6. 19, 21 (*bis*).

कृत्वे समासो वा नानापददर्शनात् ॥ २७ ॥

27. *Kṛtva* is combined or not, according to its appearance as an independent word or otherwise.

Kṛtvas occurs but three times in the Atharvan: twice it is treated as an independent word, both it and the preceding numeral having an accent; once it is combined with the numeral, the latter losing its separate accent, and it is then separated by *avagraha* from it. The commentator cites all the passages, as follows: *catúr : námaḥ : ashṭa-kṛ́tvaḥ : bhavā́-ya : dáça : kṛ́tvaḥ* (xi. 2. 9), and *tríḥ : saptá : kṛ́tvaḥ* (xii. 2. 29). After this, having not yet recovered from the impulse which made him so fertile of exposition under the foregoing rule, he continues: *nanv evam : katham : vyavasthitena vikalpena vāçabdena pratipāditatvāt*; 'now then, how is it? since a diversity of usage is taught respecting the word, by the use of the term *vā*?' and he makes reply in a lengthy citation from his metrical authority, which wanders at the end far beyond the limits of the subject in hand: *karoter daçasaptābhyāṁ tvaçabdaḥ kṛd vidhīyate : saṁkhyayā anudāttayā ashṭaçabdāt samasyate : udāttād daçasapte 'ty evam pūrveṇa vigrahaḥ : dhāparyantās taddhitā ye te 'shṭe vā 'vagraho bhavet : ato 'nyena padatve 'pi yavatyādishu taddhitam : dhātrāthātātiliçaridānīṁtaratamamatap : vamātradyubhi kṛtvāpi mayaḍkṛtvesho avagrahaḥ.* In the last verse we have an enumeration of all the suffixes thus far treated of as separable.

जातीयादिषु च ॥ २८ ॥

28. *Jātīya* etc. are also separable.

As instances of the use of *jātīya*, the commentator gives us *paṭu-jātīya*, *mṛdu-jātīya*, *paṇḍita-jātīya*, and *çobhanā-jātīya*: none of these words, however, nor any other compounds with the same final member, are to be met with in the Atharvan text. The general grammar also treats *jātīya* as a suffix, and Pāṇini's scholiasts (under v. 3. 69) give, as an example of its use, the first of the instances of our commentator. The latter farther cites, to fill out the *gaṇa* of the rule, some of the compounds of *dheya*, viz. *bhāga-dheyam* (e. g. vi. 111. 1), *rūpa-dheyam* (*rūpa-dheyāni*: ii. 26. 1), and *nāma-dheyam* (vii. 109. 6). What other frequently occurring final members of compounds it may have pleased the authors of our treatise to regard as suffixes, and to include in this *gaṇa*, I do not know: I have noted no actual suffixes as needing to be comprehended in it.

यादाविच्छायां स्वरात्कर्मनामतन्मानिप्रेप्सुषु ॥ २९ ॥

29. Also a suffix commencing with *y* and preceded by a vowel, in a desiderative form; namely, in participles, denominatives, and desiderative adjectives.

Not one of the technical terms used in this rule is known to me to occur elsewhere than in the grammatical language of our treatise. One of them, *ichá*, we have had at another place (iii. 18), and in such a connection as to show that it is employed to designate the whole class of words to which this rule applies; the others, then, are specifications under it, or a classified statement of the cases which it includes. The same thing is indicated by the commentator, who paraphrases as follows: *yáddv ichdyám svarát avagraho bhavati karma°* etc. *Karmanáma*, then, I have without much hesitation rendered by 'participle;' and *tanmánin* seems to me to mean 'implying the making or doing of that which the theme indicates,' and so to be applicable to such words as *çatrûyanti*, *aghâyanti*, where the signification is not simply desiderative: but of this I do not feel altogether confident, and I have at one time sought in the word a designation of the middle participles having the termination *mána*; *prepra* I think must belong to such derivative adjectives as *devayu*, *çravasyu*. The commentator, as usual, fails to give us any light upon these points: he only cites, as instances of the separable suffixes to which the rule relates, *adhvari-yatám* (i. 4. 1), *agha-yuḥ* (e.g. iv. 3. 2), *vṛsha-yamáṇaḥ* (ii. 5. 7), and *çatru-yatím : abhi* (iii. 1. 3): and farther, as counter-examples, *tat : nisáṣati* (xiii. 2. 14), to show that no desiderative suffix is separable unless beginning with *y*; and *yena : çravasyavaḥ* (iii. 9. 4), to show that the suffix beginning with *y* must not be preceded by a consonant.

The Vâj. Pr. has a corresponding rule (v. 10), but more briefly expressed.

वस्ववस्वप्नसुम्नसाधुभिर्या ॥ ३० ॥

30. Also *yá*, when combined with *vasu*, *ava*, *svapna*, *sumna*, and *sádhu*.

Why this rule should be necessary, after the one which precedes it, and which would include all the cases to which it is intended to apply, I find it difficult to see. It can hardly be that it was meant to exclude such words as *su-kshetriyá*, *su-gátuyá*, since these have been otherwise provided for (see under rule 12, above): more probably, forms like *mithuyá* (e.g. iv. 29. 7) and *urviyá* (e.g. v. 12. 5) are to be regarded as its counter-examples. The Vâj. Pr. (v. 20) also does a like work of supererogation in reference to sundry words of its text. The commentator repeats the words, but gives nothing of the context of the passages in which they occur: they are *vasu-yá* (iv. 33. 2), *ava-yá* (ii. 35. 1), *svapna-yá* (v. 7. 8), *sumna-yá* (vii. 55. 1), and *sádhu-yá* (x. 4. 21). The second of them is classed with the rest only by a blunder, since it is evidently *avayás*, the irregular nominative singular of *ava-yáj*, and ought to be written by the *pada*-text *ava-yáḥ*, instead of *ava-yá*.

The comment closes with another verse: *pañcâi 'vá 'vagrahán áha yáçabde çákaṭáyanaḥ : antoddttaḥ padatvaṁ ca vibhaktyarthe bhavet tu yá*; 'Çâkaṭâyana mentions five cases in which *yá* suffers separation by *avagraha*: it is accented as final, and stands as an independent element, when used as a case-ending.' I am by no means confident that I have correctly interpreted the last line.

भिर्भ्यांभ्यःसु ॥ ३१ ॥

31. Also *bhis*, *bhyâm*, and *bhyas*.

As illustrations, the commentary furnishes *pañca-bhiḥ : anguli-bhiḥ* (iv. 14. 7), *uru-bhyâm : te : ashṭhîvad-bhyâm : pârshṇi-bhyâm : pra-padâ-bhyâm* (ii. 33. 5), and *asthi-bhyaḥ : te : majja-bhyaḥ : snâva-bhyaḥ : dhamani-bhyaḥ* (ii. 33. 6). The case-ending *bhyam*, as in *tubhyam* and *asmabhyam*, is not treated as separable.

The Vâj. Pr. (v. 13) puts our rules 31 and 33 into one, declaring a case-ending beginning with *bh* separable, when following a short vowel or a consonant. This would teach the division *tu-bhyam*, *asma-bhyam*, also; but the latter is expressly declared indivisible in another rule (v. 35), and the former was perhaps overlooked.

सौ च ॥ ३२ ॥

32. Also *su*.

The commentator's instances are *anka-su* (vi. 35. 2), *ap-su* (e. g. i. 4. 4),[1] and *vayam : râja-su* (vii. 50. 7).

The Vâj. Pr. (v. 14) combines this rule with rule 34, and says that *su* is separated when its *s* is not changed to a lingual.

न दीर्घात् ॥ ३३ ॥

33. But not after a long vowel.

This restriction applies to both the two preceding rules: no case-ending is separable after a long final vowel, whether this be an original long final of the theme, or the result of a prolongation according to the rules of declension. The commentator instances *yâbhiḥ : satyam : bharati* (ix. 2. 25), *tâbhiḥ : tvam : asmân* (ix. 2. 25), *akshîbhyâm : te : nâsikâbhyâm : karṇâbhyâm* (ii. 33. 1), *gobhyaḥ : açvebhyaḥ* (iii. 28. 3), and *âsu : itarâsu* (iii. 10. 4).

Compare Vâj. Pr. v. 13, as quoted under rule 31, above.

विनामे च ॥ ३४ ॥

34. Nor where conversion into a lingual takes place.

This is an exception under rule 32, applying only to the termination *su*. The two, as was already remarked, are by the Vâj. Pr. combined into a single rule (v. 14). Our commentator cites *prati : tishṭha : dikshu* (iv. 14. 9), *namasyaḥ : vikshu : îḍyaḥ* (ii. 2. 1), *mânushîshu : dikshu* (v. 11. 8), *marutaḥ : vikshu* (viii. 4. 18), *yam : ca : vikshu* (ix. 5. 10), *pari : paçya : vikshu* (viii. 3. 10), and *su-vrjanâsu : dikshu* (xviii. 1. 46).

---

[1] The MS. adds *dap-su*, which I have not been able to identify with any Atharvan word. Possibly *drṭ-su* is intended.

वसौ ह्रस्वात् ॥ ३५ ॥

35. *Vaṅs* is separated after a short vowel.

The commentator quotes from the text the examples *cakṛ-vân* (ii. 35. 3) and *papi-vân* (xiv. 1. 3), and the counter-example *vidvân* (e. g. ii. 1. 2), and then goes on with a long citation from his metrical authority, as follows: *apade 'vagrahaḥ çishṭa ikâreṇa padâdinâ: dhâtvantâc ca vasâu hrasvâc cakṛvân papivân iti: upasargasamâse 'pi vasâv evâ 'vagṛhyate: kikiṅaurâviçesheṇa bhûte tâbhyâṁ vidhîyate: vasurvârthe tayo labdham bahulaṁ chandasi 'ti ca: vâ tayoḥ kṛtoḥ samâsâc câ 'pajâyeta vastutaḥ: avakâre padatvaṁ na pûrveṇâi 'vâ 'vagṛhyate: ahrasve 'pi padatvaṁ syât prâptas tatrâ 'py avagrahaḥ: ahrasve chândasatvât tu rutvam âhur manîshiṇaḥ.* The meaning of some of these lines is very clear, and they are seen to cover the ground of our present rule and of the two following: others are obscure, and need emendation before they can be intelligently rendered.

The Vâj. Pr. gives but one rule (v. 11) respecting the separation of the suffix of the perfect participle, combining together the specifications and counter-specifications of the three rules of our treatise.

तेनैवोपसृष्टे ऽपि ॥ ३६ ॥

36. And that, even when the form is combined with a preposition.

The cited illustrations are *pareyi-vâṅsam* (xviii. 1. 49), *praviçi-vâṅsam* (iv. 23. 1), *jakshi-vâṅsaḥ : papi-vâṅsaḥ* (vii. 97. 3), and *uttasthi-vâṅsaḥ* (vi. 93. 1). The same words (excepting *jakshivâṅsaḥ*, perhaps omitted by the carelessness of the copyist) were found cited under i. 88, and it is probably their association there which has caused the inclusion among them here of the two forms from simple roots, which are of no value as regards the matter now under treatment. But for this rule, we might expect *pra-viçivâṅsam*, *ut-tasthivâṅsam*, and so on, like *pra-vishṭam*, *ut-tishṭhataḥ*, etc. And yet, the separation as here taught is not discordant with the general principle that the last added member shall be the one which receives *avagraha*, since we may more properly regard the participial suffix as combined with the root after the latter's composition with its prefix than before: were *ta* a separable suffix, we should doubtless also have *praviç-ta*, *utthi-ta*, and the like.

उपसर्गेणावकारे ॥ ३७ ॥

37. But the preposition is separated, when the suffix shows no *v*.

That is to say, when the suffix is contracted into *ush*, in the weak forms of declension, it is no longer separable, and the *avagraha* remains where it was before, between the preposition and the verb; as in the forms cited by the commentator, *â-jagmushaḥ : anu-mata* (ii. 26. 2), and *vaçâ : pra-dadushe : duhe* (xii. 4. 35). He adds a verse: *yadâ prasâra-*

ṇaṁ tasya padatvaṁ na 'shyate tadâ : pûrveṇâ 'vagrahaḥ siddho yatas taj jîyate padam ; 'when the suffix suffers contraction, its capability of standing as an independent *pada* is not taught: the former constituent then maintains the *avagraha*, as having a superior right to it (?).'

समन्तः पूरणे ॥ ३८ ॥

38. *Samanta* is divided, when it has the sense of completion.

The commentator gives us, as instances of the separable compound, *pushkariṇîḥ : sámantâḥ* (iv. 34. 5 etc.), and *sám-agraḥ : sám-antaḥ : bhûyâsam* (vii. 81. 4); and, as instance of the separable compound, *yáthâ : vṛkshám : libujâ : samantám* (vi. 8. 1). But how the word has the sense of completion any more in the two former cases than in the latter, I quite fail to perceive. The commentator adds a farther exposition, which puts the distinction upon a safer, though still an arbitrary, ground: *samantaṁ sarvato'rthe 'ntodâttaṁ nâ 'vagṛhyate, âdyudâttam avagṛhyate : pûraṇârthaṁ pushkariṇîḥ samantâḥ ;* '*samantam*, having the sense of *sarvatas*, 'wholly,' and accented on the final, does not suffer *avagraha* ; when accented on the first, and having the sense of completion, it suffers *avagraha*, as in *pushkariṇîḥ samantâḥ*.'

अनतौ विसंभ्यां प्राणाख्या चेत् ॥ ३९ ॥

39. The prepositions *vi* and *sam* are separated from the root *an*, when the word formed is a name of the breath.

We should have expected this rule to be stated the other way; namely, that the root *an* was not separated from *pra* and *apa* (in the compounds *prâṇa* and *apâna*, which are always thus written in *pada*, without division). This would, on the one hand, be theoretically preferable, since the general rules for division would lead us to expect the *pada*-readings *pra-âna, apa-âna, vi-âna*, and *sam-âna*, and we therefore ought to have the first two denied, rather than the last two ratified, by a special rule: and, on the other hand, it would be practically more accurate, since *udâna*, which occurs in the combination *vyâna-udânâu*, is doubtless a separable compound, and is in fact so regarded by the commentator, under rule 42 below. Why *prâṇa* and *apâna* should not also be divided, it is far from easy to see.

The commentator gives us the examples *vi-ânaḥ : âyuḥ* (xviii. 2. 46), and *sam-ânam : asmin : kuḥ* (x. 2. 13). To show that it is only after *vi* and *sam* that the *avagraha* takes place before *an*, he brings up the counter-example *prâṇaḥ : apânaḥ* (xviii. 2. 46); and, to show that the compound must be a name of the breath, he cites *samânam : astu : vaḥ : manaḥ* (vi. 64. 3). The specification *prâṇâkhyâ cet*, however, is after all pleonastic, since the adjective *samâna*, 'resembling, like, accordant,' is from *sa* + *mâna*, not *sam* + *âna*.

The Rik and White Yajus treat the word *prâṇa* in the same manner as our text: *apâna* does not appear to occur in the former Veda, and in the latter it is (Vâj. Pr. v. 33, comm.) separable. Compare also Vâj. Pr. v. 36, which deals with *samâna*.

काम्याम्रेडितयोः ॥ ४० ॥

40. Also are separated *kámya* and a repeated word.

This is a strange rule. In the first place, the Atharva-Veda furnishes no ground whatever for the treatment of *kâmya* as a suffix, even though it be regarded as such in certain combinations in the general grammatical system (see Pâṇ. iii. 1. 9 etc.). We find it only in such compounds as the commentator instances by citing *açraddhâḥ : dhana-kâmyâ* (xii. 2. 51) and *anṛtam : vitta-kâmyâ* (xii. 3. 52), which would fall under rule 9 of this chapter without occasioning any difficulty or hesitation. In the second place, I can discover no possible reason for combining together in one rule things so utterly unconnected and incongruous as the occurrence of this suffix and that of words repeated in an emphatic or a distinctive sense. The dual termination, however, is our warrant that we have not here, as in the case of rules 12 and 13 of the first chapter, two rules written and explained together by the commentator. The latter cites a single passage containing two words which are *âmreḍita*, viz. *bhûyaḥ-bhûyaḥ : çvaḥ-çvaḥ* (x. 6. 5 etc.).

The Vâj. Pr. (v. 18) has the same rule respecting repeated words, and calls them (i. 146) by the same name. Pâṇini also employs the term *âmreḍita* (e. g. vi. 1. 99) in a kindred sense.

इवे च ॥ ४१ ॥

41. Also *iva*.

The commentator cites but a single instance—*sâlâvṛkân-iva* (ii. 27. 5)—of this exceedingly frequent case of combination. The Vâj. Pr. notes it at v. 16.

मिथोवगृह्ययोर्मध्यमेन ॥ ४२ ॥

42. Separation is made between two words which are each of them separable.

Or, as the commentator paraphrases it, when two words, themselves separable, are combined into a single word, separation of the middle member (*parvan*) is made. His instances are *yat : âñjana-abhyañjanam* (ix. 6. 11), *prajâ-amṛtatvam : uta : dîrgham : âyuḥ* (xi. 1. 34), and *vyâna-udânâu : vâk* (xi. 8. 4); to which we might add indefinitely, not only copulative compounds, but possessives (e. g. *âhṛta-yajñakratuḥ*, ix. 6. 27) and others.

The Vâj. Pr. finds no need of such a rule as this, nor does it seem imperatively called for, all possible cases being already disposed of by rules 10 and 12, above. Still less is to be seen the necessity of adding to it the two which next follow, and which it obviously includes.

समासयोश्च ॥ ४३ ॥

43. As also, between two compounds.

The sole example furnished in the commentary is *aghaçaṅsa-duḥçaṅsâbhyâm : kareṇa* (xii. 2. 2).

द्विरुक्ते चावगृह्ये ॥ ४४ ॥

44. As also, between a separable word and its repetition.

The commentator cites instances of repeated words occurring in five successive verses of the Atharvan text, without troubling himself about the fact that two of them are not separable: they are *karvatîm-karvatîm : eva* (ix. 5. 32), *saṁyatîm-saṁyatîm : eva* (ix. 5. 33), *pinvatîm-pinvatîm : eva* (ix. 5. 34), *udyatîm-udyatîm : eva* (ix. 5. 35), and *abhibhavantîm-abhibhavantîm : eva* (ix. 5. 36). He adds a verse: *pṛthagiṅgyasamâse ca madhye kuryâd avagraham : saṁyatîṁsaṁyatîṁ câi 'va vyânoddânâu nidarçanam*; 'separation by *avagraha* must be made in the middle of a compound made up of two severally separable words: instances are *saṁyatîm-saṁyatîm* and *vyânoddânâu*.'

वसुधातरः सहस्रसातमेति वसुसहस्राभ्याम् ॥ ४५ ॥

45. In *vasudhâtara* and *sahasrasâtama*, separation is made after *vasu* and *sahasra*.

The passages are cited by the commentator: *vasu-dhâtaraḥ : ca* (v. 27. 6), and *sahasra-sâtamâ : bhava* (iii. 28. 4). It is not without reason that the Prâtiçâkhya takes note of these cases; for, since the suffixes *tara* and *tama* are separable (by iv. 16), and are plainly the last added members, the words they form should read, in *pada*, *vasudhâ-tara* and *sahasrasâ-tama*. Comparatives and superlatives of this particular class, however, where the suffixes are appended to root words which directly govern the preceding member of the compound, are treated in the same manner by the *pada*-texts also of the Rik (e. g. *ratna-dhâtamam*, i. 1. 1) and White Yajus, and the latter's Prâtiçâkhya (V. Pr. v. 3), makes special mention of them. The commentator adds: *vasudhâtara iti : vasûnâṁ dhâtṛtaraḥ : shashṭhyantena [arthena?] samâsaḥ : samâse avagraho bhavati : vasûni vâ dadhati : vasu-dhâtaraḥ : samâse avagraho bhavati*; '*vasudhâtara* : that is, one who is in a high degree a giver (*dhâtṛtara*) of good things; composition is made with a form having a genitive sense; the compound suffers *avagraha* : or, *vasudhâtaras*, 'they bestow good things;' the compound suffers *avagraha*.' The only item of value derivable from this exposition is that some authorities regarded *vasudhâ'taraḥ* as the plural of *vasu-dhâtar*. It would be, in fact, in its Atharvan connection, much more easily interpretable in this manner, but that the accent speaks strongly for the other mode of derivation. The passage in which it occurs is shown by comparison with the White Yajus (xxvii. 15) to be curiously misunderstood and corrupted, and the Atharvan *vasudhâ'taraḥ* corresponds to *vasudhâ'tamaḥ* of the other text: we may suppose that the former means to give the plural of *vasudhâtar*, but gives it the accent which belongs to *vasudhâ'tama* and its corresponding comparative *vasudhâ'tara*. The commentator closes his treatment of the subject with a verse: *sasibhyâṁ [sâdhâbhyâm?] ca kṛdantābhyām vihitāu taddhitāu parāu: tābhyām shashṭhīsamāse ca pūrveṇa 'vagrahaḥ smṛtaḥ*: 'after *sā* and *dhā* (!), as *kṛt*-endings, *taddhitas* are declared to follow: in a compound with these having a genitive meaning, the former member is separated by *avagraha*.'

सुभिषक्तमस्तमे ॥ ४६ ॥

46. *Subhishaktama* suffers separation by *avagraha* before *tama*.

The commentator cites *subhishak-tamāḥ* (vi. 24. 2); we have also the nominative singular masculine at ii. 9. 5. He adds *çobhanaḥ bhishak: subhishak*; '*subhishak* means propitious physician;' and then again gives a verse: *bhishajā hi suçabdo 'yam puṁliṅgena samasyate: upajātas tamas tasmāt pūrveṇa* [*pareṇa*!] *'vagrahaḥ smṛtaḥ*; 'here *su* is compounded with the masculine *bhishaj*, and *tama* is farther appended: separation by *avagraha* is made of the latter.'

I can see no reason at all for any such rule as this: the case specified is simply one in which the separation by *avagraha* takes place normally, according to the general rules, and a score more of precisely similar cases might easily be quoted from the Atharvan text: instances are *bhágavat-tama* (ii. 9. 2) and *bhágavat-tara* (iv. 13. 6), *sphátimát-tama* (iii. 24. 6), *mṛtámanaḥ-tara* (vi. 18. 2), and *vṛtrahán-tama* (vii. 110. 1).

The signature of the first section, which closes here, is as follows: 47: *caturthasya prathamaḥ pādaḥ: caturādhyāyikābhāshye caturthasya prathamaḥ pādaḥ samāptaḥ*. We have found but forty-six rules in the section, but have remarked one (rule 40) which ought to have been divided and counted as two. Possibly two may have been fused together in it, in order to allow the commentator's introduction to the chapter to count as a rule, without altering the received number in the section: but I have neither been willing to allow the rank of a rule to anything in that introduction, nor ventured to divide rule 40 into two parts.

न तकारसकाराभ्यां मत्वर्थे ॥ ४७ ॥

47. The suffix *mant* and its equivalents are not separable after *t* and *s*.

The commentator cites in illustration *daívatī* (e. g. iv. 3. 2), *garutmān* (e. g. iv. 6. 3), *marutvān* (e. g. vi. 104. 3), *ūrjasvān* (*ūrjasvantaḥ*, vii. 60. 2), *payasvān* (e. g. vii. 73. 5), *ūrjasvatī* (e. g. iii. 12. 2), and *payasvatī* (e. g. iii. 10. 1). The only consonants other than *t* and *s* which are found to occur before the suffix *vant* are *n* and *ṇ*, which allow separation; instances are *dasan-vat* (vi. 12. 2), *asthan-vantam* (ix. 9. 4), *brahmaṇ-vatīm* (vi. 108. 2), etc. The rule is an exception under rule 17 above; by the Vāj. Pr. (v. 8) it is included with the general rule in one statement.

यत्तदेतेभ्यो वतौ ॥ ४८ ॥

48. Nor *vant*, after *ya*, *ta*, and *eta*.

The commentator's examples are *yâvat : te : abhi : vi-paçyâmi* (xii. 1. 33), *tâvat : sam-âitu : indriyam* (iii. 22. 5), and *etâvat : asya : prâcînam* (iv. 11. 8); and his counter-examples, which are hardly called for, are *sûnṛtâ-vat* (e. g. v. 20. 6), and *apâshṭhâ-vat* (xiv. 1. 29). This rule, also, is included in Vâj. Pr. v. 8, since in each of the words to which it refers there is an irregular prolongation of the final vowel of the theme before the suffix.

देवताद्वन्द्वे च ॥४९॥

49. Nor a copulative compound made up of the names of divinities.

The commentator gives pretty nearly the whole series of such compounds which the text furnishes: they are *indrâgnî* (e. g. i. 35. 4), *indravâyû* (iii. 20. 6), *bhavârudrâu* (xi. 2. 14), *bhavâçarvâu* (e. g. iv. 28. 1), *vâtâparjanyâ* (x. 4. 16), *agnîshomâ* (e. g. i. 8. 2), *mitrâvaruṇâ* (e. g. iii. 4. 4), *indrâvaruṇâ* (e. g. vii. 58. 1), and *indrâsomâ* (e. g. viii. 4. 1): to be added are only *somârudrâu* (e. g. v. 6. 5), *indrâpûshaṇâ* (vi. 3. 1), and *agnâvishṇû* (vii. 29. 1, 2). A number of verses follow in the commentary, in the usual corrupt condition of text: *devatânâm iha dvandve dîrghatvaṁ yadi*[1] *dṛçyate : anîngyaṁ tat*[2] *padaṁ vâcyam agnîshomâu nidarçanam :* thus much is clear, and is a virtual repetition of our rule, but with a restriction to cases in which a long vowel appears at the end of the first member of the compound, which requires a specification farther on of the single exception *indravâyû ;* what follows is more obscure, and I have not been able, with what time I have given to it, to restore the text to an intelligible form; it reads: *vâsurâṇâṁ dvandve 'py avagṛhyaṁ kathaṁ padam : çâkalyasye 'ngite nityaṁ yathâ satyânṛte* [i. 33. 2] *tathâ : brahma prajâpatis* [xix. 9. 12] *te ubhe nâ 'vagṛhyaṁ kadâ cana : ânañaḥ pratishedhaç ca vâyoç co 'bhayataḥ param : indravâyv* [iii. 20. 6] *âdishu kathaṁ dîrgho yatra tad* [na?] *dṛçyate : dvandvamâtrenashedhastvam ahorâtre nidarçanam.*

The rule of the Vâj. Pr. (v. 28), which includes also our rules 50 and 52, is to the effect that dual copulative compounds whose first members end in a vowel are not separable.

यस्य चोत्तरपदे दीर्घो व्यञ्जनादौ ॥५०॥

50. Nor one which shows a long vowel before an initial consonant of the latter member of the compound.

The instances furnished by the commentator are *ishṭâpûrtam* (e. g. ii. 12. 4), *pitâputrâu* (vi. 112. 2), *hasâmudâu* (xiv. 2. 43), *dyâvâpṛthivî* (e. g. ii. 1. 4), *dyâvâbhûmî* (xviii. 1. 31), and *ushâsânaktâ* (e. g. v. 12. 6). To these I add *çunâsîrâ* (iii. 17. 5), *sûryâmâsâu* (iii. 29. 5*), *sûryâcandramasâu* (vi. 28. 3), and *yajñâyajñiyam* (viii. 10. 13). To the same class, of *dvandvas* exempt from division, belongs *prâṇâpânâu* (e. g. ii. 16. 1), although it does not show the peculiarities of form which this rule

[1] yad. [2] anityat. * In the edition, *sûryam°* is a misprint.

demands, and therefore ought to be made the subject of a special precept: our treatise-makers and their commentator, apparently, have overlooked it. A single counter-example the commentator gives, viz. *satyánṛta iti satya-anṛta* (i. 33. 2). He adds a verse: *irâmirâpurobhyaç*[1] *ca prakṛtyâ dîrgha eva saḥ: hrasvasya yatra dîrghatvam̃ sa dvandvo nâ 'vagṛhyate;* 'after *irâ*, *amîvâ*, and *puraḥ* [*avagraha* comes in], for in those cases the vowel is long by nature; but where a short vowel is lengthened, there no division by *avagraha* takes place.' This is a very blundering statement, so far as concerns the instances given in the first *pâda: puraḥ*, of course, could form no copulative compound; *amîva* forms none such in the Atharvan, and it also, though a feminine with a long final vowel, as a separate word, always shortens its final in composition (*amîva-câtana*, e. g. i. 28. 1; *amîva-han*, e. g. RV. i. 18. 2); *irâ*, too, is found only in the compound *irâ-kshîrâ* (x. 10. 6), which is not copulative.

The implication of *dvandva* from the preceding rule seems clearly made by the particle *ca* in this rule, and is supported by the connection as shown by the two following rules: the commentator, also, inserts *dvandvasya* after *yasya* in his paraphrase. Such compounds, then, as *viçvânara*, *svârṇk*, *vîrudh*, *sûkara*, etc., which are left undivided in the *pada*-text on account of the irregularly protracted final of their first members, must be left to fall into the general *gaṇa* of rule 54.

षोडशी संदेहात् ॥५१॥

51. Nor *shoḍaçin*, on account of the interfusion of the two members of the compound.

Or, it may be, 'on account of doubt'—that is to say, of doubt as to the form to which the constituents should be restored, their mode of combination being an entirely anomalous one. It is to be observed, however, that our treatise has itself (at i. 63) given special directions as to how *shaṭ* and following *daça* are combined together, so that to the student of the Prâtiçâkhya the *pada*-reading *shaṭ-daça* ought to occasion no difficulty. That the rule reads *shoḍaçî* instead of *shoḍaça* is surprising, since both words (each in but a single passage) occur in the text: the commentator cites them, as follows: *ishṭâpûrtasya : shoḍaçam* (iii. 29. 1), *shoḍaçî : sapta-râtraḥ* (xi. 7. 11).

The Vâj. Pr. mentions *shoḍaça* in a rule (v. 37) containing a long list of indivisible words.

अहोरात्रे ॥५२॥

52. Nor *ahorâtre*.

The commentator's illustrations are *ahorâtrâbhyâm : nakshatrebhyaḥ* (vi. 128. 3), and *ahorâtre idam̃ brûmaḥ* (xi. 6. 5). The Vâj. Pr. includes the word in the same rule with *shoḍaça* (v. 37).

There is nothing in the character of either *ahorâtre* or *shóḍaça*, so far as I can discover, which should withdraw them from the action of rule 50, and render their separate mention necessary.

---

[1] MS. *idaº*.

अञ्चतिजरत्पर्वसु ॥ ५३ ॥

53. Nor the root *añc:* nor former constituents of a compound.

It is, if possible, even more surprising here than at rule 40 to find two so utterly heterogeneous matters put together in the same rule. We cannot suppose that the commentator would combine them, in statement and in exposition, unless he regarded them as composing a single precept; but, on the other hand, we have not the same warrant here as in the former case that his division is a correct one: there is nothing in the form of the rule which would absolutely forbid its simple division into two parts, without further change—although we should, in that case, expect rather *añcatâu* than *añcati*.

As illustrations of the inseparability of the root *añc*, we have given us *prâcîḥ* (e. g. v. 28. 11), *pratîcî* (e. g. iii. 27. 3), and *udîcîḥ* (e. g. xii. 1. 31). All the compounds with this root are treated as indivisible by our *pada*-text: the Vâj. Pr. also (v. 30) declares the root inseparable, with exception (v. 19) of a single derivative.

To show that, when new members are added to a compound, the existing division by *avagraha* of their former members is given up, the commentator instances *çaṁtâti-bhiḥ : arishṭatâti-bhiḥ* (iv. 13. 5): compare *arishṭa-tâtaye*, cited above, under rule 20. The principle has been already sufficiently illustrated in these notes, under rule 10. The Vâj. Pr. has nothing corresponding to this part of our rule, which is, in fact, virtually superfluous, since the directions already given for the separation of a newly-added member might be understood as involving the suspension of the ancient division.

The commentator ends with a verse which seems to say precisely the opposite of the rule of his text: *yatro 'bhe pratividhye te upajâtaṁ jaraṁ ca yat, jaratâ 'vagrahaḥ kârya ṛksâmâbhyâṁ nidarçanam;* 'when both members are severally separable, both the newly-added and the ancient, separation by *avagraha* is to be made of the ancient one: an instance is *ṛk-sâmâbhyâm.*' But this is mere nonsense, as it stands, the word cited being a case where the last-appended element is inseparable, as following a long vowel (see rule 33, above), and where, therefore, the division must be suffered to remain between the two original constituents of the compound. If the theme of declension had been *ṛk-sâman*, instead of *ṛksâma*, we should have an instrumental dual *ṛksâma-bhyâm*, which would be a true illustration of the rule. One may conjecture that the last line originally read *jare nâ 'vagrahaḥ kârya ṛksâmabhyâṁ nidarçanam*, and that it was amended to its present form by some copyist who knew that the Atharvan read, not *ṛksâma-bhyâm*, but *ṛk-sâmâbhyâm*, but who was careless enough to overlook the discordance which he thus introduced between the text and its comment.

समुद्रादिषु च ॥ ५४ ॥

54. Nor *samudra* etc.

The whole comment upon this rule is wanting in our manuscript: the copyist has again carelessly skipped from its first statement to its final repetition before the rule next following. This, however, gives us reason to believe that the commentator had performed his work in his usual brief and unsatisfactory style, and had done very little toward filling up the *gaṇa*. It would have been particularly curious and interesting to see how many and which of the words contained in the Atharvan the makers of the Prâtiçâkhya looked upon as fairly entitled to a division which the constructors of the *pada*-text had not admitted. The Vâj. Pr. (at v. 37) gives a list of such words for its text, but Weber finds it, as was to have been expected, both deficient and redundant. It is by no means easy to draw up a list which shall include all that ought to be received, and exclude all that ought to be left out; but I have looked through the Atharvan text with some care for this purpose, and trust that my filling up of the *gaṇa* of the text will be found to comprehend all or nearly all of the matter to which the rule ought to apply.

There is, in the first place, in this as in the other Vedic texts, a considerable class of compound words exhibiting an irregular prolongation of the final vowel of the former member, and which the constructors of the *pada*-text have chosen to leave unchanged, instead of separating them by *avagraha* and restoring the normal quantity of the altered vowel. Why they should be thus treated, however, in distinction from the words with which our treatise deals in the first section of its third chapter, no sufficient reason appears. They are as follows: *apâmârga* (e. g. iv. 17. 6: the word, by V. Pr. v. 21, is divisible), *apâshṭha* (iv. 6. 5: see above, ii. 95), *ashṭhîvant* (e. g. ii. 33. 5), *idâvatsara* (vi. 55. 3: cf. V. Pr. v. 32), *ubhayâdant* (e. g. v. 31. 3: divisible by V. Pr. v. 21), *ubhayâvin* (e. g. v. 25. 9: see above, under iv. 18), *ekâdaça* (v. 16. 11: cf. V. Pr. v. 37), *kakshîvant* (e. g. iv. 29. 5: cf. V. Pr. v. 37), *tatâmaha* (e. g. v. 24. 17), *dvâdaça* (e. g. iv. 11. 11: cf. V. Pr. v. 15), *narâçaṅsa* (v. 27. 3: cf. V. Pr. v. 37) and *nârâçansî* (e. g. xiv. 1. 7), *nîhâra* (e. g. vi. 113. 2: cf. V. Pr. v. 37), *prâṇâha* (ix. 3. 4), *prâvṛta* (e. g. xii. 5. 2: cf. V. Pr. v. 37), *prâvṛsh* (e. g. xii. 1. 46), *marmâvidh* (xi. 10. 26: cf. iii. 3, iv. 68), *viçvâmitra* (e. g. iv. 29. 5: cf. iii. 9 and V. Pr. v. 37), *viçvânara* (e. g. iv. 11. 7: cf. iii. 9 and V. Pr. v. 37) and *vâiçvânara* (e. g. i. 10. 4), *vîrudh* (e. g. i. 32. 1), *çvâpad* (e. g. viii. 5. 11: cf. iii. 10), *çvâvidh* (v. 13. 9: cf. iii. 3, iv. 68), *sâranga* (e. g. ii. 32. 2), *sârathi* (e. g. viii. 8. 23), *sûkara* (e. g. ii. 27. 2) *sûnṛtâ* (e. g. iii. 20. 3), *svâvṛk* (xviii. 1. 32), and *hṛdayâvidh* (viii. 6. 18: cf. iii. 3, iv. 68).

Another smaller class is composed of certain words which have as their first member a real or an apparent case of declension: such are *anyedyus* (i. 25. 4: cf. iv. 21), *âçuṅga* (vi. 14. 3), *gavishṭhira* (iv. 29. 5: cf. V. Pr. v. 37), *nârishṭhâ* (e. g. vii. 12. 2: cf. V. Pr. v. 37), *pataṅga* (e. g. vi. 31. 3), *pitâmaha* (e. g. v. 5. 1), *madhyaṁdina* (e. g. iv. 11. 12), *mâtariçvan** (e. g. v. 10. 8), and *çitiṅga* (xi. 5. 12).

The number is by no means an inconsiderable one of words whose division seems so naturally suggested by an etymology which is either incontestable or at least very plausible, that we are reasonably surprised

* At v. 2. 9, all the manuscripts have *mâtaribhvarî*, which the edition, hardly with sufficient reason, has amended to *mâtariçvarî*: it is, like the latter, left undivided.

that they were not divided by the Hindu grammarians. Of these, I name *anarvâṇa* (viii. 4. 2), *anushṭhu* (xii. 4. 45: probably regarded as formed by an inseparable suffix), *apâna* (e. g. ii. 28. 3: cf. under iv. 39), *abhishṭi* (e. g. i. 6. 1), *avarti* (e. g. iv. 34. 3), *avaskava* (ii. 31. 4), *açvatara* (e. g. viii. 8. 22: cf. under iv. 16), *asvaga* (xii. 5. 45), *âghṛṇi* (vii. 9. 2), *âdhî* (vi. 131. 1 etc.: Rik *pada*, *â-dhî*), *ânushak* (iv. 32. 1), *âprî* (xi. 7. 19), *âyudha* (e. g. iii. 19. 5: cf. V. Pr. v. 37), *ârti* (e. g. iii. 31. 2), *ârpita* (e. g. vi. 112. 3: at viii. 9. 19 only, we have *â-arpitâni*), *âçîvisha* (xii. 5. 34), *âsakti* (xiv. 1. 26), *âsikta* (xii. 3. 25: probably the absence of division is here only an error of the manuscript; we have *â'-siktam* at iv. 7. 1), *uttâna* (e. g. ix. 9. 14), *ṛtvij* (e. g. vi. 2. 1), *oshadhi* (e. g. i. 23. 1: cf. V. Pr. v. 35), *gopâ* (e. g. iii. 8. 4: cf. V. Pr. v. 37), *gopîtha* (e. g. v. 9. 7), *candramas* (e. g. v. 24. 10: cf. V. Pr. v. 37), *dâyâda* (v. 18. 6, 14), *nyagrodha* (e. g. iv. 37. 4; cf. V. Pr. v. 37), *puroḍâça* (e. g. ix. 6. 12: see i. 63: cf. V. Pr. v. 37), *prâṇa* (e. g. ii. 12. 7: cf. under iv. 39), *prâyaçcitti* (xiv. 1. 30), *vivasvant* (e. g. xi. 6. 2), *vishṭap* (e. g. x. 10. 31: cf. V. Pr. v. 41), *vishṭambha* (xiii. 4. 10: cf. V. Pr. v. 41), *vishṭârin* (iv. 34. 1 etc.), *çiñçumâra* (xi. 2. 25), *çraddhâ* (e. g. v. 7. 5), *sabhâ* (e. g. iv. 21. 6), *samantâm* (vi. 8. 1: cf. iv. 38), *samudra* (e. g. i. 3. 8: cf. V. Pr. v. 37), *surabhi* (e. g. vi. 124. 3: cf. V. Pr. v. 37), *sthapati* (ii. 32. 4), *svadhâ* (e. g. ii. 29. 7), *svapati* (viii. 6. 16), *svasti* (e. g. i. 30. 2), and *hâridrava* (i. 22. 4). It is not hard to conjecture, in the case of some of these words, reasons which may have led to their being treated as exceptional cases, but in many of them no such reason is apparent, and in a part, at least, we are compelled to suppose that the composition was fully recognized, and the division neglected for some arbitrary and unexplained cause. That the four compounds of pronominal elements *ena*, *nahi*, *nakis*, and *mâkis* were left by the *pada* in their *saṅhitâ* form is not to be wondered at: three of them are noted also by the Vâj. Pr. (v. 35, 37) as indivisible.

There yet remains quite a list of compounds and derivatives, the division of which may plausibly be supposed to have been neglected from uncertainty of etymology, anomaly of form, difficulty of restoring the original constituents, or the like: while yet, in most cases, we should not have been surprised to see the constructors of the *pada* making an attempt at their analysis. In drawing up this part of the list, especially, I may very possibly have omitted to note down some words of the text which to another would seem not less worthy of mention than those given: the series, as collected by me, is *akûpâra* (v. 17. 1), *ajagara* (e. g. iv. 15. 7: cf. V. Pr. v. 37), *adomada* (vi. 63. 1) and *adomadha* (viii. 2. 18), *anaḍvâh* (e. g. iii. 11. 5: cf. V. Pr. v. 37), *anṛkshara* (e. g. xiv. 1. 34), *abhîçu* (e. g. vi. 137. 2), *abhra* (e. g. iv. 15. 1: cf. V. Pr. v. 34), *avadya* (e. g. ii. 10. 6), *âtura* (vi. 101. 2), *âmikshâ* (e. g. ix. 4. 4), *âhanas* (e. g. iv. 30. 6), *udârathi* (iv. 7. 3), *urvaçî* (xviii. 3. 23), *karmâra* (iii. 5. 6: cf. V. Pr. v. 37), *karçapha* (iii. 9. 1), *kasarṇîla* (x. 4. 5, 17), *kucara* (e. g. vii. 26. 2: cf. V. Pr. v. 37), *kṛkavâku* (v. 31. 2), *godhâ* (iv. 3. 6: cf. V. Pr. v. 37), *jâshkamada* (xi. 9. 9), *daçonasi* (x. 4. 17), *duchunâ* (e. g. v. 17. 4: cf. ii. 61), *duradabhna* (xii. 4. 4, 19), *durâhâ* (viii. 8. 24), *druvaya* (e. g. v. 20. 2: cf. under iv. 18), *dhîvan* (iii. 5. 6), *paḍbîça* (e. g. vi. 96. 2), *paṇḍaga* (viii. 6. 16), *prâṇada* (iv. 35. 5), *maryâdâ* (e. g. v. 1. 6), *mahîluka* (x. 10. 6), *ratharvî* (x. 4. 5), *vaṅsaga* (xviii. 3. 36), *valaga* (e. g.

v. 31. 4 : cf. V. Pr. v. 35), *viçvâhâ* (e. g. vii. 50. 1 : cf. V. Pr. v. 37), *vyâghra* (e. g. iv. 8. 1 : cf. V. Pr. v. 37), *çâṇḍadûrva* (xviii. 3. 6), *sadyas* (e. g. viii. 10. 21), and *svâhâ* (e. g. ii. 16. 1).

The Vâj. Pr. (v. 37) notes a couple of words as indivisible which are found divided in the Atharvan : they are *upa-sti* (e. g. iii. 5. 6) and *puvira-vant* (iii. 17. 3). In like manner, *saṁvatsara*, which the Rik *pada* does not analyse, is in our text uniformly written *sam-vatsara* (e. g. iii. 10. 9). One or two other such cases of discordance among the several *pada*-texts are pointed out in the notes to the different rules : but there is, in general, such close agreement among them as to show conclusively that the *pada* method of text-analysis, in its details as well as in its main plan, is the production of a single teacher, or of a single school.

It may be well to add here, *per contra*, a few of the cases in which the *pada*-text makes unintelligible or palpably erroneous divisions of words : I have noted, as the most striking instances of this kind, *anam-gareḥ* (viii. 6. 22), *anapa-dyatâm* (iv. 17. 6), *jighat-svam* (ii. 14. 1), *go-pano* (xii. 4. 10), *çam-opya* (i. 14. 3), *hṛ-dyota* (i. 22. 1) and *hṛ-dyotana* (v. 20. 12). The peculiar form, accentuation, and division of two passages in the fourteenth book—*çúbham : yatîḥ* (xiv. 1. 32) and *pátim : yatîḥ** (xiv. 2. 52)—is also worthy of remark in connection with this subject.

वृद्धेनैकाक्षरेण स्वरान्तेन ॥५५॥

55. Nor is a member which has suffered *vṛddhi* separable, if it be monosyllabic and end in a vowel.

The commentator's examples of an inseparable vriddhied initial syllable are *sâpatnaḥ* (ii. 7. 2), *sâumanasaḥ* (e. g. iii. 30. 7), *sâumanasam* (e. g. xiii. 1. 19), *sâudhanvanâḥ* (vi. 47. 3), *trâiṣṭubham* (ix. 10. 1), *sâubhagam* (e. g. ii. 36. 1), and *saubhâgyam* (e. g. xiv. 1. 42). His counter-example, brought forward to show that the inseparable member must have suffered *vṛddhi*, is *su-parṇaḥ* (e. g. i. 24. 1); to show that it must be monosyllabic, they are *âirâ-vataḥ* (viii. 10. 29), *mârta-vatsam* (viii. 6. 26), and *vâdhû-yam* (e. g. xiv. 1. 29); to show that it must end in a vowel, they are *nâiḥ-bâdhyena : haviṣâ* (vi. 75. 1) and *dâuḥ-svapnyam : dâuḥ-jîvitynm* (iv. 17. 5). I add, in the farther illustration of the inseparable class, *vâimanasya* (v. 21. 1) and *prâhrâdi* (viii. 10. 22); of the separable class, *sâm-itya* (viii. 10. 6), *sâm-râjya* (xiv. 1. 43), *pâurṇa-mâsî* (vii. 80. 1), *sâurya-varcasa* (viii. 10. 27), and *avâira-hatya* (vi. 29. 3). The rule is, I believe, carefully observed throughout the whole of the Atharvan text, and the Vâj. Pr. (v. 29) has one precisely corresponding; nor have I noted any cases in which the usage of the Rik *pada*-text was not in accordance with it. Its somewhat arbitrary character, however, is patent.

The commentator again closes his exposition with a verse : *avagṛhyât padâd yasmin taddhito vṛddhimân bhavet : ekâ vṛddhisvarânteshu na câi 'vâ 'vagraho bhavet : âirâvato mârtavatsaṁ vâdhûyaṁ ca nidarçanât.*

---

* In this passage, the printed text reads *pátiṁ yatîḥ*, but without any support from the manuscripts.

A little amendment makes this mean, in restatement of our rule, 'where a *taddhita* suffix requiring *vṛddhi* is appended to a divisible word, separation is not made of a member which is monosyllabic and ends in a vowel.'

अवर्णान्तेनैकाक्षरेण प्रतिषिद्धेनाप्रयावादिवर्जम् ॥ ५६ ॥

56. Nor a monosyllabic member ending in *a* or *â* and negatived—excepting in the case of *aprayâvan* etc.

The form of statement which our treatise has adopted for its rule respecting the separability of negative compounds is not particularly well chosen. The general usage of the Atharvan *pada*-text, as regards such compounds, is as follows. The negative prefix *a* or *an* is not itself ever separated by *avagraha* from the word to which it is attached: we have *asat*, *anṛta*, etc. If, however, the word negatived is already a compound, the negative prefix is in almost all cases treated like any other added inseparable element, and leaves the prior division of the compound unaffected: we have *parâ-jita* and *aparâ-jita*, *vîra-han* and *avîra-han*, etc. A few exceptions to this mode of treatment occur, and with them it is the province of our rule to deal. The preposition *â*, with *an* prefixed, is always made inseparable: thus we find *â-srâva*, but *anâsrâva* (e. g. ii. 3. 2, 3), and, in like manner, *anâjânant*, *anâdhṛshya*, *anârambhaṇa*, *anâdishṭa*, and *anâvṛtta*. The same analogy is followed by the negative forms of compounds with *sa*, and by a single one of those with *pra*—viz. *aprajâsam* (e. g. vii. 35. 3)—and by these alone. The Vâj. Pr., then, which declares (v. 24, 25) the negative prefix inseparable when alone and when followed by *â*, leaving other rare and exceptional cases to be provided for as such, expresses more truly the usage of the text. Our commentator gives us, first, as illustrations of the rule, the only two cases of negative compounds with *sa* which are found to occur in our text: they are *asabandhuḥ* (vi. 15. 2) and *asapatnaḥ* (e. g. i. 19. 4): the latter is mentioned by the Vâj. Pr. (v. 37) in its list of indivisible words, along with *asaṃjñâta*; *asabandhu*, according to Weber (p. 305, marginal note), is treated as divisible in the White Yajus.* The commentator adds *aprajâḥ*, *aprajâtâḥ*, but neither of the words is to be found in the Atharvan. As counter-examples, he gives first *avi-dvesham : kṛṇomi : vaḥ* (iii. 30. 1), to show that the negatived member must end in *a* or *â* in order to be inseparable; secondly, to show that, if ending in *a* or *â*, it must also be monosyllabic, he gives *agne : akravya-at* (xii. 2. 3); and thirdly, as evidence that a monosyllabic member ending in the vowels specified is not separable unless negatived, he cites *yaḥ : sa-patnaḥ* (i. 19. 4). Finally, he partly fills up the *gaṇa*, with *apra-yâvan* (iii. 5. 1), *apra-mâdam* (e. g. xii. 1. 7), *apra-hitâu* (vi. 29. 2), and *apra-cankaçâḥ* (viii. 6. 16): I have noted in addition only *apra-yachan* (e. g. ii. 6. 3). To close up the exposition, is added the verse *ekâksharâvarṇântaṃ yad bhavet padam uttaram : tat padaṃ nâ 'vagṛhṇîyâd aprayâvâdivarjitam ;*

* In one of the two cases where it occurs in our own text (vi. 54. 3), the *pada* divides it, *asa-bandhuḥ* : this, however, is probably a copyist's error.

'if the word following the negative particle be monosyllabic and end in a vowel homogeneous with it, it is not to be separated, except in the cases *aprayâvan* etc.'

प्राणति प्राणन्ति ॥५७॥

57. Nor are *prâṇati* and *prâṇanti* divided.

The commentator cites *yáḥ : prâṇáti* (iv. 30. 4), *yát : ca : prâṇáti* (xi. 4. 10), *yéna : prâṇánti* (i. 32. 1), and *yásmât : prâṇáti* (xiii. 3. 3). But the rule is an exceedingly insufficient exposition of the treatment by the *pada*-text of the forms of the root *an* with the prefix *pra*. Division is, in fact, omitted only when the verb, and not the preposition, has the accent; but then, not in the two forms specified only, but also in the participles—as *prâṇát* (e. g. x. 8. 2), *prâṇaté* (xi. 4. 8), *prâṇatáḥ* (iv. 2. 2), *prâṇatâ'm* (iii. 31. 9), and *prâṇatî'nâm* (viii. 9. 9)—and in the causative, as *prâṇáyati* (xiii. 3. 3). On the other hand, if the prefix takes the accent, it is disjoined from the verb, according to the general usage in such cases, and we read *prá : ana* (iii. 31. 9), and *prá : anati* (x. 8. 19, xi. 4. 14). If the root is compounded with *apa*, also, the same usage is followed, and we have *apânaté* (xi. 4. 8) and *ápa : anati* (xi. 4. 14).

The Vâj. Pr. (v. 33), as acutely amended by Weber, gives a nearly corresponding precept, although it appears (Weber, p. 303, marginal note) that the text to which it belongs contains no verbal forms in which the division requires to be made.

संपरिभ्यां सकारादौ करोतौ ॥५८॥

58. Nor are *sam* and *pari* separated from the root *kar*, if the latter begins with *s*.

The commentator cites the only words occurring in our text in which the root *kar* has the sibilant prefixed to it, in composition with the two specified prefixes: they are *saṅskṛtatram* (iv. 21. 4), *saṅskṛtam* (xi. 1. 35), and *parishkṛtá* (e. g. ix. 3. 10).

The doctrine of the Vâj. Pr. (v. 43) is the same, so far as concerns the compounds of *sam* and *kar*; but it apparently allows the division of *parishkṛta* (which also occurs in its text: see iii. 52).

सर्वस्मिन्नेवागमसकारादौ तुविष्टमवर्जम् ॥५९॥

59. Nor is division made in any case where a *s* is inserted—except in *tuvishṭama*.

The instances which the commentator gives of the insertion of *s* as an augment (*âgama*) between the two members of a compound word, and of the consequent unresolvability of the compound, are *ataskarám* (xii. 1. 47), *táskaraḥ* (e. g. iv. 3. 2), *vánaspátiḥ* (e. g. iv. 3. 1), and *bṛ'haspátiḥ* (e. g. ii. 13. 2). Their citation under such a precept implies the acceptance of some such etymological theories of their derivation and form as are given by the Vâj. Pr. (iii. 49, 51), which explains *tas-*

kara and *bṛhaspati* as from *tat-kara* and *bṛhat-pati* respectively, with loss of *t* and insertion of *s*, and *vanaspati* as from *vana-pati*, with insertion of *s*; but it is unnecessary to remark that such explanations are futile: *taskara* is obscure, and the other two are without much doubt compounds of *pati* with the preceding genitive of an obsolete noun, being analogous with *bráhmaṇas páti*, *vácas páti*, *çubhás páti*, etc.; and they would doubtless be separated by the *pada*-text into two independent words, like these, but for their frequency of occurrence, and, yet more, the irregularity of the accent of their former members as genitives of a monosyllabic theme. The counter-example, which the commentator also cites—*indraḥ patis tuvishṭamaḥ* (vi. 33. 3: p. *tuvi-tamaḥ*)—has been made the special subject of one of our previous rules (iii. 96).

विश्पतिर्विश्पत्नी ॥ ६० ॥

60. Nor in *viçpati* and *viçpatnî*.

The commentator cites instances of the occurrence of each of these words—viz. *svaptu : viçpatiḥ* (ix. 5. 6) and *yá : viçpatnî* (vii. 46. 3)—and adds a verse in explanation of their etymology, as follows: *viçpatir viçpatnî yasya patir viçvasya viçpatiḥ: vaçabdo lupyate patyâu viçâṁ vâ patir viçpatiḥ*. This gives us our option as to whether we will take *viçpati* to represent *viçvapati* or *viçâṁ pati*: we shall not be slow to choose the latter. The indivisibility of the compound is doubtless owing to the rarity of the consonantal conjunction *çp*, and the embarrassment which would accompany the restoration of the *saṁhitâ* form from a *pada*-reading *viṭ-pati*.

ददातौ च तकारादौ ॥ ६१ ॥

61. Nor is the root *dâ* separated when it begins with *t*.

We have given us once more, under this rule, the whole series of derivatives presenting the root *dâ* reduced to the form of a simple *t* which the commentary to iii. 11, above, presented, and of which *aprattitam* (vi. 117. 1) and *parîttaḥ* (vi. 92. 2) are the only ones found to occur in the Atharvan. The difficulty of making out an acceptable analysis of them for the *pada*-text is reason enough for their being treated in that text as indivisibles.

The Vâj. Pr. marks *parîtta* as indivisible at v. 45.

उदो हन्तिहरतिस्थास्तम्भिषु ॥ ६२ ॥

62. Nor the roots *han*, *har*, *sthâ*, and *stambh*, after the preposition *ud*.

For the combination of *han* with *ud*, the commentator cites *uddhataḥ*; no such word, however, is to be found in the Atharvan, nor does any other combination of these elements occur there (except at xiv. 2. 16, where the preposition is separated from the root by the intervention of other words). For *ud + har*, the selected instances are *uddhṛtá* and *uddhriyamāṇā* (both xii. 5. 34), and *uddhṛtushu** (xv. 12. 1). The *pada*-text, however, appears to treat the combinations as inseparable only where there is actual composition, as in the participles, and as would also be the case if the unaccented preposition preceded the accented verb, for we find *út : hara* in three passages (iv. 14. 7, ix. 6. 19, xii. 3. 36). For *sthā* with *ud*, two cases are cited, viz. *utthātuḥ* (ix. 4. 14) and *utthitaḥ* (e. g. vi. 43. 2): it has already been noticed (under ii. 18) that where the preposition would be, by the general rules of combination, disjoined from the verb, it is actually so disjoined, and that the *pada* accordingly has *út : sthuḥ*, *út : sthāpaya*, etc., where the *sanhitā* has *út thuḥ*, *út thāpaya*, etc. For *ud + stambh* is quoted the only example which the text affords, viz. *uttabhitā* (xiv. 1. 1).

The Vāj. Pr. takes note of this class of cases at v. 38, but says nothing of the roots *has* and *har*; nor is any reason apparent why their compounds should be treated in this peculiar manner. One would have thought it especially desirable that the *pada*-text should separate *ut-hṛta* etc., in order to mark the forms as coming from the root *har*, and not from *dhar*.

दधातौ च हकारादौ ॥ ६३ ॥

63. Nor the root *dhā*, in a form beginning with *h*.

The commentator illustrates with *ye : dagdhāḥ : ye : ca : uddhitāḥ* (xviii. 2. 34), and we have also *uddhitā* at ix. 3. 6: no finite verbal forms of this root as compounded with the preposition *ud* are found in the Atharvan. We meet, however, with *uddhi* once (viii. 8. 22), and our *pada*-text leaves it undivided, although it does not fall under this rule, being composed of *ud* and *dhi*.

The same rule in the Vāj. Pr. (v. 38) might cover both this and the preceding one of our treatise; but no such forms as *uddhita* are there cited by the commentator.

जास्पत्यम् ॥ ६४ ॥

64. Nor is *jāspatyam* divided.

The commentator cites the only passage in which the word in question occurs: *sam : jāḥpatyam* (vii. 73. 10). This rule and one in the next section (iv. 83), taken together, show that the true *pada* reading recognized by our treatise is *jāḥpatyam*; our *pada* manuscript, however, gives *jāḥ-patyam*, with *avagraha*. The commentator adds an attempt at an etymological explanation of the form: *jāyāpatyam : yāçabdo lupyate : patyāu : asanturūshmāçu dvyaksharo jāyāḥ vā jābhāvaḥ*. Although much corrupted, it is evident that this teaches the same etymology with that given by the Vāj. Pr. (at iv. 39): *jāspatya* for *jāyāspatya*.

---

* Our *pada* manuscript writes all these words with simple *dh*, instead of *ddh*: thus, *udhṛtā* etc.

मनुष्यत् ॥ ६५ ॥

65. Nor *manushyat*.

The commentator cites the passage containing the word—*idâ manushyat* (v. 12. 8)—and adds an explanation of its form, as follows: *manushyavan manushyat: yaçabdo lupyate vakârasya ca yakârah;* '*manushyat* is properly *manushyavat; ya* is dropped, and *v* converted into *y*.' It is unfortunate that, the Atharvan form of the word being thus fully established, and its treatment having been prescribed by the Prâtiçâkhya with so much care, it should have been altered in the edited text to *manushvat*, even though the latter is theoretically decidedly the preferable reading, and is presented by the Rig-Veda in the corresponding passage (x. 110. 8).

त्रेधा ॥ ६६ ॥

66. Nor *tredhâ*.

This word, which our *pada*-text, like that of the Rig-Veda (and, I presume, the other Vedas also), always leaves undivided, is an exception under rule 13 of this chapter.

The manuscript has a *lacuna* here, omitting at least the instances cited under this rule, the first statement of the one next following, its paraphrase, and perhaps a part of the illustrations belonging to it. It is impossible to say, of course, whether a rule or two has not dropped out also, affecting one or more of the words which I have introduced into the *gaṇa* of rule 54; but this is not at all certain, nor would the loss be of much consequence, considering the quality of the rules in this part of the section.

संज्ञायाम् ॥ ६७ ॥

67. Nor a specific appellative.

The term *saṁjñâ* is evidently used by our treatise in the same sense as by Pâṇini (see Böhtlingk's glossary to Pâṇini, *sub verbo*) and the Vâj. Pr. (iv. 98): it might be tolerably rendered by our term "proper name." The commentator's illustrations—which, as remarked in the preceding note, follow immediately upon the paraphrase of rule 66, and are perhaps therefore defective—are *açvatthâḥ : nyagrodhâḥ* (iv. 37. 4: cf. V. Pr. v. 37), *kaçyapaḥ* (e. g. iv. 37. 1), and *viçvâmitraḥ* (xviii. 3. 15). He adds: *bahulam iti ca vaktavyam;* 'it should have been said that with regard to *saṁjñâ* usage varies;' and he gives, as instances of proper names which are separable, *jamadagnyâtharvaṇa* (not in AV.), *jamat-agne* (xviii. 3. 16), *bharat-vâjam* (iv. 29. 5), *parâ-çara* (vi. 65. 1), and *vâma-deva* (xviii. 3. 16). The amendment is made with exceeding good reason, for the rule is absurdly comprehensive in its form of statement. It can only be said with truth that the being a *saṁjñâ* is a circumstance which rather favors non-division, helping to excuse the *pada*-text from attempting the analysis of an obscure or anomalously formed word.

व्यधौ ॥ ६८ ॥

68. Nor is the root *vyadh* separated.

Compounds with this root have already been made the subject of one of our rules (iii. 3), and it has been there explained that the usage of our *pada*-text is to leave undivided such of them as show a protracted vowel before the root. The commentator cites here two of the three instances which the Atharvan offers, viz. *hṛdayāvidham* (viii. 6. 18) and *marmāvidham* (xi. 10. 26). The rule is too broadly stated, and should have been restricted by him, as was the preceding one: it is only when a protracted vowel precedes the root that the compound is left undivided; and we have, for instance, *vi-vyādhin*, *abhi-vyādhin* (both i. 19. 1), and *kṛta-vyadhani* (v. 14. 9).

दृशौ सर्वनाम्नैकारान्तेन ॥ ६९ ॥

69. Nor the root *dṛç*, when compounded with a pronoun ending in *a* or *i*.

The form of this rule is in one respect very unusual: such a thing as the fusion into a diphthong of two vowels of which the specification is desired is elsewhere unknown. If the reading were slightly amended, to *sarvanāmnekārāntena*, it would answer all the purposes of a rule of our Prātiçākhya, for the Atharva-Veda presents only a single one of the compounds which it appears in its present form to contemplate, viz. *īdṛç* (e. g. iii. 1. 2). The commentator, however, paraphrases as I have translated, and gives the instances *tādṛk*, *tādṛçaḥ*, *yādṛk*, *yādṛçaḥ*, *īdṛk* (iv. 27. 6), and *īdṛçaḥ*.

The Vāj. Pr. (v. 37) instances *īdṛk* and *anyādṛk* among indivisible words.

सहावाडन्ते ॥ ७० ॥

70. Nor the root *sah*, when it ends in *āṭ*.

Under this rule, the commentator gives us once more the same series of compounds of *sah* which we have had above, under rules ii. 82 and iii. 1, and which it is unnecessary to repeat here.

Compare Vāj. Pr. v. 30.

अव्ययानाम् ॥ ७१ ॥

71. Nor are indeclinables divided.

As examples of indivisible indeclinables, the commentator offers us *sanutaḥ : yuyota* (vii. 92. 1), *prātaḥ* (e. g. iii. 16. 1), *uccāiḥ* (iv. 1. 3), *uccāt* (*uccā*, xiii. 2. 36), *nīcāiḥ* (e. g. iv. 1. 3), and *nīcāt* (*nīcā*, e. g. i. 21. 2). The rule does anything but credit to the acuteness of the authors of the Prātiçākhya, for no word in the text which would otherwise be entitled to *avagraha* is left unresolved on account of its being an indeclinable.

आशा दिशि ॥७२॥

72. Nor *âçâ*, when it means 'region.'

The word *â'çâ*, meaning 'region,' comes from the root *aç*, and furnishes no ground for a division by the *pada*-text: *âçâ'*, on the other hand, meaning 'hope, desire,' is a later form of *âças*, and comes from the root *çaṅs*, with prefix *â*; hence it is divisible. The commentator cites the words and phrases *â'çâbhyaḥ* (x. 5. 29), *â'çânâm* (i. 31. 1), *â'çâḥ : âna* (vii. 9. 2), and finally, by way of counter-example, *abhi-dhâvâmi : â-çâ'm* (vi. 119. 3).

The signature of the section is merely *caturthasya dvitîyaḥ pâdaḥ*.

प्रकृतिदर्शनं समापत्तिः ॥७३॥

73. Restoration is exhibition of the natural form.

This is simply a definition of the term *samâpatti*, which I have ventured, instead of transferring, to translate by 'restoration.' It means, as the next rule will show, the reinstating, in the *pada* and *krama* texts, of that form of a word which is looked upon as the original and normal one, to the rejection of the anomalies of Vedic orthoepy. It does not occur in any other of the grammatical treatises, although its correspondent *samâpâdya* (see below, rules 117, 124) is once found in one of the later chapters of the Rik Pr. (xiii. 11, 12), in a passage so obscure, without the light which the treatment of the subject in our own Prâtiçâkhya casts upon it, that its meaning has, very naturally, been misapprehended by the learned editor.

षत्वणत्वोपाचारदीर्घटुत्वलोपान्पदानां चर्चापरिहारयोः समापत्तिः ॥७४॥

74. In the repetitions of the *pada* and *krama* texts, restoration of the natural form is made where *s* has been converted into *sh*, *n* into *ṇ*, *visarjanîya* before *k* and *p* into *s*, where a vowel has been lengthened, *t* or *th* made lingual, an element omitted, or final *n* converted into *visarjanîya*.

Most of the technical terms of this rule meet us here for the first time, and several of them are not employed elsewhere in our treatise. *Carcâ* (see iv. 123) designates the repetition, with *iti* interposed, made in the *pada*-text of a divisible compound which is also *pragṛhya*, or which ends in a vowel not subject to the ordinary rules of combination: for example, *satyânṛtê iti satya-anṛtê* (i. 33. 2); *parihâra* (see iv. 117) is the like repetition made in the *krama*-text of a *pragṛhya*, a divisible compound, a word requiring restoration to its natural form, and the last word before a pause. The former term is employed in a like sense by the Vâj. Pr. (e. g. iii. 19); the latter is peculiar to our treatise, being replaced in the others by *parigraha* and *sthitopasthita*. *Upâcâra*, 'the conversion of *visarjanîya* into a sibilant before *k* and *p*' (by ii. 62 etc.), corresponds to the *upâcâra* and *upâcarita* of the Rik Pr. (xiii. 12, iv. 14), and *ânpada* is the term employed by the same treatise (iv. 27) to designate the conversion into *visarjanîya*, and consequent loss, of a final *n* before a following vowel, as taught in our rule ii. 27. *Shatva*, *ṇatva*, and *ṇatva* are of obvious derivation and significance, nor is there anything calling for remark in their form, excepting the *u* in *ṇatva*, which identifies the term with a Pâninean symbol (viii. 4. 41: *shṭunâ shṭuḥ**).

A quite embarrassing question now presents itself, in connection with the part of the text contained in this and the following rules; namely, with reference to the constitution of the *pada*-text which they imply. The actual *pada*-text of our manuscripts is very sparing in its use of *carcâ*, or repetition with *iti* interposed: it avails itself of that expedient only in the case already referred to as prescribed by iv. 123, or when a *pragṛhya* is likewise *avagṛhya*. The Rik *pada* employs it in one additional case; namely, when a word ends in a *visarjanîya* which is *riphita*, or liable to pass into *r* before a sonant, but which does not actually become *r* in the *sanhitâ*: it would read, for example, at ii. 32. 1 (where the Atharvan *pada* has simply *antáḥ*), *antár ity antáḥ*. The Vâjasaneyi-Sanhitâ is, according to the rules of its Prâtiçâkhya (iv. 17–22)—with which, in the absence of any testimony from Weber to the contrary, we must suppose the usage of the known manuscripts to correspond—very much more liberal in its employment of the repetition; not only in the two cases where this is practised in the Rik *pada*, but also in the case of a simple *pragṛhya* (thus it says *dvé íti dvé*, where Atharvan and Rik would give simply *dvé íti*), in that of a word which contains a lengthened vowel or a lingualized consonant, and even in that of a mere divisible compound, it performs *carcâ*. In short, it repeats in *pada*-text all that is repeated in *krama*-text, excepting (by iv. 21) *su* and the final word of a sentence. The precept of the Vâj. Pr. corresponding to this one of ours is to be found implied in iii. 18, 19, where direction is given that in the repetitions of the *pada*-text the remaining rules of the chapter should not be observed—they being precisely the ones which teach the changes which our precept specifies in detail. Now when we find put forth in our treatise, as its leading and principal direction for the restoration of the natural form in *pada*, a rule like the one here given, which classes *pada* repetitions and *krama* repetitions together, and corresponds, as regards the *pada*, so nearly with the Vâj. Pr., we cannot help suspecting that it contemplates a *pada*-text in which, as in that of the Vâj. Sanhitâ, the repetitions of *krama* and *pada* extend over nearly the same classes of cases. It is actually the fact that, if we allow the *pada*-text to be of the form in which our manuscripts give it, there are but about half a dozen words in the whole Atharvan text to which this rule and the two following, all together, have any application: while, on the other hand, the Prâtiçâkhya is found to give no direction at all for

* *Shṭu* and *shatva* are also used by the little *krama*-treatise belonging to the Rig-Veda, and called the Upalekha (Upalekha, de kramapâṭha libellus. Textum Sanscritum recensuit, varietatem lectionis, prolegomena, versionem Latinam, notas, indicem adjecit Dr. Guil. Pertsch. Berlin: 1854. 8vo), to which we shall, in the sequel, have frequent occasion to refer.

the use of *iti* alone in *pada* after a *pragṛhya*, or for the innumerable restitutions of natural form which are made in words not repeated. I find myself, I must acknowledge, hardly able to avoid the conclusion that this part of our Prâtiçâkhya was framed to suit a *pada*-text in which all *pragṛhyas*, divisible words, and words requiring restoration to normal form, were alike repeated, or suffered *carcâ*: such seems to me to be the only intelligible and consistent interpretation of its rules. That the fourth section of the chapter contains a direction for *carcâ* agreeing with the nature of our extant *pada*-text, would find its explanation in the evident character of that section as a foreign addition to the main body of the work; we should have to assume that the school to which the treatise as a whole belonged, in its present form, framed its *pada*-text in the manner there taught, and probably suffered that rule to take the place of one of another character formerly contained in this section, and now omitted from it; while yet they did not so recast the section as to adapt it fully to their new method of construction of the *pada*. This may seem a violent and improbable supposition; but it appears to me, after making every possible attempt to avoid it, to involve less difficulty than the interpretation of the rules of this section in such a manner as to make them suit the *pada*-text of the manuscripts.

The true illustrations of our rule, then, would be of the nature of the following: for the conversion of *s* to *sh*, in *vasosh pate* (i. 1. 2), *vasor iti vasoḥ*; in *vidmo shu* (i. 2. 1), *su iti su*; in *vy ashahanta* (iii. 10. 12), *asahanta 'ty asahanta*: for the conversion of *n* to *ṇ*, in *pari ṇaḥ* (i. 2. 2), *na iti naḥ*; in *prá 'ṇâikshît* (ii. 7. 1), *anâikshîd ity anâikshît*: for the conversion of *visarjanîya* to *s* before *k* and *p*, in *tatas pari* (i. 10. 1), *tata iti tataḥ*; in *tokebhyas kṛdhi* (i. 13. 2), *tokebhya iti tokebhyaḥ*: for the lengthening of a vowel, in *vidmâ parasya* (i. 2. 1), *vidma 'ti vidma*; in *yâvaya* (i. 2. 3), *yavaya 'ti yavaya*: for the lingualization of dental mutes, in *bahish ṭe* (i. 3. 1), *te iti te*; in *vi tashṭhe* (ix. 10. 19), *tasthe iti tasthe*: for omission of an element, in *ut thuḥ* (vii. 52. 2), *sthur iti sthuḥ*: for the conversion of final *n* to *visarjanîya* and its consequent omission, in *mahâñ̐ asi* (i. 20. 4), *mahân iti mahân*.

One other solution of our difficulties, less satisfactory, but also less violent, deserves to be suggested. If we could omit the words *carcâ-parihârayoḥ* from the rule altogether, leaving the latter to authorize a restoration of normal form in the *pada* generally, we could perhaps make shift to get along with such inconcinnities and omissions as would still remain—of which the principal would be that the treatise made no provision for the use of *iti* after a *pragṛhya* word, and that it did not direct what form words should have in the numerous repetitions of the *krama*-text.

The commentator, offering no explanation of the rule, gives a series of compound words in illustration of it, which belong more properly under the following rules: and to the next, accordingly, I shall take the liberty of relegating them.

पूर्वपदनिमित्तानां च ॥ ७५ ॥

75. And also, where the cause of the conversion stands in a former member of a compound.

The commentator's paraphrase is simply *pûrvapadanimittânâṁ ca shatvâdînâṁ samâpattir bhavati*; 'and restoration is made of the conversions detailed in the preceding rule when their cause stands in a former member of a compound.' He cites no examples, but says *vṛtâny eva 'dâharaṇâni*, 'the illustrations are those already given:' namely, under the preceding rule. According to his exposition, then, the present rule would seem merely an explanatory appendage to its predecessor. But this is clearly inadmissible: not only ought we to have it, in that case, combined with the other, so as to form part of it, but, more especially, it would not contain the particle *ca*, 'and,' which positively stamps it as something added to the other. We cannot avoid, as it seems to me, understanding rule 74 of the abnormal changes of disjoined and independent words, and rule 75 of such as are produced by an altering influence in the prior member of a compound. The illustrations which the commentator offered under the other rule, and which do, in fact, in good part appertain to this, are as follows: conversion of *s* to *sh*, *nishevaṇam*: *nisevaṇam iti ni-sevaṇam* (i. 3. 1 etc.: our *pada*, simply *ni-sevaṇam*); conversion of *n* to *ṇ*, *parâyaṇam*: *parâyanam iti parâ-ayanam* (e. g. i. 34. 3: p. *parâ-ayanam*); conversion of *visarjanîya* to a sibilant, *adhaspadam*: *adhaḥpadam ity adhaḥ padam* (e. g. ii. 7. 2: p. *adhaḥ padam*); prolongation of a vowel, *abhîvartena*: *abhivartena 'ty abhi-vartena* (i. 29. 1: p. *abhi-vartena*); conversion of dental mute to lingual, *yo vishṭabhnâti*: *vistabhnâti 'ti vi-stabhnâti* (xiii. 1. 25: p. *vi-stabhnâti*); omission, *çepaharshaṇîm*: *çepoharshaṇîm iti çepaḥ harshaṇîm* (iv. 4. 1: p. *çepaḥ-harshaṇîm*: see above, ii. 56); and loss of final *n*, *sâlâvṛkâň iva*: *sâlâvṛkân iva 'ti sâlâvṛkân-iva* (ii. 27. 5: p. *sâlâvṛkân-iva*). The commentator does not state whether he takes his instances from the *pada* or from the *krama* text: according to the construction of our present *pada*, they could only come from a *krama*; if the conclusion drawn above as to the original *pada* contemplated by our text is correct, they may be illustrations of both. In the very rare cases in which the extant *pada*-text has occasion to repeat words showing any of the abnormal changes which the rule mentions, it restores the normal form: thus we have *dustano iti duḥ-tano* (iv. 7. 3: s. *dushṭano*), *pratisthe iti prati-sthe* (iv. 26. 1, 2: s. *pratishṭhe*), *âyushpatnî** *ity âyuḥ patnî* (v. 9. 8: s. *âyushpatnî*), *vistabhite iti vi-stabhite* (x. 8. 2: s. *vishṭabhite*), and *pathisadî iti pathi-sadî* (xviii. 2. 12: s. *pathishadî*).

The commentator adds a couple of counter-examples—viz. *parirâpiṇam iti pari-râpiṇam* (v. 7. 2) and *sutrâmâṇam iti su-trâmâṇam* (vii. 6. 3)—to show that, when the effecting cause of an alteration of form is in the same member of a compound with the alteration itself, the latter is not reversed, and the normal form restored, by the repetition and resolution of the word.

* Our *pada*-MSS. write the word as I have given it, apparently infringing the rule; but I have no question that the *sh* here is only an attempt to represent the labial spirant, or *upadhmânîya*, which the theory of the Prâtiçâkhya requires (by ii. 40) in such a place: another like case is *chandashpakshe iti chandaḥ pakshe* (viii. 9. 12: s. *chandaḥpakshe*—or, more properly, *chandaḫpakshe*—by ii. 62). Before the *iti*, where no pause of *avagraha* intervenes between the two members of the compound, they are, of course, to be put in simple *sandhi* with one another: thus, *dustano*, *çepoharshaṇîm*, and, as we ought strictly to read, *adhaḫpadam*; we have also *sadohavirdhâne iti sadaḥ havirdhâne* at xii. 1. 38.

इंग्यानाम् ॥ ७६ ॥

76. And where the compound is divisible.

That is to say, restoration to the normal form is made only in such compounds as are by the *pada*-text resolved into their constituent elements. Those words which, although they may be acknowledged compounds, are left undivided on account of special anomalies of form, retain also their irregularities of orthoepy. The commentator, in his paraphrase, represents *iñgyânâm* by *iñgyamânânâm avagṛhyamâṇânâm*, 'forms which undergo division, or separation by *avagraha*,' and adds again *etâny evo 'dâharaṇâni*, 'the examples are those already given'—namely, under rule 74 (here presented under rule 75). Of counter-examples, however, he furnishes two—viz. *parishkṛtâ* (e. g. ix. 3. 10) and *prâṇanti* (e. g. i. 32. 1)—and then cites a verse which contains two more: *aniñgyatvât samâpattir eshu nânâpadeshu tu: nishpanne 'vagrahe câ 'tra samâpattis tathâi 'va ca: sûnṛtâvad apâshṭhavad ity udâharet.* The commentator's own instances belong to the class of those in which a cause in the former member of the compound produces an effect in the latter member: the words, if divided, would read *pari-kṛtâ*, *pra-anânti*: in the other two, the irregularities are mainly in the first members themselves, and, if *sûnṛtâ* and *apâshṭha* were resolvable, we should read (according to the next rule), with restoration, *sunṛtâ-vat*, *apastha-vat*, instead of, as now, *sûnṛtâ-vat* (e. g. v. 20. 6), *apâshṭha-vat* (xiv. 1. 29). The rule, as these illustrations help to show, is not a mere additional specification to the one preceding, affecting only the cases to which the other applies: in that case it would have been incorporated with it, not made to follow it, as an independent precept; but it concerns all changes occurring in the interior of divisible words, whether in the former or the latter member, and a part of the commentator's examples, rehearsed under rule 75, belong to it, and not to the latter.

अन्येनापि पर्वणा ॥ ७७ ॥

77. In which case restoration is made, even when the word is farther compounded with another member.

That is to say: a compound which, being divisible by *avagraha*, is entitled to restoration of the normal form of its constituent parts, retains its right even when, by farther composition, the division of its original members is lost. Examples are given in the commentary as follows: *visita-stupaḥ* (vi. 60. 1: s. *vishitastupaḥ*), *abhi-nihpatan**: *api-patat* (vii. 64. 1: s. *abhinishpatan*), *vishṭhitâḥ-iva* (vii. 115. 4: s. *vishṭhitâḥ-iva*), *bṛhaspati-praṇuttânâm* (viii. 8. 19: s. °*praṇuttânâm*), *pṛshadâjya-praṇuttânâm* (xi. 10. 19: s. as before), and *durṇihita-eshiṇîm* (xi. 9. 15:

* Our manuscript writes *abhi-nishpatan*, as do also the manuscripts of the Atharvan *pada*-text in the passage cited; but I suppose here, as in the other similar cases referred to in the note to rule 75, that the *sh* is an attempt at representing the labial spirant: we have the guttural spirant, the *jihvâmûlîya*, in like manner represented by *sh* in *abhi-nishkṛta* (x. 1. 12) and *abhi-nishkârin* (x. 1. 31).

e. *durṇihitâishiṇîm*). Other instances afforded by the text are *viskandha-dûshaṇa* (ii. 4. 1), *atishṭhâ-vant* (iii. 22. 6), *sa-pranîti* (e. g. v. 11. 5), *duraṇâma-câtana* (viii. 6. 8), *anu-visiryate* (viii. 10. 33), *abhimoda mud* (xi. 7. 26), *jâgrat-duḥsvapnyam* and *svapne-duḥsvapnyam* (xvi. 6. 9), *pṛthivî-shat-bhyaḥ* (xviii. 4. 78), etc. Three exceptions to the rule are made below, in rule 96, and the text affords one more, as is there pointed out in the note. The commentator again adds a verse, but it is more than usually mutilated and obscure; it reads: *prakṛtyâ maṇatvam yad avagṛhyet tathâi 'va tat: upatishṭhanti prapaṇâdiny uddharet.*

क्रमे परेण विगृह्यात् ॥ ७८ ॥

78. In *krama*, restoration is made of a word which is taken together with another word than the disjoinable cause of its altered form.

The commentator's paraphrase is *krame pareṇa pratisaṁdhâne vigṛhyân nimittât;* which shows us—what the necessities of the case would of themselves have pointed out—that the important word to be supplied with *vigṛhyât* is, by inference from rule 75, *nimittât,* 'the cause of the altered or abnormal form.' *Vigṛhya* denotes a word which is altogether independent, and therefore disjoined from others in the *pada*-text, a *sa-nâpada*, in distinction from *avagṛhya*, which means 'divisible into its constituents (*pûrvapada* and *uttarapada*), as a compound.' In the construction of the *krama*-text, then, where each word is in succession taken along with its predecessor and its successor, a word which in *saṁhitâ* has an abnormal form, under the influence of the former or of the latter, retains that form when in the same *kramapada* with the altering word, but is restored to its natural form when making a *kramapada* along with any other word. The commentator cites a couple of passages—*âpo hi shṭhâ mayobhuvaḥ* (i. 5. 1) and *pari ṇo vṛṇdhi* (vi. 37. 9)—but does not write them out in *krama* form, so as to illustrate the rule: they would read *âpo hi : hi shṭha : sthâ mayobhuvaḥ*, and *pari ṇaḥ : no vṛṇdhi*. As counter-examples, to show that restoration of the normal form is made in a *kramapada* only when the cause of euphonic alteration stands in a separate word, and so is left out of the *kramapada*, we have given us two passages in their *krama*-form: *pṛthivyâṁ te : te nishkvaṇam : nishkvaṇaṁ bahiḥ : niṣvaṇam iti ni-svaṇam* (i. 3. 1 etc.), and *âyane te : âyana ity â-ayane : te parâyaṇe : parâyaṇe dûrvâ : parâyana iti parâ-ayane* (vi. 106. 1). Here the *sh* of *nishkvaṇam* and the *ṇ* of *parâyaṇe* are maintained wherever the words containing them enter into a *kramapada*, and only suffer restoration (by rule 75, above) to *s* and *n* in the repetition or *parihâra*.

The corresponding rules in the other treatises are Rik Pr. x. 5 (r. 5), xi. 21 (r. 44), and Upalekha iii. 3, 4. I do not find in the Vâj. Pr. any special direction upon the subject.

दीर्घस्य विरामे ॥ ७९ ॥

79. A lengthened vowel is restored to its natural form before a pause.

The illustrative passages are given by the commentator in *pada* form: as, *âpaḥ : hi : stha : mayaḥ-bhuvaḥ* (i. 5. 1 : s. *sthâ*), and *param : asya : grabhîtâ* (i. 12. 2 : s. *asyâ*). The rule, however, evidently applies not less to the *krama* than to the *pada* text, and is even intended chiefly for the former: it is our authority for shortening a protracted final when it comes to stand at the end of a *kramapada*, while it is left long when taken together with its successor: we read *hi shṭha : sthâ mayobhuvaḥ*, and *param 'sya : asyâ grabhîtâ*.

चतूरात्रो ऽवग्रह एव ॥ ८० ॥

80. In *catûrâtra*, this is done only before the pause of separation.

From rule 74, which prescribes restoration of the normal form of a lengthened vowel in both parts of a repetition, one might draw the conclusion that the word here in question should be written, when repeated, *caturâtra iti catuḥ-râtraḥ*: hence this rule, which teaches the reading *catûrâtra iti catuḥ-râtraḥ*. Our commentator cites, in *krama* form, the passage containing the word, *catûrâtraḥ pañcarâtraḥ : catûrâtra iti catuḥ-râtraḥ* (xi. 7. 11).

पदान्तविकृतानाम् ॥ ८१ ॥

81. Restoration is made of alterations taking place at the end of a word.

The commentator's paraphrase is *padântavikṛtânâṁ ca akṣarâdînâṁ samâpattir bhavati*, which would seem to show that he understands the rule as referring to the same series of abnormal alterations which was detailed in rule 74. His illustrations, however, put quite another face upon the matter: they are *pari-eti : rakshan* (iv. 38. 5) and *abhi-âimi : devâḥ* (vi. 118. 3). Here the only changes of form which have undergone restoration are the regular conversions of *i* into *y* (by iii. 39) before the following dissimilar vowel. We are thus guided to a different interpretation of the rule: whereas we have heretofore dealt with irregular or abnormal changes only, learning under what circumstances, in *pada* and in *krama*, they become reversed, and the original form restored, here we are taught that all alterations made at the end of a word, by the ordinary as well as the extraordinary combinations of the phrase, undergo restoration when the word comes to stand, in *pada* or in *krama*, before a pause (*virâme*, rule 79). It should be remarked that the final repetition of this rule is wanting in the manuscript, and that we cannot therefore be certain that we may not have lost with it other examples and farther exposition, which would have set the meaning of the rule, or the commentator's apprehension of it, in a clearer light.

अभ्यासविनतानां च ॥ ८२ ॥

82. Also of forms lingualized by the influence of a reduplication.

The Prâtiçâkhya now goes on to inform us where restoration must be made of alterations which have taken place in the interior of a word, and not under the influence of any cause lying outside of the word itself. The rules in this portion of the work are in great part the reverse of others formerly given, when the subject under treatment was the conversion of *pada* into *saṁhitá*. Thus, the present precept is the correlative of ii. 91, and it is illustrated by precisely the same series of examples; which, however, are here given in the *pada* form: thus, *susúdata* (i. 26. 4), *abhi : sisyade* (v. 5. 9), *á : susvayanti* (v. 12. 6), *sisásavaḥ : sisásatha* (vi. 21. 3), *sisásanti* (xiii. 2. 14), and *susuve* (xiv. 1. 43).

स्त्रैषूयं नार्षदेन दुष्टरं त्रैष्टुभं त्रैहायणाज्जास्पत्यम् ॥८३॥

83. Also of *stráishúyam*, *nárshadena*, *dushṭaram*, *traishṭubham*, *tráihâyaṇát*, and *jáspatyam*.

By rule 76, above, no compound was declared entitled to restoration of the natural form of its constituents, unless it was by the *pada*-text treated as divisible. The words here detailed constitute exceptions under that rule, and have their irregular alterations reversed, even though (partly by rule 55, and partly by 54, above) they are not *avagṛhya*. Our *pada*, in fact, reads *stráisúyam* (vi. 11. 3), *nársadena* (iv. 19. 2), *dusṭaram* (vi. 4. 1), *tráistubham* (ix. 10. 1: we have also other forms from the same theme in the same and the following verse), and *tráihâyaṇát* (x. 5. 22 and xii. 4. 16); and *jáḥpatyam* (vii. 73. 10) is prescribed by iv. 84, although, as there remarked, our *pada*-manuscript actually gives *jáḥ·patyam*.

अभ्यासस्य परोक्षायाम् ॥८४॥

84. Also of a reduplication, in a form of the perfect.

The term *paroksha*, 'beyond the sphere of sight, out of one's sight,' is also employed by Pâṇini (iii. 2. 115 etc.), along with *bhúta*, 'past,' and *anadyatana*, 'not on the present day,' to define the proper sphere of the perfect tense. We may suppose it here used alone as a name of the tense as being its distinctive characteristic, since the imperfect and aorist are also entitled regularly to one or both of the other designations. The commentator cites, as instances, *tatṛpuḥ* (xi. 7. 13: s. *tátṛpuḥ*) and *vavṛtuḥ* (v. 19. 13: s. *vávṛtuḥ*); and, as counter-instances, to show that the vowel is not shortened in any other tense than a perfect, he gives *lálapiti* (vi. 111. 1) and *rárajîti* (vi. 71. 2). The usage of the Atharvan texts as concerns the reduplication was fully explained under iii. 13, the only rule in which the subject is treated in the earlier part of the work.

A couple of verses follow in the commentary; they read as follows: *abhyásasya ca dîrghatvaṁ dîrghakitrti dṛçyate: na tasye 'shtá samápattir lâlapîti nidarçanam: yady abhyásasya dîrghatvaṁ nujâdînâṁ ca yaṅlakoḥ: savarṇe ca parokshâyâṁ na samâpadyate kvacit.* I have not succeeded in amending the text so as to be able to translate the whole passage.

वावृधानप्रभृतीनां च ॥ ८५ ॥

85. Also of *vâvṛdhâna* etc.

The commentator's instances under this rule are *vavṛdhânaḥ-iva* (not found in AV.), *sasahiḥ* (iii. 18. 5 : s. *sâsahiḥ*), and *vavṛdhânaḥ* (e. g. i. 8. 4). The *gaṇa* might be filled up from the material collected and presented in the notes to the first section of the third chapter, but I have not taken the trouble to put it together, as it is uncertain how much and what the authors of the treatise meant the precept to cover.

कृपिरुपिरिषीणामनह्वानाम् ॥ ८६ ॥

86. Also of the roots *kṛp*, *rup*, and *rish*, when they are *anahva*.

I can find nowhere any clue to the derivation and use of *anahva*, and the range of the cases to which the rule applies is too narrow for the induction with any confidence of a definition from them. For the root *kṛp*, either the commentator furnished no instances, or the manuscript has omitted them: the only derivative from that root, so far as I can discover, which the rule can have any concern with, is *câkḷpat* (vi. 35. 3 : p. *cakḷpat*); since *cakḷpuḥ* and *cakḷpe* would properly fall under rule 84. For the root *rup* is cited *na : rurupaḥ* (iv. 7. 5, 6 : s. *rûrupaḥ*); for the root *rish*, the two passages *enasyaḥ : deva : ririshaḥ* (vi. 51. 3 : s. *rîrishaḥ*) and *mâ : naḥ : ririshaḥ* (v. 3. 8 : s. *rîrishaḥ*). The commentator then asks *anahvâdâm iti kim artham*, 'why does the rule say "when they are *anahva*;"' and cites, as counter-examples, *na : amîmadaḥ : na : arûrupaḥ* (iv. 6. 3), *mâ : ririshaḥ : naḥ* (xi. 2. 29 : this is, however, no counter-example, but precisely analogous with the two already cited for the same word), and *sinîvâlî : acîkḷpat* (vi. 11. 3). So far as these instances go, *anahva* might be understood as designating an aorist form which has lost its accent; or, virtually, an aorist subjunctive.

The text affords one other word, *çuçucaḥ* (xviii. 2. 4 : s. *çûçucaḥ*), of the same class with those treated in this rule. Its omission must be understood as signifying, either that the verse containing it was not in the Atharvan text of the authors and commentator of our Prâtiçâkhya, or that their text read, with the Rig-Veda (x. 16. 1), *çocaḥ*, or, finally, that the word escaped their notice.

जिहीडाहम् ॥ ८७ ॥

87. Also of *jihîḍâ 'ham*.

The commentator cites the passage in its *pada*-form, *akrataḥ : jihîḍa : aham* (iv. 32. 5). Compare rule iii. 14, of which this is the reverse.

साह्याम ॥ ८८ ॥

88. Also of *sâhyâma*.

The commentator cites the passage in its *pada*-form, *sahyâma : dâsam* (iv. 32. 1). Compare the previous rule, iii. 15. He adds a verse or two:

sahyāmarjñiya sahel dīrghatvaṁ yad dṛçyate: na tasye 'hā samāpattir yaḥ çabdo dīrgha eva saḥ: ākhyāte 'sthaḥpade hrasvo na samāpadyate punaḥ. The various irregularities of form appearing in, or in connection with, the root *sah* have been the subject of several previous rules: see ii. 82, iii. 1, iv. 70.

दीदायत् ॥ ८९ ॥

89. Also of *dīdāyat.*

In the former rule (iii. 22), *dīdayat* was made the leading word of a *gaṇa* composed of forms exhibiting an irregular prolongation in the second syllable, and we are justly surprised at not finding the statement here made in a corresponding manner. The commentator, in fact, cites precisely the same cases as before, in their *pada*-form—viz. *dīdayat* (iii. 8. 3), *ushasaḥ : vīra-vatīḥ* (iii. 16. 7), and *ushasānaktā* (e. g. v. 12. 6)—just as if the rule read here also *dīdāyadīnām.*

नारकादीनाम् ॥ ९० ॥

90. Also of *nāraka* etc.

Here we have the precise counterpart of rule iii. 21, above, and the commentator cites from the text the same three cases, viz. *narakam* (xii. 4. 36), *sadanam* (e. g. ii. 12. 7), and *asataḥ : indra* (viii. 4. 8).

च्यावयतेः कारितान्तस्य ॥ ९१ ॥

91. Also of the root *cyu*, in a form containing the causative affix.

Under this rule the commentator is unusually liberal of his citations: they are *ā : cyavayantu : sakhyāya* (iii. 3. 2), *yathā : vātaḥ : cyavayati* (x. 1. 13), *aṅgāt-aṅgāt : pra : cyavaya* (x. 4. 25), *cyavayan : ca : vṛkshān* (xii. 1. 51), *devatāḥ : cyavayantu* (xii. 3. 35), and *pūshā : tvā : itaḥ : cyavayatu* (xviii. 2. 54). These are all the cases which the text furnishes of causative forms from the root *cyu*: in every instance, the *saṁhitā* prolongs the vowel of the first syllable, reading *cyāvayantu* etc.

यावयतेराख्याते ॥ ९२ ॥

92. As also of the root *yu*, if the form be a verbal one.

The commentator cites three of the numerous examples of causative forms from this root, having the long vowel of their first syllable shortened in *pada*: they are *varīyaḥ : yavaya : vadham* (e. g. i. 20. 3 : s. *yāvayā*), *asmat : yavayatam* (i. 20. 2 : s. *yāvayatam*), and *varuṇa : yavaya* (i. 20. 3 : p. *yávaya*). He does not explain the meaning of the restriction *ākhyāte* added to the rule, nor cite any counter-example. I can discover no other reason for it than the occurrence of the word *yavayāvānaḥ*, at ix. 2. 13: this may have been deemed by the authors of the treatise to contain the causative ending (*kāritānta*) *aya*, and therefore to require the rule to be so framed as to exclude it. But the word is divided by the *pada*-text *yava-yâvânaḥ*, as if composed of *yava* and *yâvan*, from *yâ*: and this seems the best account to be given of it.

वनियमिग्रथिग्लापि ॥ ९३ ॥

93. Also of the roots *van*, *yam*, *çrath*, and *glâp*.

The cases referred to in the rule are cited by the commentator, as follows: *amûm : sam : vanayantu* (vi. 9. 3 : s. *vânayantu*), *vi : madhyam : yamaya* (vi. 137. 3 : s. *yâmaya*), *madhyamam : çrathaya* (vii. 83. 3 : s. *çrâthaya*), and *sa : im : ava : glapayanta* (ix. 9. 10 : s. *glâpayanta*).

The manuscript contains no final repetition of this rule, but offers, after the last citation, the words *iṅgyavac ca*. What to make of these words I do not precisely know: they may be part of a cited verse, of which the rest, along with the repetition of the rule, is lost; or they may possibly belong to an omitted rule: but I can hardly suppose the latter to be the case, not seeing what the meaning of the phrase should be, as a rule or a part of one.

The form of our rule 93, it may be remarked, is somewhat unusual: we should expect at the end of it the genitive plural ending: thus, °*glâpînâm*.

नाष्टनः ॥ ९४ ॥

94. *Ashṭa* is not restored to its natural form.

The commentator gives the same citations as under the corresponding rule above (iii. 2): they are, in *pada*-form, *ashṭá-padî : caturḥ-akshî* (v. 19. 7), *ashṭá-pakshâm* (ix. 3. 21), *ashṭá-parṇaḥ*, *ashṭá-daṅshṭram* (these two are not found in AV.), *ashṭá-yogâiḥ* (vi. 91. 1), *ashṭá-cakrâ : nava-dvârâ* (x. 2. 31), and *ashṭá-cakram : vartate* (xi. 4. 22). He also interposes, between the first and third examples, *ashṭá-yoniḥ*; but this is a blunder, for the word is read with a short vowel in both *pada* and *saṅhitâ* (viii. 9. 21), in our Atharvan manuscripts, nor is *yoni* mentioned (iii. 3) by the Prâtiçâkhya among words before which the final vowel of the numeral is made long.

हिनोतेः ॥ ९५ ॥

95. Nor the root *hi*.

That is to say—wherever forms of this root, having the conjugational suffix *nu* or its modifications, show in *saṅhitâ* after *pra* a lingual nasal, this nasal remains lingual also in the *pada* text. The commentator's examples are *prati-prahiṇmaḥ* (x. 1. 5), *pra : hiṇomi : dûram* (e. g. xii. 2. 4), and *pra : hiṇuta : pitṝn* (xviii. 4. 40).

Rule 88 of the preceding chapter is to be compared. The *pada* usage as regards these forms is quite anomalous: I can only conjecture that it may have been adopted in order to mark the euphonic alteration as itself of anomalous and exceptional character: there being, so far as I have been able to find, no other cases in which a preposition lingualizes the nasal of a conjugational sign.

बोधप्रतीबोधौ केसरप्राबन्धाया अभ्यघायन्ति पनिष्पदातिष्ठिपं दाधार जागार मीमायेति ॥ ९६ ॥

96. ....: nor is restoration made in the words here mentioned.

The first three of the words detailed in this rule are exceptions under rule 77, above, or cases in which the normal form is not restored to a divisible compound, on its being farther compounded with another member: the *pada* writes them *bodha-pratibodhāu* (v. 30. 10: compare *prati-bodha*, e. g. viii. 1. 13), *kesara-prābandhāyāḥ* (v. 18. 11: *pra-bandha* is not found in the Atharvan text), and *abhi-aghāyanti* (v. 6. 9, vii. 70. 3: compare *agha-yantam*, x. 4. 10). The last three are exceptions under rule 84, above, being forms of the perfect tense with short vowel unrestored in the *pada*-text, which writes them like the *saṅhitā*, viz. *dādhāra* (e. g. iv. 2. 7), *jāgāra* (e. g. v. 19. 10), and *mimāya* (v. 11, 3). The text affords us once *mimāya* (ix. 10. 21), so that the rule is deficient in explicitness as regards this form, and should have cited along with it a preceding or a following word. The other two, *panishpadā* (v. 30. 16) and *atishṭhipam* (vii. 95. 2), might be regarded as falling under the first general rule (iv. 74) for restitution of original form; or they might as naturally, one would think, be looked upon as special cases, falling under no previous rule, and therefore not needing specification here.

Of the class of the first three cases is *sam-nishadya* (iv. 16. 2), which equally calls for inclusion in this rule, unless the reading in our *pada* manuscript is a copyist's error, and should be amended to *sam-nisadya*.

प्रपणः पणतेरेव ॥ ९७ ॥

97. Nor in *prapaṇa*, provided only it comes from the root *paṇ*.

The commentator cites the only two passages in which this word is to be found in the Atharvan, namely *yena : dhanena : pra-paṇam : carāmi* (iii. 15. 5), and *śunam : naḥ : astu : pra-paṇaḥ* (iii. 15. 4). I cannot in the least understand why any such rule as this should be deemed called for. There is no rule, and no principle, which should require the restoration of the *ṇ* of *prapaṇa* to a dental form, nor is there any word in the text which exhibits an element *pana* whose nasal is lingualized by a previous constituent of a compound. So far as we can see, it is merely the fear lest some one should be stupid enough to mistake the *ṇ* for an effect of the preposition *pra*, and so should commit the blunder of speaking, in *pada*, *pra-pana*, that calls out the precept. Its repetition before the one next following is wanting in the manuscript; possibly, then (as in the case of rule 81, above), we have lost something in the way of exposition or illustration which would have farther enlightened us. In his paraphrase, the commentator says *prapaṇa iti paratāirakaṁ saṁāpattir na bhavati*; but what *paratāiraka* is, I do not know.

इदमूषादिषु पदत्वात् ॥ ९८ ॥

98. Nor in *idam û shu* etc., on account of their forming together (in *krama*) a single word.

The commentator paraphrases *padatvât* by *tripadatvât*, the latter being apparently a technical designation for those *kramapadas* which, by rule 113, below, are composed of three words, instead of, as usual, two only. The rule evidently applies to the *krama*-text alone; the *pada* reading of the passages referred to does not deviate in any manner from the usual norm: we have *idam : ûṅ iti : su*, etc. But what the point of the rule is, as concerns the *krama*-text, I find it rather difficult to see. The passages cited in illustration by the commentator are nearly the same with those already twice given, under ii. 97 and iii. 4: they are *idam û shû* (i. 24. 4), *tad û shû* (v. 1. 5), *pary û shû* (v. 6. 4), *mahîm û shû* (vii. 6. 2), *anyâ û shû* (xviii. 1. 16), and *stusha û shû* (xviii. 1. 37). According as the abnormal alteration aimed at by the rule is understood to be the prolongation of the *u* or the lingualization of the sibilant of *su*, we should add to the series the farther passages vii. 85. 1 and xviii. 3. 7, or vii. 72. 2, 73. 7, and 85. 1. I presume that we must adopt the former of the two interpretations: the *û*, in these passages, is nowhere to be restored to its short form in the *krama*, since it cannot fulfill the condition required by rule 79, and appear before a pause.

ब्रह्मण्वत्यादीनाम् ॥ ९९ ॥

99. Nor in *brahmaṇvatî* etc.

The commentator cites *brahmaṇ-vatîm* (vi. 108. 2), *paçyat : akshaṇ-vân* (ix. 9. 15), *çîrshaṇ-vatî* (x. 1. 2), and *vṛshaṇyantî-iva : kanyalâ* (v. 5. 3). The irregularity which renders necessary the rule is the retention of the lingual *ṇ* as final, against the principle of rule iii. 80, above. The last case cited, however, does not belong with the rest, since the denominative ending, by rule 29, above, is separable only after a vowel, and we read *vṛshaṇyantyâḥ* (vi. 9. 1) and *vṛshaṇyataḥ* (vi. 70. 1–3), without *avagraha:* hence there is no ground for restoration.

दीर्घायुत्वादीनां च ॥ १०० ॥

100. Nor in *dîrghâyutva* etc.

The same passages which were cited under the corresponding rule in another part of the treatise (ii. 59), and no others, are here again given by the commentator: they are, according to the reading of the *pada*-text, *dîrghâyu-tvâya* (e. g. i. 22. 2), *sahasracaksho iti sahasra-caksho : tvam* (iv. 20. 5), and *barhi-sadaḥ* (xviii. 1. 45, 51).

The signature of the section is as follows: 102: *caturthasya tṛtîyaḥ pâdaḥ*; so that, unless rule 53 is to be divided into two, or unless the copyist's count is inaccurate, we have lost, somewhere in the course of the second and third sections, one of the rules of the text.

The concluding section of the treatise is occupied, first, with the recommendation of the study of the *krama* form of the text and second, with the description of its mode of construction. The way in which it is stated and explained by the commentator is altogether different from that hitherto followed. First we have presented us the whole of the text of the section, separated by marks of punctuation into the rules which compose it. Then follows the independent statement and explanation of each rule in succession; but not, as heretofore, according to the set method of restatement in paraphrase, brief and dry illustration by examples, and final repetition: we have, instead of this, a free exposition, drawn out at considerable length and with some unction, much more in the style of the known comments upon the other treatises of the class. This not only authorizes, but compels us to conclude that the remaining part of the commentary is by another hand than that which furnished the preceding. And the difference in style of the text itself no less justifies us in believing that the section was not an original part of our treatise, but is a later appendage to it. Whether or not it takes the place of another similar body of rules in the original Prâtiçâkhya, and was substituted for them as being a fuller and more satisfactory exhibition of the subject, it would not become me to attempt to say too confidently: the near agreement of the preceding chapters in respect to extent (each containing not much more than a hundred rules) would favor the supposition that it had been tacked on as new matter to the treatise, carrying with it a new division of the preceding rules of the chapter into three instead of four sections: the subject of *krama* may have been formerly disposed of in a few brief rules forming part of the last section: but our Prâtiçâkhya has in too many of its previous rules made allusion to or implication of the *krama*-text (sometimes even naming it and contemplating it alone), to allow our assuming with plausibility that the construction of that text was not from the beginning one of the subjects with which the treatise dealt.

The *krama* is not treated by the Taitt. Pr.; it is disposed of by the Vâj. Pr. in the closing rules of the final section of its fourth chapter (iv. 179–194), not occupying a whole section. In the Rik Pr. it takes up two chapters, the tenth and eleventh, each of which is by itself a complete *krama* treatise; the former giving (in fourteen verses) a concise exhibition of the subject, the latter (in thirty-seven verses) setting it forth with much greater fullness of detail. It is also the exclusive theme of the Upalekha, of unknown date and authorship, to which reference has already been made (see note to rule 74, above). The corresponding rules of all these authorities will be cited or referred to in connection with those of our own text.

वेदाध्ययनं धर्मः ॥ १०१ ॥

101. Study of the Veda is duty.

In the comment we read three times, instead of the full form of the rule, *vedâ dharmaḥ* (or *dharmam*) simply; but doubtless by a copyist's omission. The commentator adds to the rule the more detailed statement *karmaçeshabhūtāt : vedā[dhyayanaṁ] dharmam āhur yājñikāḥ*—because sacrifices are performed by means of the Veda, and sacrifice is obligatory. He makes reference to a couple of verses or sayings which inculcate the necessity or advantage of sacrifice, thus: *svargakāmo aghāyatām ity anena mantreṇa çatāudanāstakhyaṁ* [*çatāudanākhyaṁ?*] *karma kṛtvā svargaṁ sādhayed iti yājñikāmnānam.* He then anticipates and explains rule 104, below, concluding *na vinā vedāir yajñas tāyate*, 'sacrifice is not performed without the Vedas;' and he winds up his exposition with *vedādhyayanaṁ dharma ity ādisūtram*, 'this is the first rule.'

प्रेत्य ज्योतिष्ट्वं कामयमानस्य ॥ १०२ ॥

102. On the part of one desiring a condition of light after death.

Pretya, literally 'having gone forward, having departed, deceased,' is by the commentator, with many words, explained to mean 'having quitted this world and gone on to another.' Upon *jyotishṭvam* he discourses as follows: *jyotirbhāvo jyotishṭvam : uktaṁ hi : ye vā iha yajñāir ārdhnuvaṅs teshām etāni jyotīṅshi yāny amūni nakshatrāṇi 'ti : jyotir dīptibhāvam ity arthāntaram.* The next rule he introduces by the question, "is it merely the reading that is duty? the answer is, no: how is it then?"

याज्ञिकैर्यथासमाम्नातम् ॥ १०३ ॥

103. In the manner as handed down by those who understand the sacrifice.

A *yājñika* is defined as 'one who studies or understands the sacrifice' (*yajñam adhīte yajñaṁ vidur vā*). Not merely the study of the Veda, but its study according to the traditional methods of those versed in sacred things, is declared meritorious. *Āmnāna* is defined by *paṭhana*, 'reading,' and the commentator continues: "and how do the *yājñikas* read? 'with the verse *svargakāmo aghāyatām* [already referred to, under the first rule of this section] one must secure paradise:' but it is objected 'that is an act of sacrifice, not a study of the Veda: hence merit is acquired by sacrifice, not by the study of the Veda:' this, however, is not so"—as the rule which is next to be given is intended to show.

यज्ञततिर्न पृथग्वेदेभ्यः ॥ १०४ ॥

104. There is no performance of the sacrifice without the Vedas.

Hence, as the Vedas are an indispensable aid to the performance of that in which duty consists, the declaration that their study is a duty is one to which no objection can be made (*iti niravadyaṁ vedādhyayanaṁ dharma iti*).

यज्ञे पुनर्लोकाः प्रतिष्ठिताः ॥ १०५ ॥

105. In the sacrifice, again, the worlds are established.

I add the whole argument by which the commentator proves this pious proposition: *dyâur vijad avanis trayo lokâ yajñe pratishṭhitâḥ: katham: nirvâpâdisaṁskṛtaṁ havir aṅgushṭaparvamâtreṇa çakayâ 'vattam antar nidhanasvâhâkâreṇa agnâu hutaṁ jyotirdhûmabhâvena pariṇataṁ jyotirbhâvena dyâulokaṁ dhûmabhâvenâ 'ntarikshaṁ punar vṛshṭibhâvena pariṇataṁ pṛthivîṁ yâti: evaṁ yajñe lokâḥ pratishṭhitâḥ.* The properly prepared sacrifice, duly offered in the fire, becomes light and smoke: the light goes to the sky, the smoke to the atmosphere, and, becoming rain, returns again to the earth: thus it reaches all the three worlds—and, if one chooses to look upon it in that light, establishes and supports them all.

पञ्चजना लोकेषु ॥ १०६ ॥

106. As are the five races in the worlds.

The five races, the commentator says, are men: they are established in the worlds, the worlds in the sacrifice, the sacrifice in the Vedas, and the Vedas are *dharmaçeshabhûtâḥ: dharmâd âiraṭamatidâiçat karmaṇi çeshatâṁ ca gachanti:* which last sentence is corrupt and obscure. From this, he goes on to point out the necessity of the study of the *pada*-text, and, as a help to it, of the Prâtiçâkhya, anticipating the rule which is next to follow: "the connection and distinction[1] of the appellation (*abhidhâna*) and the subject of appellation (*abhidheya*) is not, without the study of the *pada*-text; the recognition of the terminations is not assured, without the study of the *pada*-text: hence, in order to an understanding of the *mantra*, its *pada*-text (*padâni*) must be studied; and, by one who studies the *pada*, the Prâtiçâkhya must necessarily be studied, in order to the resolution of doubts (*avaçyaṁ saṁçayachedâya prâtiçâkhyam adhyeyam*); and the uses of the study of the *pada* are farther set forth in the following rule."

पदाध्ययनमन्तादिशब्दस्वरार्थज्ञानार्थम् ॥ १०७ ॥

107. The study of the *pada*-text is for the sake of gaining knowledge of the endings, the beginnings, and the proper forms of words, and of their accent and meaning.

The commentator explains and illustrates this rule at considerable length, and by means of examples which are for the most part taken from our present Atharvan text. First, as he says, we are told that a rinsing of the mouth with water (*udakâcamanam*) is prescribed to be accompanied by the *pâdas* of the verse *çaṁ no devî* (*çaṁ no devyâḥ pâdâiḥ:* the verse is found at i. 6. 1); and here, without study of the *pada*, one fails to know that the first *pâda* ends with *e* (*abhishṭaye:* in *saṁhitâ*,

[1] I.—MS. *saṁbaddhâu antaraṁ ca.*

it is *abhishṭaya*). The next following example is intended to illustrate the difficulty, without the *pada*-text, of finding upon occasion the right beginning of a word: it reads *çṛtubhyas tvâ yaja ity ârtavebhyas tvâ yaja ity atrâ 'kârâdi na tu jñâyate.* The reference here is to iii. 10. 10, *çṛtubhyas tvâ 'rtavebhyaḥ . . . . yaje;* eight separate recipients of offering are enumerated in the verse, and it seems intended that, in liturgical use, *tvâ yaje*, which the verse gives once for all, should be appended to each separately; this is intimated, though obscurely, by a prefixed direction: *ashṭakâyâm: çṛtubhyas tve 'ti*[1] *vigraham ashṭâu.* Again, "without study of the *pada*, the Vedic forms of words (*vâidikâḥ çabdâḥ*) are not known: as for instance, *açravatîm strâiṣhûyam*,[2] etc.; in *sanhitâ* they have different forms, viz. *açvâvatîm* (xviii. 2. 31), *strâi-shûyam*[2] (vi. 11. 3): therefore the *pada*-text must be studied (*adhyeyâni padâni*)." The next point made is the necessity of *pada* study to the understanding and right application of the rules respecting accentuation: "the *brahmayajña* etc. (? *brahmayajñâdâdi*) are directed to be made with the employment of the three accents (*trâisvaryeṇa*): here one who does not study the *pada* is unpractised (*apravîṇaḥ*) as regards the words: here, in the passages *brahmâudanam pacati* (xi. 1. 1) etc., one is to speak not with the accents, but with monotone, at the pitch of acute (? *tatra brahmâudanaṁ pacatî 'tyevamâdishû 'dâttaçrutyâ ekaçrutyâ tâ na svareṇa adhîyîta*): now beware lest there appear here the fault of a *mantra* deprived of [its proper] accent. In the Atharvan rites, excepting the *çâga*, in the tyings on of an amulet, etc., in the performance of the sacrifice (? *yajñakarmaṇe*), the employment of the *mantras* is taught to be made with the use of the three accents." Finally, the assertion that study of the *pada* is necessary in order to the comprehension of the meaning of the text is supported with much fullness of illustration: as instances are cited *vi hara* (v. 20. 9: this, however, may be no citation, but part of the exposition), *alasâlâ 'si* (vi. 16. 4: we could wish that the *pada* actually taught us more about this obscure verse), *yavân na 'd adân* (vi. 50. 1), *ûñ iti* (passim), *sam v âmâ 'ha âsyam* (vi. 56. 3), *tad v asya retaḥ* (ix. 4. 4); and farther, with special reference to the element of accent, *yé asmấkaṁ tanvầm* (ii. 31. 5), and *svấdv adml' 'ti* (v. 18. 7): and the conclusion is "here, and in other instances, one who does not study the *pada* would spoil the *sanhitâ*; hence, for these reasons, the *pada* must be studied." I add the whole text, which in places is corrupt and obscure, and of which the value is too small to make an elaborate attempt at restoration necessary or advisable: *mantrârthaç ca padâdhyayanâd vinâ na jñâyate: vâkyaṁ hi padaço vibhaktam anuvyanakti: tac ca padâdhyâyî sandhiṁ ca pade chedaṁ tu çaknuyâd vibhaktam: vi hara: alasâlâ 'si: yavân na 'd adân: ûñ iti: sam v âmâ 'ha âsyam: tad v asya retaḥ: ityevamâdishu sanhitâyâṁ ca bhavati: ryajati 'ty atra sanhitikaḥ sa pra kuryât: tathâ udâttasvaritodayena vighâtam ojânan: ye asmâkaṁ tanvam: anyatrâ 'pi nihanyeta: svâdv admi 'ti: atra ca svaritaṁ kuryât: tathâ udâttântasya pûrvapadasyâ 'nudâttâdâv uttarapade tat tasyâ 'nusthâpattâu svaritam akshamsvarthe jânasyartha 'ty anyatrâ 'pi tat kuryât: evam âdy anyatrâ 'py apadâdhyâyî sanhitâṁ vinâçayet: tasmâd ebhiḥ kâraṇâir avaçyâdhyeyâni: kiṁ ca:*

---

[1] MS. *çṛtumabhyastveti.*

[2] MS., both times, *trâiṣhyam.*

क्रमाध्ययनं संहितापददार्ढ्यार्थम् ॥ १०८ ॥

108. The study of the *krama* has for its object the fixation of both *saṅhitā* and *pada*.

The true reading of this rule is a matter of some doubt. Prefixed to the commentator's exposition, the manuscript gives simply *saṅhitādārḍhyārtham*, and the commencement of the comment implies or requires no more than that: it might seem, then, that we had here only an addition to the last rule, "the study of *pada* is in order to the fixation of *saṅhitā*." But this would be a lame conclusion to the argument of this part of the section, which must be intended finally to bring out the importance of the *krama*-text. And as the exposition closes with pretty clearly assuming as the full form of the rule under treatment that which is presented above, and as the prefixed text of the whole section so far favors the latter as to read *saṅhitāpadadārḍhyārtham*, I think there can be little question that it is to be received as here given.

The *pada*, the commentator tells us, must be studied for the sake of the establishment of the *saṅhitā*. He defines *dārḍhya* by *dṛḍhasya bhāvaḥ*, and cites the rule of Pāṇini which teaches its formation (*varṇadṛḍhādibhyaḥ ṣyañ ca*,[1] Pāṇ. v. 1. 123). He goes on: "when here, in the *saṅhitā*, a doubt arises, the student of the *pada* will give a solution of the doubt. Then what need of a study of the *krama*? On this point, it says: 'the study of the *krama* has for its object the fixation of both *saṅhitā* and *pada*.'" What follows is corrupt, and only in part intelligible: *saṅhitā ca avasthitā na bhavati; yarāmaṇy ekapadadvipadāc ca pragṛhyāvagṛhyasandehāpanodanam.* Finally, he introduces the next rule by saying *idaṁ cā 'param kāraṇaṁ kramādhyayanasya*, 'and here follows another reason for the study of *krama*.'

स्वरोपजनस्त्वादृष्टः पदेषु संहितायां च ॥ १०९ ॥

109. And the origination of accent is not seen in *pada* or in *saṅhitā*.

That is to say—as we are doubtless to understand it—in the *pada* we have before us only the accent of the uncompounded elements; in the *saṅhitā*, only that of the combined phrase: how the one grows out of the other is shown by the *krama*, which gives everything in both its separate and combined state. The commentator defines *upajana* by *utpatti*, and declares it unperceived in *pada* (*padakāle*), while it actually takes place in *krama* (*kramakāle*). As an illustration, he takes *svādv admī 'ti* (v. 18. 7); here, in *pada*, we have an oxytone and an unaccented syllable, which form a circumflex, while in the *saṅhitā* the circumflex farther suffers depression (*nighāta*, the *vikampita* of our rule iii. 65, above), and the circumflex itself only appears in *krama* (in *svādv ādmi*, where the cause of depression of the *svarita* is not present): hence, he concludes, the *krama* ought to be studied. He adds: "now comes the description: of what sort, it is asked, is this *krama*:" the following rules of the section will answer.

[1] MS. *varṇadṛḍhādivāḥ : ḍhyañ :*

द्वे पदे क्रमपदम् ॥ ११० ॥

110. Two words form a *krama*-word.

The commentator is very brief upon this rule: he says "the study of *krama* being now assured (*prasiddha*), two combined words form a single *krama*-word; their combination will be taught hereafter [in rule 122], where it says 'according to the rules' (*yathâçâstram*)."

The corresponding rules of the other treatises are Vâj. Pr. iv. 180, Rik Pr. x. 1 (r. 2) and xi. 1 (r. 1), and Up. i. 14. With the exception of the latter, they are more comprehensive than ours, including something of what here is made the subject of following rules. The precept of the Vâj. Pr. covers our rules 110–113.

तस्यान्तेन परस्य प्रसंधानम् ॥ १११ ॥

111. With the final of this is made farther combination of the following word.

The term *antena* is explained by *avasâna*, 'close, end:' we might have rather expected the reading *antyena*, 'with the last word of each *krama*-word as already defined.' To *parasya* is supplied *padasya*, in the comment, as in the translation. The commentator takes the trouble to tell us that to the end of this following word is then to be farther appended its successor, and so on, so that one constructs the *krama* by thus successively combining the words of the text by twos. Were this rule not given, he says, the former one might be erroneously understood as prescribing that we should form our *krama*-words by taking first the first and second words of a verse, then the third and fourth, then the fifth and sixth, and so on; while this shows us that we are to take the first and second, then the second and third, then the third and fourth, and so on. We may take, as an illustration, the last line of the first hymn of the Atharvan (i. 1. 4 *c, d*), in constructing the *krama*-text of which only this simple and fundamental rule would come into action: it would read *sam çrutena : çrutena gamemahi : gamemahi mâ : mâ çrutena : çrutena vi : vi râdhishi : râdhishi 'ti râdhishi* (by iv. 117).

The Vâj. Pr. and Rik Pr. combine this rule with the preceding: the Upalekha (i. 15) states it separately, and in a distincter manner than our treatise: *tayor uttarano 'ttaram padam samdadhyât.*

नान्तगतं परेण ॥ ११२ ॥

112. A last word is not combined with its successor.

By *antagatam*, literally 'a word gone to, or standing at, the end,' is meant, in verse, the closing word of a half-stanza, or one preceding a pause: in a prose passage, it doubtless indicates a word preceding one of the pauses of interpunction by which a numbered passage, or verse, is divided into parts. A pause, which interrupts the ordinary combinations of *sandhi*, interrupts those of *krama* also: there is no need that the *krama*-text should exhibit the euphonic connection of words which in *saṁhitā* do not euphonically influence one another. The rule, as the commentator tells us, is intended to restrict the too great extension (*atiprasaktam*) of the one which precedes it. That the final word, thus left uncombined, suffers *parihāra*, or repetition, is taught in rule 117.

The corresponding rules in the other treatises are Vāj. Pr. iv. 180, Rik Pr. x. 8 (r. 9), 11 (r. 16), and xi. 21 (r. 41), and Up. i. 16.

त्रीणि पदान्यपृक्तमध्यानि ॥ ११३ ॥

113. Three words form a *krama*-word, if the middle one of them is a pure vowel.

The term *apṛkta* we have met with before (i. 72, 79), as used to designate a word composed of a single vowel or diphthong, unconnected with any consonant: the commentator, after exposition of its meaning, paraphrases it by *avyañjanamiçraçuddhakevalasvaraḥ*, 'a pure and entire vowel, unmixed with consonants.' He cites, as an instance, *dhiyā : ā : ihi* (ii. 5. 4): here the *krama* reading is not *dhiyā " : e 'hi*, but *dhiye " 'hi:* to which, by rule 115, would follow again *e 'hi*, and then, by the present and other rules, *ihy ā naḥ : ā naḥ : na iti naḥ*. The only *apṛkta* words which the text contains are the preposition *ā*, the particle *u* (p. *ūṃ iti:* see i. 72, 73), and their combination *o* (p. *o iti:* see i. 79). It is doubtless to point out and call attention to this mode of treatment of the *ā* in the *krama*-text, that our Atharvan *pada* manuscripts quite frequently write a figure 3 after the word which follows it: thus, in the instance cited, the manuscript gives *dhiyā : ā : ihi : 3*, at i. 1. 2, *punaḥ : ā : ihi : 3*, etc.*

All the *krama*-systems have this feature: compare Vāj. Pr. iv. 180, 181 (which calls such a *krama*-word, composed of three members, a *trikrama*), Rik Pr. x. 2 (r. 3), xi. 2 (r. 3), and Up. i. 17. The two latter authorities, however, except the compound *o*, and would have it treated like any ordinary word. The Vāj. Pr. is obliged to note (iv. 183), as farther instances of *trikramas*, *mo shu ṇaḥ* and *abhi shu ṇaḥ*, where, if the *krama* were performed in the usual way, the *saṁhitā* reading of lingual *ṇ* in *ṇaḥ* would not be capable of exhibition; and like reasons compel it (iv. 184) to establish, in a few cases, *krama*-words of four constituents, as *ūrdhva ū shu ṇaḥ*. The Rik systems, also, are not a little complicated by the necessity of attending to such special cases occurring in their text, and which once cause a *krama*-word to contain even five members. The fact that such complicated cases of *sandhi* do not happen to be met with in the Atharva-Veda saves our treatise the like trouble.

एकादेशस्वरसंधिदीर्घविनामाः प्रयोजनम् ॥ ११४ ॥

114. The grounds of this are the fusion of vowels into a single sound, the combination of vowels, prolongation, and lingualization.

---

* The addition of the figure is usual, but not invariable, in the first books of the text; later, it is only made here and there. The figure is never inserted after *u*.

The longer of the two *krama*-treatises incorporated into the text of the Rik Prâtiçâkhya is the only other authority which gives any reason why *apṛkta* words should not be independently reckoned in constructing the *krama*-text. It says (R. Pr. xi. 2, r. 3) that the omission takes place "for fear of nasalization;" that is, lest the particle should, if suffered to stand at the end of a *krama*-word, receive a nasal pronunciation. The entire disagreement of the two explanations offered is noteworthy, and may be taken as an indication that neither is authoritative, and as a permission to us to find a better one, if we are able. It seems to me more likely that the weakness of the vowel-words *â* and *u*, unsupported by consonants, and their liability to disappear in or become obscured by the final of the word which precedes them, as if they were mere modifications of its termination, was the cause of their exceptional treatment. A similar suggestion has already been made (see under i. 73) as to the way in which the *pada*-text deals with *u*. The commentator's exposition of the rule is elaborate, but deficient in point. To illustrate the item *ekâdeça*, 'vowel-fusion, substitution of one vowel-sound for two or more others,' he takes *dhiyâ : â : ihi* (ii. 5. 4): here, he says, by the operation of the rule *samânâksharasya* (iii. 42), *dhiyâ* and *â* become *dhiyâ*: the *â* of the latter, combined with the *i* of *ihi*, becomes *e*, and the result is the one word *dhiyehi*: *ergo*, this is the way the combination must be made, otherwise there would be no *krama*-word (*tasmâd ity anena saṁdhânena bhavitavyam: anyathâ kramapadam eva na syât*). The conclusion appears to me an evident *non-sequitur*, a mere restatement of the original proposition. For the second item, he selects the example *ihi : â : naḥ* (ii. 5. 4): here, if we compound *ihy â* and *â naḥ*, a vowel-combination (*svarasandhiḥ*) is made of the *i*, by the rule *svare nâmino 'ntuḥsthâ* (iii. 30). How this vowel-combination furnishes a ground for the *krama*-word *ihy â naḥ*, he does not attempt to point out. For the third and fourth items, the chosen instance is *idam : ûṅ iti : su* (i. 24. 4). This, too, is to be regarded as (in *krama*) forming a single word. The following text is corrupt, and I subjoin it, instead of attempting a restoration and translation: *tasyâ eva na saṁdhiḥ: tathâ hi: idamûshvâdishu asaṅhitikaṁ dîrghatvam: sarvâ 'sya tripadasya madhyabhâvâd ishyate: idamûshu ity evambhûtasyâi 'va rûpâkhyânâyâm avaçyaṁ tripadaṁ saṅkramena na bhavatitavyam: atrâi 'vâ 'padatvam: tad api tripadamadhyâvayavam.* The prolongation of the *u* in this and similar cases would indeed seem to furnish a reason for the construction of the *krama*-word out of three members, since the long vowel could not properly appear if the particle were made the final of one such word and the beginning of another; but I am unable to see how the lingualization of the sibilant should have any effect in the same direction, since there would be no difficulty in reading *u shu* as a *krama*-word, if the *u* were treated in the ordinary manner.

आकारौकारादि पुनः ॥११५॥

115. *Â* and *o* are made to begin a word again.

That is to say, after *â* and *o* have been included, as middle members, in a triple *krama*-word, they are again taken as initials of the word next following. The commentator's examples are *gopāyatā* " *'smākam : ā 'smākam* (xii. 3. 55 etc.), *dhiye* " *'hi : e 'hi* (ii. 5. 4), and *havir o shu : o shu : o ity o* (vii. 72. 2).

The same usage, as concerns *ā*, is taught also by the other treatises: compare Vāj. Pr. iv. 182, Rik Pr. x. 6 (r. 11) and xi. 18 (r. 34), Up. iv. 13.

उकारः परिहार्य एव ॥ ११६ ॥

116. *U* is merely to be repeated.

The mode of repetition of the particle is taught in the next rule but one. This rule is, as the commentator explains it, intended to forbid the combination of *u* (like *ā* and *o*) with the next following word to form a new *krama*-word (*anyayoganivṛttyarthaḥ*). As an example, he gives us *sa u sūryaḥ : ūṅ ity ūṅ iti* (xiii. 4. 5).

प्रगृह्यावगृह्यसमापाद्यान्तगतानां द्विर्वचनं परिहार इतिमध्ये ॥ ११७ ॥

117. Repetition with *iti* interposed, or *parihāra*, is to be made of *pragṛhyas*, of words admitting separation by *avagraha*, of those requiring restoration to the natural form, and of those standing before a pause.

The commentator simply expounds this rule, without bringing up any instances to illustrate it. The kinds of words specified are to be repeated, or spoken twice, in the *krama*-text (*kramakāle*), the name of the double utterance being *parihāra:* and this *parihāra* is to be made with interposition of *iti:* having performed one of the two utterances, one is to say *iti*, and then repeat the word.

The mode of repetition is, as has already been noticed (under iv. 74), called in the Rik Pr. by the related name *parigraha* (e. g. R. Pr. iii. 14). The Vāj. Pr. (iv. 187) styles it *sthitopasthita*, which title is also known to and defined by the Rik Pr. (x. 9 and xi. 15). The Up. (iv. 12) knows only *parigraha*. The forms to be repeated are, according to the doctrine of the Vāj. Pr. (iv. 187–193), a divisible word (*avagṛhya*), one in the interior of which appears a prolongation or a lingualization, a *pragṛhya*, a *riphita* of which the *r* does not appear in *saṅhitā*, and a word preceding a pause (*avasāna*). The first and the last three of these classes are, indeed, treated in the same manner by all the other authorities (compare R. Pr. x. 6–8, r. 7–9, and xi. 13–14, r. 25; Up. iv. 4–11); but, as regards the words which in *saṅhitā* undergo an abnormal alteration of form, there is a less perfect agreement among them. The Rik Pr. and Up. specify as requiring repetition in *krama* (besides sundry special and anomalous cases), words having their initial vowel prolonged, and those in the interior of which there is a change not brought about by external influences—that is to say, due to euphonic causes within the word itself. Whether the Vāj. Pr. includes among the repeatable words those having a prolonged initial, or whether any cases of this kind occur in the text to which it belongs, I do not know. Our own *krama*-system, it will be noticed, while in one respect more chary of the repetition than the others, in that it repeats no *riphita* words, in another respect is vastly more liberal of its use, applying it in the case of every word which requires restoration from an abnormal to a normal form, according to the rules given in the preceding section of this chapter. There is no limitation made, either by the text or by the commentary, of the term *samâpâdya*; so far as I can see, every word in the text which undergoes in *sanhitâ* any of the changes detailed in rule 74, above, must suffer *parihâra*. The Atharvan *krama* is thus made a more complete and elaborate index of the euphonic irregularities occurring in its text than is that of either of the other Vedas.

By way of introduction to the following rule, our commentator says, at the close of his exposition, that the words mentioned in this precept have their repetition made with a single *iti*: we are next to be told that in the repetition of the particle *u* two are required.

द्वाभ्यामुकारः ॥ ११८ ॥

118. The particle *u* requires two *iti*'s.

That is to say, when *u* is repeated, each occurrence of the word is followed by *iti*, and we have *ûñ ity ûñ iti*. None of the other treatises supports this reading: all would prescribe simply *ûñ ity ûñ*.

अनुनासिकदीर्घत्वं प्रयोजनम् ॥ ११९ ॥

119. The reason of this is its nasalization and protraction.

The commentator explains as follows: "the nasalization of this particle *u* when followed by *iti* is taught by the rule *ukârasye 'tâv aprktasya* [i. 72]; if, then, it should not be distinguished by (*âdriyeta*) a second *iti*, it would be deprived of its nasal quality—as also of its protraction [since this also, by i. 73, is prescribed only before *iti*]. Therefore, considering its prescribed nasality and protraction, *u* must always be repeated with a double *iti*."

प्लुतश्चाप्लुतवत् ॥ १२० ॥

120. A protracted vowel is, in repetition, to be treated as if unprotracted.

The commentator's exposition is: *plutaç câ 'plutavac ca parihartavyaḥ : aplutena tulyatâṁ prâvahitavyaḥ : parihârakâle : purushaḥ : â : babhûvâñ3 : atra â ity ākâraḥ plutaḥ : sa aplutavatâ parihartavyaḥ : â babhûvâñ3 iti babhûve 'ti vaktavyam*; 'a protracted vowel is to be repeated as if it were unprotracted; i.e., it is to be reduced, in *parihâra*, to equivalence with an unprotracted vowel: thus, in the passage *purushaḥ : â : babhûvâñ3* (x. 2. 28), the *â* is a protracted *a*: it must be repeated along with [or, in the form of] an unprotracted *a*; we must read *â babhûvâñ3 iti babhûva 'ti*.' The reading of the manuscript is unfortunately corrupt at the end, where the required *krama*-form is to be given: the scope and intent of the rule will be examined under the one next following, which also concerns only the passage here cited by the commentator.

अनुनासिकः पूर्वश्च शुद्धः ॥१२१॥

121. And a nasal vowel, in its first occurrence, is to be made pure.

I again add the whole comment: *yaḥ pûrvam anunâsiko dṛshṭaḥ sa parihârakâle çuddhaṁ kṛtvâ parihartavyaḥ: etad evo 'dâharaṇam: atrâi 'va purusha â babhûvâñ3 ity avasâne: iti: avasâne â iti pûrvam anunâsiko dṛshṭaḥ çuddhaḥ parihartavyaḥ: babhûve 'ti babhûvâñ;* 'the vowel first seen as nasal is, in *parihâra*, to be repeated pure [i. e. free from nasality]: the instance is the one already given: here, the vowel first appearing as nasal before the pause—by the rule *purusha â babhûvâñ ity avasâne* (i. 70)—is to be repeated pure: thus, *babhûve 'ti babhûvâñ.*' The most obvious and natural understanding of this would be that the nasalization is only to be retained in the first utterance of the word, and that in *parihâra*, by this and the preceding rules, both protraction and nasality should be lost altogether; so that the *krama* would read *â babhûvâñ3: babhûva 'ti babhûva*. But the rules in the first chapter to which the commentator refers expressly require the nasality to be retained before a pause, and forbid the protraction only before *iti*, so that they would appear to teach *babhûva 'ti babhûvâñ3;* which, as we see, is the actual reading of the commentator under this rule, while, under the preceding, the reading is too corrupt for us to understand what he intends to give us. The best manner, as it appears to me, of reconciling these apparent discrepancies is to take *pûrvaḥ* in the present rule as belonging with the predicate instead of the subject, and as indicating the former of the two occurrences of the repeated word in *parihâra*, thus making the translation such as it is given above; and farther, assuming the same thing to be implied also in rule 120, the repetition, or *parihâra*, there referred to, being, in a restricted sense, the occurrence of the word before *iti:* the Upalekha employs *parigraha*, in part, in the same sense.* It may be, however, that we ought to confess a discordance between the teachings of our treatise here and in the first chapter, and to understand the *krama* reading here prescribed to be *babhûve 'ti babhûva*—or, if *pûrvaḥ* be interpreted in the manner proposed, *babhûve 'ti babhûvañ*. A like case occurring in the Rig-Veda (x. 146. 1) is, according to the Upalekha (vii. 9, 10: the Rik Pr. seems to take no notice of it), to be treated in the manner laid down in our first chapter: *vindatîñ3*, for *vindati*, is in *krama* to be read *vindati 'ti vindatîñ3*. What is the doctrine of the Vâj. Pr. in a similar instance has been mentioned in the note to i. 97.

यथाशास्त्रं प्रसंधानम् ॥१२२॥

122. The successive combination of words into *krama*-words is to be made according to the general rules of combination.

---

* See Pertsch's preliminary note to chapter v.

The commentator expounds this rule in a clear and pertinent manner. He says: "it has been said in a former rule [iv. 111], 'with the final of this is made farther combination of the following word:' there, however, the method of combination is not taught (*saṁdhânavidhânaṁ no 'ktam*): wherefore the present rule is here added. The term *yathâçâstram* means 'according to the several rules (*yad yac châstram*):' whatever mode of combination of separate words is taught in the *pada-çâstra* (*yad yat padaçâstre padânâṁ saṁdhânalokshaṇam uktam*), that has force also here in the formation of each single *krama*-word. This is expressly stated, in order to guard against the danger of understanding a *krama*-word to be composed of disconnected vocables (*I kramapadatvâd anyaçabdaçañkayo 'cyate*): this must not be the case."

The Vâj. Pr. has no precept corresponding to this, evidently regarding it as clearly enough implied in the general direction that two words "are to be combined" (*saṁ dadhâti*: iv. 180) to form a *krama*-word. It is, however, distinctly laid down by the other treatises (R. Pr. x. 5, r. 6, and xi. 21, r. 44; Up. iii. 3–5).

प्रगृह्यावगृह्यचर्चायां क्रमवदुत्तरस्मिन्नवग्रहः ॥ १२३ ॥

123. The *pada*-repetition of a divisible *pragṛhya* is to be made in the manner of that of *krama*, with separation by *avagraha* in the latter recurrence of the word.

The commentator begins with explaining *pragṛhyâvagṛhya* to be a determinative and not a copulative compound (*yasminn avagṛhyatvam* [*pragṛhyatvaṁ ca*] *ekasminn eva yugapad bhavati*), and goes on as follows: "such a word, in its *pada*-repetition (*carcâyâm*), is to be treated as in *krama*: *carcâ* means twofold utterance (*dvirvacanam*): that takes place in the *pada*-text (*padakâle*) just as in the *krama*-text (*kramakâle*); that is, one repeats (*pariharet*) the form of the *krama*-text. In *krama*, both *pragṛhyas* and divisibles suffer repetition; in *pada* (*padesha*), on the other hand, only a divisible *pragṛhya* is repeated. In such a repetition, how is separation by *avagraha* made? The rule says, 'with separation by *avagraha* in the latter recurrence of the word:' that is, the latter or second recurrence of the word is to receive *avagraha*, and not the first: for example, *virûpe iti vi-rûpe* (x. 7. 6, 42)."

The usage of both our Atharvan *pada*-text and that of the other Vedas in regard to *carcâ*, or repetition, has been fully set forth in the note to iv. 74, above, as also the doubt which may reasonably be entertained whether the usage here taught, and followed in the extant manuscripts, is that which the rules of the preceding section contemplate.

The prescription in this rule, and in this alone, of the employment of *avagraha* in separating the constituents of a compound word when it appears for the second time in the repetition, after *iti*, seems necessarily to imply that, in the repetitions of *krama*, separation by *avagraha* is not to be made at all, either before or after *iti*, but that we are to read, for instance (i. 1. 1), *ye trishaptâḥ : trishaptâḥ pariyanti : trisaptâ iti trisaptâḥ : pariyanti viçvâ : pariyanti 'ti pariyanti*, etc. To regard the specification *uttarasminn avagrahaḥ* of our rule as in such manner retrospective as to reflect its prescriptive force, through *kramavat*, back into the rule for *krama*-repetition, or *parigraha*—understanding the meaning to be, 'in *pada*-repetitions, the second recurrence of the repeated word is to suffer division by *avagraha*; as is to be the case also in *krama*-repetitions'—would be, I should think, much too violent. Nevertheless, the Rik Pr. (x. 10, r. 16, and xi. 16, r. 31) and Upalekha (iv. 8) distinctly teach that the *avagraha* is to be used in the repetition of compound words, after *iti*. I cannot find that the Vâj. Pr. prescribes the separation either in *pada* or in *krama*, although it is regularly made by the commentator on that treatise in the examples which he cites, and Weber passes it over without remark.

समापाद्यानामन्ते संहितावद्वचनम् ॥ १२४ ॥

124. Words requiring restoration, if occurring before a pause, are to be spoken in their *sanhitâ* form.

The three last rules of the section and of the treatise concern the treatment of such words as, while they stand at the end of a half-verse, or in any other situation before a pause, also exhibit in *sanhitâ* some abnormal peculiarity of orthoepy which, by the rules of the preceding section, requires restoration to the natural form. A word of this class, instead of being combined with its predecessor into a *krama*-word, and then repeated, is, before its repetition, to be spoken once more in *sanhitâ* form. The commentator takes the example *sá vṛkshâṅ abhi sishyade* (v. 5. 9: p. *sisyade*, by iv. 82), and, without writing it out in full in the *krama* form, says that we must utter *sishyade* again, and then repeat it, *sisyada iti sisyade*. He adds: "so also may be brought forward as instances (*udâhâryâḥ*) *praṇîtaye* (vi. 23. 2: p. *pra-nîtaye*) and all other like words, having the cause of alteration within their own limits." This last restriction, as we shall see, he insists upon more distinctly under the next following rule.

This special point is left untouched in all the other *krama*-treatises.

तस्य पुनरास्थापितं नाम ॥ १२५ ॥

125. Of this, furthermore, the name is *âsthâpita*.

Weber (p. 283) regards *punaḥ* here as a part of the title, which he understands to be *punarâsthâpita*. This would not be in itself unlikely, but it is not favored by the commentator, who, both here and under the following rule, treats *âsthâpita* alone as the term designating the word to which the rule relates. He omits *punaḥ* altogether, in his paraphrase of the present rule, as being superfluous: *tasya sanhitâvad vacanasya: âsthâpitam ity evaṁ saṁjñâ bhavati.* He then goes on to state more at large the restriction hinted at under the last rule: namely, that a word which is *samâpâdya*, or liable to restoration, as being altered at its commencement by the influence of the preceding word, is not to be treated in the manner prescribed by these rules: "that is to say, where cause and effect (*nimittanâimittike*) are in one word; for instance, *sishyade*: here the conversion into *sha* produced by the reduplication holds over, owing to the fact that the reduplication and the altered sibilant are in the same word. But this is not the case in the passage *striyâm anu shicyate* (vi. 11. 2), [or, in *pada* form] *tat : striyâm : anu : sicyate:* here no repetition in the *sanhitâ* form takes place [or, the repetition does not take place in the *sanhitâ* form: *iti na sanhitâvad bhavati*]; and why? because cause and effect are declared to stand in two separate words: *anu* is a preposition; it produces conversion into *sh* by the rule *upasargât* etc. (ii. 90), and that conversion is heard (*çrutaḥ*) in a separate word; here, then, let the process not be performed (? *tendtramidibhût*): for this reason is this explanation made." It might still seem doubtful, after all this lengthy exposition, whether such a word as *sicyate* was regarded by the commentator as not to be separately spoken at all, or as to be separately spoken, only not in *sanhitâ* form, as follows: *striyâm anu : anu shicyate : sicyate : sicyate iti sicyate ;* but the latter interpretation seems to me the more probable.

स एकपदः परिहार्यश्च ॥ १२६ ॥

126. That is a *krama*-word of a single member, and is also to be repeated.

The commentary upon this rule is not so clear as the rule itself seems to be, without comment or explanation: it reads as follows, with only the most obvious emendations: *parihartavyaç ca sa âsthitasañjñapadrçaḥ* [*âsthâpitasañjñâikapadaḥ?*]: *yo 'sâu sanhitâdvirvacanena nirdiçyate: nimittanâimittikayor bhinnapadasthatvât : sa parihâryaç ca bhavati.* If the intent of this is to limit the application of the rule to those words whose cause of alteration is situated in a preceding independent word, it can hardly be accepted. What follows is still more corrupt and less intelligible: *sanhitâvad viçâci bahulam iti yaç chandasi 'ti: varṇalopâgamahrasvadîrghaplutâ âtmanesha parasmâi vibhâshâ api yanti.*

Finally, to close up the commentary, two verses are given us, but so much mutilated that hardly more than their general sense (and even that only in part) is recognizable: *natakîbadhyâ nacaçâstra dṛshṭyâ yathâmnânam anyathâ nâi 'va kuryât: âmnâtam parishannasya çâstram dṛshṭo vidhir vyatyayaḥ pûrvaçâstre: âmnâtavyam anâmnâtam prapâṭhe 'smin rkvâcatpadam : chandaso 'parimeyatvât parishannasya lakshaṇam : parishannasya lakshaṇam iti.*

The signature of the chapter and of the work has been already given in the introductory note, but may be repeated here: *iti çâunakîye caturâdhyâyike caturthaḥ pâdaḥ: caturâdhyâyîbhâshyam samâptam: çrir astu: lekhakapâṭhakayoḥ çubham bhavatu: çrîcaṇḍikâyâi namaḥ: çrîrâmaḥ: samvat 1714 varshe jyâishṭhaçuddha 9 dine samâptulikhitam pustakam.* I may also be permitted to add the propitiatory heading of the manuscript, which was, by an oversight, omitted to be given in its proper place: it reads *oṁ namaḥ sarasvatyâi namaḥ: oṁ namo brahmavedâya : athângirasaḥ.* The last word is, as I cannot doubt, a copyist's error for *atharvângirasaḥ.*

Additional Notes.

1. *Analysis of the Work, and Comparison with the other Prâtiçâkhyas.*

So far as concerns the agreement or disagreement of the other Prâtiçâkhyas with that of the Atharva-Veda in respect to the doctrines taught in the latter, the comparison has already been made in detail in the notes to the text. I have thought, however, that it would be advisable to append here a systematic view of the contents of our treatise, and a brief statement of the correspondences of the rest, in order to exhibit more clearly the sphere of the former, and to show how far those of the latter coincide with it, and how far they cover more or less ground than it occupies.

I. Introductory and explanatory.

Introductory, object of the treatise, i. 1, 2; definition of terms, i. 3, 42, 43, 46, 49, 92, iv. 73, 125; interpretation and application of rules, i. 95, iii. 88.

II. Phonetics and Euphony: production, classification, properties, and combination of sounds.

1. *Simple sounds:* formation and classification of consonants, i. 10–13, 18–31; do. of vowels, i. 27, 32–41, 71; quantity of vowels and consonants, i. 59–62; accents, i. 14–17.

2. *Sounds in combination, and resulting modifications:* possible finals, i. 4–9, ii. 8; final vowels not liable to euphonic change (*pragṛhya*), i. 73–81, iii. 33; syllable, i. 93; division of syllables, i. 55–58; quantity of syllables, i. 51–54:—kinds of independent circumflex accent, iii. 55–61, 65; kinds of enclitic do., iii. 62–64; evocation and modification of accents in words and sentences, iii. 67–74:—conjunction of consonants, i. 49, 50, 94, 98, ii. 20; *abhinidhâna*, i. 43–47; *yama*, i. 99, 104; *nâsikya*, i. 100, 104; *svarabhakti*, i. 101, 102, 104; *sphoṭana*, i. 103, 104, ii. 38; *karshaṇa*, ii. 39; euphonic duplication of consonants (*varṇakrama*), iii. 26–32.

III. Construction of combined text, or saṅhitâ.

Prolongation of initial, final, and medial vowels, iii. 1–25:—combination of final and initial vowels and diphthongs, iii. 39–54, ii. 21–24, i. 97; resulting accent, iii. 55, 56, 58, 65, 66; resulting nasality, i. 69; final vowels not liable to combination, iii. 33–38:—combinations of final and initial consonants: final non-nasal mutes, ii. 2–8, 13, 14, 38, 39; final nasals, ii. 9–12, 25, 26, 28, 30–37, iii. 37, i. 67; final semivowels, ii. 19, 21–24, iii. 20; final *visarjanîya*, ii. 21, 24, 40, 43–52, 54–59, 62–80; initial consonants, ii. 7, 15–18:—final nasal before a vowel, ii. 27, 29, i. 68, iii. 27; final *visarjanîya* before a vowel, ii. 41, 42, 44–53, 56:—lingualization of *t* and *th*, ii. 15, 16; do. of *n*, iii. 75–95; do. of *s*, ii. 81–107:—insertion of *s*, iii. 96.

IV. Construction of krama-text.

Importance of *krama*-text, iv. 108, 109; its construction, iv. 110–122, 124–126, 74–100, i. 70, 97.

V. Construction of disjoined, or pada-text.

Importance of *pada*-text, iv. 107; combination or separation of verb and preposition, iv. 1–7; do. of suffixes, iv. 13–37, 46–48, 53, 65, 66; do. of compounds, iv. 8–12, 21, 22, 27, 28, 38–45, 49–64, 67–72; restoration of the original form of words, iv. 74–77, 79, 81–97, 99, 100; repetition in *pada*, iv. 123; special cases, i. 72, 78, 81, 82; enclitic accent in *pada*, iii. 68, 69, 72, 73.

VI. Summaries, special cases, etc.

Study of Veda recommended, iv. 101–109:—special irregularities of formation, i. 83–86, ii. 25, 60, 61, iii. 7, 45; special case of accent, i. 96; list of protracted vowels, i. 105; quantity of nasalized vowels in interior of word, i. 88–91.

In regard to the matters embraced in the first of the general divisions here laid down, it may be said that our treatise is much more curt and concise, and more ready to pass without notice what may be assumed as already known, than either of the others. Definitions of terms are far from numerous, and the whole department of *paribhâshâ*, or explanation of modes of phraseology, of extent, bearing, and application of the rules, and the like, which in all the other Prâtiçâkhyas occupies considerable space, is here almost wholly wanting. This is in part owing to the simpler and less artificial mode of arrangement adopted in our work.

In the division of Phonetics and Euphony, the discordances among the different authorities affect chiefly matters of detail, and are not of a character to call for notice here. The other three treatises include or imply a list and enumeration of the sounds of the spoken alphabet, which is wanting in our own. All, also, after treating the subject of the formation of articulate sounds in the outset in a manner nearly according with that here followed, return to it in their later and less genuine chapters, and discuss it anew with a straining after greater theoretic profundity. The niceties of consonantal combination, as *abhinidhâna* etc., make nearly the same figure in all the four: for minor differences, see the notes on the text. The Rik Pr., to its specification of possible finals (which is wanting only in the Tâitt. Pr.), adds that also of possible initials, and of compatible or conjoinable consonants (xii. 1–4).

Under the head of the conversion of *pada*-text into *sanhitâ*, the authorities differ only on minor points, or by the treatment of special cases appertaining to the text with which each has to deal.

Thus far, the subjects treated are those which no Prâtiçâkhya can pass over in silence: those which remain are not essential to the completeness of a work of this class, and are accordingly found altogether wanting in one or more of the treatises. Thus, the IVth general division, the construction of the *krama*-text, is not touched upon in the Tâitt. Pr., and the parts of our own and of the Rik Pr. which concern it are open to the suspicion of being later accretions to the text. The Vth division, the construction of the *pada*-text, receives still more scanty attention, being entirely passed over in the Tâitt. Pr., and represented in the Rik Pr. only by a few scattering rules relating to special cases, analogous with those found in the earlier chapters of the Ath. Pr.; only the Vâj. Pr. joining the latter in treating it at large, although in a less complete and elaborate manner.

A more detailed comparison will be necessary under the last head, that of miscellaneous and extra-limital additions to the body of the work, of matters more or less akin with its proper substance, and auxiliary to its object, yet omissible without detriment to its completeness as a Prâtiçâkhya. As concerns the study of the Veda, the first subject mentioned in our analysis, the Rik Pr. offers a very interesting chapter (xv. 1–16) on the mode of instruction followed in the schools of Vedic study; the Vâj. Pr. recommends Vedic study (viii. 35–42), and tells (i. 20–26, viii. 32–34) who should pursue it, and under what circumstances. All the other treatises give explanations of single irregular and exceptional words and forms, of which the list will be more or less extended according as we include in it all those words which the *pada*-text does not analyze, or only such as are of especially anomalous character. The Rik Pr. alone among them (i. 6) catalogues the few protracted vowels occurring in its text. Like our treatise, it also teaches (in a late chapter, xiii. 7–10) when interior nasalized vowels are long: the Tâitt. Pr. (xvi. 1–31) goes farther, and laboriously catalogues all the nasalized vowels contained in its text, short or long, which are not the result of euphonic combination. Of this same class of appendices, which are designed to call attention to points in the text where especial liability to error is held to exist, are the following: the Rik Pr. (ii. 5) gives a list of instances of hiatus within a word; the Vâj. Pr. attempts (in part, in a bungling manner, and with very sorry success) to point out words which do not end with *visarjanîya* (iv. 26–32), which contain one *y* or two (iv. 149–159), or single, double, or triple groups of consonants (vi. 25–30); the Tâitt. Pr. adds to its list of nasalized vowels only (xiii. 8–14) that of words showing an original lingual *n*. The Vâj. Pr. (iii. 1, viii. 50, 51) defines a word, and both it (i. 27, viii. 52–57) and the Rik Pr. (xii. 5, 8, 9) distinguish and define the parts of speech, while all the three give a list of the prepositions (R. Pr. xii. 6, 7; V. Pr. vi. 24; T. Pr. i. 15): and the Vâj. Pr., after its fashion, carries the matter into the domain of the absurd, by laying down (viii. 58–63) the divinities and the families of *ṛshis* to whom the several classes of words, and even (viii. 47) of letters, belong. The Rik Pr. (x. 12, xi. 12) and Vâj. Pr. (iii. 148, iv. 77, 165–178, 194) treat of the *samaya* or *saṁkrama*, the omission of verses or phrases which have already once occurred in the text. Such omissions are abundantly made in all the manuscripts of the Atharva-Veda, *saṁhitâ* as well as *pada*, but the Prâtiçâkhya takes no notice of them. The Rik Pr. has a chapter (xiv. 1–30) on errors of pronunciation, from which, by careful comparative study, important information on phonetic points may be drawn. It also, in its three closing chapters (xvi–xviii), treats with much fullness the subject of metre, which no one of the others even hints at. The Tâitt. Pr. devotes a single brief chapter (xviii. 1–7) to the quantity and accent of the auspicious exclamation *om*. The Vâj. Pr. has an interesting, although rather misplaced, series of rules (vi. 1–23) respecting the accentuation of verbs and vocatives in the sentence, and also makes a foolish and fragmentary attempt (ii. 1–45, 55–64) to define the accent of words in general. With its rules respecting the ritual employment of different tones and accents (i. 127–132) is to be compared what the Tâitt. Pr. (xxii. 12, xxiii. 12–20) says of tone and pitch. The Vâj. Pr., finally, remarks briefly and imperfectly (iii. 17, 137, 138) on the omission in the Vedic dialect of certain terminations.

It is thus seen that the Atharva-Veda Prâtiçâkhya does not greatly differ in its range of subjects from the other treatises of its class; being somewhat less restricted than the Tâitt. Pr., and somewhat less comprehensive than the remaining two, the Vâj. and Rik Prâtiçâkhyas. Its style of treatment is marked by sundry peculiarities, of which the most striking and important is the extensive use which it makes of *gaṇas* in the construction of its rules. It is this which has enabled it, while including so much, to be at the same time so much the briefest of the four works. This approximates it, also, to the character of the general Sanskrit grammar, as finally and principally represented to us by Pâṇini. The close connection between the two is farther shown by many other circumstances which have been pointed out in the notes upon the text —by the contemplation in numerous rules, both general and special, of phenomena of the general language rather than those of the Atharvan vocabulary alone, by a more liberal introduction of grammatical categories than any other of the Prâtiçâkhyas makes (the Taitt. Pr. is its antithesis in this respect), and by the exhibition (not the use, as significant) of some of the indicatory letters employed by Pâṇini himself. It is very sparing of its references to the opinions of other authorities, Çâunaka and Çâkaṭâyana being the only grammarians whom it cites by name. The latter of the two appears, both from the text and the commentary, to have stood in an especially near relation to the authors of our treatise. Çâunaka, although his opinion is rejected in the only rule where his name appears, is yet mentioned in a way which may be regarded as implying his special importance as an authority; it being thought necessary to teach expressly that his *dictum* upon the point referred to is not binding. There is nothing, at any rate, in the mode of the reference, which should militate against the claim apparently implied in the name of the work, that it represents in the main the doctrines of a Çâunaka, and belongs to a school which derives its name from him.

Whether the peculiarities pointed out are of a nature to determine the chronological relation of our treatise to the other Prâtiçâkhyas is a difficult and doubtful question. The discussions of this point hitherto made appear to me nearly barren of any positive results. They are all more or less based upon the assumption that the appearance in a Prâtiçâkhya of a later phase of grammatical treatment or of grammatical phraseology is an unequivocal evidence of later composition. That this is so is not readily to be conceded. Since Prâtiçâkhyas are no complete grammatical treatises, but only the phonetical text-books, and the manuals of rules for conversion of *pada* into *saṅhitâ*, belonging to special schools, and since they imply a vastly more complete grammatical science than they actually present, it is not to be denied that any one of them might include more or less of the form and the material of that science, as its compilers chose, or as the traditional usage of their school required. Thus, for instance, there would be no implausibility in supposing that the Tâittirîya Prâtiçâkhya, though so much more limited in its grammatical horizon than those of the Vâjasaneyi and Atharvan, was actually composed at a later date than either of them, and deliberately adopted the method of treating its material according to the letter rather than the meaning, as being better suited to the character of a Prâtiçâkhya, which concerns itself only with phonetic form, and not with sense. If such a supposition admits of being proved false, it can only be so by a more searching and wary investigation and comparison than has yet been made, or than is possible before the full publication and elucidation of all the treatises. It is very doubtful whether any one of the Prâtiçâkhyas has escaped extensive modification, by alteration, insertion, and addition, since its first substantial construction. The fact that in the Rik Pr. all that is essential to make out such a treatise is contained in the first half, or chapters i-ix, is strongly suggestive of the accretion of the later chapters, and the character of more than one of them lends powerful support to such a suggestion. That the Vâj. Pr. has suffered interpolation and increment is the opinion of its editor, and we cannot help surmising that its weakest and most impertinent portions, especially those in which the expression seems intended to conceal rather than convey the meaning they cover, are the work of a very late hand. None of the other treatises is disfigured by such features. In point of dignified style, and apparent mastery of the material with which it deals, the first rank belongs unquestionably to the Rik Prâtiçâkhya; with what inaccuracies and deficiencies it may have to be reproached, its editors have not ascertained for us: a careful testing of the rules by the text whose phenomena they were meant to present in full will have to be made for all the treatises before their comparison can be rendered complete. The results of such a testing as regards the Atharva-Veda are to be found scattered everywhere through the notes upon the text, and do not need to be summed up here. I fulfil, however, a promise previously given (note to i. 1), by making summary reference below to the rules in which our treatise oversteps the limits of the subject which it is treating, or of the sphere of such a work as it professes to be, or in which it contemplates euphonic combinations and words not to be found in its text.

Treatment of matters purely concerning the *pada*-text, in the portions properly devoted to *sanhitâ*, is made in rules i. 72, 73, 81, 82, iii. 64, 68, 69, 72, 73: a like thing is done for the *krama*-text at i. 70, 97, iv. 74 etc., 96. Combinations not Atharvan are had in view at i. 47, ii. 9, 11, 12, 14, 15, 26, iii. 27, 48; words not Atharvan, at i. 77, 86, 87, ii. 25, 51, iii. 2, 92, iv. 28, 62, 89. The bounds set in the first rule of the work are transgressed, by the inclusion of matters of word-formation and derivation, and the explication of forms which have no other qualities in *pada* than in *sanhitâ*, at i. 63–66, ii. 19, 33, 34, 52, 59, 60, 61, 62, 87, 89, iii. 1, 2, 3, 7, 8–11, 43, 49, 57, 59, 60, 61, 75, 76, 87, 90. Among these last cases, a few are palpably and grossly out of place; but the greater part may be explained and excused by supposing that the *pada*-text implied by the Prâtiçâkhya is an ideal one, which our established and recorded *pada*-texts nearly approach, but do not altogether coincide with.

2. ***Relation of the Prâtiçâkhya to the existing Text of the Atharva-Veda.***

In attempting to determine the relation of our treatise to the only known text of the Atharva-Veda, by the help of the citations which the former contains, it is necessary, of course, to consider as one the text and its commentator, since the *gaṇa*-method pursued by the treatise relieves it from quoting more than a small part of the words and passages to which it was intended to apply. And even with the help of the commentator, since he fills out the *gaṇas* but in part, we are able to find references to no more than a portion of the phenomena of the text to which the view of the makers of the Prâtiçâkhya was directed. This state of things deprives our investigation of much of the definiteness and certainty which it ought to possess, and which would attend a similar examination of any other of the Prâtiçâkhyas by means of its Veda; yet it is desirable even here to make the comparison, which will be found not barren of valuable results. The index of passages in the Atharvan text cited by the Prâtiçâkhya and its commentary, to be given later, furnishes in full detail the principal body of the material of investigation; and from that we derive at once the important information that to the apprehension of the Prâtiçâkhya the Atharva-Veda comprehended only the first eighteen books of the present collection. The two single apparent references to passages in book xix, the one made by the commentator (under ii. 67), the other by an authority whom he cites (under iv. 49), are of no account as against this conclusion: the absence from the rules of the treatise of any notice of the numerous irregularities of the two closing books, and the want of other citations in the commentary than the two equivocal ones referred to, are perfectly convincing. This testimony of the Prâtiçâkhya, moreover, agrees entirely with that which we derive from a consideration of the character of those books and the condition of their text: no *pada*-text of book xix and of those portions of book xx which are not taken bodily from the Rig-Veda is known to be in existence, and it is not at all likely that there ever was one; the text could hardly, in that case, have become so corrupt. The citations run through all the other books of the Atharvan; they are more numerous, as was to be expected, in the earlier books, and in parts of the text they are but thinly scattered; yet no extended portion of the first eighteen books can with plausibility be supposed not to have lain before the commentator for excerption. As regards single passages, there is room for more question: although our lack of the complete *gaṇas* greatly interferes with a full discussion of this point, we are able to discover phenomena in the existing text of which the Prâtiçâkhya, even as at present constructed, plainly fails to take notice. Some such cases of omission the commentator himself has perceived, and calls attention to,* but those which have escaped his notice also are much more numerous.† Many, probably the greater part, of these are to be set down to the account of the authors of the treatise, as results of their carelessness or want of accuracy: but that all of them can be thus disposed of does not appear to me likely; it seems a more probable supposition that in our authors' Atharvan single passages and single readings were wanting which are met with in the present text. The question, however, hardly admits of a positive solution: it would aid us not a little in coming to a conclusion upon it, did we know precisely what is the completeness and accuracy of the other treatises, as tested by their respective texts.

Differences of reading offered by the manuscripts as compared with the Prâtiçâkhya form another main branch of the evidence bearing upon the question under consideration. That which I have collected, how-

---

* See under ii. 68, 88, 101, iii. 60, iv. 16, 18, 67.

† All, so far as my own search for them has been successful, have been set down in the notes on the text, above: see under ii. 63, 72, 93, 96, 97, 101, 108, iii. 5, 12, 13, 25, 32, 45, 61, 80, iv. 13, 16, 39, 50, 57, 62, 68, 86, 96.

ever, is not of decisive character, and hardly furnishes so much ground for suspicion of a discordance between the present text and that of the authors and commentator of our treatise as was derived from the citations. That the manuscripts neglect the refinements of Vedic orthoepy, such as the *yama*, *nāsikya*, *svarabhakti*, and *sphoṭana*, and the duplications of the *varṇakrama*, is a matter of course. Other theoretical niceties of a similar character, as the aspiration of a final mute before a sibilant (ii. 6), and insertions between a mute and sibilant (ii. 8, 9), we are equally prepared to see neglected in the written text, and we should not think of founding upon their absence the suspicion that the manuscripts represented the Veda of another school. Some peculiarities of euphonic combination—the insertion of *t* between *n* and *s* (ii. 9), the assimilation of *n* to *j* (ii. 11), the omission of a mute between a nasal and another mute (ii. 20), the conversion of *m* to nasal *l* before *l* (ii. 35), the retention of *visarjanīya* before a sibilant and following mute (ii. 40)—have been noted as followed or disregarded by the copyists of our codices with utter irregularity and absence of rule. Their treatment of *a* or *ā* before *ṛ* (iii. 46) is a more distinctive trait, and may possibly rest upon a difference of scholastic theory. Their writing of *ḍhḍh* or *dh* for *ḍḍh* (i. 94) is of no significance, being more or less common in all Vedic MSS., while opposed to all sound phonetic theory and doctrine. Nor do I regard as of importance the great discordance of the manuscript treatment of the *visarjanīya* with that which the Prātiçākhya teaches (ii. 40)—viz. the neglect of the guttural and labial spirants, and the retention of *visarjanīya*, instead of its assimilation, before a sibilant: all the written Vedic texts, so far as I know (with, at least, but rare and unimportant exceptions), follow in these respects the usage of the later language, and not the requirements of the Vedic phonetic grammars. A few single cases have been pointed out in the notes, where all or nearly all the manuscripts give readings of words differing from those which the rules of the treatise require: but most of these* are of a kindred class with those last noted, or concern the conversion or nonconversion of *visarjanīya* into a sibilant, and are therefore of doubtful value: upon such points our Atharvan manuscripts, closely connected as they are with one another in origin, not unfrequently disagree. These being set aside, only two or three indubitable cases of violation of the Prātiçākhya rules in the existing *çākhā* of the Atharvan remain,† and these admit of ready and plausible explanation as errors of copyists.

We come now to consider the remaining department of the evidence, or that afforded by the references and citations in the text and commentary which furnish words and phrases not to be found in the extant Atharvan text. Such references and citations are very numerous, occurring in or under nearly a fifth of the rules which the treatise contains.‡ Much the greater part, however, of the considerable body of

* See under ii. 62, 72–76, 80, 86, 98, 107, iv. 75, 77.

† See under iii. 76, 79, iv. 64.

‡ See the notes to i. 4, 14–16, 20, 25, 28, 44, 47, 49, 52, 56, 58, 65, 68, 77, 78, 86, 87, 89–91, 98; ii. 3, 5, 6, 9, 12, 14, 16, 19, 20, 25, 26, 28, 31, 40, 41, 47, 50–52, 58, 64, 74, 82, 83, 84, 90, 102; iii. 1, 2, 5, 8, 11, 20, 27, 30, 32, 37, 39, 40, 42, 44–46, 48, 50, 51, 53, 54, 55, 56, 64, 75, 77, 78, 90, 92; iv. 18, 26, 28, 34, 61, 62, 67, 69, 85.

non-Atharvan material thus presented us is recognizable at first sight as of no force to show any discordance between the Atharva-Veda of the Prâtiçâkhya and that of the existing manuscripts. It is, as has been often pointed out in the notes, a peculiarity of the authors of our treatise to give their rules a wider scope than the vocabulary of the Atharvan requires, in many instances contemplating and providing for combinations of sounds which are found nowhere in the whole body of the Vedic scriptures, and for which, accordingly, the commentator is obliged to fabricate illustrations. Moreover, even where the Atharvan furnishes numerous or innumerable examples of the application of a rule, the commentator sometimes prefers to draw upon his own fancy, instead of citing its text (notable instances of this are to be found especially under iii. 42–50). This being the case, it is evidently impossible to draw any distinct and certain line of division between what may be cited from an Atharvan text not agreeing with the one which we possess, and what is derived from other sources. But there are a certain number of sentences, among those given by the commentator, which have more or less clearly the aspect of genuine citations from a Vedic text; and although some among them might be regarded as instances of carelessness on his part, he quoting by memory from another source than his own Veda, we cannot plausibly extend this explanation to them all: it must remain probable that in part, at least, they were contained in some hitherto unknown *çâkhâ* of the Atharva-Veda. The sentences referred to are as follows: *prá 'mú ca roha* (i. 14–16), *punâ raktaṁ vâsaḥ* (i. 28, ii. 19, iii. 20), *çṛṇur çṛṇubhiḥ* (i. 68), *ami açaçre* (i. 78), *tad abhûtam* (ii. 2), *dhâtar dehi savitar dehi punar dehi* (ii. 47), *samaho vartate* (ii. 50), *yad aho rûpâṇi dṛçyante* (ii. 51), *yadâ 'ho rathaṁtaraṁ sâma gîyate* (ii. 51), *bhuvo viçveshu savaneshu yajñiyaḥ* (ii. 52: found in Rig-Veda, x. 50. 4), *dvish kṛṇute rûpâṇi* (ii. 63), *dyâush pitar yavaya adharân* (ii. 74), *vi sṛpo virapçin* (ii. 102), *tatarsha puroḍâçam* (iii. 32), *vârshyodakena yajeta* (iii. 32), *sahasravarcam iḍa atra* (iii. 54), *svargeṇa lokena* (iii. 78), *mahi tvam* (iv. 26), *jamadagnyâtharvaṇa* (iv. 67), and *vavṛdhânaḥ-iva* (iv. 85). In two instances these citations are directly referred to in a rule of the text (ii. 51): in all the other cases where the treatise itself mentions or implies words not found in the Atharvan,* it seems to me unnecessary to see anything but the tendency of the rule-makers to give their rules a wider bearing than the nature of the case required.

The identity or near correspondence of many of the fabricated illustrations furnished by the commentator with those given by the scholiasts to Pâṇini has been remarked in many instances,† and is a very noteworthy circumstance, as adding a new proof to those already elsewhere given of the more intimate relation of the grammatical system of our treatise than of that of any other of the Prâtiçâkhyas with the general Sanskrit grammar; and also, as indicating the antiquity and the persistence in use of at least a part of the examples selected to illustrate the Pâṇinean rules.

---

* They are i. 77, 88, 67, ii. 25, iii. 2, 92, iv. 28, 62.

† See under i. 58, ii. 14, 25, 40, 52, 62, 89, 90, iii. 27, 30, 32, 39, 40, 44, 46, 48, 50, 51, 63, 77, 90, iv. 23; analogies might also be pointed out in Pâṇini for the examples under i. 49, 98, ii. 6, 9, 26, iii. 42, and a more thorough and careful search than I have made would doubtless bring to light additional correspondences.

8. *The Consonantal Combinations of the Atharva-Veda, and their Phonetic Form according to the Rules of the Prâtiçâkhya.*

In the course of the notes upon certain portions of the text of the Prâtiçâkhya, I found it highly desirable, or almost necessary, to ascertain how many consonantal combinations of certain classes were to be found in the Atharva-Veda, and with what frequency they occurred. I was hence led to draw out a complete list of all the combinations of consonants which the text contains. Later, in examining and comparing with one another the nicer points in the phonetic theory of the treatise, particularly those which the written alphabet does not attempt to represent, I thought it worth while to make a practical application of all the phonetic rules to the collection of combinations already drawn up, writing each one out in the form which the rules would require it to assume. The result is the following scheme, which has seemed to me of sufficient interest to be worth appending to the present work.

To make out a complete list of the consonantal groups of our text is a work only of time and patience: to determine in every case what is the Prâtiçâkhya's doctrine as to its true phonetic form is less easy, since it involves the application of rules which sometimes appear to trench upon each other's spheres, and of which the reconciliation cannot always be satisfactorily effected. I have not, however, been willing to assent to the opinion which Weber (p. 247) expresses, that any of the modifications prescribed are absolutely inconsistent with, and exclude, one another. It is not easy to see how, in that case, the phonetical treatises should present them side by side without any apparent misgivings, and without notifying us that the application of certain ones exempts us from the necessity of making certain others. At any rate, I shall here follow as accurately as I can all the directions which our Prâtiçâkhya gives, expressing now and then such doubts as may suggest themselves respecting the mutual limitations of the rules: if the resulting combinations sometimes look strange, intricate beyond measure, and unutterable, the fault will lie with our Hindu authorities.

One circumstance deserves to be specially noted here: namely, that the loss of a rule or rules from the midst of the passage of the Prâtiçâkhya treating of duplication (see under iii. 28) doubtless loads our list with a few more doubled consonants than it should properly bear. I do not venture, however, to fill out the *lacuna* by conjecture: a suggestion or two will be made farther on as to what the lost rules may in part have contained.

I. Groups not liable to phonetic modification. These are, α, of two consonants: *cy, chy, jy, ts, pv, bv, bhv, mr, yy, ll, ll, ṅk, ṅkh, çc, çch, çy, çç, shṭ, shṭh, shṇ, shsh, st, sth, sn, ss, ḥp, ḥph*; β, of three consonants: *tsm, tsy, tsv, ṅkl, ṅkr, ṅksh, çcy, ççm, ççy, ççr, ççl, ççv, shṭy, shṭr, shṭv, shṭhy, shṇy, shṇv, sty, str, stv, sthy, ssk, sst, ssth, ssn, ssp, ssm, ssy, ssr, ssv, ḥpr, ḥpl*; γ, of four consonants: *ṅkshr, shṭry, sstr.*

This class, it will be noticed, is composed of combinations containing two consonants of the same organ (*sasthâna*), where, by iii. 30, no duplication is made—the constitution of the group being, at the same time, not such as to necessitate *abhinidhâna*, or any of the euphonic insertions taught at i. 99–104. To the groups containing, in the printed text, a final *visarjanîya* as their first member, I have given the form required by the Prâtiçâkhya at ii. 40, representing (after Müller's example) the *jihvâmûlîya* spirant by χ, and the *upadhmânîya* by φ, as I have also done in one or two isolated cases in the notes on the text.

II. Groups suffering *abhinidhâna* only (by i. 44). These are as follows: α, of two consonants: *kk, gg, ggh, ṅk, ṅkh, ṅg, ṅgh, ṅṅ, cc, cch, jj, ñc, ñch, ñj, ḍḍh, ṇṭh, ṇḍ, ṇḍh, tt, tth, dd, ddh, nt, nth, nd, ndh, nn, pp, bb, mp, mph, mb, mbh, mm*; β, of three consonants: *kksh, ṅkr, ṅkl, ṅkv, ṅksh, ṅkhy, ṅgy, ṅgr, ṅgl, ṅghr, cchr, cchl, cchv, jjy, jjv, ñchy, ñchr, ñchl, ñchv, ñjy, ḍḍhy, ṇḍy, tty, ttr, ttv, ddy, ddr, ddv, ddhy, ddhr, ddhv, nty, ntr, ntv, nts, ndy, ndr, ndv, ndhy, ndhr, ndhv, nny, mpr, mpl, mps, mbr, mbhr, mml*; γ, of four consonants: *ṅkshṇ, ṅkshv, ntry, ntst, ntsth, ntsp, ntsv, ndry.*

All these groups are of such a character that, by the rule already referred to (iii. 30), they are not subject to duplication of their initial consonant; which latter, however, by i. 44, must, as being followed by another mute, undergo the weakening process of *abhinidhâna*. Representing, as I propose to do, this weaker utterance by a type smaller and set a little lower, the pronunciation will be *kk, kksh, ṅkshṇ*, etc.

III. Groups suffering duplication only: 1st, with duplication of first consonant; α, groups of two consonants: *yv* (as *yyv*), *lk, lg, lp, lph, lb, lm, ly, lv, vn, vy, vr, çn, çp, çm, çr, çl, çv, shk, shp, shm, shy, shv, sk, sp, sph, sm, sy, sr, sv*; β, of three consonants: *lgv* (as *llgv*), *çrv, çvy, shkr, shpr, shmy, sphy, smy, svy*;—2nd, with duplication of second consonant; α, groups of two consonants: *hy* (as *hyy*), *hr, hl, hv*; β, of three consonants: *hvy* (as *hvvy*).

IV. Groups suffering duplication and *abhinidhâna*. 1st, with *abhinidhâna* of one consonant; α, groups of two consonants: *ky* (as *kky*), *kr, kl, kv, ksh, khy, gy, gr, gl, gv, ghr, ghv, ṅy, ṅv, jr, jv, ṭy, ḍy, ḍr, ḍv, ḍhy, ḍhr, ḍhv, ṇy, ṇv, ty, tr, tv, thy, thv, dy, dr, dv, dhy, dhr, dhv, ny, nr, nv, py, pr, pl, pç, ps, br, bl, bhy, bhr, my, mr, ml, lç, lh*; β, groups of three consonants: *kshṇ* (as *kkshṇ*), *kshm, kshy, kshv, ghry, ṅvr, try, trv, dvy, dvr, dhry, nvy, nvr, psy*; γ, of four consonants: *kshmy* (as *kkshmy*);—2nd, with *abhinidhâna* of two consonants; α, groups of two consonants: *kc* (as *kkc*), *kt, kth, kp, gj, gd, gdh, gb, gbh, ṅj, ṅt, ṅd, ṅdh, ṅn, ṅp, ṅm, ṅh, ṭṭ, ṭp, ḍb, ḍbh, ṇṇ, ṇm, tp, tph, dg, db, dbh, np, nb, nbh, nm, nh, pt, bj, bd, bdh, mṇ, mn*; β, of three consonants: *kty* (as *kkty*), *ktr, ktv, kthy, kpr, gdhy, gdhv, gbhy, ṅty, ṅtv, ṅdhy, ṅpr, ṭṭv, ṭpr, ḍbr, ḍbhy, ṇny, tpr, tpl, dbr, dbhy, dbhv, npr, nps, nbr, nbhr, nmy, pty, ptv, bdhv, mny.*

V. Groups suffering one or both the above modifications, with interposition of *yama*. 1st, with *yama* and double *abhinidhâna*; α, groups of two consonants: *jñ* (as *jj̄ñ*), *tn, thn, dn, dhn, pn*; β, of three consonants: *cñy* (as *cc̄ñy*), *jñy, tny, dhny, sthn* (as *sthth̄n*);—2nd, with *yama* of second consonant, and triple *abhinidhâna*: *ṅghn* (as *ṅghgh̄n*), *jjñ, ñjñ*;—3rd, with duplication of first consonant, *yama*, and triple *abhinidhâna*; α, groups of two consonants: *kṇ* (as *kkk̄ṇ*), *kn, km, khn, gn, gm, ghn, jm, ṭm, tm, dm, dhm, pn, bhṇ, bhn*; β, groups of three consonants: *kny* (as *kkk̄ny*), *gny, ghny, dmy, pny*;—4th, with duplication of first consonant, *yama* of second, and quadruple *abhinidhâna*: *kthn* (as *kktht̄hn*).

The Vâj. Pr. (iv. 111) has a rule expressly prohibiting duplication of the first consonant in a case like the last, where a consonant suffering *yama* follows it. Such a precept is very possibly one of those lost in the *lacuna* exhibited by our MS. after iii. 28; and I should hope that the Prâtiçâkhya might have extended the exemption from duplication also to any consonant of which *yama* is made, thus including our 3rd division, and allowing us to say simply *kṅn*, etc. There were enough of duplication, one would think.

VI. Groups suffering one or more of the above modifications, with interposition of *nâsikya*; viz. duplication of second consonant, *nâsikya*, and *abhinidhâna*; *α*, groups of two consonants: *hṇ* (as *h"ṇṇ*), *hn*, *hm*; *β*, groups of three consonants: *hṇy* (as *h"ṇṇy*), *hny*.

VII. Groups suffering the interposition of *svarabhakti* only: 1st, of the longer *svarabhakti*: *rç* (as *r°ç*), *rsh*;—2nd, of the shorter; *α*, of three consonants: *rjy* (as *r'jy*), *rts*, *rshṭ*, *rshṇ*; *β*, of four consonants: *rtsy* (as *r'tsy*), *rshṇy*.

I have assumed that, in the last class of cases, the rule forbidding the duplication of a consonant before another of the same class prevailed over that prescribing the duplication after the *r*. In the absence, however, of any direction as to this point in either the text or its commentary, I am by no means confident that my understanding is the true one.

VIII. Groups suffering *svarabhakti*, together with one or more of the preceding modifications. 1st, with *svarabhakti* (shorter) and *abhinidhâna*: *rtt* (as *r'tt*);—2nd, with *svarabhakti* and duplication; *a*, with longer *svarabhakti*: *rh* (as *r°hh*); *b*, with shorter; *α*, groups of two consonants: *ry* (as *r'yy*), *rl*, *rv*; *β*, groups of three consonants: *rvy* (as *r'vvy*), *rvr*, *rçv*, *rshm*, *rshy*, *rshv*, *rhy*, *rhr*, *rhv*;—3rd, with *svarabhakti* (shorter), duplication, and *abhinidhâna*; *α*, groups of two consonants: *rk* (as *r'kk*), *rg*, *rgh*, *rc*, *rch*, *rj*, *rṇ*, *rt*, *rth*, *rd*, *rdh*, *rn*, *rp*, *rb*, *rbh*, *rm*; *β*, groups of three consonants: *rksh* (as *r'kksh*), *rgy*, *rgr*, *rṇy*, *rty*, *rtr*, *rtv*, *rdy*, *rdr*, *rdv*, *rdhy*, *rdhr*, *rdhv*, *rny*, *rpy*, *rbr*, *rbhy*, *rbhr*, *rmy*; *γ*, groups of four consonants: *rkshy* (as *r'kkshy*), *rtry*;—4th, with *svarabhakti* (shorter), *yama*, and double *abhinidhâna*: *rtn* (as *r'ttn*), *rdhn*;—5th, with *svarabhakti*, duplication, *yama*, and triple *abhinidhâna*: *rtm* (as *r'ttm*).

Two or three of these combinations are liable to the doubt expressed after the last class. It may also excite a question whether *r* and *h* are to be duplicated when following one another: I have, however, in classifying such groups, interpreted the first part of rule iii. 31 as meaning '*r* and *h* are not liable to duplication when either is the first consonant of a group:' this would leave each free to be doubled when preceded by the other.

IX. Groups liable to *sphoṭana*, together with some of the preceding modifications: viz. to duplication, double *abhinidhâna*, and *sphoṭana*; *α*, groups of two consonants: *ṭ'k* (as *ṭṭ°k*), *t'k*, *t'kh*, *d'g*, *d'gh*, *p'k*, *p'ch*, *b'g*, *b'j*, *n'k*, *n'kh*, *n'g*, *n'gh*; *β*, groups of three consonants: *ṭ'kr* (as *ṭṭ°kr*), *ṭ'kv*, *t'ksh*, *d'gr*, *n'kr*, *n'ksh*, *n'gr*.

With regard to the question whether the groups commencing with *n* are to be ranked in this class, see the note to ii. 38. If denied *sphoṭana*, they would fall under IV. 2. *a*.

It would seem most natural to regard a mute as relieved by *sphoṭana* of its modification by *abhinidhâna;* and if any of these subtle euphonic changes mutually exclude one another, the two in question must certainly do so. It is not absolutely impossible that the Hindu grammarians may have regarded the name *sphoṭana* itself as implying suspension of *abhinidhâna*, and so have saved themselves the trouble of specifically teaching the fact of such suspension: yet I cannot think this likely, and so have combined the modifications as they are given above. The admission of a nullifying effect in the *sphoṭana* would remove merely the *abhinidhâna* of one consonant; changing, for instance, *dᵉg* to *ddᵉg*.

It remains only to take notice of a peculiar class of cases, where a final surd mute comes to stand before an initial sibilant, and their combination undergoes (according to the rules ii. 6, 8, 9) certain euphonic modifications, which are not usually represented in the manuscripts or in the edited text.

X. Combinations of a final surd mute with an initial sibilant. 1st, with aspiration of the surd: *t·s* (as *ths*), *t·sy*, *t·sr*, *t·sv*, *t·str;*—2nd, with aspiration, duplication, and *abhinidhâna: k·s* (as *kkhs*), *ṭ·ç*, *p·s*, *k·sth*, *p·sv;*—3rd, with insertion and *abhinidhâna: ṭ·s* (as *ṭṭs*), *ṭ·sv*, *ṅ·s* (as *ṅks*), *ṇ·sh*.

Akin with a part of this last class is the combination of *n* and *s*, with insertion of *t;* I have not brought it in here, because the inserted letter is regularly given in the printed text. It might be made a question whether all these inserted mutes are not liable to be converted into aspirates by the action of rule ii. 6, so that we ought to speak *ṭths*, *ṅkhs*, *nths*, etc. But, considering the want of explicitness of the treatise upon this point, and the uncertainty whether the inserted mute is properly to be regarded as appended, in the character of a final, to the former word, I have thought myself justified in adopting for the combinations in question the simpler mode of utterance.

In order to facilitate the determination, with regard to any given group, of its occurrence in the Atharvan text and of the phonetic form to which the rules of the Prâtiçâkhya reduce it, I add an alphabetical list of all the groups, each followed by its theoretic mode of pronunciation, and by a reference to a passage of the text where it occurs. As in the preceding examples, a sound which has suffered *abhinidhâna* is marked by a smaller letter; a *yama*, or nasal counterpart, has a straight line above it; the *nâsikya* is expressed by a superior *n;* the two *svarabhaktis*, shorter and longer, by a heavy dot and a little circle respectively; the *sphoṭana*, by a superior *ᵉ*. Where a group has the phonetic form given it only when composed of final and initial letters taken together, the division between final and initial is made by an interposed period.

I. Groups of two consonants:

kk (*kk*: iv. 19. 6), *kc* (*kkc*: i. 6. 3), *kṇ* (*kkk̄ṇ*: viii. 10. 18), *kt* (*kkt*: i. 23. 1), *kth* (*kkth*: i. 10. 3), *kn* (*kkk̄n*: i. 23. 1), *kp* (*kkp*: i. 14. 1), *km* (*kkk̄m*: i. 23. 1), *ky* (*kky*: ii. 33. 2), *kr* (*kkr*: i. 12. 1), *kl* (*kkl*: ii. 33. 3), *kv* (*kkv*: i. 27. 1), *kṣh* (*kkṣh*: i. 2. 3), *k·s* (*kkhs*: iii. 1. 4); *khn* (*kkhk̄hn*: v. 31. 8), *khy* (*kkhy*: iii. 3. 2); *gg* (*gg*: ii. 36. 7), *ggh* (*ggh*: iii. 19. 6), *gj* (*ggj*: iv. 15. 2), *gd* (*ggd*: iv. 3. 1), *gdh* (*ggdh*: i. 10. 2), *gn* (*ggḡn*: i. 6. 2), *gb* (*ggb*: iii. 27. 6), *gbh* (*ggbh*: iii. 6. 6), *gm* (*ggḡm*: ii. 2. 3), *gy* (*ggy*: vii.

44. 1), *gr* (*ggr*: i. 10. 1), *gl* (*ggl*: iv. 4. 7), *gv* (*ggv*: iv. 19. 5); *ghn* (*gghghn*: i. 28. 4), *ghr* (*gghr*: iv. 3. 1), *ghv* (*gghv*: xix. 55. 5); *ṅk* (*ṅk*: i. 12. 2), *ṅkh* (*ṅkh*: iv. 10. 1), *ṅg* (*ṅg*: i. 12. 2), *ṅgh* (*ṅgh*: iv. 11. 10), *ṅṅ* (*ṅṅ*: v. 22. 2), *ṅj* (*ṅṅj*: v. 4. 8), *ṅṭ* (*ṅṅṭ*: xvii. 17), *ṅd* (*ṅṅd*: xiii. 2. 20), *ṅdh* (*ṅṅdh*: i. 25. 1), *ṅn* (*ṅṅn*: ix. 1. 3), *ṅp* (*ṅṅp*: xii. 2. 1), *ṅm* (*ṅṅm*: v. 1. 1), *ṅy* (*ṅṅy*: v. 26. 12), *ṅv* (*ṅṅv*: iii. 4. 1), *ṅ's* (*ṅks*: iv. 11. 8), *ṅh* (*ṅṅh*: iv. 19. 7).

cc (*cc*: iv. 1. 3), *cch* (*cch*: iii. 12. 3), *cy* (*cy*: i. 3. 6); *chy* (*chy*: ix. 5. 4); *jj* (*jj*: i. 11. 4), *jñ* (*jjñ*: i. 7. 6), *jm* (*jjm*: iii. 30. 6), *jy* (*jy*: i. 1. 3), *jr* (*jjr*: i. 7. 7), *jv* (*jjv*: iii. 24. 2); *ñc* (*ñc*: i. 4. 1), *ñch* (*ñch*: iv. 3. 4), *ñj* (*ñj*: i. 2. 4).

ṭ'k (*ṭṭ'k*: iv. 18. 3), *ṭṭ* (*ṭṭ*: i. 11. 1), *ṭp* (*ṭṭp*: v. 14. 8), *ṭm* (*ṭṭm*: viii. 6. 15), *ṭy* (*ṭṭy*: xix. 44. 6), *ṭ'ç* (*ṭṭhç*: ix. 5. 21), *ṭ's* (*ṭṭs*: xi. 1. 2); *ḍḍh* (*ḍḍh*: vii. 97. 7), *ḍb* (*ḍḍb*: vi. 96. 2), *ḍbh* (*ḍḍbh*: xii. 2. 48), *ḍy* (*ḍḍy*: ii. 3. 1), *ḍr* (*ḍḍr*: xi. 7. 11), *ḍv* (*ḍḍv*: iii. 11. 5); *ḍhy* (*ḍḍhy*: i. 18. 4), *ḍhr* (*ḍḍhr*: vii. 95. 3), *ḍhv* (*ḍḍhv*: viii. 8. 11); *ṇṭh* (*ṇṭh*: x. 9. 15), *ṇḍ* (*ṇḍ*: ii. 7. 3), *ṇḍh* (*ṇḍh*: xix. 29. 6), *ṇn* (*ṇṇn*: v. 20. 11), *ṇm* (*ṇṇm*: i. 13. 3), *ṇy* (*ṇṇy*: i. 9. 2), *ṇv* (*ṇṇv*: i. 13. 4).

t'k (*tt'k*: i. 24. 2), *t'kh* (*tt'kh*: iv. 11. 10), *tt* (*tt*: i. 9. 1), *tth* (*tth*: i. 8. 4), *tn* (*ttn*: i. 9. 2), *tp* (*ttp*: i. 12. 2), *tph* (*ttph*: vi. 124. 2), *tm* (*ttm*: i. 18. 3), *ty* (*tty*: i. 7. 4), *tr* (*ttr*: i. 1. 1), *tv* (*ttv*: i. 7. 6), *ts* (*ts*: i. 15. 3), *t's* (*ths*: i. 13. 3); *thn* (*tthn*: ii. 30. 1), *thy* (*tthy*: iii. 4. 7), *thv* (*tthv*: xiii. 2. 22); *dg* (*ddg*: i. 27. 3), *d'g* (*dd'g*: i. 2. 3), *d'gh* (*dd'gh*: v. 21. 8), *dd* (*dd*: i. 28. 1), *ddh* (*ddh*: i. 7. 7), *dn* (*ddn*: vii. 45. 2), *db* (*ddb*: ii. 29. 1), *dbh* (*ddbh*: i. 20. 1), *dm* (*ddm*: i. 2. 1), *dy* (*ddy*: i. 1. 1), *dr* (*ddr*: i. 3. 8), *dv* (*ddv*: i. 2. 2); *dhn* (*ddhdhn*: i. 14. 1), *dhm* (*ddhdhm*: i. 22. 1), *dhy* (*ddhy*: i. 8. 2), *dhr* (*ddhr*: iii. 12. 2), *dhv* (*ddhv*: i. 4. 1); *n'k* (*nn'k*: i. 14. 2), *n'kh* (*nn'kh*: v. 19. 3), *n'g* (*nn'g*: ii. 1. 2), *n'gh* (*nn'gh*: iii. 10. 11), *nt* (*nt*: i. 15. 2), *nth* (*nth*: i. 27. 1), *nd* (*nd*: i. 7. 1), *ndh* (*ndh*: i. 4. 3), *nn* (*nn*: i. 7. 5), *np* (*nnp*: i. 25. 1), *nb* (*nnb*: v. 26. 6), *nbh* (*nnbh*: ii. 8. 4), *nm* (*nnm*: i. 10. 4), *ny* (*nny*: i. 2. 1), *nr* (*nnr*: ii. 35. 2), *nv* (*nnv*: i. 1. 1), *n'sh* (*ntsh*: viii. 9. 17), *n's* (*nts*: viii. 5. 16), *nh* (*nnh*: i. 12. 2).

p'k (*pp'k*: viii. 9. 20), *p'ch* (*pp'ch*: vi. 48. 3), *pt* (*ppt*: i. 1. 1), *pn* (*pppn*: ii. 11. 1), *pp* (*pp*: iii. 17. 5), *pm* (*ppm*: iii. 31. 1), *py* (*ppy*: i. 14. 3), *pr* (*ppr*: i. 7. 2), *pl* (*ppl*: iii. 6. 7), *pv* (*ppv*: iii. 2. 5), *pç* (*ppç*: vi. 2. 2), *ps* (*pps*: ii. 2. 3), *p's* (*pphs*: i. 6. 2); *b'g* (*bb'g*: xviii. 2. 6), *bj* (*bbj*: viii. 4. 1), *b'j* (*bb'j*: xix. 21. 1), *bd* (*bbd*: ii. 24. 6), *bdh* (*bbdh*: v. 18. 4), *bb* (*bb*: xix. 21. 1), *br* (*bbr*: i. 6. 2), *bl* (*bbl*: xi. 9. 19), *bv* (*bv*: xiii. 1. 15); *bhṇ* (*bbhbhṇ*: iii. 8. 6), *bhn* (*bbhbhn*: x. 3. 3), *bhy* (*bbhy*: i. 4. 3), *bhr* (*bbhr*: i. 1. 1), *bhv* (*bhv*: v. 2. 7); *mṇ* (*mmṇ*: ii. 36. 2), *mn* (*mmn*: ii. 25. 2), *mp* (*mp*: iii. 26. 5), *mph* (*mph*: x. 6. 8), *mb* (*mb*: i. 4. 1), *mbh* (*mbh*: i. 6. 2), *mm* (*mm*: iii. 30. 1), *my* (*mmy*: i. 11. 2), *mr* (*mmr*: ii. 24. 3), *ml* (*mml*: viii. 6. 2), *mv* (*mv*: vi. 56. 3).

yy (*yy*: i. 1. 3), *yv* (*yyv*: i. 11. 4); *rk* (*r'kk*: iii. 3. 2), *rg* (*r'gg*: vi. 69. 2), *rgh* (*r'ggh*: i. 22. 2), *rc* (*r'cc*: i. 2. 3), *rch* (*r'cch*: xx. 34. 12), *rj* (*r'jj*: i. 2. 1), *rṇ* (*r'ṇṇ*: i. 10. 4), *rt* (*r'tt*: i. 28. 2), *rth* (*r'tth*: i. 7. 6), *rd* (*r'dd*: i. 22. 2), *rdh* (*r'ddh*: i. 9. 3), *rn* (*r'nn*: i. 1. 3), *rp* (*r'pp*: i. 2. 1), *rb* (*r'bb*: i. 1. 1), *rbh* (*r'bbh*: i. 11. 2), *rm* (*r'mm*: i. 4. 1), *ry* (*r'yy*: i. 3. 5), *rl* (*r'll*: i. 18. 1), *rv* (*r'vv*: i. 2. 2), *rç* (*r°ç*: iv. 4. 7), *rsh* (*r°sh*: i. 5. 4), *rh* (*r°hh*: i. 8. 4); *lk* (*llk*: v. 17. 4), *lg* (*llg*: ii. 36. 1), *lp* (*llp*: iii. 8. 1), *lph* (*llph*:

x. 2. 1), *lb* (*llb*: iv. 2. 8), *lm* (*llm*: ii. 30. 3), *ly* (*lly*: vi. 11. 3), *ll* (*ll*: ii. 32. 5), *l̄l* (*l̄l*: iv. 36. 8), *lv* (*llv*: ii. 31. 1), *lç* (*llç*: vi. 30. 2), *lh* (*llh*: v. 22. 5); *vn* (*vvn*: vi. 2. 3), *vy* (*vvy*: i. 3. 1), *vr* (*vvr*: ii. 1. 1).

χk (*χk*: i. 4. 3), *χkh* (*χkh*: i. 6. 4); *çc* (*çc*: i. 5. 4), *çch* (*çch*: ix. 3. 14), *çn* (*ççn*: i. 11. 4), *çp* (*ççp*: iv. 5. 6), *çm* (*ççm*: i. 2. 2), *çy* (*çy*: i. 7. 5), *çr* (*ççr*: i. 1. 2), *çl* (*ççl*: i. 31. 3), *çv* (*ççv*: i. 1. 1), *çç* (*çç*: i. 5. 2); *shk* (*shshk*: i. 11. 3), *shṭ* (*shṭ*: i. 3. 1), *shṭh* (*shṭh*: i. 2. 4), *shṇ* (*shṇ*: i. 13. 4), *shp* (*shshp*: i. 1. 2), *shm* (*shshm*: i. 12. 3), *shy* (*shshy*: i. 14. 1), *shv* (*shshv*: i. 2. 1), *shsh* (*shsh*: xi. 5. 2); *sk* (*ssk*: i. 13. 2), *st* (*st*: i. 1. 2), *sth* (*sth*: i. 16. 1), *sn* (*sn*: v. 5. 8), *sp* (*ssp*: i. 1. 1), *sph* (*ssph*: iv. 7. 3), *sm* (*ssm*: i. 1. 4), *sy* (*ssy*: i. 2. 2), *sr* (*ssr*: i. 2. 4), *sv* (*ssv*: i. 2. 3), *ss* (*ss*: i. 4. 2); *φp* (*φp*: i. 1. 1), *φph* (*φph*: iii. 15. 4).

hṇ (*h'ṇṇ*: ii. 34. 5), *hn* (*h'nn*: ii. 33. 3), *hm* (*h'mm*: i. 8. 4), *hy* (*hyy*: i. 8. 4), *hr* (*hrr*: iv. 15. 14), *hl* (*hll*: xviii. 3. 60), *hv* (*hvv*: i. 4. 3).

II. Groups of three consonants:

kksh (*kksh*: xix. 24. 2), *kty* (*kkty*: i. 12. 3), *ktr* (*kktr*: iii. 30. 6), *ktv* (*kktv*: iv. 31. 4), *kthy* (*kkthy*: vi. 9. 1), *kthn* (*kkthn*: xx. 136. 4), *kny* (*kkny*: i. 23. 3), *kpr* (*kkpr*: ix. 1. 10), *kshṇ* (*kkshṇ*: ii. 33. 3), *kshm* (*kkshm*: vii. 89. 1), *kshy* (*kkshy*: i. 8. 3), *kshv* (*kkshv*: ii. 2. 1), *ksth* (*kksth*: xx. 134. 3); *gdhy* (*ggdhy*: iv. 33. 1), *gdhv* (*ggdhv*: v. 16. 10), *gny* (*ggny*: ix. 1. 12), *gbhy* (*ggbhy*: x. 6. 12); *ghny* (*gghny*: iii. 30. 1), *ghry* (*gghry*: xii. 2. 4); *ṅkr* (*ṅkr*: v. 20. 9), *ṅkl* (*ṅkl*: vi. 136. 1), *ṅkv* (*ṅkv*: x. 7. 1), *ṅksh* (*ṅksh*: i. 5. 4), *ṅkhy* (*ṅkhy*: iv. 16. 5), *ṅgy* (*ṅgy*: iv. 37. 2), *ṅgr* (*ṅgr*: xiv. 1. 36), *ṅgl* (*ṅgl*: iv. 38. 3), *ṅghn* (*ṅghghn*: vi. 76. 4), *ṅghr* (*ṅghr*: xiii. 1. 46), *ṅty* (*ṅkty*: xiii. 3. 5), *ṅtv* (*ṅktv*: xviii. 2. 60), *ṅdhy* (*ṅdhy*: viii. 3. 6), *ṅpr* (*ṅkpr*: x. 8. 18), *ṅsr* (*ṅksr*: xv. 18. 5).

cchr (*cchr*: iii. 12. 2), *cchl* (*cchl*: x. 3. 1), *cchv* (*cchv*: xviii. 8. 18), *cñy* (*ccñy*: xii. 4. 30), *jjñ* (*jjñ*: ii. 12. 7), *jjy* (*jjy*: vi. 61. 1), *jjv* (*jjv*: iii. 11. 8), *jñy* (*jjñy*: xiv. 1. 44); *ñchy* (*ñchy*: xi. 9. 17), *ñchr* (*ñchr*: iv. 8. 3), *ñchl* (*ñchl*: xviii. 1. 33), *ñchv* (*ñchv*: xi. 10. 23), *ñjñ* (*ñjñ*: iii. 14. 4), *ñjy* (*ñjy*: i. 9. 1).

ṭtv (*ṭṭtv*: iii. 4. 1), *ṭpr* (*ṭṭpr*: xi. 4. 12), *ṭsv* (*ṭṭsv*: viii. 9. 9); *ḍḍhy* (*ḍḍhy*: xi. 1. 31), *ḍbr* (*ḍḍbr*: xi. 8. 30), *ḍbhy* (*ḍḍbhy*: iii. 3. 4); *ṇḍy* (*ṇḍy*: vi. 136. 2), *ṇny* (*ṇṇy*: vi. 77. 2).

t'kr (*tt'kr*: ii. 12. 6), *t'kv* (*tt'kv*: ix. 9. 17), *t'ksh* (*tt'ksh*: ii. 8. 2), *tty* (*tty*: v. 6. 10), *ttr* (*ttr*: vi. 107. 1), *ttv* (*ttv*: i. 23. 4), *tny* (*ttny*: ii. 12. 1), *tpr* (*ttpr*: ii. 34. 2), *tpl* (*ttpl*: v. 5. 5), *try* (*ttry*: ii. 8. 2), *trv* (*ttrv*: vi. 40. 2), *tsm* (*tsm*: vii. 82. 2), *tsy* (*tsy*: xi. 3. 37), *t'sy* (*thsy*: iii. 13. 4), *t'sr* (*thsr*: xii. 4. 34), *tsv* (*tsv*: ii. 5. 4), *t'sv* (*thsv*: iii. 3. 1); *d'gr* (*dd'gr*: ii. 10. 6), *ddy* (*ddy*: iv. 19. 6), *ddr* (*ddr*: ii. 10. 1), *ddv* (*ddv*: vi. 107. 2), *ddhy* (*ddhy*: xii. 2. 3), *ddhr* (*ddhr*: vi. 87. 3), *ddhv* (*ddhv*: iv. 14. 2), *dbr* (*ddbr*: i. 32. 1), *dbhy* (*ddbhy*: ii. 33. 5), *dbhv* (*ddbhv*: xviii. 4. 26), *dmy* (*ddmy*: v. 23. 13), *dvy* (*ddvy*: iv. 19. 6), *dvr* (*ddvr*: vii. 90. 1); *dhny* (*ddhny*: iv. 1. 1), *dhry* (*ddhry*: iv. 29. 4); *n'kr* (*nn'kr*: ii. 31. 2), *n'ksh* (*nn'ksh*: x. 4. 8), *n'gr* (*nn'gr*: viii. 7. 11), *nty* (*nty*: i. 3. 7), *ntr* (*ntr*: i. 3. 6), *ntv* (*ntv*: i. 4. 2), *nts* (*nts*: viii. 6. 8), *ndy* (*ndy*: ii. 14. 2), *ndr* (*ndr*: viii. 8. 9), *ndv* (*ndv*: ii. 11. 3), *ndhy* (*ndhy*: vi. 25. 3), *ndhr* (*ndhr*: iv. 16. 7), *ndhv* (*ndhv*: v. 13. 7), *nny* (*nny*: v. 5. 5), *npr* (*nnpr*: i. 10. 2), *nps* (*nnps*: x. 3. 14), *nbr* (*nnbr*: i. 29. 1), *nbhr* (*nnbhr*: v. 22. 12), *nmy* (*nnmy*: xi. 10. 13), *nvy* (*nnvy*: iv. 3. 1), *nvr* (*nnvr*: xv. 3. 1).

ply (*pply*: i. 28. 4), *ptv* (*pptv*: iv. 5. 6), *pny* (*ppṇy*: iv. 9. 6), *psy* (*ppsy*: x. 9. 7), *psv* (*pphsv*: i. 4. 4); *bdhv* (*bbdhv*: i. 8. 2); *mny* (*mmny*: iv. 7. 5), *mpr* (*mpr*: i. 7. 4), *mpl* (*mpl*: ii. 33. 4), *mps* (*mps*: x. 5. 43), *mbr* (*mbr*: i. 6. 4), *mbhr* (*mbhr*: vi. 120. 2), *mml* (*mml*: vi. 66. 3).

rksh (*r'kksh*: xviii. 2. 31), *rgy* (*r'ggy*: ix. 2. 14), *rgr* (*r'ggr*: iii. 2. 5), *rjy* (*rjjy*: vii. 22. 1) *rṇy* (*r'ṇṇy*: ii. 25. 1), *rtt* (*r'tt*: ii. 7. 5), *rtm* (*r'ttm*: i. 1. 3), *rtm* (*r'ttm*: iii. 8. 6), *rty* (*r'tty*: iii. 31. 2), *rtr* (*r'ttr*: x. 1. 30), *rtv* (*r'ttv*: i. 4. 3), *rts* (*r'ts*: v. 7. 1), *rdy* (*r'ddy*: vii. 6. 1), *rdr* (*r'ddr*: vii. 28. 1), *rdv* (*r'ddv*: v. 12. 5), *rdhn* (*r'ddhn*: iv. 39. 1), *rdhy* (*r'ddhy*: vi. 94. 3), *rdhr* (*r'ddhr*: vi. 88. 1), *rdhv* (*r'ddhv*: iii. 26. 6), *rny* (*r'nny*: ii. 14. 3), *rpy* (*r'ppy*: ix. 2. 22), *rbr* (*r'bbr*: iii. 20. 5), *rbhy* (*r'bbhy*: i. 12. 4), *rbhr* (*r'bbhr*: v. 1. 1), *rmy* (*r'mmy*: iv. 5. 5), *rvy* (*r'vvy*: iii. 17. 3), *rvr* (*r'vvr*: i. 16. 1), *rçv* (*r'ççv*: ii. 33. 3), *rshṭ* (*r'shṭ*: iv. 18. 7), *rshṇ* (*r'shṇ*: x. 2. 1), *rshm* (*r'shshm*: iii. 4. 2), *rshy* (*r'shshy*: vi. 16. 1), *rshv* (*r'shshv*: xviii. 3. 2), *rhy* (*r'hhy*: iii. 1. 2), *rhr* (*r'hhr*: xii. 5. 29), *rhv* (*r'hhv*: vii. 58. 3); *lgv* (*llgv*: xii. 3. 32).

ṅkt (*ṅkt*: ii. 2. 5), *ṅkr* (*ṅkr*: ii. 32. 1), *ṅksh* (*ṅksh*: ii. 8. 5); *çcy* (*çcy*: x. 1. 13), *çrv* (*ççrv*: xiv. 2. 26), *çvy* (*ççvy*: viii. 3. 15), *ççm* (*ççm*: v. 31. 8), *ççy* (*ççy*: v. 5. 6), *ççr* (*ççr*: iii. 17. 2), *ççl* (*ççl*: v. 20. 7), *ççv* (*ççv*: viii. 5. 11); *shkr* (*shshkr*: ii. 34. 1), *shṭy* (*shṭy*: i. 12. 1), *shṭr* (*shṭr*: viii. 2. 27), *shṭv* (*shṭv*: i. 22. 3), *shṭhy* (*shṭhy*: i. 9. 3), *shṇy* (*shṇy*: i. 3. 1), *shṇv* (*shṇv*: iii. 19. 5), *shpr* (*shshpr*: iv. 10. 4), *shmy* (*shshmy*: ii. 32. 3); *sty* (*sty*: ii. 32. 3), *str* (*str*: i. 8. 1), *stv* (*stv*: i. 10. 3), *sthn* (*sthn*: iv. 12. 1), *sthy* (*sthy*: iv. 12. 3), *sphy* (*ssphy*: xi. 3. 9), *smy* (*ssmy*: iv. 32. 6), *svy* (*ssvy*: v. 28. 10), *sk* (*sk*: ix. 7. 3), *sst* (*sst*: i. 8. 3), *ssth* (*ssth*: i. 31. 2), *ssn* (*ssn*: vi. 115. 3), *ssp* (*ssp*: iv. 16. 4), *ssm* (*ssm*: v. 22. 10), *ssy* (*ssy*: ii. 10. 7), *ssr* (*ssr*: ii. 3. 3), *ssv* (*ssv*: i. 19. 3); *ḥpr* (*ḥpr*: i. 7. 5), *ḥpl* (*ḥpl*: ix. 7. 12).

hṇy (*h"ṇṇy*: x. 8. 16), *hny* (*h"nny*: vi. 110. 3), *hvy* (*hvvy*: iv. 17. 2).

III. Groups of four consonants:

kshmy (*kkshmy*: i. 18. 1), *ṅkshṇ* (*ṅkshṇ*: v. 20. 1), *ṅkshv* (*ṅkshv*: iii. 12. 6); *t'str* (*thstr*: vi. 11. 1), *ntry* (*ntry*: ii. 31. 4), *ntst* (*ntst*: ii. 35. 2), *ntsth* (*ntsth*: v. 2. 4), *ntsp* (*ntsp*: viii. 8. 7), *ntsv* (*ntsv*: iv. 5. 1), *ndry* (*ndry*: x. 2. 9); *rkshy* (*r'kkshy*: vii. 85. 1), *rtvy* (*r'ttvy*: viii. 10. 22), *rtsy* (*r'tsy*: x. 1. 21), *rshṇy* (*r'shṇy*: vi. 24. 2); *ṅkshv* (*ṅkshv*: viii. 8. 7), *shṭry* (*shṭry*: iv. 1. 2), *sstr* (*sstr*: vii. 95. 3).

There is no group of five consonants in the Atharva-Veda: if, however, the order of two words in i. 8. 1 had been reversed, we should have had a group of six, viz. *ntstry* (*pumānt stry akaḥ*). The fact deserves to be remarked here, although familiar to all students of the Vedas, that by no means all the groups of four and three consonants, or even of two, were, in all the cases of their occurrence, actually such groups to the makers of the hymns: in a majority of the passages where a *y* or *v* follows two or three other consonants, and very frequently where they follow a single consonant only, they are, as the metre shows, to be read as *i* or *u*, or *ī* or *ū*, constituting separate syllables. Those combinations which seem most difficult of enunciation are thus often relieved of a part or the whole of their harshness. Rarely (as at v. 28. 10), an apparent group of three consonants is to be resolved into two separate syllables.

4. *Longer Metrical Passages cited by the Commentator.*

In the notes on the text, I have passed over two extracts of considerable extent, made by the commentator from unnamed sources, and I now offer here the text of them. The first is found under rule i. 10; it runs as follows:

apara âha: caturtho hakâreṇe 'ti:

I\. 1. *pañcâi 'va prathamân sparçân âhur eke manîshiṇaḥ,*
teshâṁ guṇopasaṁcayâd ânyobhâvyaṁ pravartate.
2\. *jihvâmûlîyaçashasâ upadhmânîyopañcamâḥ,*
etâir guṇâiḥ samanvitâ dvitîyâ iti tân viduḥ.
3\. *ta eva saha ghosheṇa tṛtîyâ iti tân viduḥ,*
ûshmaṇâ ca dvitîyena caturthâ iti tân viduḥ.
4\. *prathamâḥ saha ghosheṇa yadâ syur anunâsikâḥ,*
tân âhuḥ pañcamân sparçâṅs tathâ varṇaguṇâḥ smṛtâḥ.
5\. *na tu hi vyañjanasaṁdhir asaṁyogo bhavet punaḥ,*
saṁyogaç ca prasajyeta kramo vâcyaḥ punar bhavet.
6\. *dvitvaprâptiç caturtheshu hakâro hy atra kâraṇa,*
dvitîyeshu tu tan nâ 'sti sasthâne tannivâraṇât.
7\. *pippalyâdishu yad dvitvaṁ svare chabdavidhiḥ kṛtaḥ,*
jñâpakaṅç ca dvitîyânâṁ dvitvaprâpter iti sthitiḥ.
8\. *guṇamâtrâ nu tatrâi 'shâm apûrṇaṁ vyañjanaṁ kvacit,*
apûrṇe vyañjane kramaḥ saṁyogaç ca kuto bhavet.
9\. *pṛthaktvatvâni paçyâmas tulyaliṅgâni kâni cit,*
na teshâṁ liṅgasâmânyâd ekatvam pratijâyate.
10\. *sattvapṛthaktvâd dvâiliṅgyaṁ yad eteshu nibaddha tat,*
tathâi 'va pañcavargeṇa guṇamâtreṇa tulyatâ.

The other passage is the commentator's introduction to the fourth chapter:

samâsâvagrahavigrahân pade yatho 'vâca chandasi çâkaṭâyanaḥ; tathâ vakshyâmi catushṭayaṁ padaṁ nâmâkhyâtopasarganipâtânâm.

II\. 1. *âkhyâtaṁ yat kriyâvâci nâma sattvâkhyam ucyate,*
nipâtâç câdayaḥ sarva'[1] *upasargâs tu prâdayaḥ.*
2\. *nâma nâmnâ 'nudâttena samastaṁ prakṛtisvaram,*
na yushmadasmadvacanâni na câ "mantritam ishyate.
3\. *nâmâ 'nudâttam prakṛtisvaro gatir anucco vâ nâma cet syâd*
udâttam, kriyâyoge gatiḥ pûrvaḥ,[2]
samâso yâvanto 'nuccâḥ samarthâṅs tân samasyate.
4\. *yatrâ 'neko 'nudâtto 'sti paraç ca prakṛtisvaraḥ,*
âkhyâtaṁ nâma vâ yat syât sarvam eva samasyate.
5\. *sopasargaṁ tu yan nîcâiḥ pûrvaṁ vâ yadi vâ param,*[3]
udâttena samasyante tathâi 'va supratishṭhitam.
6\. *udâttas tu nipâto yaḥ so 'nudâttaḥ kvacid bhavet,*
samasyante tathâ vidhim itihâso nidarçanam.
7\. *naghârishâṁ sumake 'ty evamâdiny udâharet,*
sahe 'ty anenâ 'nudâttaṁ paraṁ nâma samasyate.
8\. *anudâttena co 'dâttam svabhâvo yatra co 'cyate,*
sahasûktavâkaḥ sântardeçâḥ çatakrato nidarçanam.

---

[1] *câdayo sarva.* [2] *gatishûrvaḥ.* [3] *pûrvaṁvâyadivâparaḥ.*

9. *anudâtto gatir*[1] *madhye pûrvaparâu prakṛtisvarâu,*
pûrveṇa vigrahas tatra purashe 'dhi samâhitâḥ.
10. *udâttânugatir yatrá 'nudâttam paraṁ padam,*
pûrveṇa vigrahas tatra saṁ subhûtyâ nidarçanam.
11. *yatro 'bhe prakṛtisvare pûrvaṁ yac ca paraṁ ca yat,*
varjayitvâ "dyudâttâni sarvam eva samasyate.
12. *nâ "khyâtâni samasyante na câ "khyâtaṁ ca nâma ca,*
nâma nâmno 'pasargâis tu sambandhârthaṁ[2] *samasyate.*
13. *na yushmadasmadâdeçâ anudâttât padât pare,*
nâmopasargagatibhiḥ[3] *samasyante kadâ cana.*
14. *mâm anu pra te pra vâm ityevamâdiny udâharet,*
etadarçanudâttâni idam asya tathâi va ca.
15. *nâmopasargagatibhiḥ*[3] *samasyante kadâ cana,*
bṛhann eshâṁ ya enâṁ vanim âyanti pary enân pary asye 'ti nidarçanam.
16. *anudâtto gatiḥ sarvâiḥ samastaḥ svaritâdibhiḥ,*
saṁsrâvyeṇa[4] *durarmaṇya âcârye 'ti nidarçanam.*
17. *pra-parâ-ni-sam-â-dur-nir-avâ-'dhi-pari-vini ca,*
aty-abhy-api[5]*-sû-'d-apâ ya upâ*[6]*-'nu-pratir viṅçatiḥ.*
18. *ekâkshare udâttâ âdyudâttâs tathâ 'pare,*
abhî 'ty anta upasargâḥ kriyâyoge gatis tathâ.
19. *âdyudâttâ daçâi 'teshâm uccâ ekâksharâ nava,*
viṅçater upasargâṇâm antodâttas tv 'abhî 'ty ayam.
20. *achâ-'ram-astam-hasta-lâṅgûla*[7]*-tiraḥ-puraḥ*[8]*-punar-namaḥ*[9]*-*
-kshiti-râti[10]*-phali-hiñ-srug*[11]*-vashaṭ-prâdur*[12]*-ulâ-kakojâ-*
-svâhâ-svadhâ-çrat-svaralala 'ty upasargavṛttîni yathâstâta-
svarâṇi.

Of this passage, the preliminary sentence (or verse) has been already translated, in the introductory note to the fourth chapter. The first verse gives a definition of the four parts of speech—or rather, a definition only of the verb and noun, the prepositions and particles being referred to as the two series commencing respectively with *pra* and *ca* (compare Pâṇ. i. 4. 57, 58, and the lists of prepositions in the other Prâtiçâkhyas). Thenceforward, from the second to the sixteenth verse, inclusive, the extract is occupied with giving directions for the combination or non-combination, in the *pada*-text, of the various parts of speech, as they stand in juxtaposition with one another in connected discourse. The text of the Veda is assumed as existing in an utterly disjoined state, each independent element being known in its phonetic form (including its accent), and as such and such a part of speech; and the attempt is made to define the cases in which the elements form compounds with one another. The problem, however, is evidently much too extensive and difficult to be so briefly solved—if, indeed, any solution of it is possible without taking into account also the inflectional forms of the nouns and verbs—and the system of rules laid down is only fragmentary: but I have not taken the trouble to test them by the text, so as to

[1] *anudâttonugatir.*
[2] *sarvasadhârthaṁ.*
[3] *samasy.*
[4] *saṁsadvyaṇi.*
[5] *abhyapi.*
[6] *apdyânuiîyapd.*
[7] *hastolâṅgûlaṁ.*
[8] *puraḥ.*
[9] *puraḥ.*
[10] *nikshiti.*
[11] *hiñsvaḥ.*
[12] *prâdur.*

determine where their deficiencies lie. The second verse informs us that a noun which has its natural accent is compounded with another which is unaccented, except in the case of an enclitic pronoun of the first and second persons, or a vocative; thus we must combine *tri : saptā́ḥ* (i. 1. 1), *çatá : vṛshṇyam* (i. 3. 1), into *tri-saptā́ḥ*, *çatá-vṛshṇyam*. The next verse and the one following treat of the combination of nouns and verbs with prepositions and other words employed as prepositions: these receive here and in what follows the name *gati*, which Pāṇini also (i. 4. 60 etc.) uses. Verse five has for its subject such compounds as are instanced by *súpratishṭhitam* (xii. 1. 63: p. *sú-pratishṭhitam*). The sixth verse applies to compounds into which a particle enters as a constituent, and cites *itihāsáḥ* (xv. 6. 4: p. *itiha-āsáḥ*) as an example; and the first line of the next verse adds the farther instances *naghārishā́m* (viii. 2. 6; 7. 6: p. *nagha-rishā́m*) and *sā́saha* (vi. 64. 3; p. *sá-saha*). Hence to the end of verse 8, compounds with *saha* (and its substitute *sa*) are defined, the chosen illustrations being *sahásūktavākaḥ* (vii. 97. 6: p. *sahá-sūktavākaḥ*) and *sā́ntardeçāḥ* (ix. 5. 37: p. *sá-antardeçāḥ*): *çatakrato* is also added, but apparently only by a blunder; or rather, the reading is probably false and corrupt, as the metre helps to show. Verse 9 prescribes the mode of combination in such a case as *púrushā́ 'dhi samā́hitāḥ* (x. 7. 15), where an unaccented preposition stands between two others, both of which have their proper accent. The next verse takes for its example *sáṁ súbhūtyā* (iii. 14. 1), where two accented prepositions precede an unaccented noun, and the former of them is to be made independent. Verse 11 has no example, and, although easily enough translated, its meaning is to me obscure. We are then told what combinations are possible: verbs are not compounded with verbs or with nouns; but nouns with nouns and with prepositions. A verse and a half follows, denying the enclitic forms of the first and second personal pronouns the capability of entering into compounds, and citing as instances *mā́m ánu prá te* (iii. 18. 6) and *prá vām* (e. g. vii. 73. 5): and three additional lines extend the same exception to the enclitic demonstrative pronouns, and give the examples *bṛhánn eshām* (iv. 16. 1), *yá enáṁ vanim āyánti* (xii. 4. 11), *páry enān* (ix. 2. 5), and *páry asya* (xv. 12. 7). The sixteenth verse declares an unaccented preposition capable of composition with a following word, however accented, but illustrates only their composition with a circumflexed word, as *samudravyáṇa* (e. g. i. 15. 1), *durarmaṇyā̀ḥ* (xvi. 2. 1), and *ācāryā̀ḥ* (xi. 5. 3 etc.). The subject now changes, and verses 17–19 give us a list of the twenty prepositions and a definition of their accentuation. Finally, the last verse (or prose passage) attempts to give a list of those words which are treated as if they were prepositions, although properly belonging to other classes. This list is a somewhat strange one, with regard both to what it includes and what it omits. A part of the forms which it contains are in frequent use, and familiarly known as bearing marked analogies with the prepositions proper. Such are *achā*, *tiraḥ*, *puraḥ*, *punaḥ*, *kiṁ*, *prāduḥ*, and *çrat*. Others, as *aram* and *astam*, are more remotely connected with the same class. *Vashaṭ*, *svāhā*, and *vāṭ* are in the Atharvan compounded only with *kāra* and *kṛta*, and hardly in such a manner as should require their inclusion in the list. *Svadhā* and *sruk* form no other compounds than *svadhâkâra* and *srukkâra* (ix. 6. 22); *phalî* forms *phalîkaraṇa* (xi. 3. 6); *kakajâ* forms *kakajâkṛta* (xi. 10. 25). *Namas* enters into *namaskâra*, *namaskṛta*, and *namaskṛtya* (vii. 102. 1), which last affords actually good ground for special treatment, as does *hastagṛhya* (e. g. v. 14. 4), on account of which *hasta* is ranked with the others. For *lâṅgûla*, *kshiti*, and *ulâ*, I can find nothing at all in the Atharvan: there is room in the case of the two last, and especially of the third, to suspect corrupted readings. What may be hidden in *svaralalâ*, I have not been able to discover, nor how the last word in the extract, which apparently has to do with the accent of the words treated of, is to be amended into intelligibility. There are two words which we especially miss in this list of *upasargavṛttîni*, and can hardly believe to have been originally absent from it: they are *antaḥ* and *dviḥ*: I cannot, however, find by emendation any place for them in the text as it stands.

5. *Corrections and Emendations.*

I add here a rectification of certain errors in the body of the work, which have attracted my attention as I have been engaged in preparing the indexes; as also, corrections of such errors of the press as I have hitherto discovered.

At p. 25, rule i. 24, for सिगुग्र्यं read सिगुरां.

At p. 41, rule i. 47, translation, for *palatal* read *lingual*.

At p. 46, l. 16, for *kârpanyam* read *kârpaṇyam*.

At p. 79, in commenting upon ii. 15, 16, I failed to notice that the implication in the former rule is of *cuṭavargâbhyâm*, 'after palatal and lingual mutes,' and mutes only: hence this rule has nothing to do with any cases practically arising in the conversion of *pada* into *saṁhitâ*, and rule 16 covers all the lingualizations of *t* and *th* after *sh*, whether in the same or a different word.

At p. 89, rule ii. 29, at the end, for °द्रौनासु read °द्रौनाम्.

At p. 106, comm. to ii. 62, l. 4, the hyphen representing the *avagraha* has dropped out from *viçvataḥ-pâṇiḥ*.

At p. 106, comm. to ii. 62, l. 28: another like instance of repetition is found at xx. 132. 12, where all the MSS. read *punaḥ punaḥ*.

At p. 107, rule ii. 64, translation: for *is* read *does*.

At p. 112, rule ii. 76, at the end, read °पर्रे (broken letter).

At p. 118, under rule ii. 92, I was so heedless as to refer to *vy âsthan* (xiii. 1. 5) as an anomalous form from *sthâ*, forgetting for the moment that it was, in fact, the irregular aorist of the root *as*, although I had formerly interpreted and indexed it as such. The *pada*-reading is *vi : âsthan*, as given by our manuscript; but it seems to require amendment to *vi : âsthat*, having *rohitaḥ* as subject.

At p. 120, rule ii. 97, comm., l. 3: for *stusha u shu* read *stusha û shu*.

At p. 126, comm. to iii. 5: a compound analogous with *oshadhi-ja* is *pṛthivi-sad* (*pṛthivishadbhyaḥ*: xviii. 4. 78), which has also a claim to the attention of the Prâtiçâkhya in this part. Its *sh* was prescribed by ii. 100.

At p. 184, at the top, introductory note to chapter iv, I have expressed myself in a manner which misrepresents and does injustice to the Vâj. Pr. Although that treatise does not make the restorations of normal form in *pada* the subject of detailed treatment, yet its rules iii. 18, 19 (as pointed out in the note to iv. 74, above) virtually cover the ground, with more or less completeness.

At p. 209, under rule iv. 53, I have omitted the reference belonging to *ṛkṣâmâbhyâm:* it is xiv. 1. 11.

At p. 214, rule iv. 59 would have been more accurately translated "nor is division made before any member having an inserted *s* as its initial," etc. Whether, however, there is any propriety in regarding the inserted sibilant of *tuvishṭama*, and of the other words cited, as the initial of the second member of the compound, is very questionable.

At p. 253, l. 39, for *vavrdhânaḥ-iva* read *vavṛdhânaḥ-iva*.

The indexes call for but a few words of explanation.

Into the first I have admitted all distinct references to single passages of the Atharva-Veda, made by either the text or the commentary of the Prâtiçâkhya, distinguishing those of the latter always by an appended *c*. Words or brief phrases found at two or more places in the Atharvan (and so referred in the notes to the first of them, with a prefixed *e. g.*) are made no account of unless they are of peculiar and distinctive character; and, when noticed, they are marked here also by an added *e. g.*, or, if found only in a series of passages occurring in the same connection (as in different verses of the same hymn), by an added *etc.* I have also included in the index all passages to which important reference has been made in the notes on the text, as for the purposes of amending a reading, giving account of an emendation made in the edited text, stating the manuscript authority favoring or opposing a given reading, or the like: these are distinguished by an *n* affixed to the Prâtiçâkhya reference.

The second, or Sanskrit index, comprises, in the first place, the whole vocabulary of the treatise itself, both its grammatical phraseology and its citations from the Atharvan, the latter being denoted by a prefixed *a*. I have added as much of the vocabulary of the commentary as seemed to me worth the trouble, adding always a *c* to the reference. The pseudo-citations of the commentator, or the illustrations which he fabricates or derives from other sources than the Atharva-Veda, are also (excepting the phrases given in the latter part of add. note 2) included in the index, and marked with a prefixed *q*. This same indicatory letter is set before the few words quoted in the text of the treatise which are not found in the Atharvan.

In the third index it has not seemed to me worth while to make detailed references to the doctrines of the other treatises referred to in the notes; they may always be found stated in connection with the treatment of the related subject by our own Prâtiçâkhya.

INDEXES.

1. Index of Atharvan Passages,

Cited or referred to in the Text, Commentary, and Notes.

An *e. g.* added to the Atharvan reference marks it as denoting one of two or more passages where the word or phrase cited is found; an *etc.*, as denoting the first verse of a hymn or passage to which the reference applies. A *c* added to the Prâtiçâkhya reference marks it as belonging to the commentary; an *n*, to the editor's note. The passages of the commentary given in add. note 4 are indicated by 4. II. 16 etc.

AV. iii.	
14.1	ii. 32c, 4. ii. 10.
3	iii. 53c.
15.4	iv. 97c.
6	iv. 97c.
16.1	ii. 48c.
7	iii. 17c, 29c, iv. 89c.
17.1	ii. 55c.
18.1	iii. 6c.
5	iv. 85c.
6	4. ii. 14.
19.6	ii. 7c.
20.6	i. 75c, ii. 22c, iii. 83c, iv. 49c.
10	ii. 103.
21.1	iii. 54c.
3	ii. 40n.
5	iv. 4c.
6	iii. 64c.
22.5	iv. 48c.
23.4	ii. 84.
6	ii. 74n.
25.1 etc.	iii. 65c.
4	iii. 3c.
28.3	iv. 23c.
4	iv. 45c.
5	ii. 85c.
29.1	i. 63c, ii. 3c, iv. 51c.
3 etc.	ii. 85c.
6	iv. 50n.
30.1	iv. 58c.
5	ii. 82c.

AV. iv.	
1.1	ii. 44c, 103c.
5	ii. 5c, iv. 71c.
3.4	iv. 29c.
4.1	ii. 56, iii. 6c, iv. 75c.
7	iii. 16n (to i. 4. 5), iii. 40n.
8	iv. 16c.
6.2	ii. 48c.
3	iv. 86c.
5	ii. 95.
6	ii. 84c.
7.5	ii. 62c, 85c.
5, 6	iv. 86c.
6	ii. 84c.
8.6	iii. 94c.
9.9 e.g.	ii. 67c.
10.1	ii. 67c.
3	iv. 5c.
4	ii. 62n.
11.3	iv. 12c.
7	iii. 9c.
8	iv. 48c.
9	ii. 54c.
12.4	i. 69c.
13.2	ii. 88c.
5	iv. 53c.
14.5	ii. 87c.
7	iv. 31c.
9	iv. 84c.
15.11	iii. 84c, 86c.
15	i. 98, 99n, 105.
16.1	ii. 5c, iii. 34n, 4. ii. 15.
17.3	ii. 40n.
5	ii. 81c, iii. 84c, iv. 55c.
18.6 e.g.	i. 66.
19.2	iv. 63.
7	i. 47c.
20.3	ii. 39c.
5	ii. 59c, iv. 100c.
5 e.g.	ii. 68c.
7	ii. 80c.
21.4	iv. 58c.
22.3	ii. 65c.
4	i. 82c.
23.1	i. 84c, iv. 85c.
24.1	iii. 91c.
5	ii. 83.
25.3	i. 81c, iii. 67c.
5	i. 74c.
6	i. 81c, iii. 40c.
27.1	iii. 21n.
4	ii. 69c.
5	iv. 65c.
29.1, 2	iv. 18c.
5	iv. 67c.
6	iv. 16c.
30.4	iv. 57c.
6	iv. 11.
31.3	iii. 60n.
3	i. 77n, 94c, iv. 26c.
4	i. 31c.
32.1	iii. 15, iv. 83.
3	iii. 56c.
5	ii. 47c, iii. 14, iv. 87.
6	i. 69c, 81c, ii. 29c.
7	i. 69c.
33.2	iv. 12c, 80.
34.1	ii. 105c.
3	iii. 46c.
5 etc.	iv. 39c.
8	ii. 80n.
36.1	ii. 9c, iii. 18c.
5	ii. 31c.
37.1	i. 28c, ii. 19c, iii. 20c.
4	iii. 59n, iv. 67c.
38.5 e.g.	ii. 85c, iv. 31c.
39.1 etc.	iii. 49c.
2	ii. 6c, 48c.
3 etc.	ii. 73.
4	ii. 20c.
9	ii. 62c.

AV. v.	
1.1	ii. 5c.
3	i. 76c, 77n.
5	i. 76c, ii. 97c, iii. 4c, 13c, iv. 98c.
2.8	ii. 40.
9	iv. 54n.
3.8	iv. 86c.
9	ii. 70c.
10 (?)	ii. 102c.
4.1	iii. 39c, 66c.
3	iv. 14c.
6	iii. 27c.
10	ii. 68c.
5.3	iv. 92c.
4	ii. 65c.
5.9	ii. 91c, 103c, iv. 83c, 104c, 125c.
6.4	iv. 94c.
9 e.g.	iv. 95.
7.3	iv. 1c, 75c.
6	i. 75c, ii. 22c, iii. 83c, 86c.
7	ii. 53c.
8	iv. 80.
8.5	iv. 1c.
7	ii. 11c.
11.3	iv. 95.
6	iii. 90c.
7	i. 68c, ii. 29c.
8	iv. 84c.
12.3	iv. 14c.
5	iii. 71c.
6 etc.	ii. 97c, iv. 82c.
8	iv. 63.
13.5	i. 81c.
6	i. 69c, ii. 42c, iii. 23.
8	iii. 72c.
9	iii. 3c.
14.7	iii. 31.
11	ii. 101c.
16.3-4	i. 27c, 53c, 88c, ii. 57c.
6	ii. 59c.
17.1 (?)	iii. 52c, 55c.
4	ii. 61c.
5	ii. 2c.
18.7	iv. 107c, 109c.
11	iv. 95.
13	ii. 55c.
19.1	iv. 22c.
3	ii. 40c.
4	iv. 4c.
7	iii. 2c, iv. 94c.
8	ii. 61c.
13	iii. 13c, iv. 64c.
20.2	iv. 18c.
6	ii. 69c.
8	ii. 7c.
9	iii. 59c, iv. 107c.
10	ii. 62.
11	ii. 23, 62c, iii. 1c, iv. 70c.
21.6	ii. 42c.
22.1	ii. 63c.
5	i. 34c.
6	ii. 85c.
7	ii. 40c.
9	i. 46c.
14	ii. 11c.
23.7	i. 103c, ii. 88c, iv. 25c.
24.1	iii. 91c.
25.6	ii. 104c.
9	iv. 18c.
26.8	iii. 34n.
27.6	iv. 45c.
9	ii. 47c.
28.14	i. 71c, ii. 18c.
29.3	iv. 15c.
2, 3	ii. 77.
11	i. 86c.
30.9	iii. 7.
10	iv. 95.

AV. xii.	
3. 28	ii. 68.
29	iv. 29c.
30	ii. 18c.
33	iii. 34.
35	iv. 91c.
37	iv. 2c.
39	ii. 62c.
41	iii. 23c.
43	i. 28c, ii. 19c, 20c, iii. 20c.
52	iv. 40c.
53	iv. 91c.
55 etc.	iv. 115c.
58	iii. 55a.
4. 4	iii. 66a.
11	4. 11. 13.
18	ii. 63c.
29, 30	i. 86c, 80a.
30	ii. 15a.
35	iv. 87c.
36	iii. 55a.
38	iii. 31, iv. 50.
41	iii. 59a.
43	i. 97, 103.
47	iii. 53a.
5. 7	ii. 4c.
20	ii. 102c.
21	iii. 65a.
34	iv. 53c.
44	ii. 11c.
48	iii. 92c.
50	i. 103.

AV. xiii.	
1. 4	ii. 9a, 46c.
13	iii. 65a.
16	i. 50c.
23	ii. 107c.
25	iv. 75c.
34 (?)	i. 16c.
35	ii. 84c.
45	iii. 52a.
2. 8	iv. 6c.
14	ii. 91c, iv. 29c, 55c.
20	iii. 37c.
28	ii. 63c.
35 (?)	iv. 71c.
37	ii. 69c.
46	ii. 108c, iii. 67c.
3. 3	iv. 37c.
6	ii. 9a.
10	iii. 17a.
16	iii. 65a.
19	iv. 13a.
4. 5	ii. 91c, 94c, iii. 85c, 86c, iv. 116c.
10	iv. 13a.
25 (?)	iii. 63c.
28	i. 74c.
41	iii. 38c.
47	ii. 71.

AV. xiv.	
1. 1	ii. 14c, iv. 62c.
3	iv. 85c.
6	i. 50c.
11	iv. 53c.
12	iv. 34c.
18	ii. 65c.
24	iv. 18c, 49c, 76c.
36	ii. 93.
41	ii. 54.
43	ii. 91c, iv. 88c.
44	ii. 88c, iii. 60c.
57 (?)	i. 93c.
2. 3	ii. 70.
12	ii. 31c, iii. 95c.
14	ii. 54c.
17	ii. 83c.
20	ii. 65c.
28	iii. 60c.
34	ii. 90c.
37	i. 76c.
41	iii. 60c.
43	iv. 50c.
44	ii. 81c.
52	iv. 54a.
61	ii. 14c.
73	iii. 18c.

AV. xv.	
2. 1 etc.	i. 90c, ii. 25c.
3. 3	iii. 53c, 55c.
6. 4	4. 11. 6.
8. 1	iii. 53c, 55c.
10. 7	iii. 40c.
12. 1	iv. 62c.
7	4. 11. 13.
13. 1	iii. 6c.
14. 3	iii. 55a.
15. 4	iii. 43a.
7	ii. 21c, 34c, iii. 85c.
18. 3	iii. 53c, 56c.

AV. xvi.	
1. 1	ii. 102c.
2. 1	4. 11. 16.
3. 5	iii. 45c.
4. 5	iii. 55a.
6. 6	ii. 71c.
7. 11	ii. 58c.

AV. xvii.	
28	ii. 50c.

AV. xviii.	
1. 1	i. 79c.
4	ii. 7c.
5	iii. 84c, 86c.
10	iii. 8c.
16	ii. 97c, iii. 4c. iv. 94c.
20	iii. 73c.
21	iii. 25.
23	ii. 40c.
30 (?)	iii. 80c.
31	iv. 50c.

AV. xviii.	
1. 22	i. 74c, ii. 43c.
29	ii. 17c.
37	ii. 97c, iii. 4c, iv. 94c.
39	i. 74c.
45 etc.	ii. 59c, iv. 100c.
46	iv. 84c.
49	i. 88c, iv. 36c.
51	ii. 100c.
54 e. g.	iii. 86c.
55	ii. 51c.
2. 3	ii. 70.
4	iv. 98a.
6	i. 103c, ii. 38c.
13	ii. 100c.
23	iii. 25c.
25	ii. 31c.
31	iii. 17c, 40a, iv. 107c.
33	ii. 52c.
34	iv. 68c.
35	ii. 7c.
46	iv. 38c.
54	iv. 91c.
3. 8	iii. 79c.
14	i. 80c.
15	iv. 67c.
16	iii. 9c, iv. 67c.
21	iii. 25c, iv. 18c.
39	i. 80c.
42	i. 94a.
44	i. 80c, 84c, ii. 84c, 85c, 86a.
46	iii. 13a.
55	iii. 10c.
61	iv. 17c.
63	i. 94c, iii. 9c, 9a.
70	ii. 47c.
71	ii. 7c.
4. 1	i. 94a, iii. 65c.
2	ii. 63c.
4	i. 74a.
5	ii. 85c.
15	iii. 55a.
37	iii. 39c, 66c.
40	i. 88c, iv. 95c.
50	iii. 79a, iv. 2c, 7c.
51	i. 87c.
54	iii. 9c, 9a.
56	i. 94a.
58	iii. 84a.
59	i. 65c, ii. 10c, 17c.
60	iii. 86c.
67	ii. 98c.
78	ii. 100c.

AV. xix.	
6. 5	ii. 22a.
9. 13	iv. 49c.
13. 1	ii. 22a.
39. 1	ii. 67c.
40. 4	i. 77a.
44. 5	iii. 65a.

9. Sanskrit Index.

A prefixed *a* marks a word or phrase as a citation from the Atharva-Veda; a prefixed *q*, as a quotation in the text or commentary not taken from the Atharvan. Other signs are used as in the preceding Index.

3. General Index.

The references are as in the preceding Indexes.

[From Journal of the American Oriental Society, Vol. X, No. 1, 1872.]

COLLATION OF A SECOND MANUSCRIPT

OF THE

ATHARVA-VEDA PRÂTIÇÂKHYA.

By WILLIAM D. WHITNEY,
PROFESSOR OF SANSKRIT IN YALE COLLEGE.

The Atharva-Veda Prâtiçâkhya was published by me, with a translation and notes, founded mainly on the native comment, in the seventh volume of this Journal (1862). The edition was based upon a single manuscript, of a very incorrect and somewhat defective character, but the only one known to be in existence: and the publication was not made until after the failure of an attempt to obtain new manuscript material in India (as is explained in the introductory note to the work). Early last year, however, I was informed by Professor Weber of Berlin that Dr. George Bühler of Bombay had recently purchased on behalf of the Government of Bombay, along with other Atharvan material (see the complete list in the Monatsbericht of the Berlin Academy for February, 1871, pp. 76–7), a copy of this treatise; unfortunately, not accompanied by a commentary. I lost no time in sending to Dr. Bühler a request for a transcript of the new manuscript, and, by his kindness, I received the desired transcript, carefully verified by himself, in the course of the summer. The results of its collation are here presented.

The signature of the manuscript, giving the scribe's name, and the place and time of writing, is as follows:

granthasaṁkhyā 180. *pañcolināgajitsūnunā kaṇvālayanivāsinā bhavadevene 'daṁ granthaṁ likhitaṁ; saṁ* 1718 *kārttikaçudi* 11 *budhe.*

The date is in the autumn, A. D. 1660.

The title of the treatise is everywhere given as *caturādhyāyikā* simply, with no mention of Çaunaka. The ending of each of the four chapters is *ātharvaṇe caturādhyāyikāyāṁ prathamo* (etc.) *'dhyāyaḥ;* and at the end of all is farther added, in more extended phrase, *âtharvaṇe saṁhitâlakshaṇagranthe caturâdhyâyikâvyâkaraṇaṁ saṁpûrṇaṁ.* The endings of the sections are also marked in entirely uniform manner, *prathamasya prathamaḥ pâdaḥ*, and so on. There is nowhere any trace of an enumeration of the rules.

The form of the name as before accepted by me is therefore established beyond the reach of question; and the responsibility for its inconsistency with grammatical rule is to be put upon the shoulders of its authors or transmitters, whose errors, if such there be, we are not called upon to amend in a matter of this kind.

The opening invocation, *oṁ namaḥ çrîbrahmavedâya*, is in close accordance with that of the other manuscript (see p. 575, or 245 of the separate impression).

I begin now a detailed collation, with statement of the results following from it. With this I incorporate, here and there, a few corrections, in great part derived from a notice and criticism of the former work given by Weber in the Literarisches Central-Blatt, No. 29 (1863), and reprinted by him in the second volume of his Indische Streifen (pp. 280–288). For the sake of brevity, I denote the new manuscript everywhere by B., and refer to the other as A.

After the invocation, already quoted, follows next *oṁ athâ 'ṅgirasaḥ*. This, then, is evidently the first rule of the treatise as at present constituted, and my conjecture (p. 575 [245]), that it was "a copyist's error for *atharvâṅgirasaḥ*," and so a part of the invocation, is proved erroneous. Being, however, unexplained in the commentary (like the metrical and other appendages to the third and fourth chapters, to be noticed later), its right to stand as an original part of the treatise may be questioned. Its form, too, is suspicious: *athâ 'ṅgirasaḥ* would be a proper heading for the Atharvan text itself, rather than for such a treatise as this. Nor do we expect a Prâtiçâkhya to begin with defining the text to which it relates; a mere *evam iha*, as in the next rule but one, is all the definition that is called for.

i.2. B. divides into two rules, by a line of interpunction inserted after *ca*. A. does the same in the final repetition of the rule. This is not an evidence of much consequence, as there are several cases later (namely i.94, ii.65, iv.96, 109) where B. blunderingly inserts a mark of division in the midst of a rule. The exposition of the whole as one connected rule by the comment in A. (though not unattended with difficulties) is of much more weight. The point would hardly be worth dwelling upon, save that the admission of *athâ 'ṅgirasaḥ* as a rule seems to demand that, in order to make out the number of forty-one rules in the section, we throw rules 14–16 into one (see below), and then find one extra rule somewhere; and there would appear to be no other place to find it than here. I will not undertake to decide the point absolutely.

i.4. B. has *anṛkāraḥ* . . . . , as has A. also in every place but one, where it reads *annṛkāraḥ*. There can be no question that the amendment to *anṛkāraḥ* is a necessary one.

i.8. B. . . . . *tṛtīyāntān iti çāu-*: a mere copyist's error.

i.14–16. These are given in B. as a single rule, and should doubtless count as such. It was not quite correct to state that A. treated 12 and 13 together, as one rule; a renewed examination shows me that there has been, rather, a complete falling out of the comment to 12, so that 12 is stated, and then 13 explained and repeated. As to how the required number of rules shall be found in the chapter, see above, under rule 2.

i.19. B. . . . . *adharakaṇṭhyaḥ*; A. has the same in the rule and its final repetition, but *-ṭhaḥ* both times in the comment.

i.25. B. . . . . *adharāushṭhyam*; A. has *-ṭhyam* in rule, paraphrase, and repetition, but not in the interpretation.

i.30. B. . . . . *antasthānām*; and so in every other like case hereafter (with an exception or two which will be noted in passing); A. has the same almost uniformly; I adopted the reading *antaḥsthā* etc. because the rules of the Prātiçākhya itself do not authorize the omission of *visarjanīya* before a sibilant followed by a surd mute.

i.33. This rule is probably to be understood as *eke 'spṛshṭam* (as suggested by F. M. Müller, Sanskrit Grammar, §57, note †). The commentary reads (a little amended) *eke 'spṛshṭaṁ svarāṇāṁ karaṇaṁ bruvate, apare vivṛtaṁ*. What, however, should be the difference between *aspṛshṭam* and *vivṛtam* except as a verbal question, of choice between synonyms, it is not easy to see. Possibly a difference in the implied degree of openness is to be recognized.

i.39. B. *salakāra ṛvarṇam*; A. everywhere *sabhakāraṁ*, followed by *ṛvarṇam, ṛv-*, and *ṛv-*; that the true reading is that given in the edition is not, of course, to be questioned.

i.42. B. has, apparently, *-shṭānaḥ* amended to *shṭhānaḥ*.

i.43. B. . . . . *hīnaḥ çvāsanādaḥ*: doubtless an error of the scribe.

i.63. B. *shaṭparasor* . . . . : an obvious blunder.

i.66. B., in fact, has . . . . *aṅgurim*, which I pointed out as being undoubtedly the preferable reading.

i.68. B. *parosh-*; a scribe's error.

i.73. B. *dīrgha pra-*: also doubtless an error of transcription.
It is to be noted that the Tāittirīya-Prātiçākhya (at x.24) makes the same prescription as the others do respecting the exemption of a "*pragraha*" vowel from phonetic alteration.

i.74. B. *ikār-:* a mere slip of the pen.

i.77. B.....*co 'dāttaḥ;* and A. has the same reading. My reading *udāttāḥ* was, I think, a simple oversight; since the singular, used in a collective way, is obviously not less admissible than the plural.

i.82. B.....*iti paraḥ*, like A. I should, however, still defend the reading of the edition as a called-for emendation.

i.85. B. has *pāñcanadīs-* by first hand, but alters, erroneously, to *pāñçu-*.

i.94–95. B. divides, erroneously, *soshmaṇi: pūrvasyā 'nūshmā 'ntaryeṇa vṛttiḥ*.

In the edition, *'nushmā* is an error of the press for *'nūshmā*.

i.96. B.....*khāimakhās ity*.....: an oversight of the scribe.

i.98. B.....*avavetāni*.....: a blunder merely.

i.99. B.....*'nuttamā sp-:* also nothing more than a blunder.

I am inclined to think that the expression *yathāsaṁkhyam* in this rule distinctly implies the existence of four *yamas* only, and prescribes the insertion of them after the various mutes "in accordance with the number" of the latter: that is to say, of a first *yama* after a "first" mute, a second after a "second," and so on.

i.104. B. *pūrvaḥ svar-*, which seems to me a false reading. I have no new light to cast upon the construction and meaning of this very obscure rule.

i.105. B., like A., runs all these extracts into *sandhi* together. It writes *çreshṭhās* and *prāçthā* (putting the figure after the *visarjanīya*); A. had dropped out the sign of protraction in these two words (as also that in *prāçīas*, where B. reads with the edition). It also has *avaçe 'ti*, without the sign, in accordance with what I had pointed out to be the requirement of rule 97. It adds a double stroke of interpunction after the *ç* of *daiçā*, before the figure. Finally, along with A., it omits the *iti* after *tāsā* in the last citation; this I either admitted from the Atharvan text by an inadvertence, or inserted by way of an (unnecessary) emendation.

B. adds, as final rule of the chapter, *ita uttaram adhikam*, one of the phrases reported in the edition as constituting a part of the comment. There was nothing whatever in its appearance in A. to suggest the idea of its being a rule.

The full rehearsal of the cases of protraction in rule 105 is not in accordance with the general style of the treatise, which is wont to dispose of such a matter by a *gaṇa*, like *khanvakhāsī 'tyādi plutam;* and this circumstance, taken in connection with the peculiar mode of treatment of the two last rules by the commentator, is calculated to suggest the suspicion that whatever follows rule 104 is a later addition to the text. The Tāittirīya-Prātiçākhya, at least, deems it no part of its duty to give a statement of the protracted vowels of its text, and in the Vājasaneyi-Prātiçākhya (ii.50–53) such a statement is made only incidentally.

ii.9. B. *hananemaḥ* . . . . : mere blunder.

ii.16. B. *shakdrāntān nānāp-*: an equivalent reading.

ii.18. B. *lopo daṅ shāh stambhoḥ* . . . . : the most blundering version of a rule that is to be found in the whole manuscript.

ii.22. B. *nakār-*: slip of the copyist's pen.

ii.26. B. *nakārasya catatavargeshu* simply; and it has been pointed out already by Weber (in the review referred to above) that this is the true reading of A. also, I having allowed to blunder into the rule three words that in fact belonged to the comment. Of course, the inference which I drew in the note to the preceding rule from the repetition of *visarjanīyaḥ* in this one falls away as unfounded.

ii.47. B. . . . . *rodviv-*: error of copyist.

ii.58–59. B. runs these two rules together, and adds *ca* at the end. The *ca* may be a genuine difference of reading, but the rules must at any rate be separated, as no *na* is implied in the latter.

ii.61–62. B. again accidentally omits the pause between these two rules.

ii.65. B. puts a *virāma* under the *t* of *karat*, and adds a pause, thus dividing the rule into two; but it is an obvious blunder.

ii.73. B. has *pitush pi-*, which is the better reading; but it also gives erroneously *piturī*.

ii.75. B. *āyush pra-*: again a preferable reading.

ii.77. B. *paridhish pa-*: once more, as in the two preceding cases, the true reading, since the Prātiçākhya ought by all means to follow its own prescriptions.

ii.82. B. . . . . *sāḍrūpasya*: an equivalent reading.

ii.86. B. *sṛtasyasvapishu*: copyist's error.

ii.89. B., *pr. manu*, had *nārṇadenope*; but it is amended to an accordance with the edition.

ii.92. B., *pr. manu*, had . . . . *akāravyadhāye* . . . . , but is amended to *akāsya* (for *akārasya*?) *vyavāye*.

ii.94. B. supports the peculiar expression *-mebhyo*.

ii.102. B. has in margin *pāṭha mṛṣi*.

iii.6. B. *vyavadhāv* . . . . : mere copyist's blunder.

iii.20. B. *ralope pūrvasya*: a real difference of reading; acceptable, but not necessary.

iii.27. B. *-padhā svare*: error of the scribe.

iii.28. The *lacuna* pointed out as existing here in A. turns out to have involved two rules, which B. gives thus:

chakâraç ca;

pippalyâdishu pûrvât.

In the former of these, there is doubtless continued implication of *svarât*, and the rule teaches that *ch* is doubled, or changed to *cch*, after any vowel. To this no other restriction applies than that taught in rule 30; and that one, only in the combination *chy*. The corresponding rules in the other Prâtiçâkhyas are as follows. The Rik Prât. (vi.1, r. 3, ccclxxx.) teaches that *ch* is doubled as well when it is not the first consonant of a group as when it is; while a couple of later rules (vi.3, r. 12–13, ccclxxxviii.-ix.) rehearse a number of exceptional cases in which the duplication does not occur. The Vâj. Prât. (iv.24) prescribes the invariable insertion of *c* between *ch* and a preceding vowel, and excepts (iv.25) but three cases. The Tâitt.-Prât. (xiv.8) prescribes the duplication only in certain specified cases.

The second rule declares that 'in *pippali* etc. there is duplication after the first vowel of the word.' The cases here contemplated, judging from the word taken as example, are of a wholly different character from the others to which the rules of duplication relate, being such as have a double letter as part of their original and proper orthography. I do not, therefore, think it at all worth while to look through the Atharvan text in order to pick out the other words which may have been included in the *gaṇa*. In every occurrence of this particular word, it may be noticed in passing, a part of the Atharvan manuscripts read *pishpali*.

The next following rule is *na visarjanîyaḥ*, and with it begins the rehearsal of exceptions.

The hope which I before expressed (p. 584 [254]), that the restoration of these lost rules would lessen somewhat the list of duplications, is not realized: not a single one of the consonant groups treated in the third additional note requires to have its form as there given modified; we have only to extend the simple letter *ch*, in a host of cases, to the group *cch*.

iii.33. B. . . . . *prakṛtyâḥ:* a blunder only.

The Tâitt.-Prât. also has a corresponding rule (x.24).

iii.39. B. . . . . *'ntasthâḥ;* and the omission of the *ḥ* and the treatment of the word as a singular were an oversight on my part, since my copy of A. reads in the rule *-sthâḥ*, and in the comment *antasthâ bhavanti.*

iii.53. B. . . . . *pûrvapadâder* . . . . A. has the same reading in the rule, and *pûrvaḥ* was my emendation, suggested partly by the apparent necessities of the case, partly by the paraphrase of the commentator, which runs *pûrvo bhavati: padâder akârasya.* I do not see how the desired meaning can be obtained without reading *pûrvaḥ;* although, even then, the expression is very difficult and peculiar.

In the comment to this rule and to 55, we are doubtless to read, as Weber suggests, *te 'bruvan* for *te 'kravan.* The phrase, however, does not occur in the Atharvan text.

iii.54. B. has .... *prakṛtyâḥ* again, as in rule 33 above.

The passage introductory to the third section of this chapter, and which, in the edition, I treated as a part of the commentary, is found in B., as if belonging to the text. That it belongs to the text, however, as an original and proper part of it, is by no means to be believed; it is, rather (along with the two similar passages to be noted later), the interpolation of some reworker. This is evidenced both by its own character and by the fact that the comment takes no notice of it; it did not belong to the treatise which the commentator took in hand to explain. Rather than report various readings merely, I give the whole passage precisely as it stands in B.:

shaḍ eva svaritajâtâni lakshaṇâni pratijânate:
*pûrvaṁpûrvaṁ dṛḍhataraṁ mradiyo yadyad uttaram.*1.
abhinihitaḥ prâkçlishṭo jâtyaḥ kshâipraç ca tâv ubhâu:
*tâirovyañjanapâdavṛttâv etat svaritamaṇḍalam.*2.
sarvatîkshṇo 'bhinihitas tataḥ prâkçlishṭa ucyate:
*tato mṛdutarâu svârâu jâtyaḥ kshâipraç ca tâv ubhâu.*3.
tato mṛdutaraḥ svâras tâirovyañjana ucyate:
*pâdavṛtto mṛdutara iti svârabalâbalam.*4.

aparaḥ prâha: tâirovyañjanapâdavṛttâu tulyavṛtti ity udâttaḥ pûrva paro 'nudâttaḥ svarita saṁdhiḥ:

iii.55. B. *'kâraḥ* instead of *'kâraṁ*, which relieves the grammatical difficulty pointed out in the note.

iii.56. B., as everywhere else, *prâkçlishṭaḥ*, sometimes writing the *k* with *virâma*, sometimes combining it with the *çl*.

iii.59. B. *antapade* ....: an error of the scribe.

iii.60. B. supports A. in the reading *ukârasya*, but it cannot be otherwise than false.

iii.62. B. *-vyapetas* ....: a mere slip of the pen on the part of a copyist.

iii.65. B. again has *-prâkçlishṭa-*; also *anumâtrânighâto*, which, as Weber has pointed out, is the true reading of A. also.

iii.71. B. *udâttam udâttaçrutiḥ.* This, except the final *ḥ*, is the true form of the rule, and deducible (as Weber shows) from A. also. In constructing the text, I overlooked the fact that, from 67 onward, the implied subject is *aksharam*, not *svaraḥ*.

iii.73. *vidhaḥ* had been added in the original of B. after the *ca* of this rule, but was struck out again.

The concluding remarks upon this section, like the introduction, are given in B. as part of the text, and I repeat them here in their form as B. presents them:

asvarāṇi vyañjanāni: svaravati 'ty ānyatareyāḥ. kiṁ saṁdheḥ svaritam: pūrvarūpam ity ānyatareyaḥ: uttararūpaṁ çāṅkhamitriḥ: kim aksharasya svaryamāṇasya svaryate. ardhaṁ hrasvasya pādo dīrghasye 'ty eke: sarvam iti çāṅkhamitriḥ: aksharasyāi 'shā vidhānaṁ vidyate yad visvarībhāvaḥ: ṛgardharcapadāntāvagrahavivṛttishu mātrā kālaḥ. Weber notes that *visvarībhāva* is the reading in A.

iii.80. The *lacuna* in A. after this rule proves to be of nearly the dimensions that I conjectured; it includes, namely, five rules, which are given in B. as follows:

nasap ca;
dhātusthād ayakārāt;
uru;
brahmaṇvatyādīnām;
nipātasya svaḥ.

The form of these rules is in part very questionable, nor do I find it possible to make them fit the phenomena presented by the Atharvan text.

The first rule, *nasap ca*, must mean 'the *n* of *naḥ* also is changed to *ṇ* after *pra* and *parā*.' So far as *pra* is concerned, this is well enough; the cases of *pra ṇaḥ* are twelve in the Atharvan; they are all mentioned in the note to rule 80. But the text offers no example of *naḥ* after *parā;* while, on the other hand, there are eight cases (counting xii.3.55–60 as but a single case) in which *naḥ* follows *pari* and is changed to *ṇaḥ*, all the manuscripts agreeing. The form of rule 80, then, as here implied, needs absolutely to have been *praparibhyām*, instead of *praparābhyām*. How to get over the difficulty I do not see. We cannot amend rule 80 to *praparibhyām*, because there is in the Atharvan a single case of *ṇa* after *parā*, and a single phrase (repeated) in which it remains *na* after *pari;* both are quoted by the commentator under rule 80.

Of the remaining rules, one, *brahmaṇvatyādīnām*, is clear enough in its bearing; it applies to the cases (referred to also in iv.99, and there rehearsed in the note) in which, against iii.89, a *n* becomes *ṇ* (in *pada* as well as *saṁhitā* text) even when final.

The other three have the aspect of representing the three items of a rule of Pāṇini, *naç ca dhātustho-'ru-shubhyaḥ* (viii.4.27), and of having had their form determined rather by that principle of general grammar than by the requirements of the Atharvan text. To the form of the last of the three, indeed, great exception is to be taken. It appears capable of meaning only 'of the particle *su*,' while it ought to mean 'after *shu*, when a particle,' and so to read *nipātāt shvaḥ*. If the particle *su* in its unaltered form were given in the rule, it ought to be represented by *suñ*, as once before (ii.97); and in that case *suñaḥ* would be enough of itself to constitute the rule; while if (as is obviously preferable) the altered form be taken, and written as *shvaḥ*, the added qualification *nipātāt* would be needed, to exclude the case-ending *shu* in *gṛhashu naḥ*, and any other similar case that might occur. There is then the further and not unimportant objection that no example of *ṇ* for *n* after *shu* is to be found in the text. The altered *shu* is not once followed by *naḥ*; the only initial *n* that comes in contact with it is at xviii.1.37, where we have *stúsha ā shu nṛtamâya* (R. V. viii.24.1, *stusha ū shu vo nṛtamâya*), not a single manuscript reading *ṇṛtamâya*. Unless, therefore, all the manuscripts are wrong here, and we have to alter to *ṇṛtamâya*, I cannot see what purpose this rule answers. In the Rig-Veda, it is to be observed, *shu* has an altering effect only on *naḥ* (R. Pr. v.26); but the putting of the precept here in question after *brahmaṇvatyâdînâm* in our Prâtiçâkhya seems to dissociate it from *naḥ*, and mark it as applying to any word whatever with initial *n*. A number of illustrative cases are given in the comment to Pâṇini, all of them taken from the Rig-Veda, and falling under the rule of its Prâtiçâkhya already referred to. In the same comment is given as counter-example *gṛheshu naḥ*, the phrase which (as noted under rule 80 of the Prâtiçâkhya) occurs twice in the Atharvan, most of the manuscripts reading each time *ṇaḥ*. I think that, in view of the absence of authority for this reading in the Prâtiçâkhya, the adoption of *naḥ* in the edited text is to be approved.

The rule *uru* affords fewer difficulties of interpretation. But the only passage in which *naḥ*, or any other word beginning with *n*, follows *uru*, is *uru naḥ kṛṇota* (v.3.6), where P. M., to be sure, have *ṇaḥ*, but E. I. H. read *naḥ*, which was received into the edited text, because the passage is found also in the Rig-Veda, and is expressly exempted by the Rik Prât. (v.27) from the operation of the rule requiring in general *ṇaḥ* after *uru* (v.26). If this rule of our own treatise is to be respected, the correct Atharvan reading is *uru ṇaḥ*. Possibly *urûṇasâu* (xviii.2.13), which I had regarded as included in the *gaṇa* of rule 76, is to be brought under the present precept.

There remains the rule *dhâtusthâd ayakârât*, which can hardly signify anything else than 'after an altering letter contained in a root, unless combined with *y*,' and must be understood as applying only to *naḥ*. But the only case of altered *n* in the text falling under the rule as thus understood is *çikshâ ṇo asmin* (xviii.3.67: the passage is also found at R. V. vii.32.26, and falls under one of the specifications of R. Pr. v.26, but one that is quite otherwise constructed than in our treatise): all the manuscripts read *ṇo*. But the specification *ayakârât*, if I interpret it correctly, can only be intended to exclude *urushya* (vi.4.3); and there all the *sanhitâ* MSS. save E. give *urushyâ ṇaḥ*, which has accordingly been received into the edited text. And, on the other hand, we have *mîmṛsho naḥ* at iii.15.4, and *rîrisho naḥ* at xi.2.29, in which *ṇ* is not read by a single manuscript. And these are all the cases occurring in the text to which the specification *dhâtustha* applies.

It will have been made plain by this discussion how radical and even irreconcilable a discordance exists between the facts of the text as we have it and the rules of the Prâtiçâkhya, upon this particular point. Considering the state of things, we must greatly regret that we have not the native comment on the rules, that we might see how the commentator would deal with the difficulties involved. In order to cast any possible additional light upon them, I will here state, more fully than was done in the former note on iii.80, what the manuscripts do in various cases offered by the Atharvan text.

The reading *āçīr ṇaḥ* was received into the edited text at ii.29.3, because it was found in all the manuscripts without exception. But it is questionable whether this was anything more than an accidental agreement in error. There are thirty-four other similar cases in the text, where *naḥ* is preceded by a *r* altered from the final *s* of a form of declension, though no other in which the *r* represents a *s* that belongs to the radical part of the word; among these, H. reads *arātir ṇaḥ* at ii.7.4, and P. M. W. have *sindhur ṇaḥ* at iv.31.2. Further, H. has *pitre ṇaḥ* at i.31.4, and E. H. have *sarve ṇaḥ* at v.7.6; H. has *atra ṇaḥ* at vi.104.2. Of the two cases of *gṛheshu ṇaḥ* I have already spoken. If (as I do not at all suppose to be the case) the term *dhātustha* required to be understood as applying to an altering letter contained in the radical part of a noun-derivative, so that it would authorize *āçīr ṇaḥ*, then the following cases would also fall under it: *dvesho naḥ* (iv.33.7), *vāiçvānaro naḥ* (vi.35.1,2; 53.2; 119.1), *rayiṁ naḥ* (vii.20.4; 79.1), *kshayāya naḥ* (vii.26.3), *ushā naḥ* (vii.69.1; also xix.46.2; 50.7), *viçvarūpo naḥ* (ix.4.22), *adhyaksho naḥ* (x.1.6), and, in the nineteenth book, *pāshā naḥ* (xix.10.9). No manuscript reads *ṇ* in any of these passages.

There are a few such cases as *pari pāhi naḥ* (vii.84.1), but these are to be excluded from the operation of the rules by a reasonable understanding of the terms of the latter, as prescribing alteration only in words immediately following that containing the altering cause, without intervention of other words.

iii.81. The reading of this rule is in fact *punar ṇayāmasi*, as restored by conjecture in the edition.

iii.83. B. *duryāṇaḥ*: a blunder merely.

iii.86. The corruption of A. at this point was greater than I imagined, and B. gives three rules between our 85 and 87, namely:

pra minanti;
na minanti;
nabheḥ.

Of the last of these, A. also has preserved a remnant, reading *nabheḥ* instead of *bhānoç ca* as the first statement of rule 87; but as there immediately followed a comment on *bhānoḥ*, with *bhānoç ca* repeated at the end, I regarded *nabheḥ* as merely a copyist's error. In this I doubtless showed a want of acuteness; yet, I hope, only to an excusable degree; for, although the forms *pra nabhasva* and *pra nabhatām* (vii.18.1,2) needed to be exempted from the operation of rule 79, above, I regarded them as included in the *gaṇa* of rule 92, where they would be not less in place than the forms of *naç* with *pari* which are, according to the commentator, actually contemplated there.

The other two rules are attended with much greater difficulty. The facts in the text to which they must be meant to apply are fully stated in the note to rule 86; we have *pra minâti*, *pra minanti*, and *pra minâ*, each once only, besides *pramiṇâma* in the nineteenth book (with which the Prâtiçâkhya does not concern itself). All these would be sufficiently provided for by a single rule, *na minâteḥ*, letting the third person singular present, as so often elsewhere, represent the root of which it is a form. We can, indeed, make shift to get along with *na minanti*, since the third plural might, in an exceptional way, be used as representative of the verb (there appears to be one other such case, at iv.39; see below), and it might be irregularly left uninflected though used in a genitive relation. But what to do with *pra minanti* besides I do not see, unless we may simply regard it as a blundering repetition of the other rule; and this is a very daring thing to do, as regards a manuscript so careful and generally accurate as B. Here, again, we must greatly regret our deprivation of the aid which the comment would give us in explaining the apparent anomalies of the text.

It was noted under rule 86 that A. also reads *na minanti*.

iii.89. B. *padântât parç-*: a mere blunder, so far as I can see. We might be glad to amend the rule to *padântasparçayuktayoḥ* or *padânte sparçayuktasya ca*, but the ablative *padântât* is wholly unmanageable.

iii.93. B. . . . . *çashaldiḥ*: copyist's error.

iii.95. B. *padenâ* "*varjitena*, which is doubtless the true reading.

The long introductory passage at the head of the fourth chapter, given in full in the fourth additional note to the edition (p. 591 [261] ff.), is found in B. as part of the text of the chapter. I reproduce it here, precisely as read in the manuscript (but prefixing to the verses the same numbers as in the note referred to).

oṁ samâsâvagrahavigrahân pade yatho 'vâca chandasi çâkaṭâyanaḥ: tathâ pravakshyâmi catushṭayaṁ padaṁ nâmâkhyâtopasarganipâtânâm.

1. *âkhyâtaṁ yat kriyâvâci nâma satvâkhyam ucyate:*
   nipâtâç câdayo satva upasargâs tu prâdayaḥ.
2. *nâma nâmnâm udâttena samastaṁ prakṛtisvaram.*
   na yushmadasmadvacanâni na câ "mantritam ishyate:
3. *nâmâ 'nudâttaṁ prakṛtisvaro gatir*
   anucco vâ nâma cet syâd udâttam.
   kriyâyoge: gatipûrvaḥ samâso
   yâvanto 'nuccâḥ saṃarthâs tân samasyet:
4. *yatrâ 'neko 'py anucco 'sti paraç ca prakṛtisvaraḥ:*
   âkhyâtaṁ nâma vâ yat syât sarvam eva samasyate.
5. *sopasargaṁ tu yan nîcaiḥ pûrvaṁ vâ yadi vâ 'param.*
   udâttena samasyante yathâ 'tat supratishṭhitam.
6. *udâttas tu nipâto yaḥ so 'nudâttaḥ kvacid bhavet.*
   samasyate yathâvidham itihâso nidarçanam:

7. *naghârishâṁ sasahe 'ty evamâdîny uddharet :*
sahe 'ty enâ 'nudâttaṁ paraṁ nâma samasyate.
8. *anudâttena co 'dâttam abhâvo yatra co 'cyate :*
sahasûktavâkaḥ sântardeçâḥ çatakrato nidarçanam.
10. *anudâtto 'nugatir yatrâ 'nudâttaṁ paraṁ padam :*
pûrvena vigrahas tatra saṁ subhûtyâ nidarçanam.
11. *yatro 'bhe da prakṛtisvare pûrvaṁ yac ca paraṁ ca yat :*
varjayitvâ "dyudâttâni sarvam eva vigṛhyate :
12. *nâmâkhyâtâni samasyante na câ "khyâtaṁ ca nâma ca :*
nâma nâmno 'pasargâis tu saṁbandhârthaṁ samasyate.
13. *na yushmadasmadâdeçâ anudâttât padât pare :*
nâmopasargagatibhiḥ samasyante kadâ cana :
14. *mâm anu pra te putram ity evamâdîny uddharet :*
etadaç câ 'nudâttânî 'danuç ca tathâi 'va ca :
15. *nâmopasargagatibhiḥ samasyante kadâ cana :*
bṛhann eshâm ya enâṁ vanim âyanti pary enân pary asye
'ti nidarçanam :
9. *anudâtto 'nugatir madhye pûrvaparâu prakṛtiḥsvarâu*
pûrvena vigrahas tatra purushe 'dhi samâhite :
16. *anudâtto 'nugatiḥ sarvâiḥ samasta svaritâdibhiḥ :*
saṁrâvyena nir durarmaṇya âcârye 'ti nidarçanam :
17. *pra-parâ-ni-sam-â-nir-dur-avâ-'dhi-pari-vî 'ti ca :*
aty-api-sû-'d-apâ-'bhî 'ty upâ-'nu-prati viṅçatiḥ :
18. *ekâksharâ udâttâ âdyudâttâs tathâ 'pare :*
abhî 'ty anta upasargâḥ kriyâyoge gatis tathâ :
19. *âdyudâttâ daçâi 'teshâm uccâ ekâksharâ nava :*
viṅçater upasargâṇâm antodâttas tv abhî 'ty ayam :
20. *achâ-'ram-astaṁ-hasto-lâṅgûlaṁ-tiraḥ-puraḥ-punar-naçaḥ-çyenî-vâlî-phalâ-hiṅ-srag-vashaḍ-rulâ-kakajâ-svâhâ-svadhâ-prat-svarakâ ity upasarga-vṛttîni yathânâmnâtaḥ svarâṇi.*

The variations of reading here presented are in hardly any instance of a nature to throw further light upon the meaning of the passages in which they occur; and I think it accordingly superfluous to enter into any new discussion of the extract. That it forms no proper part of the substance of the Prâtiçâkhya is sufficiently obvious.

iv.3. B. *anarthakakarm-;* and this is probably the true reading in A. also, as the commentary has *anarthakâiç ca karmapravacanîyâiç ca* etc.

iv.6. B.... *plutaḥ svarasyâ 'siddhatvât ;* and A. also has *plutaḥ*, *plutasvarasya* being my own conjectural emendation, and one to which I should be inclined still to adhere: at least, I do not see how to construe *plutaḥ*. But *asiddhatvât* is probably correct, and is to be understood as having the virtual meaning of 'anomalousness.'

iv.12. B. reads distinctly *aniṅgena*, thus refusing its support to Weber's conjecture of *aliṅgena*. I have no new light to cast upon the interpretation of the rule.

iv.16. B. reads plainly *taratamayoḥ*, not *-poḥ.*

iv.18. Weber conjectures, in the commentary, in place of *vijño*, the reading *vineḥ*, i. e. 'of the *taddhita*-ending *vin*.'

iv.20. B. *tâtaye:* a real and rather surprising difference of reading. I cannot now tell whether *tâtaye* would cover all the cases that occur in the Atharvan text, but know nothing to the contrary. We have *tâtibhiḥ* more than once, but that is differently divided, *tâti-bhiḥ*, by iv.31.

iv.21. B. *ubhayâ[d] dyusi:* doubtless the true reading.

iv.29. B. has, erroneously, *svasvarât*, instead of *svarât;* also *tanvâni*, but amended to *tanmâni*. Respecting the latter word, see the St. Petersburg lexicon, under *mânin.*

iv.36. B. has .... *'paspṛshṭe 'pi*, as also A. in the rule, but *-sṛshṭe* in the comment. If *upaspṛshṭe* is the actual reading of the treatise, it can hardly be anything but a corruption of *upasṛshṭe*, which is plainly used as equivalent to *upasargayukte.*

iv.39. B. *anantâu;* and A. has the same in the commentary and repetition. Probably, then, this is the true reading, and we have here a second instance (as in iii.86) of the adoption of a third person plural instead of singular as representative of the root.

iv.44. B. .... *vâ 'vagṛhya:* doubtless a blunder merely.

iv.48. B. *subhishaktame:* also, I presume, an error of the copyist.

iv.53. B. does not divide this medley; and it reads *pûrvasu* for *parvasu.*

iv.56. B., by a slip of the pen, *avarṇâtendi* ....

iv.61. B. omits *ca:* a better reading.

iv.62. B. *udo* for *udo;* and so also A. in the rule, but *udaḥ* in the commentary. I do not see how we can help accepting *udo.*

iv.66–7. B. omits the mark of division between these two rules, but doubtless only by an oversight. The *lacuna* in A. makes its evidence a little less valuable, perhaps; yet I can hardly question that the rules are correctly divided in the edition.

iv.69. B. reads *dṛçi* instead of *dṛçâu*, as does A. also in the rule and its repetition. I altered the reading to *dṛçâu*, to accord with *vyadhâu* and *sahâu* in the preceding and following rules, on the authority of the comment, which has *dṛçâu ca sarvanâmnâ ukârântena ikârântena ca.* B. has, by accidental omission, *-rânta* at the end.

iv.73. B. *prakṛtir darç-:* a blunder merely.

Overlooking, it may be remarked in passing, the definition and use of *samâpatti* and the kindred word *samâpâdya* in our treatise, Professor Müller has failed to comprehend the latter as met with in the Rik Prâtiçâkhya (xiii.11,12).

iv.74. B. *shatvaṇatvopacāradīrghaplutvalopāpadānām* ..... *Upacāra* is doubtless an error of transcription; and *āpadānām*, although A. has distinctly the same reading, cannot be anything else.

iv.86. B. reads also, with the utmost distinctness, ... *anaḥvānām*. Weber acutely suggests emendation to *anaṭkānām*, 'being without augment' (*aṭ* being the Paninean designation for the augment), and I can hardly doubt that the latter is the true reading.

iv.93. B. at end *glapinām*, which would probably have been the reading of A. also, but for the corrupt condition of the text along here.

The words *iṅgyavac ca* are in fact found in B. as the next rule; but, in the absence of a comment and illustrations to show what is the meaning, I do not venture to attempt the interpretation of a phrase so indefinite.

iv.96. B. has .... *kesarapräbandhāyām*, with *virāma* under the final *m*, and a pause added, thus dividing the rule into two; in both respects, evidently in the wrong.

iv.98. B. *-shu tripadatvāt:* doubtless the true reading. Weber points out that it is to be plausibly inferred from A. also.

iv.100. B. *-tvāyādīnāṁ ca:* probably the true reading.

The restoration of *iṅgyavac ca* (after rule 93), and the reckoning of the introduction to the chapter as a rule, would make out the number 102, given in A. as that of the rules in the first three sections.

iv.107, comment (p. 565 [285], l. 22). Read *tānasvarena*, 'with prolonged tone' (as pointed out by Weber, Ind. Stud. x.432).

iv.108. My solution of the difficulty here was not quite the right one. The present rule stands as I gave it; but there is found before it another, namely *saṁhitādārḍhyārtham* (B. has in both rules *-dāḍhy-*), which is an additional specification to the preceding rule, and which we have reason to be surprised at not finding pointed out as such by an added *ca:* 'and for the sake of fixing the *saṁhitā*-reading.' The presence of *ca* would have made evident the value of the phrase as a rule; although it must be confessed that I ought (notwithstanding the imperfection at this point of the prefixed body of rules, which gives for both the rules together only *saṁhitāpadopadādyārtham*) to have been acute enough to infer that value for it as things actually were. The rules and comment read in A. as follows (somewhat amended):

saṁhitādārḍhyārtham: saṁhitādārḍhyārthaṁ ca padāny adhyeyāni: dṛḍhasya bhāvo dārḍhyam: varṇadṛḍhādibhyaḥ shyañ ca: tatra padādhyāyī saṁhitāyāṁ saṁdeha utpanne saṁ-payachedanaṁ kuryāt. yadi padādhyayanena saṁdehāpanayo bhavati tarhi kiṁ kramādhyayanena: tatrā "ha:

kramâdhyayanam saṁhitâpadadârḍhyârtham: saṁhitâ ca svasaṁsthâ ca bhavati:
and so on, as given in the edition.

iv.109. B. has . . . . *câ 'dṛshṭaḥ*, and adds a double pause, breaking the rule into two: an obvious error.

iv.112. B. *nâ 'ntargataṁ* . . . . : a blunder.

iv.117. B. *-samâpadyântargatânâṁ* . . . . : both the variations of reading from the edited text being evidently erroneous.

It is made sufficiently plain, I think, in the note on this rule, that my pronouncing the Atharvan *krama* a more complete index of the irregularities of its text than is that of the Rik depends upon the suggested understanding of the term *samâpâdya*, as applying to all words which require a restoration of natural form in any of the respects mentioned in iv.74, without the restriction, laid down in Rik Prât. x.7, to those whose alteration is *ananyakârita*, 'not having its cause in another word.' Whether *samâpâdya* actually has so wide a meaning is another question, which I admit to be doubtful. It is easy, by leaving out of sight the difficulties that beset the interpretation of rule 74 and its successors, to render a facile decision as to what is there signified. Doubtless, if we had a *krama*-text which we knew to be constructed according to the directions of our Prâtiçâkhya, we should be able to make the former explain the latter. But, as things are, a renewed careful study of the rules and their bearings, while it has made me less certain as to some of the conclusions which I before reached, has not brought me to so assured a solution of the difficulties involved that I think it worth while to discuss the subject here anew.

iv.122. B. *-tra pras-:* without doubt, an error, although A. has once the same reading in the commentary.

iv.123. It would be easy, by understanding *pragṛhyâvagṛhya* in this rule as a copulative instead of a determinative compound, meaning '*pragṛhyas* and divisibles' rather than '*pragṛhya* divisibles,' to make it teach nearly the same extent of repetition in *pada*-text as appears in the Yajur-Veda, and as was conjectured above (under rule 74) for the Atharvan also. Yet it is possible so to understand rules 74–6 as to make them imply a *pada*-text like that found in the manuscripts. Rule 74, namely, would, so far as the *pada* was concerned, teach restoration only in *dustano iti duḥ-tano* and the few other cases rehearsed on page 552 [222]; while rule 75 would apply to such *pada* words as *ni-secanam*, meaning 'even where there is no repetition, the same reversal of the specified alterations is made, when these occur in the latter member of a compound as effects of a cause contained in the former member;' and rule 76 would add the farther restriction that the words so treated must be not merely theoretically divisible, but divided in the actual usage of the *pada*-text.

iv.126. B. repeats *parihâryaç ca*, to signify the conclusion of the treatise.

As I have noticed and reported the various corrections and conjectures made by Weber in respect to matters of detail, in his valuable notice of the Prâtiçâkhya, I will say a word or two here also upon points of a more general character in that notice.

Weber says: "Between *bahlika*, 'of Balkh,' and *valhika*, from the root *valh*, there is doubtless a distinction to be made. Both words may well enough have existed side by side, but have then been variously confounded with one another." These remarks are not quite intelligible to me. In the three passages where the word occurs in the Atharvan text, it is plainly a geographical name, and doubtless designates 'them of Balkh;' it was, therefore, a matter of interest that the Prâtiçâkhya proved *balhika*, and not *bahlika*, to mean 'of Balkh;' thus tending to show that the latter form of the word, wherever met with, is a mere orthographical blunder. The St. Petersburg lexicon, it may be added, takes my view of the matter, and knows nothing of any word *valhika* from *valh*.

My objection to recognizing the Atharva Prâtiçâkhya as demonstrably the most modern of the treatises of its class was only that I did not consider the fact quite so satisfactorily demonstrated as some had been inclined to claim. Against the conclusion itself, as a matter of sentiment, I have not the least objection; but would only guard against an undue estimate of the force and conclusiveness of the evidence bearing upon the point.

Weber pronounces it "completely impracticable" (*völlig unthunlich*), in attempting to determine the relation of the Prâtiçâkhya to the existing Atharvan text, to combine the citations of the commentary with those of the Prâtiçâkhya itself. To me it still seems quite impracticable to do otherwise. There is no possibility, in the case of any of these treatises, of reaching a precise and absolute conclusion in regard to such a point, because the Prâtiçâkhya does not in general cite passages, but rather determines principles and instances words. But in the present treatise especially, where the rules often give only the initial word of a list, the case is even more hopeless than elsewhere: to test the text by the Prâtiçâkhya alone would lead to no result that was worth deriving or stating; we have to choose between nothing at all and a conclusion which, being founded on both treatise and commentary, is liable to the uncertainties arising from the introduction of an uncertain element—everywhere, of course, avoiding the assertion respecting the treatise itself of anything which really depends on the comment: as I was careful to do. In the reprint of his notice, Weber allows in an added note that "in the indexes" the text and commentary are sufficiently distinguished: which evidently implies that elsewhere there are instances of their confusion. In this, however, he does me injustice: any one who will take the trouble to look carefully through the second additional note will find that there is not there made a single statement or item of statement in which the two are not held distinctly apart.

www.ingramcontent.com/pod-product-compliance
Lightning Source LLC
Chambersburg PA
CBHW032042230426
43672CB00009B/1434

* 9 7 8 3 7 4 1 1 8 4 6 6 6 *